A War of the People

The men that Captured the
battle flags have gone home on leave
in 30 days, Sergt Woodbury Co "E"
& Private Sweeny Co "H".

Genl Custer started for
Washington today with Colors captured
by the (1st Corps) (8) eight in number
I shall be in Command of the
Division untill he returns, which
will be within a week, he also
told me that he should recommend
me to the Sec of War for a
promotion to Brig Genl, and that
he should urge the thing strongly,
that I had earned the Star if
any one ever had,

Now is the time for
my friends to work for me, if
they ever intend too,

Mr Gillingham
help me very much if he will
through Senators Collamer & Foot, also
Woodbridge, Morrill & Baxter. Letters
them to the President would help

A War of the People

Vermont Civil War Letters

Jeffrey D. Marshall, Editor

Foreword by Edwin C. Bearss

University Press of New England ★ Hanover and London

University Press of New England, Hanover, NH 03755

© 1999 by Jeffrey D. Marshall

Printed in the United States of America

5 4 3 2 1

CIP data appear at the end of the book

Frontispiece: From William Wells letter dated October 21 [20], 1864. William Wells Papers, carton 1, folder 34. UVM.

Contents

Illustrations

Figures

Maps

Foreword

In the six years since 1993 I have been privileged to write forewords for two outstanding publications on Vermonters in the Civil War, both by my friend Howard Coffin, whose antecedents in the Green Mountain State date back five generations. The first of these, *Full Duty: Vermonters in the Civil War*, is a critically acclaimed narrative history of Vermonters during those years. The second Coffin book, *Nine Months to Gettysburg*, centers on Brigadier General George Stannard's nine-month brigade, and especially on the troops' last four weeks in uniform when men of three of the five regiments were in the eye of the Confederate hurricane on Gettysburg's Cemetery Ridge.

The Coffin publications reinforced my interest in and appreciation for the Green Mountains, Lakes Champlain and Memphramagog, and the northern frontier and its people, an interest that was seeded in the mid-1930s by Kenneth Roberts's *Saturday Evening Post* serial titled "Rogers' Rangers." In the autumn and winter of 1941–42, this childhood fascination was honed when I read and enjoyed Roberts's *Arundel* and *Rabble in Arms*.

By September 1955 I was an historian with the National Park Service and duty stationed at Vicksburg, where my horizons broadened and I became a Civil War enthusiast. I was surprised to learn that four Vermont units—the 7th and 8th Vermont Infantry regiments and the 1st and 2nd Vermont batteries—saw hard service in Union campaigns to capture Vicksburg and Port Hudson and to secure control of the Mississippi River from Cairo, Illinois, to the Gulf of Mexico. Soldiers from no other state could have been confronted by such a drastic change in environment as these boys from the Green Mountains.

In view of my longtime interest in Vermonters and their military history, I was delighted to receive the draft of Jeffrey D. Marshall's manuscript, "A War of the People: Vermont Civil War Letters." The more I read, the more enthralled I became. Marshall's approach was similar to that used by Coffin in compiling *Nine Months to Gettysburg*, but different in certain essentials. Coffin's story treats one brigade numbering fewer than one-tenth of the more than 30,000 Green Mountain men and boys who answered "Father Abraham's" call. Marshall paints with a far broader brush. He employs soldiers' letters with a sprinkling of correspondence from loved ones and those on the home front to give an excellent overview of the war as seen by Vermonters in all theaters of the war and in all branches of service, as well as those at home. Marshall primarily relies on personal correspondence intended for family and friends whereas Coffin's chief sources are published memoirs, reminiscences, unit histories, and newspapers.

A key element responsible for much of today's ever-increasing popularity of the Civil War—with all its tragedy, pathos, and self-sacrifice —is the soldiers' correspondence, particularly with the homefolks. Unlike the rank and file in our nation's earlier wars, the majority of those wearing the blue, as well as many of those in gray, were literate and frequent letter writers. Equally important, unlike in the big wars of the twentieth century, the correspondence of military personnel in combat zones was not censored. Because the censor in these later wars was usually the soldier's, sailor's, marine's, or airman's platoon leader or immediate superior, letters, besides being devoid of military information, avoided mentioning morale and sex or making adverse remarks about senior officers, politicians, or other units. Troops going overseas were warned that keeping a diary or a camera were military crimes punishable by court martial. In contrast, the Civil War soldiers' correspondence has proved to be an almost inexhaustible treasure trove for historians and the reading and viewing public.

Vermont born, reared, and educated, with degrees in anthropology and history, Jeffrey Marshall first became a manuscript curator at the Massachusetts Historical Society and in 1989 returned to Burlington to become University Archivist and Curator of Manuscripts at the Bailey/Howe Library. This situation boded well for all those interested in an overview of the Civil War as seen by Vermonters in the camp, on the march, in battle, or on the home front. Melding the talents of an archivist, historian, and writer, he permits us, at the threshold of the third millennium, to step back more than thirteen decades. Marshall, as an historian and editor, employs a light touch. His introductory remarks at the beginning of each chapter set the stage but do not overwhelm. It is after all what the Vermont participants, in what has been called the American Iliad, thought and saw that will command the reader's attention, and that is why this book will be of lasting interest not just to Vermonters but to all Civil War buffs and to the generalist.

Edwin C. Bearss
Historian Emeritus
National Park Service

Preface

Correspondence between soldiers and the folks at home reflects the concerns most in the minds of the writers when they had the chance to write. Although it was a common practice to publish parts of soldiers' letters in local newspapers, only one of the letters in this volume—the March 8, 1864, letter of Louden S. Langley—was written expressly for publication. Letters home are generally more candid, less full of patriotic pronouncements, and closer to the heart than letters written for the papers. Some of the letters in this collection contain sentences and whole paragraphs that have nothing to do with the war, yet it was the circumstance of separation that forced each writer to remark on otherwise mundane topics. A soldier might, in one paragraph, write of the horrors he had seen on the battlefield, and, in the next paragraph, laugh at a private joke lost to time. To omit the "irrelevant" parts would leave the reader wondering whether ordinary people caught up in extraordinary events had any everyday interests and concerns. Therefore, each of the letters in this volume is presented in its entirety. Each is a reflection of the person who wrote it; each a story in itself.

Letters were selected for their unusual perspectives and quality of expression, not for their grammatical standards. The preservation of the spirit and integrity of the letters calls for a minimum of editorial interference. Any alterations of spelling or grammar are supplied within brackets. Usually, a misspelled word that sounded like, or looked substantially like the intended word was left alone. Missing or illegible words that could be inferred reasonably have been supplied in brackets. In the case of fabulous misspellings, the inferred word is supplied in brackets next to it. Many letter writers used dashes for commas and periods. These have not been changed, but spaces were inserted after dashes that serve as periods to indicate the end of a sentence. Likewise, letters lacking punctuation altogether have been supplied with spaces to indicate breaks in the stream of thought. Ellipses have been added within the letters only to indicate the removal of words unintentionally repeated or mistakenly placed where they make no sense.

Although the spelling, grammar, and content of the letters have been faithfully reproduced, no attempt was made to replicate the physical appearance of the letters. Paragraph indentations were sometimes supplied where writers ended a sentence, and a thought, far from the right margin, but failed to begin the next sentence with an indentation. Printed text on stationery generally was ignored, as were metatextual comments such as "continued on next page" at the bottom of a page.

Some of the letter writers made no attempt to disguise their contempt for African-Americans. The passage of more than a century does not excuse their offensive remarks and hateful attitudes, or make them any more palatable today. For the most part, I believe, these attitudes were the product of ignorance and fear. Most of the soldiers from Vermont had never seen a person of color before they went off to fight, and the popular culture of the time provided few positive images. I decided to include the letters with offensive remarks because it would be dishonest to pretend they did not exist, and because they are all honest, if regrettable, expressions of the writers' states of mind.

Acknowledgments

A work of this kind is truly a collaboration between the editor and the archivists, curators, and local historians who provide access to manuscript collections. I am grateful for the generous and knowledgeable services provided to me by the professionals and volunteers in numerous libraries and historical repositories. Barney Bloom and Paul Carnahan patiently endured my requests for materials during dozens of trips to the Vermont Historical Society. Nancy Rucker at the Sheldon Museum graciously assisted me with the Robinson Family Papers and other collections. William R. Erwin Jr. and staff at the Special Collections Library of Duke University, Richard Sommers and David Keough at the U.S. Army Military History Institute Archives, and Philip Cronenwett and Anne Ostendarp at the Dartmouth College Special Collections Department all provided friendly, professional service. Jane Williamson at Rokeby Museum, Elaine Purdy at the Rutland Historical Society, Clare Sheppard and Donald J. Minor at the St. Albans Historical Museum, Ruth Levin at the Bennington Museum, and Corinne Biggs at the Park-McCullough House all went out of their way to accommodate my requests, and provided me with valuable advice.

Many individuals offered me the use of their personal collections, including Gertrude Mallary of Bradford, Donald Johnstone of Colchester, Walter C. Munson of Colchester, Brad and Sue Limoge of Morrisville, and Peter Mallett of Georgia. Jim Fuller brought to my attention the letters in various newspapers from Vermont's African-American soldiers, and provided copies. Christina Bauman kindly translated Louis Lavallée's letter from the French. Bill Dilillo, Sally McCay, and Sharon Fosbrook at the University of Vermont Photo Service did excellent work with illustrations, often at very short notice. Many others provided valuable information, including Ed Irwin of Burlington, Margaret Stone of Brookfield, Tom Ledoux of Swanton, Art Ruitberg of Germantown, Maryland, and Mary N. deJong of Philadelphia, Pennsylvania.

Special thanks go to my colleagues in the UVM Library Special Collections Department—Connell Gallagher, Karen Campbell, Elizabeth Dow, Ingrid Bower, Sylvia Knight, and David Blow—who cheerfully covered for me while I was on sabbatical leave, and often when I wasn't. Many others at UVM have offered encouragement and support, including Rebecca Martin, Dean of Libraries, and Ralph Swenson, Assistant to the Dean of the Graduate College.

I am especially grateful for the financial support provided by the Friends of Special Collections, the University Committee on Research and Scholarship, and a private donor who prefers anonymity.

I owe my biggest debt of gratitude to several individuals who provided inspiration, encouragement, and constructive criticism at important points along the way. Foremost among them is Howard Coffin, whose books *Full Duty: Vermonters in the Civil War* and *Nine Months to Gettysburg: Stannard's Vermonters and the Repulse of Pickett's Charge* shaped my understanding of Vermont's role in the Civil War. Howard gave generously of his time, advice, and encouragement for this project, and whatever success shines upon it must reflect largely on him. My former colleague J. Kevin Graffagnino provided encouragement and advice on virtually every aspect of the book. Professor Emeritus Samuel B. Hand read my first scribblings and, as he has done for so many others, helped me to say what I really mean to say. Coffin and Graffagnino also read the manuscript, as did Jack Anderson, Gene Sessions, Sarah Reid, and my brother, Dan Marshall. Their many corrections of grammar, style, fact, and interpretation are very much appreciated. Of course, any errors that remain in the book should be attributed solely to me.

Most important, I thank my wife Tina for her patient support and many sacrifices. To her this book is lovingly dedicated.

November 1998   J.D.M.

Abbreviations

Sources

Duke	Rare Book, Manuscript, and Special Collections Library, Duke University, Durham, North Carolina.
MHI	U.S. Army Military History Institute Archives, Carlisle Barracks, Pennsylvania.
Sheldon	Sheldon Museum, Middlebury, Vermont.
UVM	Special Collections, University of Vermont Library, Burlington, Vermont.
VHS	Vermont Historical Society Library, Montpelier, Vermont.

Ranks (from lowest to highest)

Pvt.	Private
Cpl., Corpl.	Corporal
Sgt., Sergt.	Sergeant
Sgt. Maj.	Sergeant Major
Lieut., Lt.	Lieutenant
Capt.	Captain
Maj.	Major
Lieut. Col., Lt. Col.	Lieutenant Colonel
Col., Coln.	Colonel
Brig. Gen.	Brigadier General
Maj. Gen.	Major General
Lieut. Gen., Lt. Gen.	Lieutenant General

Military units

Co.	Company. Normally one hundred men, commanded by a captain.
Bat., Bn.	Battalion. Four or five companies, commanded by a lieutenant-colonel, major, or senior captain. Normally a tactical unit only.
Regt., Reg.	Regiment. Ten companies (twelve for some cavalry and heavy artillery regiments), commanded by a colonel.
Brig.	Brigade. Normally five regiments, commanded by a brigadier general.
Div.	Division. Normally three brigades, commanded by a major general.
A.C.	Army Corps. Normally three divisions, commanded by a senior major general.

Other terms

Adjt., Ajt.	Adjutant
Arty.	Artillery
Bvt.	Brevet
Com. Sgt.	Commissary Sergeant
Cav.	Cavalry
Ma.	Militia
Qr. Mr., Qmstr.	Quartermaster
Vols.	Volunteers

A War of the People

Introduction

"This war is a war of the *people*," William Young Ripley of Vermont wrote to his son William after the humiliating Union defeat at Bull Run in July 1861. "The men at Washington—will find that they are only agents in the matter," he warned. A prominent citizen of Rutland, and a member of his state's emerging class of industrial leaders, Ripley represented a swelling tide of dissatisfaction with the military and political leadership in Washington. Before the war ended four years later, Ripley would exchange hundreds of letters with his three sons in the army, sharing home-front reactions to war news and receiving frank assessments of the conflict's progress from the front.[1] The story of this "war of the people," fought by citizen-soldiers and supported by the extraordinary sacrifices of citizens at home, unfolds in countless letters written from the battlefront and the home front.

The Civil War left no Vermonters untouched and few families free from pain. The widely-held, powerful conviction that the Union must be preserved made it a true war of the people, but so did the widespread suffering that resulted. Americans understood during the Civil War that nothing so meaningful or so devastating had happened to the country since the Revolution, or was likely to happen for generations to come. Evidence of that understanding exists in the mementos—spent bullets and shells, muskets and swords, uniforms, photographs, and especially letters—carefully saved after the war. Handed down from generation to generation, many of the letters eventually found their way to public institutions. The Wilbur Collection at the University of Vermont holds close to three thousand Civil War soldiers' letters, the Vermont Historical Society owns more than four thousand, and there are thousands more in Vermont's local libraries, private collections, museums and historical societies, and in out-of-state research libraries. Altogether, the Vermont letters in public repositories represent nearly 350 soldiers, or 1 percent of those Vermont sent to war.

Perhaps nothing more powerfully demonstrates the Civil War's effect on the American consciousness than the value we have placed since 1861 on preserving the letters that document the experience.

Letter writing provided a crucial link between the Vermont soldier and his family. At no point in the state was the Confederacy closer than 325 straight-line miles. If the South was not precisely a foreign land to the men of Vermont, the distance from home and the hardships of camp life made many a Green Mountain boy yearn for home. Vermonters had few ways to allay that yearning. A soldier lucky enough to get a furlough often spent the larger part of his leave on the road. Family and friends might take the train to Washington in hopes of visiting a soldier in a nearby camp, but the expense of travel and lodging was prohibitive for most. Mail was the only realistic means of communication between the soldier and his home.

Soldiers corresponded with family and friends for a variety of reasons. Maintaining the bonds of affection, sharing news of sickness and reassurances of health, and reporting on daily activities are the most obvious. Many of the men wrote to wives or parents to advise them on the management of farms and family finances. "If folks come to you for money," Private Frederick Field wrote to his wife from camp in September 1862, "you tell them that you have not got eny to spare . . . be as independent as a hog on ice." Some wrote letters in the form of a journal, with an eye toward history, and with the expectation that parts of their letters would be quoted in a newspaper. A few soldiers, such as Lieutenant George G. Benedict of the Twelfth Vermont Infantry, served as newspaper correspondents while they served their country. A private in Benedict's regiment advised his family to read the *Burlington Daily Free Press* for news of the Twelfth, "as Mr. Benedicts letters are very interesting and they tell the thing Just as it is." In the midst of warfare, correspondence with family and friends provided a thread of sanity, a diversion from discomfort, and sometimes a reminder of the principles that led a soldier to enlist.[2]

Mail day, Sergeant Isaac Watts of the Tenth Vermont Infantry declared, was "the greatest day we have,"[3] but always it was a disappointment for some. Letters from Vermont might reach soldiers near Washington in as little as three days, but for those who were on the march or stationed in distant camps, delivery sometimes took weeks. Soldiers serving in the Department of the Gulf (of Mexico) relied on sailing ships and steam packets to bring news from home, frequently a month out of date. While postal reforms, such as the expansion of mail sorting on trains, gradually improved service in the East during the war,[4] soldiers also sent and received mail through private carriers. Civilian visitors, agents of relief societies, and furloughed or discharged soldiers often carried letters, money, and other valuables. In the other direction, private express companies delivered the most prized mail of all: boxes from home containing items unavailable in the war zone or too expensive for the enlisted man to purchase, including cheese, apples, maple sugar, boots, and clothing. "If there is anything that can make a soldier's heart glad," Edwin C. Hall assured his parents, "it is a box from home." Some enterprising soldiers made small fortunes through the illicit sale of liquor packed carefully in boxes from home.[5] Boxes sometimes proved more of a burden than a relief to soldiers who changed camps frequently, but military authorities apparently put few limits on shipments from home as long as they did not interfere with military operations and discipline.

Whether the mail they received brought the physical comforts of home or just comforting words, soldiers on all fronts made a ritual of reading and writing. Leroy Griswold of the Ninth Vermont wrote that "One great source of enjoyment to me is reading letters from home & writing in answer. When I get a leasure I read them over a second & third time." Lieutenant Colonel Charles Cummings of the Seventeenth Vermont asserted that there was "not an officer or soldier" he had seen "but what prizes a letter from home as the greatest pleasure of which he is susceptible of enjoying." Private Andrew H. Norton of the Third Vermont Light Artillery concurred. "Letters is all the comfret that we hav here," he wrote to a friend from his camp near Petersburg, Virginia, in early 1865. The Eighth Vermont's Major John L. Barstow had trouble deciding what to include in his letters. "I could write you a thousand things that would, no doubt be interesting but events that at home would have been of startling interest and would have almost been considered as eras in my life—occur here, in numbers *every* day, and in trying to write a Letter I hardly know what to select to write about—& so generally let *details* alone."[6]

To follow the story of the Civil War through the letters of the participants is by no means to follow the unerring narration of faithful eyewitnesses. On the contrary, enlisted men generally knew little about the broad strategies or even the strategic results of the military activities in which they participated. Soldiers received information from newspapers when available, from official proclamations, and from rumors, which outranked all other sources in abundance if not in accuracy. "We hear a great deal of news here," Private Benjamin Hatch wrote from Washington, "but thare aint one word of it true."[7] Not all Vermont soldiers were as skeptical as Private Hatch, but their letters frequently contain news that, in retrospect, is clearly false. Letters lacking accuracy, though, sometimes tell a great deal of truth, for rumors, embellishments, and wishful thinking reveal the soldiers' motivations and states of mind.

Aside from battle narratives, financial advice, and accounts of camp life, the letters of the Vermont soldiers contain expressions of deep commitment to the cause of Union and an increasing acceptance of the necessity for abolition. Citizens of the Green Mountain State shared with their Yankee neighbors strong feelings of patriotism and aversion to slavery, but it was a sense of state patriotism that fueled their response to the war, for Vermonters regarded an attack on the United States as an attack on Vermont. They drew upon a rich tradition of belligerent independence. From the beginning of the American Revolution Vermont had aligned itself with the cause of the United States, while maintaining its own struggle for independence from New York. The men who pinned snips of evergreen boughs to their caps as they marched south in 1861[8] styled themselves after Ethan Allen and the Green Mountain Boys, who won Vermont's independence from New York and the British empire in the 1770s and 1780s. Vermont's admission to the United States in 1791 brought to an end its fourteen-year experiment as a self-declared independent republic. This dual tradition of regional independence and national loyalty was an important part of Vermont's identity in the middle of the nineteenth century.

The Vermonters who went to war to save the Union knew of the disputes that had culminated in Vermont's independence. Among the most widely read books in nineteenth-century Vermont was Daniel P. Thompson's novel *The Green Mountain Boys* (first published in 1839), a national bestseller that celebrated Ethan Allen's Revolutionary exploits.[9] As war loomed in the spring of 1861, newspaper editors and public speakers around the state drew patriotic parallels between that earlier struggle and the growing threat to the Union. "Ethan Allen was in the van in the days that tried men's souls," a writer for the *Burlington Times* observed, "ready to strike at British tyranny 'in the name of the great Jehovah and the Continental Congress[.]' Will the Green Mountain Boys of to-day fail to emulate that bright example and strike a blow for the Independence 'Old Ethan' and his associates so signally helped to achieve? 'Up and at them.'" In one of many citizens' meetings across the North, the people of Fairfax resolved, "That the indications from every part of our State, show conclusively that the descendants of Ethan Allen, are yet alive, and that the Green Mountain Boys are wide awake, and in every village, town and hamlet, they are demanding an opportunity to go and fight the battles of their country." Many an anxious parent echoed the words of a Craftsbury father when he sent his son off to war with the plea "I hope you will maintain the honor of the Green Mountain Boys of Vermont."[10]

If there was irony in Vermont's opposition to Southern independence, it was lost on the Vermonters. Issues of state sovereignty mattered little to ordinary citizens, after all; the issues of personal liberty, loyalty, and commonwealth motivated Vermonters to fight for the Union. Vermont's motto, "Freedom and Unity," signified the desire of her founders to establish and preserve common ground with others who loved liberty. Vermonters wanted nothing more in 1791 than to join the United States and share in its promises of liberty and prosperity. "Freedom and Unity" lost none of its relevance to Vermonters in the seventy years that followed the state's admission to the Union.[11]

Love of liberty and a general attitude of tolerance made the state a haven for runaway slaves: there is little reliable evidence that fugitives were pursued into or apprehended in the state in the three decades preceding the Civil War. In 1840 the Vermont General Assembly passed a law requiring anyone who apprehended an alleged fugitive in Vermont to prove his case before a jury. Three years later, the state forbade citizens and officials from assisting in the apprehension of fugitive slaves. Legal roadblocks and popular hostility toward slavery made the pursuit of runaway slaves a difficult venture.[12]

Vermont's constitution of 1777 prohibited slavery, but abolition as a national cause provoked mixed reactions in the Green Mountains. Vermont claimed twenty local anti-slavery societies in 1834, the year the Vermont Anti-Slavery Society adopted a constitution calling for the immediate emancipation of slaves. Vermonters had always disliked slavery, but few were prepared for the radical reforms proposed by William Lloyd Garrison and the apostles of abolition. When abolitionist speakers began to tour the state in the early 1830s, they frequently encountered mobs, threats of violence, condemnation from the mainstream newspapers, and ministers and local officials who refused to provide meeting halls for anti-slavery rallies.[13] Some active opposition to abolitionism came from those who favored more gradual schemes of emancipation such as the repatriation or "colonization" of American blacks to Africa. Gradually, abolition gained the support of Green Mountain religious and political leaders despite the early and highly visible opposition. By the late 1840s the doctrine of immediate emancipation had won the endorsement of Vermont's Protestant churches and many of the state's prominent politicians.

The sentiments of the people at large were less consistent. Social historian David Ludlum claimed that by 1848 Vermont's anti-slavery consensus made "a conflict with the South [seem] irrepressible." But when the war came in 1861, most of Vermont's volunteer soldiers enlisted to save the Union, not to fight slavery. Though they hated slavery, many Vermonters apparently had little love for African-Americans. "I loath them and can not help it," Lieutenant Alfred Keith wrote in 1864. "This feeling against the negro is not one that I make—it is natural— and if the Lord has put such an aversion against them in my heart I can not help it." Private Edward Robie shared Keith's prejudice, writing, "I have seen enough of [the blacks] to see them all hung for I dont think they are worth enough to make all this trouble." Robie blamed "them damned Abbilishinesst" for putting the welfare of blacks ahead of the welfare of soldiers. Corporal Willie Stevens, an anti-slavery man himself, declared in 1862 that abolition crusader Wendell Phillips was "not in good repute among the soldiers. . . . He has done much to bring on this war, but has he ever done anything to bring it to a close?" The attitude of Vermont soldiers toward blacks and their most fervent advocates, the abolitionists, provides a sobering perspective on Vermont's role in ending slavery. Lieutenant Roswell Farnham, after his first brush with battle in 1861, expressed the view of many soldiers when he wrote, "I never was in favor of slavery, but I could see no means of freeing them and was satisfied to see it restrained within proper limits."[14]

Although the preservation of the Union provided the immediate inspiration for the Vermont Volunteer Infantry, in the end it became obvious that slavery played a central role in the rebellion. As the war progressed, more and more soldiers came to see the abolition of slavery as a necessary and inevitable step toward peace. After President Lincoln's Emancipation Proclamation took effect in January 1863, Private Moses Leach declared that he favored no compromise on the question of slavery, the "curs[e] of all curses." He advocated a "clean sweep in the way of humanaty and we may be shure of final success." The proclamation freed slaves only in the states waging war against the Union, and thus could not be enforced effectively. But in issuing the proclamation, as historian Stephen W. Sears points out, Lincoln made the world understand that the Union stood for freedom, the Confederacy for slavery. In effect, if not intent, the abolition of slavery became a legitimate goal of the northern war effort. Vermonters joined the national transition. When Congress passed the Thirteenth Amendment abolishing slavery in January 1865, Private Henry Dunbar wrote, "*Slavery is dead*, & *past resurection*, & that.s what we have been fighting about."[15] Soldiers who had enlisted to save the Union became the reluctant champions of a liberated people.

Vermont's commitment to the Union resulted in staggering sacrifices by her soldiers. According to postwar adjutant general Theodore S. Peck, Vermont suffered a higher percentage of military deaths from "all causes" (principally disease and battle casualties) than any other Union state. George G. Benedict, a lieutenant in the Twelfth Vermont Infantry and later the author of the first full history of Vermont's participation in the war, claimed that Vermont had the North's highest percentage of men killed in action. Peck figured that Vermont had the second highest; only Pennsylvania, by his reckoning, had a higher proportion of men killed in action and mortally wounded.[16]

In all, Vermont raised seventeen infantry regiments, one cavalry regiment, three batteries of light artillery, and three companies of sharpshooters. These units accounted for most of the nearly 35,000 soldiers Vermont sent to war, though hundreds served in the regular U.S. Army, Navy, and Marines, and in regiments raised by other states. Vermont provided the U.S. Colored Troops with 104 white officers, most of

MAP 1. (Opposite.) The seat of war in Virginia. Guernsey and Alden, *Harper's Pictorial History of the Civil War*, vol. 2, 636. UVM.

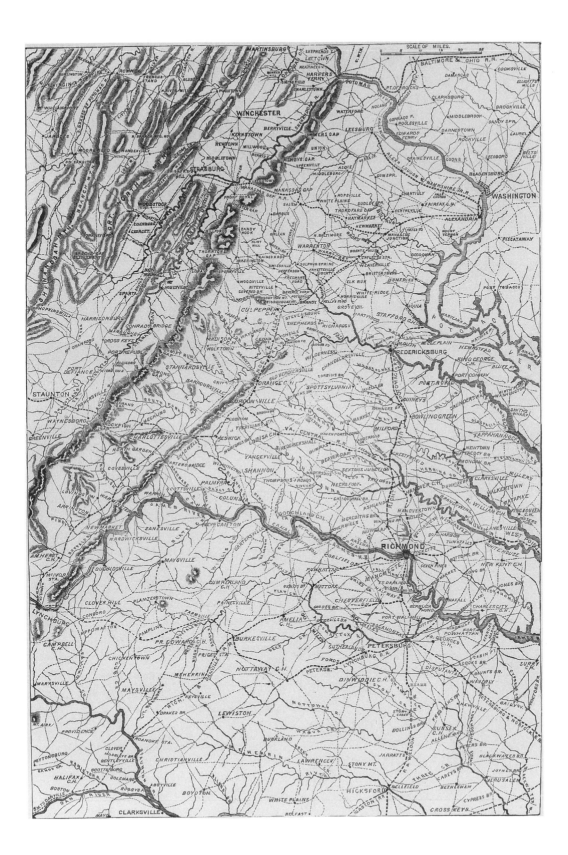

them commissioned from the ranks of enlisted men in the volunteer regiments. It also supplied 150 African-American soldiers to the Union cause, 68 of whom served in the famous Fifty-Fourth Massachusetts Infantry, and the rest in regiments of the U.S. Colored Troops. An unknown number of Vermonters—probably fewer than 100—fought for the Confederacy.[17] As demonstrated amply in their letters, the experiences of the Vermont soldiers varied greatly. The First Vermont Cavalry and the infantry regiments of the First Vermont Brigade, all three-year-enlistment regiments destined to fight in most of the hard battles in the East, grew tougher even as their ranks dwindled from battle casualties, disease, and desertion. Two infantry regiments (the Seventh and Eighth) and the First and Second batteries of light artillery fought in the lower Mississippi Valley, where they suffered from disease, heat exhaustion, and low morale. By contrast, the soldiers of the Second Vermont Brigade served most of their nine-month terms in relative comfort and safety near Washington before proving their fighting abilities at Gettysburg.

Instead of forming new regiments every time Washington issued a call for more soldiers, in the last two years of the war Vermont assigned most of its enlistees, draftees, and substitutes to fill vacancies in the ranks of the old regiments. The Seventeenth Infantry and the Third Light Artillery were the only new Vermont units to take the field after 1862. The old regiments frequently assigned officers to recruiting duty in Vermont, giving them some control over the quality of men to be added to their units. Nevertheless, the recruiting officers often found themselves scraping the bottom of the barrel. Out of fifteen new men assigned to Company C, Third Vermont Infantry, in September 1863, "four of them are in the Hospital and two of them are fools and the rest of them are out of som por house" complained Corporal Hosea B. Williams. "Som of them have no teath and the old Soldiers hafter chaw . . . for them and I for one dont like to do it." The old soldiers regarded with suspicion and envy those who enlisted for high bounties later in the war. Lieutenant Colonel Valentine G. Barney of the Ninth Vermont thought little of these "*eight hundred dollar patriots*" but admitted he would be "happy to get a few of them to fill up our regt." When all was said and done, Vermonters took pride in their state's promptness and consistency in meeting federal quotas. Reports of this success led Samuel Pingree, in the winter camp of the Fourth Vermont Infantry early in 1864, to write of "a peculiar joy here at seeing the proud position our state has taken and will hereafter hold in history . . . I believe it hardly finds a rival even in the days of the bold Allens."[18]

Congress approved conscription to raise troops in the spring of 1863. Provost marshals in each congressional district (Vermont had three) compiled and submitted to Washington enrollment lists of men eligible for the draft. Quotas based on these lists were issued to each district and subdistrict (townships and cities in Vermont) in each of the ensuing four drafts.[19] Many Vermont towns had to resort to the draft to fill quotas, even though compulsory military service seemed to contradict the Vermont tradition of personal liberty. Aversion to conscription induced some town officials to raise bounties, making enlistment more attractive at the price of runaway bounty inflation. Few of the old soldiers, though, had any qualms about the draft. "I hope they will go in big," wrote cavalry quartermaster Lorentio King after passage of the conscription act. "I want to see men enough out here to eat all the Rebs, and do it up quick." Counting the days remaining in their nine-month enlistments, the men of the Second Vermont Brigade considered themselves lucky to be exempt from further service in three-year regiments. Richard Irwin of Burlington summed up the brigade's situation: "The weather for the past few days has been very damp and rainy and the mud is as deep as ever, but I tell you what it is Mother. I had rather be down here in the Va mud, than up in the Vt draft."[20] In all, Vermont sent only 437 conscripts to war. Drafted men could furnish substitutes or pay a three-hundred-dollar commutation fee to avoid service, until commutation was abolished for all but conscientious objectors in July 1864. Approximately 1,250 Vermonters hired substitutes and 1,971 paid the fee.[21]

Those who could not find a substitute or pay the commutation fee might find refuge in Canada, or face arrest if they failed to report for duty. Henry Vaughn of Middlesex attempted to elude the authorities after he was drafted in the summer of 1863, but soon found himself in a Rutland jail. He wrote to his brother that "there is no use in a poor devil thinking to get off here, unless he sticks a hundred dollar greenback in the Dr.s pocket, for unless he does, if he has got one leg and one arm he has got to come." Conscripts were kept under armed guard while en route to the front. Some volunteers received rough treatment as well. Moses Parker, who enlisted in a sharpshooter company in 1864 after recovering from an illness that caused his discharge from the Third Vermont Infantry, found himself thrown in with bad company on his way to the front. "We are shut up here in [Camp Fairhaven, Connecticut] like so many sheep with all the subs and conscripts of the meanest characters of N.Y. thieves and cut throats A man cannot go out of his barrack without having his pocket picked by one of these chaps hundreds of dollars are stolen every day and there is scarcely a night but what some one is shot in trying to make their escape."[22]

Conscripts and volunteers alike faced a life of deprivation in the army. Clothing and shelter were frequently inadequate. Poor food and unclean water were typical wherever armies camped, and nearly everyone suffered occasional spells of fever and diarrhea.[23] When sent out on picket duty, soldiers had to bear whatever weather came along, without shelter, and to stay alert for hours on end. "It kills more men in proportion than fighting" the Twelfth Vermont's George Hagar insisted. Hard-marching columns always left behind a roadside residue of men disabled by sunstroke, exhaustion, and dehydration. "It is a dog's life to live," Private Stephen Brockway wrote to a friend, advising him not to enlist. "Dont for Gods Sake enlist," another soldier warned, "unless you can get the position of Major General."[24]

The sick received less care and sympathy than they could expect at home. "I tell you it is hard to be sick in the army," Rufus Lanpher wrote. "If one is well right along he gets along very well but the sick have no sympathy at all   the surgeon dont care whether they live or die." Vermont sent some of its finest physicians, such as Waterbury's Henry Janes, to serve as regimental surgeons. Dr. Janes treated the soldiers of the Third Vermont, supervised the field hospitals at Gettysburg, and later was in charge of Montpelier's Sloan Army Hospital. One of the Third's assistant surgeons, however, did not measure up to Dr. Janes, in the estimation of Private Peter Abbott: "[Dr. Janes] is a good docter [but this] one is not fit to wait on the oald Herry himself." Some of the surgeons, a soldier in the Tenth Vermont Infantry wrote, had "no more feeling for us then the Hogs that run around here."[25]

Men became inured to death. Funeral formalities such as military processions, salutes, and graveside services were abandoned as deaths from disease and battle grew. "How soon the dead are forgotten!" Roswell Farnham lamented. "At home they are forgotten soon enough, even with every effort to preserve their memory, but here in war men die & are buried where they fall & no one remembers them." Private William Cheney observed that "a man soon becomes hardened so he has not but little feeling for himself or any body else." The bodies of the dead were handled "just the same as you would load a piece of beef & then one goes in gets his over Coat & mittens & takes the train & starts off as unconserned as can be."[26]

Army food did little to boost morale. The ubiquitous, and sometimes only, army ration was hard tack, a hard cracker that exercised a soldier's jaws and provided "an extra allowance of fresh meat in the way of worms," as one officer put it. "O! they *are* hard," Willie Stevens wrote his sister Mary. "I have thought of sending some to Mother to pave her walk to the Dairy house with, for they are so clean and white they would look neatly and there would be no end to the *wear of 'em*."[27] Fresh meat, fruit, and vegetables often could be purchased from civilians, but just as often they were stolen (or "foraged"). "Chickens some how have a way of getting fastened to our saddles as we go past the farm houses here in Virginia," Assistant Surgeon Joseph Rutherford of the Tenth Vermont reported, "and once in a while a hog will follow some of the soldiers off, and whenever a sheep *bites* the boys they will kill him and I tell you the boys say that these Va sheep are terrible things to bite." Dr. Rutherford himself boasted of foraging "a large fat turkey . . . from a bloody *Reb*" for Christmas dinner.[28]

Some Vermont recruits adapted poorly to the hardships of army life, but most found ways to make it tolerable or even enjoyable. For entertainment, soldiers played cards, chess, and ball games. In winter camp, snowball fights between whole regiments sometimes occupied the soldiers' leisure time. Some of the boys from Vermont encountered for the first time temptations such as drinking, gambling, and the company of prostitutes. "Camp is a place which tries a mans principles very hard," cavalryman Albert Sawyer wrote his aunt, "and he has to contend with a great many adversaries to all that is good." Proscriptions against drunkenness, gambling, and other vices received uneven enforcement from one regiment to another. Dr. Rutherford claimed that gambling was unknown and intemperate drinking uncommon in the Tenth Vermont, but Private Tabor Parcher thought that no regiment had a worse reputation for stealing from civilians. Virtue did not seem to be a notable characteristic of the Green Mountain boys. "There is no restraint on man here and there seems to be no fear of man or God," Aldis Brainerd confided to his sister from the Union army camps outside Richmond in the spring of 1862. "The V[ermonter]s," he added, "are as bad as any."[29]

Regimental chaplains made little headway in their struggle against sin. Few soldiers attended the infrequent Sunday meetings. Sunday was generally the busiest day of the week in the army, with morning inspections and afternoon parades. In November 1862, the Reverend Edward Stone confessed that none of the chaplains to whom he had spoken were sure they were of any use. The Reverend Charles C. Parker of Waterbury, sent to the winter camps by the U.S. Christian Commission in 1864, claimed some success in evangelizing the soldiers. One "precious meeting" in particular, he wrote, "rewarded me a thousand fold for all that I have done or endured in coming to the army," as ten soldiers confessed their sins or spoke about the power of Christ to sustain them in their trials. Parker's reports of success were disputed, however, by Waterbury's Tabor Parcher, a private in the Tenth Vermont. "I doant think that Parker started many revivles in the armey," he wrote his wife, "as at least what you wrote is the first that I herd about it   I did not go to hear him while he was here   I doant go to meating much."[30]

Those at home experienced their own hardships during the war. The anxiety shared by all Vermonters for the welfare of the soldiers sharpened to grief for the families of the 5,237 men who died. The army had no official protocol for informing families in case of a soldier's death, though by common practice company officers wrote to next-of-kin when soldiers under their command died. Frequently, family and friends first received the bad news at local newspaper offices from telegraphic dispatches listing battle casualties. The seriously ill had no such means for communicating their plight, and often no one to write for them. Franky Brown of Craftsbury waited for many desperate weeks to hear from her brother Elijah after the battle of Fredericksburg. When she finally received his letter informing her that he was sick but alive, she immediately wrote back, elated—only to have her letter returned two months later with a short, cruel message scrawled on the back: "said to be *dead*."

For some, neither patriotism nor frequent reassurances from the front could ease the dread caused by war's separation. Henrietta Parker of Vergennes found the absence of her son, Adjutant Charles Parker of the Seventh Vermont Infantry, unbearable. "I am sick sick Heart sick, of this War, and I want my Son out of it and I must have you out of it. Do my dear Charlie make this your decision that when your Reg comes North, you *will resign*. I cannot sacrifice you to this Unholy War. They accomplish nothing but the slaughtering of thousands, and to all appearances it is all they will accomplish."[31]

The war also brought financial difficulties. Families who depended on the labor of the men gone to fight often found hired help scarce and expensive. New taxes for war expenses added further burdens to household finances. Asahel Hubbard of Whiting noted in May 1863 that the 3 percent federal income tax along with his state tax of fifty-six dollars made "a good smart War tax." Enlistment bounties proved especially burdensome in some towns. In the patriotic flush of 1861, no bounties were necessary to entice recruits. By the summer of 1862, with casualties mounting and little progress evident in the fight against secession, volunteers were not so numerous. Even before the first draft in 1863, Vermont issued quotas to each town to meet federal calls for troops. By 1862 the towns began offering bounties to induce enlistments. Inequitable quotas and the inability of certain towns to compete with others for recruits resulted in wide disparities in bounties from one town to another, especially after drafting began. Silas Hall, a farmer in Brookfield, complained in August 1864 that the town would have to offer bounties between four and six hundred dollars to compete with neighboring towns, "And few want to go for that   There is no patriotism left   Tis all for money now & those towns that pay the most soonest fill their quota." As the number of recruits dwindled, town bounties rose accordingly, from the low hundreds in 1862 to as much as one thousand dollars in 1864—more than three years' pay for a farm laborer.[32]

As the toll in lives and money rose, some Vermonters began to question the need for war. Hundreds of marble quarriers in the Rutland area banded together to drive away officials who arrived to enroll them for the first draft in July 1863.[33] No other such disturbances in Vermont have been documented, but soldiers and civilians alike grumbled in the privacy of their correspondence. Many blamed military leaders and Washington for the Union army's string of defeats and incomplete victories. Nellie French was "brim full of wrath" against politicians. "It is pretty hard work to keep up *courage*, when ones husband is risking his life and health for these *wranglers* who do not care a fig for their country," she wrote. Captain Alfred H. Keith asked in April 1863, "Can you expect us to be energetic patriotic and every thing when we see such incivility displayed at Washington?" Asahel Hubbard's brother Frank, a musician and gunner in the Second Vermont Light Artillery, believed the Union generals were "lin[ing] their pockets with out regard to loss of lives or property," and thought they all ought to be hanged or shot. Patriotism wore especially thin after the battle of Fredericksburg in December 1862. "It was a bloody battle as I ever was in and I for one dont want to fite eny more for my country," wrote Hosea Williams of the Third Vermont. "I will tell you plainly," George Howard declared, "that the North can never conquer these Rebels and the sooner we find it out the better."[34]

Civilians in Vermont experienced war first-hand on October 19, 1864, when a squad of Confederate raiders robbed three banks in St. Albans and mortally wounded a man during their getaway. The raiders, all Confederate soldiers who had escaped to Canada from Union prison camps, returned to Canada with more than two hundred thousand dollars in cash and securities. As a military event the raid hardly merits notice, but its effect on civilian morale was significant. Outraged citizens throughout the northern half of Vermont began reporting to the authorities suspicious characters, some of whom were arrested. Governor J. Gregory Smith authorized a "Frontier Cavalry" to patrol the border. The need for vigilance restored some of the sagging morale brought about by war weariness. War against the Union, Vermonters were reminded, meant war on Vermont.[35]

The psychological effects of the war on families and individuals defy measurement, but letters provide a good deal of insight. Henry McAllister, pious and indomitable in spirit, left his studies at the University of Vermont in 1861 to join what he believed to be a noble cause. He lost a leg at Fredericksburg and suffered through years of slow and painful recovery, but never lost hope or thought himself unfortunate. Joseph C. Rutherford viewed the rebellion as a threat to his family. As an assistant surgeon in the Tenth Vermont, he grieved over the death of his child at home, far from his healing hands, in September 1864. The doctor grew increasingly bitter toward the enemy and the "traitors" at home who failed to support the war effort to his satisfaction. Rutherford was not the only Vermonter pushed to patriotic extremes. Commenting on the intransigent pacifism of some Quaker conscripts from Vermont, Major Stephen M. Pingree of the Fourth Vermont wrote, "I do not think a man is entitled to have any

FIGURE 1. "News from Home." Broadside collection, Special Collections, University of Vermont.

religion in times like these—if it interferes with the duty he owes his country."[36]

The war posed a particular dilemma for Vermont's Quakers, bound by conscience to resist both slavery and war. Willie Stevens found the cause of righteousness more compelling than "the Quaker principle" of his East Montpelier family and joined the Fourth Vermont in August 1861. A year later, the Society of Friends read him out of meeting. Like most of his comrades, Stevens changed during the course of the war, particularly during his five months as a prisoner of war from October 1863 to March 1864. Willie's resentment toward the Friends and his desire for revenge upon the rebels deeply disappointed his mother, Rachel, as did his abandonment of the Quaker manner of speech. "I shall not cease to regret that thy mind has become so soured against friends," she wrote. "I must think if thee understood the whole thing, thee would feel differently—it really sounded cold to me to have the[e] close thy letter 'your loving son.'"[37]

Rachel Stevens held fast to pacifism but agreed to knit socks for the soldiers. She declined an offer to "preside over a society for knitting etc. for the soldiers" on the grounds that "the Quaker way of doing things was quiet" and the work could be done just as well "without a society & constitution & by laws." Willie's sister Ann apparently shared his view of the war as a necessary evil but regretted that women were left so helpless to influence its outcome.[38] If she shared her most candid views on the war with anyone but Willie, she did not suffer the censure that Willie endured for following his conscience.

Writing from an army hospital bed on September 16, 1862, the eve of the bloodiest day in American history, Henry McAllister observed that "The true history of this war must come in a measure from the rank and file."[39] The Vermont slice of that history emerges most immediately, and often most candidly, in the letters of soldiers like Mc-

Allister, Joseph Rutherford, and Tabor Parcher, and civilians like Ann Stevens and William Ripley. Unvarnished and unrevised, the words of the men and women who experienced the war reveal the mindsets, beliefs, and emotions that shaped Vermont's response to the Civil War. Their letters reveal few unanimous opinions, nor do they suggest that Vermonters faced the war with greater righteousness or heroism than others. Rather, they tell a story of men and women motivated by a heritage of independence and a love of liberty. Their voices speak of personal tragedies and triumphs, of families torn apart and drawn closer together, of hopes demolished and new worlds discovered.

Chapter 1

Spring 1861

The bombardment of Fort Sumter on April 12, 1861, settled beyond any doubt the question of peacefully resolving America's sectional conflict. In Vermont, as in most of the North, citizens rallied to the cause of the Union. Public meetings throughout the state drew large crowds, and the state legislature quickly voted to raise one million dollars to help finance the war effort.[1] Young men rushed to enlist in Vermont's first infantry regiment, or waited impatiently for new regiments to form. Few believed that the war would last long, and opportunities for glory would vanish for those who procrastinated. As James McPherson observed, Americans held a romantic view of warfare, both in the North and the South.[2] In the popular mind, a question of principle could be settled once and for all in a short, heroic struggle. This was the war Vermonters expected in April 1861: brief, perhaps bloody, but decisive.

Vermont and her prospective soldiers were ill-prepared for war. Only a few hundred men in seventeen militia companies scattered around the state had experience in military drill and marching. Ten of these companies were incorporated into the First Regiment, Vermont Volunteer Infantry. On May 8 they entered the service of the United States for a term of ninety days, under the command of Colonel John W. Phelps of Brattleboro, a West Point graduate and Mexican war veteran. Peter T. Washburn of Woodstock, who was to spend most of the war as Vermont's adjutant general, received the commission as lieutenant colonel.[3] Traveling by train and steamer, the First Vermont arrived at Fortress Monroe, a federal stronghold on the Yorktown Peninsula of Virginia, a week after mustering. For the first week the troops occupied a hotel, an Old Point Comfort resort in more peaceful times, next to the fortress. Late in May the regiment moved ten miles to Camp Butler, near Newport News, where it remained for the rest of its service in Virginia.

"The Peninsula," already renowned in American history as the

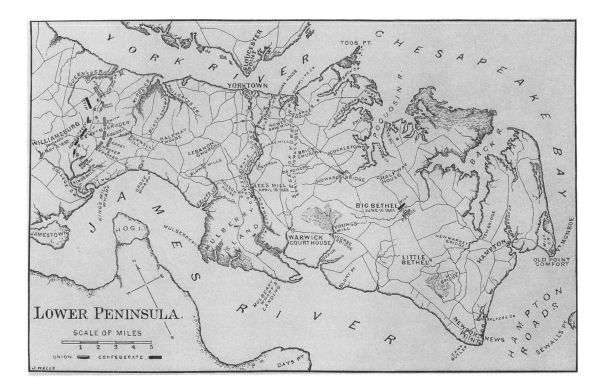

place where Washington cornered Cornwallis in 1781, gained further fame in General George McClellan's campaign of spring 1862, but in 1861 it served as an arena for only a few nervous skirmishes. On May 24 the Vermont regiment marched to Hampton, where rebels were reported to be building defenses against the Yankee invaders. After an exchange of words between Colonel Phelps and the colonel of the opposing force, and a bungled attempt by the rebels to burn the bridge leading into town, the Vermonters marched into Hampton to find no further sign of the enemy.[4]

A more serious engagement took place on June 9 and 10. The First Vermont, commanded by Lieutenant Colonel Washburn (Colonel Phelps had been put in charge of Camp Butler) was part of a small force sent to destroy enemy fortifications at Big Bethel, about ten miles from Newport News. Marching at night in hopes of surprising the enemy, the men approached Big Bethel in two columns. Some of the soldiers became disoriented in the dark and fired on their friends, thus eliminating the element of surprise. Daylight came, and with it, exaggerated reports of the enemy strength. The attack proceeded, and the Northern men traded fire with the Southerners for several hours with little result. Washburn's men probed the left flank of the enemy's works late in the morning but were soon ordered to withdraw. There were few casualties, none among the Vermonters, and the entire affair was of no military significance. It was, however, one of the first infantry en-

MAP 2. The Yorktown peninsula, showing the locations of the battles of Big Bethel (June 1861), Lee's Mill (April 1862), and Williamsburg (May 1862). *Battles and Leaders of the Civil War*, vol. 2, 188. UVM.

gagements of the war, and it received a good deal of newspaper coverage.[5]

Meanwhile, as spring ripened into summer, the raising of troops continued at home. In April the Vermont General Assembly had authorized the formation of six regiments of volunteer infantry. The Second Vermont Infantry made its first camp (Camp Underwood) in Burlington early in June at the old fairgrounds near Battery Park, while the Third assembled at Camp Baxter in St. Johnsbury in June and July. The remaining regiments would not take the field until the fall.

Raised initially to help protect Washington in the days following the bombardment of Fort Sumter, the First Vermont Infantry was in a sense obsolete by the time it reached the field. There was little use for a ninety-day regiment once it became clear that Washington was safe from immediate attack. But the First Vermont and other early volunteer regiments served notice on the Confederacy that the North would not back down from its pledge to preserve the Union. Furthermore, the brief service of the ninety-day regiments gave the best men field training that would prove of great value in the new three-year regiments. More than 600 of the First Vermont's men reenlisted, and 250 of them received officers' commissions.[6]

FIGURE 2. Ann Stevens. Rokeby Museum.

1. Rokeby Museum, Robinson Family Papers, box 41, folder 11, Sheldon.

2. The Reverend John Gleed (1785–1870) was pastor to several Congregational churches in northern Vermont before he retired in Morrisville.

"That which we have so dreaded has come upon us."

Ann Stevens to her brother William, April 21, 1861.[1]

A young Quaker from East Montpelier, Ann Stevens taught school at People's Academy in Morrisville.

Morrisville .. Vt. 4 .. 21 .. 1861 ..

My Dear Brother:—

Do not think because I have not written to thee, I have not valued thy letters, though anyone, who did not know how much I have to do might draw that inference. I have had a very hard cold the past week that I caught at the Falls a week ago, and have coughed so much, my head aches very hard and I am sore and old all over, it makes a pretty large sore doe'nt it? Mary writes thee is some better, how glad I am to hear it. maybe the journey if not the physician will do thee good. Thee must be very careful and still keep good courage, though Prof. Lee says thee will never lose that, which is a very desirable thing where there are so many *dis*-couraging things to be met. through all storms may the bird of Hope sing on sweetly as ever. We have been to hear Grandpa Gleed preach to-day.[2] he prayed long and earnestly for our Nation, and that civil war and bloodshed might be stayed, and peace be restored to the country. May the prayers of him and the thousands of others In the pulpit by the home fireside and in the camps prevail before Him who is the God of battles.— The war seems to be inevitable. There is scarcely anything else thought or talked about here, men gather in the streets and a crowd is ever in the bar room, talking hotly concerning the state of affairs. Last evening there was a very spirited meeting at the Hall, where resolutions were passed giving their wealth, strength and life if need be to the cause of freedom, Mr. Gleed was President. I will send an account when they are printed. Mr. Blanchard and Thomas Gleed have sworn to go to the battle.[3] Blanchard says he will be ready the day after school closes, if more volunteers are called for. There will [be] a company formed in a few days here. They do not wilfully rush to battle and destruction but calmly and considerately give themselves for their country. Mrs. Whipple with red eyes says she will give her husband up for her country. I think she is a noble woman. That which we have so dreaded has come upon us. May God direct us all.

We cannot think of anything else. We hurd last night from Philip he was going to enlist. the Northfield company passed through Richmond and three young men had already gone from that place. Young man from the Park. [Hyde Park, Vt.] hurd of the surrender of Fort Sumpter, dropped his work and the next day shouldered his knapsack and started for Charlestown. Forty of the Students of Middlebury have enlisted. The Green Mountain State will not have withholden her support in so necessitous a time. The Lord have mercy and turn the thunderbolt from this land. I visited at Susan's the other day, she is such a good woman. Uncle Pollos is quite sick has had the Lung fever, [   ] has returned, so as to stay there nights. She brought us up some hulled corn & we had Mr. & Mrs Blanchard in here and had quite a party, George Doty is going to the war. O dear, what sorrow! what sorrow! Susan wants one of thy pictures   I do not know which on[e] to leave her   I like the Photographs very much. took the liberty to give one to Mrs. B. who was very much pleased with it. I am afraid Jay will not pay me the visit he expected to. I think he is a good boy and always shall, let [Leeve?] sputter all he is a mind to, and he will make a smart man, and I think a good one, I expect to hear Isaac and Levi have gone to the South, do not have very much fears concerning my own relatives excepting Timothy, for I hope the Quaker principle is strong enough to restrain them.[4] I worry a good deal about Timothy. I am going to write to him to-day if I feel able to, though by that another need not think I am very near my grave, though I feel some as though its rest would feel pretty good, and welcome. I have received a beautiful letter from Nancy. she talks of being heare at the close. Unless the excitement cools down some I am afraid there will not be much but a close, Mrs.

3. Thomas Gleed, a prominent lawyer and son of John Gleed, apparently never enlisted; Andrew J. Blanchard, principal of People's Academy, joined the Third Vermont Infantry as captain of Company E, but resigned in October.

4. Ann's brother Timothy spent the war on the western plains; whether he served in the military is unclear. See his letters in the Robinson Family Papers, Sheldon Museum.

Blanchard has copied that piece Horace likes so well, onto sheets and is going to have it sung   they rehearsed it last night. it is splendid

> "Calm all commotion
>   That may arise,
> Increase devotion
>   Strengthen our ties .††
> God save the Union,
>   God save our Land,"

There is no news to write as I know of. There was some talk of a factory's being built in this place, using two hundred hands, but if the times are not more settled this will not be done. Susie Burnette has been to Mrs. Whitney's all the spring   it has occasioned a good deal of talk, but she is not the one to stop for that. Fannie has written 16 pages to Mary, at Mt Holyoke.. she can write two pages to my one. My school is not near as large as the fore-part of the term, a good many are sick . . — Will not some of you come up at the close? Aunt Mary has sent a pillow case and a pair of shoes to mother, suppose by Amos,— they were left here, anyway. How do uncle Timothy's folks get along?— It causes me many pangs to think Laura T. is at Charles: alas that she will seem beautiful to him, I fear. Please excuse this poor letter, and this long delay. Love to all, Farewell, Thine

forever Ann

Rhoda Wing is Mrs Presiding Elder   Wonder of all wonders thank thee very much for that Harpers, very correct likeness in it

"My life is at my countrys disposal"

1. Joseph L. Perkins Letter, Manuscript Files, UVM.

Joseph L. Perkins to his brother, April 23, 1861.[1]

Perkins, of Barre, was a medical student at the University of Vermont.

Burlington Apr. 23/61

My Dear Brother,

I have just recd. and perused your truly welcomed letter   I will reply as well as my exhausted powers will permit. I have had but little sleep for severall nights on account of the excitement and my making preperation for war. Nearly all are drilling.

Now my brother allow me to speak plain that you may truly judge my motives. I believe tis no common tie that binds our hearts togather—my feelings being the criterion. When this great national crisis came—when I *felt* that I *must go* to my country's rescue, among my first thots were *we* would go togather, side by side, and if needs be die in each other's defence.

Would it not be much easier to die in the arms of one we loved? Would not the death struggle be mitigated if we felt a heart near our own that shared all our joy and sorrows?

Forgive me my brother if when I learned of your endeavors to enlist and no invitation to go along with you, forgive the pang of jealousy that shot through my heart. It was uncalled for, but by it I was the better enabled to realise the depth of that friendship. Since learning of your rejection I have nearly ceased hoping that we might go togather and half an hour since I pledged my word with a classmate that I would go with him   tis not certain yet on his part as his friends are all strongly opposed to it. he is of the right mettle—is true. If we can get into the best company here I think that he will go—otherwise will probably wait awhile. Now if he does not go can I get into the Bradford Guards,[2] how many more will they take. I thot of writing to Blodgett but shall not til this is decided.

I will not go without *one friend*. I am acquainted with some of the Bradford company and would feel more at home there than here.

In reply to your question—yes, I have well considered this step thru days and nights of sad, sober thot. I am aware that my constitution will not endure much hardship and as you say I might be a burden rather than a help. I *hope* that my life is of too much value to throw away for nought   In answer to whether it is dear to me I would refer you to my hopes of the future—to the love I bear her whose life is two fold dearer than my own and perhaps that stimulates me to action— What would be the pleasure of homes without Liberty? Twould not be home—we were born free let us die freemen. Shall we hold back the good we might do because we cannot do more? Tis a foolish war truly, I think we'd better ask the heathen to pray for us—to send us missionaries etc. Well let the cause be what it may we have a Constitution—laws. We have elected a president   Shall we support him in doing his duty—in executing the laws or desert him? We the light of the world toward which all nations are gazing   shall we allow it to be extinguished becaus demons prefer drkness? *No!* So long as there courses [in our] veins a drop of American blood so long the Palmetto[3] flag cannot cast its damnable shadow ore New England homes.

Can there be found a man so depraved with soul so small that there cannot be arroused a spirit of self defence or that will not raise an arm to save a countrys fall—. This stirs my whole soul to action— My life is at my countrys disposal and if possible should be given ten thousand times ere I'd be ruled by tyrants and *much less traitors*. I didn't know before what it was to *feel* patriotic—like the electric shock it goes

2. The Bradford Guards, one of the best-trained of the prewar militia companies, became Company D, First Vermont Infantry.

3. The Palmetto flag, South Carolina's state flag, was an early symbol of Southern secession.

through ought my whole system absorbing all things else—no I cannot say all things I must make *one* exception   It has been said that man rules the world and woman rules man   I never knew the philosophy of that but it has just come into my head how it is and it can be clearly demonstrated—"logically"   Woman is equal with man yet is termed the weaker vessel—well she is physically therefore she must possess some other quality in greater digree to keep the ballance— We will go back a little now, we say knowledge is power, well Eve first bit the Apple of Knowledge then Adam but Eve took the largest mouthful concequently was wiser and most powerful   So they do to this day possess a power which we have no means of overcoming.

 I dont wish to be rash in this but I want to find the right place and do the right thing. I dont know but it would be better for us who are not accustomed to severe exercise and labor to drill here awhile ere we join a company   We have a drill master. I mean to pursue the right course   I could but weep when I read your letter. My noble hearted brother! If every northern man but possessed that Spirit this war would soon end for want of traitors with whoom to fight   a week's time would give them each a hemp neck tie   or, if not a *blue* pill[4] one that would make them *feel blue*   When you spoke of another's tears —had I been suddenly immerced in ice water the chill would not have been more apparent. Womens tears conquer me.

 Will you reply by return mail   please write a long letter and tell me of *our folks*—love to them.

> Your brother
> J. L. Perkins

P.S. I made a mistake in the date. the 24th came in nearly three hours ago—we have to carry our lette[rs] the night before as the mail goes early and the P.O. is not open til after the mail goes—

4. "Blue pill" was a common term for a bullet.

"War has commensed and great excitement prevailes"

1. Fitch Family Papers, carton 1, folder 13, UVM.

Samuel Sumner to his father, April 27, 1861.[1]

Sumner was a schoolteacher in Kentucky before the war called him home to Troy, Vermont.

Bourbon Co Ky Apr 27/61

Dear Father

 I received yesterday your letter dated the 15th inst [i.e., of the current month]   I am s[t]ill going on with my school the same as ever but war has commensed and great excitement prevailes here. A company of 100 men left Cynthianna last monday to join a regiment at Louisvill subject to the orders of Jeff Davis and on wednesday they left L to join the confederate army   Military companys are formeing evry where most of them are what they call home gards   At some places they are hoisting the Secession flag at some the Stars and Stripes and at other some both   They are raseing money and sending to France for arms I have not and do not intend to join any company and although I do not think that the North have done right yet I have no notion of becomeing a Southern Mercenary   Had the North accepted the Critiden ammendments this scheme of secession would have proven abortive[2]   The advocates of disunion would have been robed of their thunder and I do not bealieve that a single State with the exception of South Carlina would have left the Union but now I bealieve that the 15 Slave States will go to gether   When an old Patriot like J C Crittenden offered messures of reconciliation the North should have offered to the South garentees that they did not intend to interfear with the instution of Slavery eather directly or indirectly. Borrow now trouble on my account   I am as safe here as I would be at home and if bad should come to worse I can return home at almost any time.

> Your Son
> Samuel Sumner

2. Senator John J. Crittenden of Kentucky proposed amendments to the Constitution early in 1861 that would have prohibited slavery north of 36° 30′ but protected it elsewhere. (See McPherson, *Battle Cry of Freedom*, 252–54.)

"It is hard for us to study or do anything but get excited"

Henry McAllister to Willie Stevens, April 30, 1861.[1]

McAllister, of Stowe, was a member of the class of 1862 at the University of Vermont.

1. Rokeby Museum, Robinson Family Papers, box 41, folder 11, Sheldon.

U.V.M. North Hall April 30. 1861.

My Dear Friend—

Your letter was received last night. I was not expecting it. but I have been looking for you instead for a few days. Yet for all this it was welcome but you would have been more so. The term is drawing to a close. Next Saturday sets us free for awhile. The Summer Term will commence the 16th May. At that time Sophomores will be expected to appear in public. The present excitement operates badly for our performance. Erhardt & Loomis have already left,[2] and the rest are too excited to do justice to themselves. My piece is nearly completed. I am in hopes to do nearly as well as I could under more favorable cir-

2. Joel Erhardt served as lieutenant and captain in the First Vermont Cavalry. William Loomis enlisted in the First Vermont Infantry and later served as a lieutenant in the Twelfth Vermont Infantry (Peck, *Revised Roster*, 22, 223, 462).

3. John T. Drew received a commission as captain of Company G, Second Vermont Infantry, was captured at the first Battle of Bull Run, and eventually paroled (Peck, *Revised Roster*, 53).

4. The English drillmaster, William F. Hart, is not listed on the muster rolls of the "Light Brigade," which made its ill-fated charge at Balaklava on September 20, 1854 (according to correspondence with the Public Records Office in Kew, Surrey, in the possession of the editor). Hart received a commission as captain in the Fourth New York Cavalry and was killed at Raccoon Ford on September 16, 1863.

cumstances. It is hard for us to study or do anything but get excited. Patriotism is above par. The Stars and Stripes float over the old U.V.M. and many of the students will be ready to go when they think there is a call for them. I have not enlisted yet, and I hope it will not be necessary but if it becomes so I shall go if I can get the consent of my creditors. I wrote home to see if father and Uncle would let me go. Uncle wouldn't let me go because it would annul my life policy and father said the greatest objection he had was that people might lose their money and their confidence in me. Further than that he didn't know why I shouldn't go as well as others. I do not wish to go unless it is necessary for it would be too great a sacrifice, but when my debt to my country becomes greater than those to my friends I hope I shall discharge the larger obligation first. Drew has left College and is Captain of a company forming in town.[3] The College boys are all under drill. We can beat any company here in field evolutions. Our drill master is an Englishman   He has seen ten years service, was in Crimea, and in the charge of the 600 at Balaklava.[4] We like him very much. Those who stay here during vacation are going to march to Underhill and camp out a week. They will have a nice time, but I can't go with them. Next Friday or Saturday I shall go to Uper Jay [New York] to get some of my things. I shall return sometime next week and go home. Can you come down here at our Exhibition? I want to see you very much during vacation. Can you go to Stowe with me? I shall find it impossible to go to Morrisville at the close of the term. I have not been to the Dr's yet, when I shall I don't know. I shall be very busy this Summer. I have some loose ends to bring up, but with my present health I can do considerable work. Dr. Foote is helping me as usual. If I can get money to take another course after this I think I shall feel *well*. Please write me within a week and tell me where you will be the last of next week and whether you can come here at our exhibition. I *must* see you during vacation or shortly after.

With kind regards to your people I remain

Your Friend
Henry

P.S. You need not send my things at present. bring them if you come down.

"We have got to stand it, so there is no use grumbling"

1. Valentine G. Barney Papers (MS 104), folder 1, VHS.

Sergeant Valentine G. Barney of Swanton, Company A, First Vermont Infantry, to his wife, Maria, May 19, 1861.[1]

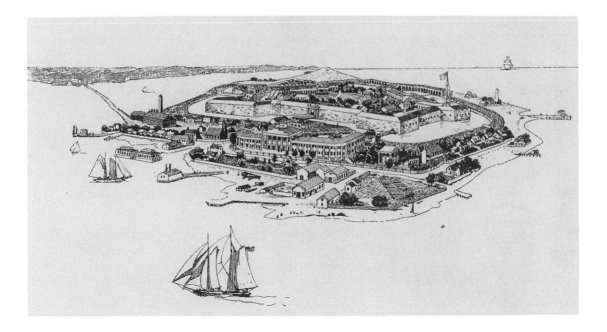

Sunday May 19th 1861

Dear Maria

It is now one week to morrow morn since we came to this fortress and a long week has it been. I wrote and sent you a lot of mixed stuff a few days since but have heard nothing from you yet. I recd a letter from Father yesterday which was dated the 10th and glad was I to hear from home, but this does not suffice. I am very anxious to hear from you and know about the children and your health. Day before yesterday we changed our quarters from the northern to the south western side of the fort. We are now in more comfortable quarters but how long we are to remain here is not certain. We (the Regiment) ocupy a large Hotel situated just outside the fort. and on old point Comfort This point is or has been a great summer resort for Southern Gentlemen but now the same great Hotel is occupied (as they say) by northern barbarians. The building covers over a large piece of ground and is finished off very nicely but is only two stories high Our Company ocupy nine rooms so that nine men have one room for their benefit. We have to sleep on the floor which comes rather tuff but we have got to stand it so there is no use grumbling No one is allowed to eat drink or smoke in the house nor even spit on the floor. there is a Cook tent a short distance from us and we have to go there and get our grub (which I dont hanker after) and sit down on the ground and eat We pay W. H. Bell 25 cts extra each month from evry mans wages to do the Cooking washing dishes etc for the Company and he hires an assistant Every day some Company is at work mounting cannons for the de-

FIGURE 3. Fortress Monroe. *Battles and Leaders of the Civil War*, vol. 2, 144. UVM.

fence of the fortress and while we are at work the Enemy is not idle. Yesterday they were discovered in building a sand batery on the shore about five miles from here on the oposite side of the bay and a little Steamer with Three guns ran over there but before they got very near them, the Enemy fired at the Steamer but did no harm the Steamer then let drive at them some Twenty or Thirty times and the report is that some 18 or 20 of the Enemy were killed but how true it is is not known by me but we could see the firing and hear the report plainly There are Two large war vessels lyeing here with about 25 guns each, and one of them would have gone over but the water is to Shallow for them to get very near but as the little Steamer done the business and routed them it was just as well. These little Steamers are very active and are on the lookout all the while for batteries Smuglers etc. Most evry day they bring in one or two prizes (as they call them) that is they bring too vessels occupied by the Secessionists and fetch them into port—. There is some 15 or 20 of them now lying here— It is said that Gen Butler of Mass is coming on here with some 8 or 10 thousand men and that there is to be an army formed here to march out into the interior of the State but all reports are not to be relied on[2] The most of our boys are pretty well but young Spencer continues Sick at the hospital. Rugg is not very well but is able to be about. I have not felt first rate for a few days and have taken some medicine but I am able to be on duty and perform all my labor which is not little I should like to be at Danby to day and spend the Sabbath with my dear little family but I hope it is for the best as it is now I think of you and the children much and I can imagine that I see Freddy nodding his head and saying bye bye and Carrie too repeating her verses and asking her mother where Pa has gone. It seems a long time to look forward to the time when we shall be together again but the time will soon pass and I will be with you in our little home. I tell you Maria I never before realized so forcibly the comforts of a home and the kindness and goodness of my loveing Wife and children as at the present and I hope and trust that I may be more attentive to them in the future than I have been in the past. I shall expect to hear from you soon and I hope good news will accompany your letter. As I gave you the directions before where to write in a bungling form I will now give them again— Direct your letters "In care of Fairbanks & co. New York, 1st Co. 1st Regt. Vt Vols Fort Monroe Va." Give my love to all the folks and kiss the children for me often. I will now Close and go to dinner which is ready and bid you a good bye until I write again

> Your Aff Husband
> V. G. Barney

2. General Benjamin F. Butler, former governor of Massachusetts, took command of forces at Fortress Monroe on May 22 (Benedict, *Vermont in the Civil War*, vol. 1, 38).

"We hear every day of large bodies of men near but when we look for them they were not there"

Captain William Y. W. Ripley of Rutland, Company K, First Vermont Infantry, to his wife, Kelie (Cornelia), May 26, 1861.[1]

Out in the country near
Fortress Monroe
    Sunday May 26

Dear Kelie

Your dear letter of 19 May was recd day before yesterday. I think I must have recd all the letters you had written before that one. You do not know how much good your letters do me. When the mail comes in the boy's all flock to my tent so anxiously, & those who get letters are so happy & those who get none feel so disapointed that it is sad to see them. You see that we have left our comfortable quarters at the Hotel and gone into camp again. We moved yesterday and have just got nicely fixed. We are on good, high ground near the woods & Every tent has a cool comfortable little porch of green boughs in front of it which is a great addition to our comfort but alas, we have today recd orders to move again. We do not know where we are to go or what we are to do, so do not be disapointed if you do not hear from me as often as you have. I shall write you as often as I can but do not know how I shall send the letters. You must write me often & direct as before, they will reach me some way.— Last night we were twice called up by attacks of scouting parties upon our piquets. We have two Regts besides ours on this ground, one from Troy among which are many of my old friends of the Troy Citizens Corps as officers   Larry Kingsley—Den's Brother, Father will recollect him, is with this Regt. & came to see me the first thing. ask Father to tell Den that Larry is well & hearty.— The other Regt is a Zouave Regt from Brooklyn. they wear the regular Zouave uniform which is very handsome but too conspicuous for service. The 4th Mass Regt is to go with us tomorrow. Day before yesterday our Regt was ord[ered] out to Hampton to drive in four Cos said to be entrenching themselves there. My co was on guard that day & of course could not go. but I could not see the Vt Regt go out for active service & stay at home myself & went as Aid de Camp to [Lieut.-]Col Washburn.

The town is approached only by a long bridge which was defended by three light guns, when we got within about 1/2 mile of the bridge we were met by an aid of the Col commanding who wanted to know what we were after, & asked if we intended to fire on any of the inhabitants, Col Phelps replied that he should fire on no party who did not first fire

FIGURE 4. William Y. W. Ripley, Jr. Rutland Historical Society.

1. William Young Ripley Papers, Duke.

on him but that any armed party must disperse. The Aid replied that they were in arms to defend their homes and would not allow us to cross the bridge, he then turned & rode off at Top speed & in less than five minutes the bridge was on fire. The only order Col Phelps gave was "forward, double quick" & the leading Co advanced at a run & tore up the planks & threw them in the river. there was a party posted on the opposite side with three guns but when the head of our column reached the bridge they dismounted one and threw it in the river & ran off with the other two. a party of citizens standing near recd an intimation from Col Phelps that they had better assist in putting out the fire or he would fire on them. they took hold with a will & soon put out the fire, We crossed the river & marched through the town & all around it, but every secession flag was down & not an armed man in sight. We hear every day of large bodies of men near but when we look for them they were not there. You ask what we do for recreation & what are our duties, well, we rise at five & ans[wer] to co roll calls. breakfast at seven. in the interval between roll call & breakfast the men put their camps in order bathe, mend their clothes etc.

At 1/2 past seven co Drill which lasts till eight (I mean half past eight) from half past eight till 10 nothing, from 10 till 1/2 past 11 battallion drill. dinner at one, & lay off till half past four, then battalion drill till half past six then dress parade & dismiss for supper at 7, tattoo at 9, when all retire. This is our standing order varied of course by circumstances. Tomorrow we take the field & commence the campaign in good earnest. You may hear of fighting soon—if you do, do not dear Kelie, worry about me—what I mean is, do not give yourself needless alarm till you have certain knowledge of the facts, after a battle few people have the time to write letters and as capt of a co I have perhaps less time than others. I will of course let you hear from me as soon as I possibly can, but if you do not hear from me in a week or even two or three weeks, do not consider me as among the killed or wounded— Mails will of course be disarranged & every body busy so that if I got time to write I might not be able to get my letter off— The Havelocks have just come, & I have just distributed them to the men. Many of them were marked for particular individuals and as they recd them many an eye was glossy with tears. They are just what we need and must be very comfortable indeed. if we had time we might pass votes of thanks but as it is the Ladies must rest satisfied with the knowledge that we are very gratefull to them for their kindness. I am glad that you go to see Mrs Coppins often & I wish that you would see Mrs Clark as often as you can—they need & ought to rec[eive] a great deal of sympathy. I do hope that some body is visiting & caring for the families of my men. We are all well except a few trifling colds & slight cases of diarrhea. we have no one in hospital   other cos have in all twenty seven— There is great complaint about Sanborn & he does act

FIGURE 5. A havelock. Lossing, *Pictorial History of the Civil War in the United States of America*, vol. 1, 575. UVM.

strangely, but he may be right, it does not appear so to me however.[2] time will tell— It is warmer now than when I wrote you last. 90° in the shade & 100° in the sun & it does not seem to me as warm as I have felt in Vt when it was only 75 or 80   the sea breeze is fine here. It must be pleasant here in the summer when the fort & Hotels are full of company, but except soldiers the place is deserted now. It has been so hot today that we have had no service. at 6 1/2 we have our dress parade & after that we have service. The men enjoy the sunday service much, & it is interesting. The Regt is formed in square by division & faced inward, the singers are invited to the center & usually some 90 or 100 come out. Last sunday we sang a hymn set to "home sweet home" Many of the singers & others wept freely— They are none the less men for that.

I wish I could be with you in the cong[regational] church this pleasant afternoon. dear little Bessie, how quiet she is at church for such a little thing. I am glad you give her a little mint & such things, but I would not get her into the habit of eating any thing upon her bread. When will you wean Willie? this summer? he must be a great boy when I come home— & Bessie must grow a great deal—I hope she will not forget me. Why dont you take the old cat down to the house? she never was a great favorite of mine but I dont care to have her suffer. I feel as you do about any thing that we had about us in our dear little home. we shall be as happy there again however, so dont worry yourself sick dear— Tell Mother that the Havelock she made for me gives me more pleasure than any thing she has done for me since my first pair of breeches. I think it will be very comfortable. I have it on now. Coppins & Clark & the others were very glad of theirs & seemed to take great pleasure in thinking that they were made by their wives & friends— I do hope with all my heart that they will be well cared for, I wish somebody would see W B Thompson's wife, he is feeling badly about her. she lives on West street I think. Now darling I must close my letter. Kiss Each & Every one of my dear friends for me & give our little ones a great many. do not let Bessie forget me & if Willie begins to talk I know you will teach him to say Papa. Write me often

> Your aff husband
> Wm. Y. W. Ripley

"The blunders of political generals"

Second Lieutenant Roswell Farnham of Bradford, Company D, First Vermont Infantry, to Charles Harding, June 15, 1861.[1]

2. Dr. Eben Kimball Sanborn, Surgeon of the First Vermont Infantry, was accused of drunkenness and of neglecting his patients, but Phelps and Washburn defended him against the charges. (Benedict, *Vermont in the Civil War*, vol. 1, 59).

1. Roswell Farnham Papers, box 20, volume 37, UVM.

Camp Butler, Newport News, Va.
Saturday June 15th, 1861

Friend Harding:—

You have probably by this time read a great variety of accounts of the battle of Great Bethel. You will probably never hear all the facts, or rather nine tenths of what you do hear will not be fact. The newspaper accounts that we have seen here thus far have not come within gun shot of the truth. All sorts of absurd mistakes are made. From the N. York papers you would suppose that Col. Bendix had command of the detachment that went from this post. They fall into the mistake by supposing that a Lieut. Col. cannot rank a Col., not knowing that Lieut. Col. Washburn is acting as Col. and that he in fact had the command of the expedition from here. Col. Bendix had but three companies and they were stationed at the fork of the road and made the fatal mistake of firing into their friends—tho' perhaps Bendix and his men are not to be too much blamed for that.[2] Among other little items I saw that one man was wounded with a bayonet! The fact is there was no bayonet fighting, and none of our men came near enough to the enemy to be bayoneted, unless the enemy had guns from four to six rods long. Our boys engaged them nearer than any body else, for we were not more than four or five rods off. You will see that the New York papers ignore our fighting at all. The fact is while we were fighting the other regiments were withdrawing from the field, and we were so far to the right (our right) that we were lost sight of. We could not see one of the other regiments, nor were we in the least sustained. When the order to retreat came, the wonder is that we were not all cut off, for the enemy had already outflanked us on our right, instead of our outflanking them, and gave us a peppering of grape and canister as we withdrew. It is well they did not follow us at once, for if they had, we should have been in danger of being entirely cut off. The only reason they did not, is because we had poured such a storm of lead upon them for the few moments we were engaged that they did not dare to. When we got out of the woods the whole army was in full retreat. Whose fault was this? You will ask. The papers have got one thing right. They blame Gen. Pierce, and he is the man on whose shoulders a great portion of the blame should rest.[3] Who is Gen. Pierce? Where did he come from? I never heard of him before. He did not seem to know any thing. When officers came to him for orders his reply was, "Act your own judgement, gentlemen." The papers say that Butler cursed him to his face. I presume he did.

I am writing this letter on the supposition that you have read the account of the battle I wrote my wife. Can you imagine what a labor we performed that day on four crackers, on an average? Col. Phelps says that in all his experience in Mexico and elsewhere he never performed

2. Lieutenant Colonel Peter T. Washburn had command of the regiment after General Butler put Colonel Phelps in charge of Camp Butler. Colonel John E. Bendix commanded the Seventh New York Infantry.

3. Brigadier General Ebenezer W. Pierce of Massachusetts.

and he dont remember ever hearing such a march, so long and desperate a fight, and such a retreat on the amount of food we had.

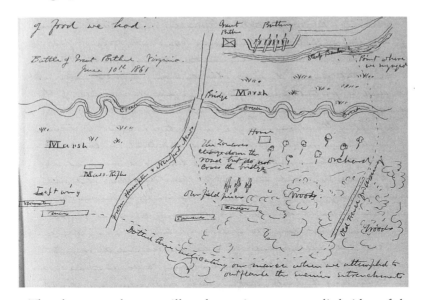

FIGURE 6. The Battle of Big Bethel: drawing from Roswell Farnham's letter of June 15, 1861. UVM.

The above rough map will perhaps give you some little idea of the position of matters during the fight at Great Bethel. You will see that we formed the left wing at the beginning of the battle, but that when we came in contact with the enemy, it was at the extreme right. We had five companies from our Regt. but only three were ordered to march, Bradford, Woodstock and Northfield. The other two were ordered to remain in their position. Some of the Mass. Companies were with us, and on the road thro' the woods we picked up a few Dutchmen.[4] We were half an hour in getting into a good place—or rather in getting far enough to the right. The woods between the Zouaves & the point of attack are much more extensive than they appear in the sketch, and we came out twice before we had got far enough. Fortunately we fell upon the trench and that run in the right direction and afforded us a good deal of protection. When we came into the vicinity of the entrenchments, we had to run up a steep bank to get sight of the enemy. They were posted in a sort of trench in advance of their works. The most that we could see was their heads, while they could have full sight at us. But we soon made it so hot for them that they did not want to get sight very often. We certainly sent some to their account. The number of the enemy has been variously estimated at from 500 to 6000. Whatever it was, if we had been well backed, and had we received the order to do what many of the boys were ready to do, when we got to the top of the bank, that is rush right along, we should have taken the place at once, and history would have had no occasion to blush at the blunders of political generals. We feel that as a company and officers of a company we have done our duty, and that Bradford has no occasion to be

4. The "Dutchmen" Farnham refers to were German-Americans belonging to a New York Zouave regiment.

ashamed of us—further than that I have nothing to say. Few men know how terrible a thing a battle is, and the man is worse than foolish who places himself where he may have charge of a battalion, in a fight, without experience. Remember me to all and write soon. Yours etc.

Roswell Farnham

"i feell as lonsom as the very Devil"

Musician James E. Hart of Pittsford, Company B, Second Vermont Infantry, to his friend, Nellie, June 16, 1861.[1]

1. Edwin Horton Papers (MSS 21-16), VHS.

Burlington June 16th 1861

My Deares Nellie

As it is sunday and I [have] Nothing to think of but friends that ar absent you may Judge my feeling here   A sunday without the pleasure of any society Except that of man   I will be a perfect Barbarian if [I] should stay hear 3 years but that is out of the Question for i Never Will Stay so long   probably this co Will be disbanded in the fall   I Never will leave til i get an honerable Discharge if it [is] for 3 years   Nellie you dont know how bad i felt that Night i left you   I tryed to conceal it from you but i thought my heart would break to think of leaving for so long a time   Nellie if you only knew how bad I wanted your likeness you would send it to me   Now please send it the first opertunity. I had a letter From Cynthia   She said the folks ar all well. I am going to write to Lana by this Mail. I dont know what to write for i feell as lonsom as the very Devil to say as i think but there is No use of complaining for there is others the same as myself   there is one shure thing that if i Ever live to Return I will Rais a dust   if i Never do Return it will be all the Same in [Duch][2] for it will give some one a chance to ware my old shoes if they se fit   Rob Caldwel and myself tryed to get a pass to go to castleton but could Not as we dont know how soon we will leave this for Washington   All potter did Not go home as he said he would but was able to come up to the camp on foot this morning he is improving very fast. there is a large audeance of spectators here most of the time   We have a Picnic this afternoon   the people of Burlington use us better than them of castleton. I went down to port Henry [New York] yesterday and see some of my old friends   As you will probly like to know our location i will try and give you an idea [Each] company has 18 Tents set in 2 files the captains at the End of the street   the music[ians] all tent to gather at the Extream Right corner

2. Hart seems to be accepting a "Dutch consolation," or very little consolation at all.

of the Regiment   there is 24 in the Brass Band & 20 in the Martial makeing 44 in all   the music Marches in front of the Reg all togather Except when in action, then in the Rear   the Musicians ar Each armed with a sword & Revolver. the Name of this . . . camp is under-wood   the P.O. address this company whare Ever they are as follows. Co. B. 2d. Reg. V. V. which stands for Company B. 2d Regiment Vermont Volunteers   Each co has a letter to Distinguish them apart Now if you complain of this short letter i will write a Quire the Next Now get a sheet of foolscap and fill it full to answer this   it Rains here Today but our tents do Not leak a drop and ar very comfortable   Answer this soon as we will probaly leave soon   I will write after we get to Washingto[n] and tell you all the News so good by

From your Ever true friend
J. E. Hart

Chapter 2 Summer 1861

As the First Vermont Infantry regiment finished out its service in July 1861, the Second Infantry arrived in Washington in time for the first major battle of the war, Bull Run. The regiment had been brigaded soon after its arrival with three Maine regiments under the command of Colonel Oliver O. Howard. Howard's Brigade approached the battlefield on July 21 after a long and exhausting march toward the enemy's left flank. As the New Englanders came under fire some of the men—officers among them—wavered, held back, or hid behind trees. Most of the soldiers marched on and formed ranks as they had been trained to do. Corporal Russell Benjamin of Brattleboro was struck and killed by an artillery shell, earning the distinction of being the first Vermonter killed in action. The same shell mangled the right arm of Burlington's Sergeant Urban Woodbury, future governor of Vermont. The brigade advanced in formation but found the enemy too strong to dislodge from its position. With the tide turning against the federal army the brigade was ordered to fall back, but the Vermonters refused to withdraw. Finally the regiment retreated, at first in good order but soon, like most of the Union army, in a great panic, every man for himself. Two Vermonters had been killed and thirty-five wounded. Thirty-one men, of whom twenty-one were wounded, found themselves prisoners.[1]

The idea that one grand battle might end the Civil War died at Bull Run. Blame for the disaster fell upon Union field commander Irvin McDowell, General in Chief Winfield Scott, and President Lincoln, though many held the prowar Northern press responsible for pressuring the government to act before the army was ready. The Confederate victory revealed serious flaws in the organization and leadership of the Union army, but instead of dampening Northern war fever, Bull Run stiffened Northern resolve. Volunteers soon swelled the ranks of the three-year regiments mustering throughout the North.[2] Within days, President Lincoln put the soldiers in Washington under the command of General George B. McClellan, a promising young officer who had been credited with winning a series of small but important battles in western Virginia.[3]

At Camp Baxter in St. Johnsbury, the Third Vermont Infantry began training and preparing for its journey south. Poor discipline and inadequate leadership led to a number of disturbances in and out of the camp. On the eve of the Bull Run battle, a soldier was shot and killed trying to break into a camp sutler's "refreshment saloon" with a mob of his comrades.[4] The regiment shipped out a few days later, much to the relief of the citizens of St. Johnsbury.

Fortunately, the Third's reputation did not precede it. Shocked and angered by the Bull Run defeat, people turned out in town after town to cheer the regiment as the troop train rolled south through the Connecticut River Valley. The scene was repeated with equal fervor as the Third made its way through New Jersey and Pennsylvania. The men were treated to sumptuous meals in some of the larger cities. Only when the regiment reached Baltimore, which was sullen and hostile to the Northern cause, did the sober realities of war begin to sink in.[5]

William F. Smith of St. Albans received a commission as colonel of the Third Vermont Infantry, and joined the regiment after its arrival in Washington on July 26. A career army officer and 1845 West Point graduate, Smith stayed with the Third for less than three weeks. In August he was commissioned brigadier general; eventually he rose to the rank of major general of volunteers, in command of an army corps.[6]

The Third Vermont Infantry participated in some minor skirmishes in the late summer and early fall. On September 11, the Third and part of the Second Vermont Infantry ventured into rebel territory near Lewinsville as part of a small reconnaissance force. On their return, since they were in the rear, the Vermonters bore the brunt of a surprise attack by Jeb Stuart's rebel cavalry. The Third proved as cool under fire as the Second had at Bull Run, standing fully exposed to the enemy artillery until support could be brought up. A single shell killed a Vermonter and wounded eight others, one mortally.[7]

"they must run or die or surender one of the three pretty soon"

Private James W. Bromley of Danby, Company B, Second Vermont Infantry, to friends, July 6, 1861.[1]

1. James W. Bromley Papers (MSC 5-18), VHS.

Alexandra July the [6th]

Dear friends   I received your letter last night   it was verry exceptable   I was glad to hear that you was all well   I am well and hope

2. The Fire Zouaves (the Eleventh New York Volunteer Infantry), were composed of New York City firemen.

3. Most rifles used in the Civil War fired the "minié ball," a lead bullet loaded from the end of the barrel.

these few lines will find you all enjoying the same blessing   I am as tough as a negro   We are now 6 miles from fairfax Court house   we are going to start for manatia [Manassas] Gap to morow morning at 1 o'clock   I think that we shall have a little brush then if the southerners have got any spunk   they have left the Court house and I think that . . . they will leave richmond or else they will get whiped   we have 35 thousand men with in five miles of us   we are all going to start and march right along   there is 2 thousand in the same meadow with us here now   the fire souaves[2] are clost to us now   they caught 1 secesioner yesturday and brought him into camp   he was one of the first lieutenants   the mishigan rigement caught 3 of the rebels night before last   they had caught one of them two times before and now they think that he wont get away again   they are stout looking men   they was well armed   they had the miny[3] rifle musket and one revolver each and a boa knife   there was 15 secesionest in one party and 3 of the souaves chased them into the mishigan rigement   the souaves had not any arms with them   they was out looking for some sheep and came a crost these rebels and chased them   the rebels was so scart that [they] did not show fight   they asked them why they did not shoot   they said that they did not have time   they said that they did not know that their pickits extended so far south before   we shall let them know that we shall be further south before next saturday night than they ever thought of   they must run or die or surender one of the three pretty soon   I haint got much more time now   you must write soon   tell me all of the news   direct as before   this is a fine farming country   plenty of unions and tobacco raised here   we are now encamped on one of the old planters farms   he has got 12 hundred acres in it   he is in the southern army   now we are after him [   ]   there is thousand of acres of wheat here cut and shocked and left in the field uncle sam is the owner   I hant got any more time now   I will tell you the particulars when I get back

      Write soon
      youres
            for
                  Ever
      James W Bromley

      Alexandra
          Va

"It was a disgraceful affair the whole of it"

Second Lieutenant Chester K. Leach of Fletcher, Company H,
Second Vermont Infantry, to his wife, Ann, July 23, 1861.[1]

FIGURE 7. Chester K.
Leach. U.S. Military
History Institute Photo
Archives.

Alexandria July 23d 1861

Dear Ann

The last time I wrote I wrote that we expected hot works & I think
we have had it, but thanks to God *some* of us are yet in the land of the
living, I suppose it will be good news to you to know that I am unhurt,
but still there are a number missing from our company. Woodbury was
wounded in the arm, which was amputated & Streeter in the knee
(But to the particulars)   We were ordered to march saturday the 20th
at 6 PM but the orders were countermanded & set at 2 OC sunday
morning   We were up at half past one & ready to march but there being so many to move it was six O clock before we got fairly started &
it was 12 O clock or more when we reached the battle ground & we
were all worn out with fatigue & the want of water but we did the best
we could   In marching to our place of attack we had to pass over an
elevation of ground where the canon balls played upon us pretty hard,
Woodbury was wounded at this place with a grape shot or rifle ball,
One of our color guard was . . . wounded in the knee about the same
time by a canon ball, Our brigade made a stand an hour or an hour
and a half when a retreat was ordered   The rebels canons were entrenched & their men were concealed in the woods so that we had no

1. Chester K. Leach Papers,
box 1, folder 1, UVM.

FIGURE 8. *The Second Vermont at Bull Run*, by James Hope. Mary Stewart Baird and Howard Coffin.

2. The captain of Company H was William T. Burnham of Montpelier and the first lieutenant was Jerome B. Case of Fletcher; both resigned within a few months. Leach replaced Case as first lieutenant (Peck, *Revised Roster*, 56).

chance at all, Some of the wounded were left behind, what their fate is I cannot tell   report is that they were all killed, but that is uncertain

Our Capt did not reach the battle ground at all & after passing where the canon balls raked us so hard Case failed up so there was no officer when we made a stand but me with our company,[2] Our boys feel almost disgraced by the battle   there must be as many as one hundred missing from our regt   Some are killed some wounded and left behind & some probably taken prisoners. some six or eight from our company are missing but I believe none from Fletcher, It was a disgraceful affair the whole of it   Nearly all of our baggage is lost, and a great many of our guns & almost every thing we had with us   I have thought a great many times that I was tired but I never knew what it was to be tired before, when we came off the field I could hardly stand up, but we were 8 or 10 miles from our camp, I reached there about 10 OC PM & had been there about 3/4 of an hour when we were ordered to retreat to Alexandria which place we reached about eleven AM on monday   making a march of about 40 or 50 miles & without any rest for about 36 hours   I think some of the missing will [p]robably get in yet

write as soon as you get this

Ever yours   C K Leach

"We shall never retreat again"

1. Brown Family Papers (Miscellaneous File Additions), VHS. See Franky's letter to Elijah, February 8, 1863, p. 133.

Private Elijah S. Brown of Craftsbury, Company F, Second Vermont Infantry, to his sister, Franky, July 26, 1861.[1]

Alexandera July 26/61

Dear Franky My Sister

Received your letter this morning & was hapy to hear from you the day you wrote your letter I was in the hardest Battle ever known our Vt 2 Rigt went on to the field to fight & two maine Regts come on to the field after we did & we was the last to Retreat & we had the order to Retreat & we wuld not go   we fired some five or six rounds & had the order Again to Retreat & Co A from Benington & our Co F from the Capitol marched the whole length of the field & then fired again on the Retreat   the canon balls & baum shels flew like hale stones & there was an emensed shour of rifle balls & some of them took affect but not many of them   there was one of our men shot through the head by my side & three wounded & my canteen was shot of from my side & in our Regt 2 Vt loss is 34 killed & 35 wounded & lost   part of our brigade was cut of at bulls run & the whole loss on our side killed & wounded & not accounted for is about two thousand in all & the enemy loss is supposed to be 5 to one but we dont know sertain but we drove them something like A mile   I say we I mean our forces   when we went on to the field they was in the woods & they marched to the right of the woods into A corner that was cleared & waved there little palmito [palmetto flag]   it is about two feet square it is A very inferior looking thing & we made them leave that place in les than half A minute & they fled to the right of us & opened on us with canons & we had nothing but muskets & they was so hot that we could not touch the barrels   I loded my gun after the second order retreat was given & before I got the cap on it went of & when left we scatered in all directions   I was run over by our own Cavelry & knocked down & was steped on by one of the horses & jamed into the mud but was not hurt but A little   You can see the rest of the news in the papers   my health is good as usual   I am very tired & lame from the march   it was so long it was about 50 miles   tel Clem that waren Smith sends his compliments to him   give my best wishes to all that inquire after me   Bill Stowe is well & [   ] as ever   Direct to the 2 Vt Regt Co F   Elijah S. Brown

wright soon
direct to Washington D C

E S Brown

we have moved back to Clermont to day   we probably Shall have an other fight in a few days & we shall give them just what they deserve or we will be killed on the Spot   we Shall never retreat again our Colonel hid behind A rock for protection & left us to our selves the Capt Stood by us like A lion[2]

2. Colonel Henry Whiting, never popular with his troops, was accused in the newspapers of "showing the white feather at Bull Run," in Benedict's words (*Vermont in the Civil War*, vol. 1, 89). The captain, Francis V. Randall, subsequently won commissions as colonel of the Thirteenth and Seventeenth Vermont regiments.

"This war is a war of the people"

William Young Ripley of Rutland to his son William, July 29, 1861.[1]

Ripley owned and operated marble quarries in West Rutland. His daughter-in-law Cornelia (nicknamed Kelie or Keelie) and her two children lived with him while her husband, William Jr., served in the First Vermont Infantry.

1. William Young Ripley Papers, Duke.

FIGURE 9. William Y. Ripley, Sr. Rutland Historical Society.

2. Horace Greeley edited the *New York Tribune* and Henry J. Raymond edited the *New York Times.*

Centre Rutland July 29, 1861

My Dear William

Keelie has just received your letter of the 24th—you wrote feeling much as I did, when we got the first news from Bull run—if it had been half true, we might well have despaired—our first reports were that the army was completely cut up, and annighilated—but in an hour or two, we had other reports—and felt much relieved—and now we feel—although we are ashamed, at the causeless & senseless panic which seized our men, that the apparent defeat, was substantially a *victory*—and that the army and the country are stronger to day, than they were the day before the battle—the army is fully reorganized—and is stronger than before—as it has done more to arouse throughout the North a stern determination, to prosecute the war to the bitter end, at whatever cost of men or money, than even the attack on Sumter did—there is no doubt, that there has been a great want of energy, and *pluck* at Washington—they have been very much afraid of hurting the feelings of the gentlemen traitors—and they must soon learn that . . . if the war is to be prosecuted—that the men they fight are enemies—and when taken are to be treated as such— It is I believe the first time in the history of the world—that rebels and traitors—taken with arms in their hands— have been treated to a good moral lecture—have the oath of allegiance administered to them *again* & . . . dismissed—to take their places in the ranks, to fight again, as many of them do— If the government do not reform that—I predict that the army will, and that speedily— And there is one other thing that they ought to do, and must do—if they expect to make any movement, without having the enemy fully advised of their plans—and that is to hang every newspaper reporter, and editor, that they find within ten miles of Washington or any military post— I have no doubt that Greely Raymond[2] etc. etc.—have done as much . . . to keep the enemy fully advised of all the movements and intentions of the government, as their agents & spies have—and there are plenty of them, all around the army & Washington—

This war is a war of the *people*, and the men at Washington—will find that they are only agents in the matter—if they go ahead and lead, with vigor, the people will follow & support them—if they falter—another Cromwell or Napoleon—will make his appearance on the stage, and tell them to make room for more competent men— I have no doubt that Gen Scott & the administration, were hurried on to the attack of manassas, by the senseless clamor of the press—led by Greely etc. with the war cry "onward to Richmond" before they were ready— and it is a mistake that probably will not be repeated— You say that we have terribly underrated the resources & courage of the South— you know what my opinion was six months ago, about that—its not changed now—they had the advantage of us in the start—they brought out all their rescources—and were ready, before we began to prepare—and when we have brought out all, and more than all that they can do—no impression will have been made on the strength and rescources of the North—we shall have a reserve that will overwhelm them—if the blockade had been made effectual—and it is now a mere sham—they would have been subdued in twelve months, without firing a gun— You say that Gov Fairbanks has offered you a position in the 4th Regt. but dont say *what*— I was in a measure prepared to hear it—we had a rumor about town, some days ago—that he had, or would offer you the command of the 3rd—he has not been fortunate in his Col of the 2nd—and no one will be surprised to hear of the failure of the Lieut Col of the 3rd—there was a time when I was rather inclined to wish, that you would accept some of the offers made you—for I supposed that you would make your *mark* under competent leaders—but if the army is to be commanded by politicians, and stump orators—your chance of gaining a good reputation is as good here, as in the army—

But enough of this— Keelie went over the river this morning to put the house in order, and have it ready for you—but after getting your letter she is a good deal dispirited, she has not much courage—and is a good deal afraid that you will not come home to stay— I wish she had a little more ambition, or that you had less of the military in you—she is a dear good girl—and wants nothing beyon[d] her house— You write as thought little Bessie was sick—she has been a little unwell—as children often are, but nothing of much consequence. some time ago you spoke of something like a *fit* she had— I suppose that it was nothing but holding her breath—as you recollect Charly used to when small— You need have no fears about her knowing you—she will call you as far as she can see you, when you come—if you shave as much as usual—she talks about you constantly, and when she sees me coming from the Post office, she calls to know if there is a letter from Papa— Willie is *one of the Boys*, wide awake, and full of life and fun as he need be—he is a fine strong boy—and has grown and improved a great deal since you left— I intend that they shall meet you at the Depot, if you know when you are coming— We hear from your mother often— Helen is gaining, but slowly   the poor child has had a hard time— We have had a fine season, crops good, and the country looks finely— We have just got through repairing all the mills—both sides of the river & in Mendon— Business has been as good or better than we expected it would be— I have bought a 4 year old St Lawrence colt, that I think will suit you— We shall look with a great deal of anxiety for news from Newport [News]—but I cannot make myself believe that they will attack you there— write as often as you can— May God protect & spare you is the prayer of your affectionate Father

Wm Y Ripley

"it was nothing but one continual ovation"

1. Solomon Heaton Papers,
Manuscript Files, UVM.

**Private Solomon Heaton of Brighton, Company D, Third
Vermont Infantry, to his parents, July 30, 1861.**[1]

Camp Lyon near
  Washington
  July the 30 1861

Dear Father & Mother

I now take my pen in hand to write a few lines to you   I am well &
hope that you are the same   I have enjoyed myself very much   I will
try and give you a little account of my Journey   when we left camp
Baxter there were not much feaalings among the people but when we
gut down to Bradford the cannon rattled away pretty good but [we]
did not stop and when we gut down below White River Junction it was
nothing but one continual ovation and when we gut down to Bratle-
burough there we stopt and got some refreshments & stop about one
half hour and then we went on as far as Springfield Mass and then
stopt about one hour and there we was received with great pleasure
there was about 5 thousand people to see us and the fireman there gave
us a good treat and from there we went to Hartford Conneticut and
there we had a good time I tell you and from there we went to New
Haven   it bein dark we did not have such a good time as in some
other places but there was a Great number of folks to see us although
it bei[ng] dark   and from there we went to Jersey City and there we
stopt about 4 or 5 hours and from there we went to Philadelphia and
when we reached there I cant discribe the fealings that was shown to
our soldiers there   when we got there and got of from the cares we
marched up on to Washington street and when we got there a nice supper was waiting for us and I never see such a crowd of Ladies and Gentleman reddy to take us by the write hand and with tears in there eyes
bid us god speed   we stopt in that city all night and our cares was sur-
rounde[d] all most with the admireing crowd and [when] we left there
the people said that they wished [we] could stopt there longer   I shall
always remember that city as long as I live and from there we went to
Baltimore and a more quite place I never see   we see the six rigament
was atacked[2] and from there we went to Washington and from there
we went to our present camp which we occupy   we . . . have the most
advance post on the Potomac   some [of] our Officers expect an attack
soon   we are under the orders of Major General McLeland   we are
about 14 miles from buls run   we dont expect to commence an attack
till about the first of Octtober and then if you dont hear of some hard
fighting then we Vermont boys [didn't] fight   my health is first rate   I

2. The Sixth Massachusetts
Infantry had been attacked by
mobs of Southern sympathizers
on its march through Baltimore
on April 19, 1861.

never felt better in my life   If I should live to git out of this scrape I
dont no as I shall come home at all   I like this climate first rate   I
dont no of any more to write at present   So good by for the present

Solomon Heaton

ps direct your letter to Camp Lyon near Washington
    Georgetown District of Colombia

"I couldnt help thinking how I should turn up my nose at <u>such a supper</u> in Vermont"

Corporal Henry E. Dunbar of Newbury, Company C, Third Vermont Infantry, to his father, July 31, 1861.[1]

1. Henry E. Dunbar Papers, MHI.

7 miles from the United States Capitol
    Headquarters 3rd Regt., Vt. Vols. Camp Lyon   Co. C.
    Chain Bridge, D.C.   July 31st 1861

Dear Father, I have but precious little time to give to writing, but I
promised to write to you so I will try & fulfill my promise, & first I am
well & pretty tough considering this hot climate, for I must confess (al-
tho we have tried to make ourselves believe to the contrary) that it is
somewhat hotter here than any weather that I have ever seen in Vt that
is, for any length of time, perhaps some of our hottest days & for a few
hours in the day, it might possibly come up to this. Dont know how hot
it is here for I.ve not seen or heard of a Thermometer *guess they cant
get one long enough*. However we have a cool breeze once in a while,
to last a few minuets which is *delicious* & also quite cool nights, so
that after all we stand it pretty well & I think after getting accustomed
to it I shall like it first rate. one thing is sure I have not had the least bit
of a cold since I came here which is more than I could say of Camp
Baxter for I got cold there every night. Our greatest trouble yet is to get
good water. the most of it the more we drink the more we want & we
have to drink so much that it makes us feel mean enough, but I found
a new place to day where it is very good & cold & tastes like our water at Home. We are just getting somewhat settled down to Camp life
& I begin to enjoy it first rate, have got very good Camping Ground &
in quite a pleasant Country, it dont look so very much different from
some parts of Vt., is quite hilly & plenty of woods close by tho *they* are
not like *our glorious old Woods* in Vt. They are mostly southern Pine
& Scrub Oaks, tho there are some Walnut & Chestnut & occasionly a
big Sycamore. The soil is a kind of a reddish sand & Gravel & bakes

down hard as a *brick* except when it rains, then its soft enough & muddy as fury, & we have some specimens of Southern showers & when they come which they do *all in a minuet* we have to spring to our tent poles, The first one we had it took 5 of us to hold our tent from blowing away & us with it, but they go off about as quick as they come, & then the sun come out as hot as ever. They dont frighten me at all tho the lightning is very sharp & thunder heavy & as I wrote to Mary I think I should like to live in tents all the time, especialy in this country   We have got a very important position here & mean to hold it too, some consider it the advance Guard of the Army, There are none of our troops beyond us in at least two or 3 directions & 12 miles from us. There are some 12 to 15 thousand rebels encamped, right in sight a little east of us there is a Reg.t of Maine troops & a Cavalry & heavy Artillery company. 200 of our men & as many more of the Maine men & a Cavalry Co. went out over the Chain Bridge & followed the main road some 7 miles into Virginia & went within 5 miles of the rebel Camp. They came in sight of a few of their Cavalry but they fled as soon as discovered & kept out of sight afterwards. while I am writing a Cavalry Co. is crossing the Bridge to see if they can catch one of the villains, but I guess they are bound to keep a proper distance. I think we shall stay here a month or two & perhaps longer to keep the *Scamps at bay* & be drilling all the while. I have 4 Privates in my tent, Kidder—Stimson—Howes & Paddock, & they are very good Boys. Our Col. (Smith of St Albans) we dont know much about yet, as he has not officiated but a day or two, but he appears to be smart & I guess pretty strict, if a man is late at Roll Call he goes in the Guard house. They are grumbling some about our rations, Especially the Officers. Yesterday all we had was *Gutta Percha*[2] Beef & hard Bread & coffee for Breakfast, last night you ought to have seen my supper. I tell you it made me *think of home*, I[t] was a small piece of hard dry boiled beef & one hard biscuit & a dipper of Tea without milk   I couldnt help thinking how I should turn up my nose at *such a supper* in Vermont & I expect we shall see tougher fare even than this before our 3 years are out, but there is necesitty for it, & when we get up to a *proper pitch* we shall *flare up*, & perhaps thats all the good it will do. However they say we are going to have some good bakers bread & fresh beef for Breakfast this morning. It has been *pouring down* (the rain) for an hour like soap, & the cooking is all out of doors so you see we shant have our breakfast very early   I must stop for the mail goes out at 7 1/2. *Now do please write* as often as you can & not wait for me. Direct to H.E.D. Wash, D.C. Camp Lyon 3rd Regt Co. C. Affectionately your son H.E. Dunbar

2. A form of rubber derived from the latex of certain tropical trees.

"They have got my rifle to crow over"

Private Moses A. Parker of Concord, Company C, Third Vermont Infantry, to Eliza Hale, September 19, 1861.[1]

1. Parker Family Papers, folder 6, UVM.

Camp Advance Sept 19

Dear Friend Eliza

I received your kind and ever welcomed last night and hasten to answer it in my poor feeble way. would I could write one that would compare with the one I rec'd but shall fail in hand as well as in orthography and syntax   I assure you I was very very glad to hear from you so soon and I beleive that you are a *true* friend and one that will prove and remain so in adversity as well as in prosperity. will you not   I think I hear you answer yes (Eliza I feel so down hearted today and have a very lame arm that I dont beleive I had better try to write for I dont think you can read it)   Doubtless you have heard of the skirmish we had the other day therefore I shall not give the details very particularly   We were sent out to protect the surveyors who were surveying that day some infantry a company of cavalry and four pieces of cannon   Our pickets had been ordered in and were about for starting to camp when the enemy began to pour in uppon us from a masked battery As our regt. marched out in front of course it would be in the rear comming back   We were marching by fours when Co C stood directly under their guns for ten or fifteen minutes and all we could do was to stand and take it   the balls and shells flying one after annother over our heads thicker and faster but we succeeded in dogging them for some time. At length a well directed shell told dreadfuly uppon some of our poor boys   It burst directly behind me killing the one . . . behind me and my left hand man in rank wounding the other at my right also myself besides knocking down two or three more   A piece of the shell passed between my arm and side inflicting a severe bruise on the latter; annother piece struck on my back but did not [hurt] me much   I [was] stuned so for a minute I did not know where I was or how I came there I was supported from the field by two comrads; took an ambulance and went to Geo. Town hospital   I did not like [it] there very well although I received the best of care but I was not at home among friend so I beged off as soon as I could   Where the boys I beleive were glad to see me   I did not stop there only a week I am getting along very well now. I think I can do duty in a few days   You can [see] Eliza, that it was pretty close dogging for me to have a shell pass between my arm and side, and I think none but a Divine hand directed it   But I will return to field of battle a few minutes   As soon as our flying artillery reached the spot the rebel battery was silenced in less than no time   our

2. Moses Parker's brother, Stephen Madison Parker, served in the same company. Madison died in January 1862 of disease (Peck, *Revised Roster*, 82).

brave boys stood their ground to the last man to defend our battery in case of a charge of infantry   It is reported that rebel loss 100 killed and wounded our loss 7 killed 9 wounded   The bodies of the killed wer left at a house near by and Jacob Goodell and one more was to guard them through the night and wer taken prisoners   To bad for Jacob   They have got my rifle to crow over; but I trust they wont get annother unless I go with it   There are a great many sick in this reg.t I think I never saw so many before   Madison[2] has got better has done duty three days   Sam is not much better although he was discharged from the hospital last night   I beleive they will kill the regiment if they [don't] stop working us so   Every man that is able have to stand on picket one half of the time

Two of our boys in Co. C. are under arrest for going to sleep on picket Our clothes stand it pretty well although some are pretty ragged owing in part for the want of care   I have kept mine mended as well as I could   the [ ] finding almost every day that that little kit of tools are very useful you gave me; so much so that I did not half express my thanks to you for them   I am *verry verry* much obliged to you for those stamps and paper and hope I shall be able to return the compliment sometime   We have not been paid a cent since we left Vt and are dead broke for money. I should liked very much to have been to that camp meeting I heard so much about there   That feamale was not thoughtful enough to send her daguerreatype to me, and I was not thoughtful enough to ask her for it or indeed think of it until you reminded me of it
I guess you will not be ashamed of your letter when you come to see this   But I will close by wishing you a welcome good night and pleasent dreams

From your sincere friend
Moses A Parker

Camp Advance

Autumn 1861

Chapter 3

General George B. McClellan brought hope and confidence to the army in Washington—soon to be named the Army of the Potomac—after the Bull Run disaster. McClellan, historian Shelby Foote wrote, was the Union's answer to the rebel hero of Bull Run, General P. G. T. Beauregard—dashing, energetic, and self-assured.[1] He issued proclamations to his troops with Napoleonic grandiosity and won the nearly universal admiration of his men. McClellan also proved to be a skillful military organizer; he labored to supply the army with better food, clothing, shelter, and equipment. Morale improved dramatically during the last half of 1861, and the men grew impatient to meet the enemy in battle.

The morale of the Vermont troops improved as well, in part because of a plan to combine five regiments of Vermont infantry into a Vermont Brigade. Conceived by Brigadier General William F. Smith, the Vermont Brigade would intensify the state pride that motivated Vermont soldiers and provide Smith with a brigade command of fellow Vermonters. General McClellan approved the plan in the fall, but Smith never took command. By this time, he had been promoted to the command of a division, of which the Vermonters would soon comprise one of four brigades. William T. H. Brooks, a career army officer from Ohio, took charge of the Vermont Brigade in October.[2]

The brigade—consisting of the Second, Third, Fourth, Fifth, and Sixth Vermont Infantry regiments (the First having disbanded in August)—assembled by steps. The Second Vermont Infantry, detached from O. O. Howard's brigade in August, joined the Third at Camp Lyon in Georgetown. The two regiments then moved across the Potomac to establish Camp Advance, where the men worked for several weeks building forts to protect the capital. These earthen structures, part of a ring of defenses around Washington, were named Fort Ethan Allen and Fort Smith (later renamed Fort Marcy).[3] The Fourth and Fifth regiments arrived in late September, and in early October the four regiments moved to the large Union encampment near Lewinsville called Camp Griffin. Here, late in October, the Sixth regiment joined them at last, and the Vermont Brigade was complete. Over the next three and a half years, the Vermonters would participate in most of the hard battles of the eastern theater and gain a reputation as one of the best fighting brigades in the Union army.

For the time being, though, the Vermont soldiers at Camp Griffin faced a foe deadlier than rebel soldiers. Disease struck the Vermonters severely, killing 197 between October 1, 1861, and March 23, 1862, the day the brigade boarded transports at Alexandria, Virginia, for the spring campaign. Of the five thousand men in the Vermont Brigade, as many as one thousand at a time were sick at Camp Griffin, a ratio far out of proportion to that of the camp as a whole. Among the diseases common at the camp, measles and mumps infected those who had never been exposed before and were now living in close quarters. More serious and often fatal diseases such as typhoid fever, malaria, and dysentery devastated the Vermonters as well. In December 1861 Governor Holbrook dispatched the eminent Vermont physician Edward E. Phelps to investigate sickness among the Vermont soldiers at Camp Griffin. In his report, Dr. Phelps speculated that the continuous occupation of the site by a large number of men caused the area to become impure, but he found no explanation for the disproportionate suffering among Vermont men.[4]

Vermont raised only one regiment of cavalry, but it was to see as much action, win as much glory, and suffer nearly the same rate of casualties as the Vermont Brigade. The First Vermont Cavalry mustered into service at Camp Ethan Allen in Burlington, on ground formerly occupied by the Second Vermont Infantry. Supplied with horses and sabres, the cavalry left Burlington on December 14, 1861, in 153 railroad cars, arrived in Washington on December 17, and on Christmas Eve received orders to march to Annapolis, Maryland, for training. Awkward and overburdened with personal baggage, the cavalry straggled into camp after an exhausting two-day march.[5]

As the year came to a close, six thousand Vermont soldiers settled in for a cold winter at Camp Griffin and Annapolis. General McClellan fended off strong suggestions from Washington that he put the army in motion. There would be no fighting in this cold and snowy winter, but drilling and guard duty continued regardless of the weather. The sick lists grew, and the soldiers waited impatiently for the chance to fight, unaware of the grim harvest that 1862 would produce.

"I feel that I am in the right and have not felt differrently since I enlisted, at all"

Private William B. Stevens of East Montpelier, Company G, Fourth Vermont Infantry, to his mother, Rachel Stevens, October 9, 1861.[1]

His sister Ann worried that her brother Timothy might abandon the Quaker principle of nonviolence, but it was brother Willie who enlisted.

10th 9th 1860 [1861]
Camp Advance, Chain Bridge Va.

My Dear Mother

I must write thee a very few lines to night, to let thee know of our affairs; we have not had many adventures since I wrote thee before. Mc[2] and I have both been a little unwell for a day or two, but both are now feeling well as we have in some time. The Reg. had orders to march this morning at day light; we were left here to see to the things in the tents till we were sent for, or till they came back; now have orders to get up one days rations and be ready to start at daylight with all the baggage of the Co. Most likely we are to go straight along to the South; the Federal army knows no such word as retreat now, they are ready for war now and *will go on*. We shall go tomorrow, and shall probably go into action ere tomorrow night. I feel that I am in the right and have not felt differently since I enlisted, at all; I *may not be*; If I am *wrong*, I hope to be forgiven; I may not go into battle. I spoke to Dr. Allen[3] the day before yesterday and he said he should want me in a very few days, and if the Reg. goes into action before we get there I shall be called on; if I am not I shall do what I think is my duty to God and my Country; If I fall I fall with a firm purpose; I do not have the least ill feeling toward any living being. Troops have been passing here ever since we had the orders, and now the artillery wagons are rumbling by in the dark. Some like 20 000 men have passed here since noon; no doubt there will be 300 000 men under arms tomorrow on our side; they go sure of a victory, and I do not expect to see thiss camp till we have seen Richmond, and some other parts of the South, if I live to go with the Army. I hope to see home again; I may not, I may never even write thee again. Give my love to all my friends. I have not time to write to Mary now but will, if I get a chance. I have just written to Ann, and the letters will go in the morning, I suppose.

I must bid you-all farewell; it may be *forever*; it *may not*; I trust it *is* not; if it is I do not fear to meet my fate.

FIGURE 10. William B. Stevens. Rokeby Museum.

1. Rokeby Museum, Robinson Family Papers, box 40, folder 6, Sheldon. See Ann's letter to Willie, April 21, 1861, p. 18.

2. "Mc" was Stevens's friend Henry McAllister.

3. Dr. Samuel J. Allen of Hartford was surgeon of the Fifth Vermont Infantry.

Dear Mother Farewell. Thomas, Charly, Mary, Horace, Howard, Jane, Melissa, all, Farewell.

In much love to all,
William B.

FIGURE 11. George H. Randall. Special Collections, University of Vermont.

1. George H. Randall Papers, Manuscript Files, UVM.

"to day one of our ladyes is to be sent home A corpse"

Musician George H. Randall of Glover, Company D, Fourth Vermont Infantry, to his wife, November 8, 1861.[1]

November 8th
Headquarters 4th Reg't. Co. I
Camp Grifin   1861

   Dear wife   take my pen in hand to write A few lines to let you know that I received your letter dated November 3thd and was glad O how glad to hear that our little Hattie was so much better   O how I wish I could see her and her mama to   I am so hoarce that I cant speak loud more than half the time   my throat is very sore   it is A disease that wee all have   there is one man in the third reg that has not spoken A loud word for three months   my back has been groing weak for about two weeks   it is pretty lame now but I think I shal get over it in corse of A week or so and then be tough as A not   there are about four hundred on the sick list in our regiment now   probably there are twenty five that will get A discharge and some eight or ten that will die   ther was one man buried yesturday and to day one of our ladyes is to be sent home A corpse   there was two ladys in our regiment[2]   both had husbands the one that died was sister to the others husband   they are all going home with her   the company that she belong to feel her loss very much   they were both good women   I sent Hattie my picture in A letter but it was A miserable thing but I could not make them take it over again now but I will send A better one by and by   old ike was up to see me yesturday and I went home with him   I wrote to Hattie to send me some things   our boys are geting boxes of good things every day and I tell you it makes my mouth watter to see them   you see it does not cost any thing to send A box to the soldiers only to new york   it comes free after it gets there so it dont cost much   it has to be paid in advance   we expect to be paid off next monday and I will send you some money   O how I wish I could bee at home to day wee would have A good time   I have never said any thing about my bad writing but you take A board and go out in the door yard sit down on the chips put the board on your knees curl up like A sick monkey in

2. It is unclear whether the wives had actually enlisted disguised as men. Some such cases have been documented, but not in the Vermont regiments. Family members were sometimes allowed to board with officers in or near camp, but the privilege generally was not extended to enlisted men.

A sour aple tree and then write and you will not find falt with my writing   well I am going to write to Hattie on an other sheet so good by to you my sweet good wife
direct as before

this from your old Hen

"I cannot feal as bad as his Mother when she gets the sad inteligance"

Corporal Henry H. Wilder of Weybridge, Company F, Fifth Vermont Infantry, to his mother, November 11, 1861.[1]

Camp Griffin Nov 11th

Dear Mother

It is 10..oclock at night and a solemn time it is for the ambulance has just drove a way from in front of my tent dore and what do you think that it left there   it left one of my tent mates a corps   Adam Potter of Cornwell and a good boy he was when he was alive but he is gon to his home with[out] any friendes to console him and comfort him in his last hour   his remains are to be watched to night before my tent   to morow morn we pay the last respects to him [w]home we did hope but ashort time agoe would get well and goe thorough this War with us and be able to meete his friends again with some of us but it was not Gods will and t[h]erfore we cannot have him for a tent mate but it is well we know for it is Gods will but sad and lonly as it is with me I cannot feal as bad as his Mother when she gets the sad inteligance he left a Mother that is with out a Husband and more with noe consent and with out her knolage of his cumming   he enlisted the morning that we left Midd[lebury]   he first had the measles then he got cold and then he had a feaver and at last the cuick concumpsion and this morning at five o clock he died   there is another one in this Comp that is not expected to live   how do you and Father and Horty do   I hope you are all well   I am well as usual   pleas do not trouble your self about me for if I am unwell I will let you know   give my love to Dea Sampson people and tell them that M[errill] is well and is very healthy give my love to Mrs Lathrop and tell her that I am agoing to write to [her]   I wrote to Uncle Nelson yesterday   how do all the people do in Was [u]sual I suppose   it is late and soe good by Mother   write when conveniant   from your ever afectionate

Son..Henry..H..Wilder

FIGURE 12. Henry H. Wilder. Special Collections, University of Vermont.

1. Henry H. Wilder Papers, folder 1, UVM.

"the Vermont Regiments are all well provided for but a soldiers life is hard"

FIGURE 13. Samuel Sumner, Jr. Vermont Historical Society.

1. Fitch Family Papers, carton 1, folder 13, UVM. See Sumner's letter of April 27, 1862, p. 22.

2. The battle of Ball's Bluff, on October 21, 1861, was another Union blunder. Though of minor military importance, it damaged Union morale. (See Foote, *Fort Sumter to Perryville*, 104–108.)

3. The Fifth Vermont Infantry camped at St. Albans for two weeks before leaving for Washington. T. D. S. Bassett suggests that jobbers in Vermont made out even better supplying some of the other regiments with food and other necessities at the mustering camps (*Urban Penetration*, vol. 2, 492).

Second Lieutenant Samuel Sumner of Troy, Company D, Fifth Vermont Infantry, to his parents, November 12, 1861.[1]

Although he had been ambivalent about the war several months earlier, Sumner soon after accepted a lieutenant's commission.

Camp Griffin Nov 12 1861

Dear Parents

I have received a Montpelier paper from farther which I was glad to receive as it was from home but we are pretly well supplyde with papers here   Captin Benton takes Waltons Dailey Journal and our first Lieut the Daily Green Mountain Freeman and the News Dealer comes to our camp regular besides we get the Washington Daileys evry morning by 8 and the New York Papers the day after they are ishewed but the News Boys have not been allowed to visit Camp to day from some cause or other   thair has been such instance before which was the day after the battle at Ball Bluff[2]   I suppose that you are anxious to know how we fair   the men all have woolen Shirts and drawers one pair of pants a coat and a thin spencer we call a blouse an over Coat Shoes and socks the socks are of no account but the most of them have home made socks   the men have each a bed tick which they have filled with husks or hay and a woolen and rubber blanket   they sleep together so that they have two or three blankets over them at night   they have fires in thair tents in what we call California fire places which is constructed as follows   a trench is dug about 16 inches square extending from the interior to the exterior of the tent   it is covered over with the exception of a foot at each end the inside serving as a fire place and the outside end is covered with a headless barrel serves as a chimney   our living is better than it was at St Albans   thair we were let out to jobers who [made] out of us in 10 days over expenses $1800.[3] here our rations are good and we have more than we use which we sell back to the comisary department   I must say that our living is better than I expected it would be   the men are all provided with clothing which is new and good and by the way the third are geting new Clothing to day the Vermont Regiments are all well provided for but a soldiers life is hard   he is exposed to all weather and frequently has to remain on duty all Day in the rain   I have been out on picquet when it rained all night and we could have no fire or shelter   the Vermont Regiments have been kept in the advance and have had to [do] a great deal of picquet duty besides have worked on fortes and have fallen a great many acers of trees

We bearyed one of our men a few days ago by the name of Sco[t]t from Woolcot   he died with a feaver   was a man of a strong constitution and one of the best soldiers we had   I went to Washington Saturday the first time I have left camp   I stoped at Georgetown to see our sick at the hospital thair   they are all better than they were when they went thair   Charley Bachelor who has been very sick is so he sits up most of the time and Gib Porter I found round helping the rest   Lieut Stiles has gone home   we have an other appointed the Sargent Major who I think will make a good officer

> Yours Affectionately
> Samuel Sumner Jr

"clothe your self warm & be careful of your health"

Perry Ayer of Goshen to his brother Dana, a private in Company C, Sixth Vermont Infantry, November 17, 1861.[1]

Goshen   Nov 17 1861

Dear brother

I received your letter last night   was very glad to hear from you & to hear that you was well   I hav ben down to fathers to day   he seemed pleased to hear from you   I will giv you a scetch of your goin away   I worked with Wilber Allen the day after he came back   he told me he saw you to montpeler   I was very sory to hear that you had [en]listed I think you ant old enuf   I went down to let father no you had gon he swore all sorts   he swore you should not go   when he found out he cood not stop you without goin to your captin then he wood hav your wages   I was afraid he cood get the 7 dollars[2] but I soon lernt he cood not get that he gut my mind in full   if I cood seen you before you went it wood of ben a grait consolation to me   I should advised you & I must now Obay your oficers   get the good will of them   dont gamble & drink   you have grait temptations before you   be a good boy   Volney is coming to morow   one advise more & I will close that is to send your money to some one to me or lo or some one that you hav confidence in   keep what you need   Volney does so mikel [Michael?] does so   you are in more danjer   it can be sent with a check & [p]ut in the bank   rite your feelins about that next time   the boys are gon to bed   thay hav miletary caps   we hav had an awful wind hear   I am goin to chopin to morrow   ned has hired out to Z[ ] Allen for one year   we have about 3 inches of snow now   Dana if thare is any

1. Dana Ayer Papers, Gertrude Mallary Collection, Bradford, Vermont.

2. The State of Vermont supplemented each soldier's monthly federal pay of thirteen dollars with seven dollars from the state treasury. This sum was intended to support the soldier's family and usually was signed over to a family member designated by the soldier.

thing you need footins gloves or any thing I will send them   we herd you was asistant coock   clothe your self warm & be careful of your health   it is about bed time & I must close   dont fail to rite   rite evry week   I will as often as you will   I was goin to rite to day & see if I cood get one to you   rite as soon as you get this   so good by for this time

> Yours Truly
> Perry Ayer

"May I go home … may I go down town … May I go some whare, that is the talk here in Camp all the time"

Captain William Wells of Waterbury, Company C, First Vermont Cavalry, to his parents, December 8, 1861.[1]

1. William Wells Papers, carton 1, folder 20, UVM.

Burlington Vt
Camp Ethan Allen
Decr 8th 1861—

Dear Parents

Having learned a little more about our leaving for Dixie thought I would write you.

Next Thursday 12th inst afternoon the Regt is to be presented with a stand of *Colors* by Gov Holbrook, who by the way is a *bully* man for us   he says we have the best Regt that has been raised in the State.

Thursday 12th inst night there is to be a Grand Ball at this place   I understand it is to be a free thing to the Officers of the Regt. I hope it will be *free*   if it is I shall attend.

The Gov has set next Saturday as the day for our departure. we strike tents at 3 a.m. hope to leave by 8 a.m. get to New York Sunday forenoon. the RR. folks say they can carry us to N.Y. in 24 hours, but guess it will take 30 to 36 hours. we shall stop there untill Monday forenoon   We do not know whare we shall be stationed this Winter, are ordered to report ourselves to Washington. the Gov is going with us, to try and help us to get some good quarters.

Lieut Col. Kellogg, Maj Bartlett Surgn Gale & Asst Surgn Edson, Lieuts Page & Holden & myself board just outside the Gate, commenced last T[h]ursday, we live tip top. had Turkey for Dinner today have Buck Wheat Cakes every morning   I tell you it seems like home.

Their cannot be got up another as good mess in Camp as we have got. I do not know how we shall mess when we leave here, but the Maj has agreed to mess with Lieuts Page Holden & myself   we shall try to get Lieut Col with us. Every one in the Regt likes Maj Bartlett   he is going to make a tip top officer   his being Maj does not do our Co any harm.[2]

I wish you could get Ruggles down here as soon as Friday, for we want him to go with us.

Mason has been unwell for a few days   is now getting out again. he will be able to do duty soon. he had a bad cold. Carr is as tough as a *brick*. tell Mrs Carr he is all right,

Does Ned write any thing more about coming home. their is not much show for him here at this recruiting office I think. will do all I can for him   such chances as he wants are picked up & one needs to go himself & see the Recruiting Officer. he cannot tell untill he sees the man what he will do for him. perhaps if Ned was here he might stand some *show*. Their has nothing presented itself in this Reg whare I could help him   I will keep my eyes open for all chances.

May I go home, my wife wants I should, may I go down town, to get my boot fixed. May I go some whare, that is the talk here in Camp all the time. I am getting them dried up in a great degree about going down town, but the (Going home) is as often asked as you please & sometimes oftener, if I let one go I must let more, orders are not to let only ten be gone at once   I shall be glad when we leave this place, whare Furloughs will be plaid out   I am to late for the mail. I will close & write more tomorrow. their is to be a meeting of Capts at the Cols tent   perhaps I may learn something new. we are to put 8 Horses & 8 men in a car. the Horses will then get good care. we go by the way of Rutland & Troy.

Lieut Holden went home Saturday, returns tomorrow. I shall not go home before we leave the State. the men all feel good about going away. One of our men is going through Waterbury   I will send this by him. I am well have gained several pounds since I have been here

Let me hear from you before I leave the State.

Should be pleased to see you down here before we go.

Send Ned Dillingham down here.

I must close & go over to the Cols tent & help him eat a chicken *pie*.

Your affectionate Son
William

Lieut Page & Orderly Cheney wish to be remembered

Wid

I have not time to look this over

2. Major John D. Bartlett of Montpelier had been the original captain of Company C; Wells replaced him as captain upon Bartlett's promotion to major (Peck, *Revised Roster*, 230).

FIGURE 14. "Camp of the Second Vermont Volunteers at Camp Griffin, Va.," by George H. Houghton. Special Collections, University of Vermont.

1. Hiram Hunter Letter, Civil War Miscellaneous Collection, MHI.

2. Seth Bumps of Company D was Hunter's brother-in-law, Maria's husband.

"be of good chear for gods will must be done not ourn"

Private Hiram M. Hunter of Albany, Company D, Fifth Vermont Infantry, to his sister, Maria Bumps, December 22, 1861.[1]

Camp Griffin Va

Dec the 22 1861

Absent sister   I seat my self to write afew lines to you under rather painfull sircomstanses   Seth has departed this life[2]   he died last night about five oclock   he will be berred to morrow   I would like to have sent his remaines home but sircomstances for bid   if it is your wish I will try to have him sent home   it will cost about sixty dolars to send him home   there is six dollars that he had that will be sent to you as soon as we can git the bills on it   he had the lung feaver and then the typhorid feaver sat in   John is quite unwell but I think that he will be well again in a few dayes   he is so that he is around but is not able to do duty   I think that you had better stay on the hill this winter   if you want any thing I will try to send you some money so that you wont suffer   I supose that father will draw Johns sevan dolars amonth but ask for seths   I doant know how that will be but I think that you can draw his pay as long as you live or at any rate untill the three years are out   be of good chear for gods will must be done not ourn   evry thing is for the best imust close this time so good by this time   this from your afectionate brother Hiram M Hunter

to Maria Bumps   West Albany

Winter 1862

Chapter 4

The Vermont Brigade stayed at Camp Griffin from October 1861 to March 1862, a longer period of time than it would spend at any other camp. Over the long winter of 1861–1862 the troops drilled daily and gradually adjusted to the rigors of army life. Sickness maintained its grip on the Vermonters through January before loosening in the latter half of the winter. Many factors contributed to the improved health of the soldiers, including an increase in the number of surgeons, better clothing and camp conditions, the removal of infected soldiers to central hospitals, and the natural immunity acquired by those who recovered.[1] The Vermonters in the Army of the Potomac would never again encounter a season of sickness as severe as the one they endured at Camp Griffin.

At home, severe winter weather early in 1862 did not delay the mustering of the Seventh and Eighth Vermont Infantry regiments, both bound for service in the Gulf of Mexico. The Eighth had been recruited expressly to serve under General Benjamin F. Butler in the Department of the Gulf, but the officers and soldiers of the Seventh expected to serve in the Army of the Potomac and were bitterly disappointed to be assigned to Butler. It was the first in a series of misfortunes to befall the Seventh, Vermont's "hard luck" regiment.[2]

The two Gulf-bound regiments embarked on four sailing ships, leaving Boston and New York between March 9 and 14, and arrived at Ship Island, off the southern shore of Mississippi, between April 7 and 10. After enduring three weeks of storms and seasickness, many men set down their trembling feet on the warm sand of Ship Island, barren though it was, with a great sense of relief.[3]

Aboard one of the ships that carried the Eighth regiment was the First Vermont Light Artillery battery, 150 men armed with eight cannon. The Second Vermont Light Artillery battery had already arrived a month before. All four of the Vermont units on Ship Island were assigned to the brigade of John W. Phelps, the Vermonter who had charge of the state's First Infantry regiment a year before.[4] Phelps had established the Union base on the island in the fall, but by the time the Vermont units arrived, General Butler had assumed control of the Gulf Department.

Vermont produced three companies for service in the two federal sharpshooter regiments under the command of Colonel Hiram Berdan. Considered one of the best shots in the country, Berdan proved to be far less talented as a military officer. This deficiency was made up to some degree by officers of lower rank, notably Lieutenant Colonel William Y. W. Ripley of the First U.S. Sharpshooters, who had commanded a company of the First Vermont Infantry in 1861.[5] Ripley strove to earn the respect and loyalty of his men, and his efforts paid off, to some extent, during a crisis that enveloped both regiments that winter. The men had been promised Sharps rifles, highly accurate rifles with a much greater effective range than the muskets in general use. When the sharpshooters were issued inferior Colts rifles instead, virtual mutiny ensued. Ripley persuaded the Vermont company of his regiment (Company F) to take the Colts rifles as a temporary measure, but the rest of the regiment refused to accept the guns. Eventually all the sharpshooters received Sharps rifles, but Company F got the first allotment.[6]

In Washington the pressure grew on General McClellan to make use of the mighty army he had built. Reluctant to assault directly the Confederate fortifications near the Bull Run battlefield, he proposed to move his troops by water to a position behind the rebels, who would then be forced to attack the Yankees instead. Before McClellan could move, however, the rebels abandoned their Manassas fortifications. The Union general quickly occupied them, only to find they had been far weaker, and much less strongly occupied, than he had imagined. With the rebels falling back, McClellan abandoned his first campaign plan and proposed a plan to assault the rebel capital via the Yorktown Peninsula. More than one hundred thousand federal troops were to land near Fortress Monroe and fight their way to Richmond, seventy miles to the northwest. This approach presented many advantages over a direct route south by land: There would be less land to cover and gunboats and water transports might be used close to the rebel capital. The York and James Rivers would provide natural protection on either flank to within a few miles of Richmond. And, from all appearances, there were fewer natural or man-made obstacles blocking the southeast approach. Lincoln was skeptical of the plan, fearing it would leave the road to Washington open to a rebel advance, but he approved it. Preparations for the massive military operation began immediately.[7]

By the end of March Vermont soldiers were on the move in three regions. The Vermont Brigade and the sharpshooters broke camp in mid-March and took transports from Alexandria, Virginia, to the peninsula. The First Vermont Cavalry rode to the Shenandoah Valley of western Virginia to help General Nathaniel P. Banks oppose Stonewall Jackson's small but aggressive rebel army. And out on the stormy Atlantic, Vermont soldiers were sailing for the Gulf of Mexico.

"I have been quite buisy in staking off the ground for the camp"

Adjutant Charles E. Parker of Vergennes, Seventh Vermont Infantry, to his parents, January 8, 1862.[1]

Rutland Jan. 8th 1862
10 O'clock P.M.

My dear Father & Mother,

You would, no doubt, be pleased to hear from your *Adj't* although he has been absent but a very short time. The first day of my residence here in an official capacity there was very little for me to do, in the afternoon however I went with the Colonel to the Town Hall to assist in organizing the Rutland Company. They elected their Co Officers (i.e.) commissioned Officers, and determined their name as the Green Mountain Guards.

To day I have been quite buisy in staking off the ground for the camp, arranging it for six tents to a company and the streets 20 ft wide, but as this including the streets and space between the tents with the surface they occupy does not make the camp line long enough to draw up the Regiment in line of battle by some 100 ft I am to stake it over and widen the streets 10 ft. Our tents are very nice ones Sibley patent, conical in form and about 18 ft diameter at the base. I am to have one for myself and possibly two as I am entitled to two one to be used as Adjutants office which I occupy during the day in the performance of my duties, the other as my private tent when I sleep, besides a letter A tent for my servant.

We have now in camp Two Companies the Brandon & Rutland they went in to day at noon. the Swanton Company goes in tomorrow or Friday I think. The soldiers have very good Barracks and the culinary department is very well arranged so the boys will be well fed while here   I cannot tell when I shall go into camp, that depends upon the rapidity with which the Companies come in, probably as soon as 6 or 7 companies arrive the duty of guard mounting etc. will be commenced and I shall be obliged to be on the grounds most of the time, so that it will be more convenient to occupy permanently my tent   I am

FIGURE 15. Charles E. Parker. Special Collections, University of Vermont.

1. Charles E. Parker Papers, carton 1, folder 8, UVM.

be at home before you left, untill I learned you had gone. this was a great disappointment to us, but we were very much disappointed in not getting a letter from you, after you received that box. Zulma received a letter Saturday night, but we had none   I wish you would be more particular the next time you write and let us know in what condition the things were in that you received and what you did with what was left when you was called away. Did you receive the two dollars we sent in a letter by Matot. I hope you will answer *all* these questions if you live to write us again, and be sure and tell us about your sea voyage whether you was much sea sick or not   I want Franklin that you should make a practice of writing a little every day to me that when you send a letter I may get a good full one and know something about what you are doing, for you may rest assured that we have a great deal of anxiety on your account, that you are not forgotten but often thought of, and often spoken of in the family. I hope my dear Son, as you are so far seperated from all your friends and relatives, with no one to counsel or advise you, that you will deeply feel the importance of so *living*, and *doing*, as you will wish you had when called to die. You are in a spot where you can have any sort of society but do not mingle with those you would be ashamed of here, or with those who would exert a bad influence over you. Do not I beg of you seek the company of the rough, the profane, the intemperate the gambler or any other immoral person, but seek the society of those who will exert a good influence over you   Oh Frank I have many fears for you. I dread the influence of a camp life over you; you are in a spot where danger besets you on every side. If you stay at the south through the warm weather you will be subject to disease but remember that it is very important you keep yourself your body and clothes as clean as possible. change your shirts often   be particular about this if you wish to keep well. wash your body often. I do not know how it will be about writing, whether we can get letters often from you or you from us but let us try to exchange letters as often as we can. write all the particulars, do not send short letters so far, and we will do the same   Good bye my son.

from your affectionate Mother

I hear Mason Goodell is in your company, how does he manage

"we 'Pitched tents'—1/2 mile from the Capital in a grave yard"

Private William H. Daniels of Barton, Company I, First Vermont Cavalry, to his friend Blake, February 16, 1862.[1]

1. Warren S. Leslie Papers, Manuscript Files, UVM.

From the Vt Cavalry Regiment
Camp Harris
Annapolis Md Feb 16th 1862.

Friend Blake:—

In accordance with your wishes I will respond simply, giving you a limited account of our journey from Vermont to Washington our stay while there removal to Annapolis our condition and present situation. We left Burlington Saturday December 14th last en rout for New York arived at said place at 10 o clock Sunday morning and being that no preperations had been made for our reception we were quartered in what is known as *"the house of Refuge"* with no accommodations save what might be expected from this disconsilate reserve, but owing to a dissatisfaction on the part of the [   ] to be quartered in this lugubrious place they were granted the privalige of retiring for the night in a barn with their horses with a little straw as a substitute for a bed. however but little complaint was manifested except that the rats made quite too frequent calls;— According to order on monday morning all appeared mounted ready to march   after passing through a few of the principal streets inclu[d]ing *broadway* we reached the wharf. we there boated our horses and crossed over to Jersey City and as there was no [depot] we had to ride our horses a distance of 15 miles to reach such at Elisabath Port, which place we gained about 7 a clock P. M. and being that we had to car our horses again we did not get started untill 12 N. Tuesday   we passed through a portion of Pennsylvania and reached the Capital at eve.   Wednesday morning about 8 o clock we struck the lines of Maryland, and arived at Baltimor 11. a clock but as our cars each of them had to be drawn through the City by horses we did not get ready to March till 9 o clock   We reached Washington 5 o clock Thursday morning. one would think that our journey was greatly prolonged from New York to Washington. It was owing to being hindered by other trains. After unloading our baggage and horses, we *"Pitched tents"*—1/2 mile from the Capital in a *grave yard* which may seem to be rather *tough* nevertheless it was true. Our horses while there were Picketed out exposed to storm which togeather with a long and fatigu[ing] ride caused many deaths. (I think 29)   Of the men but one death has occured since we left Vt. Our winter quarters wer not designated while here untill the day before we left & yet It was intimated pretty strongly that we were to move in the direction of Camp Grifin   on the

24 of Dec last we recevied orders to march for Annapolis   on the 25th and with every head beaming high at the thought of being removed from this to some place whare suitable means could be obtained for drilling and preparing us for service, all excepting those sick and those left in charge of them started and after one days march we reached Marlboro and camped for the night in an open piece of woods. The next morning we resumed our march and reached our camp ground about 2 miles from Annapolis about 7 o clock P.M.   here we encamped in the open air on a corn field with but *little* to eat and *nothing* to drink and had it not been for the generosity of the New York 5th [Cavalry] who supplyed us coffee and hard bread we should have suffered greatly and not only them but the New Yorkers generaly will we remember for their generosity and kind regards for us. Our tents here are Pitched on a tobacco plantation commanding a beautiful appearance. Since we have been here we have Stockaded our tents built barracks for our horses and have been preparing our camp ground which adds much to its appearance. for the last four weeks we have been under a course of drill. Mounted in the fore noon and dismounted in the afternoon at which time we practice the sabre exercise. our streets are formed in row of one company each[,] each company 100 feet apart and each Squadron composed of two companies a distance of 150 feet apart. on the right of each company uniformely the line officers are stationed and on the right of these (the line officers) uniformely are stationed the field officers   It is surmised here in camp now that our colonel is to resine and that Capt Holiday is to take command an officer from the regular service. The state of the weather since we have been here has been very stormy, and as a mater of course being that considerable teaming has been performed evry day has caused mud in abundance from 12 to 15 inches in depth in and about Annapolis City the news of the victory of our arms at Rhonoke iland[2] caused much excitement in camp and by order of Genl Hatch there was to be a salute at the naval Academy at Annapolis on Saturday last in honor of said victory but on account of storm was delaid also the probability of our troops capturing Fort Dolanson with from 15 to 20 thousand prisoners, including Genrals Pillow and Johnson[3] which we are waiting patiently to hear from caused equal excitement and our captain this morning after telling us of this victory said that he had a *"hurah"* in him as big as a wild cat, but being Sunday he would make no *demonstration* of it. The general health of our Regiment has been very good, also our company. we have Divine Services in camp generally evry Sabath and here can we learn (no less at home) the way to live to fulfill a manly course here but to qualify us for a higher state of existance. one word for Maryland and its citizens. A finer tract of country no State can boast of and facilities for making it one of the first in the union, but during our journey from Washington to Annapolis not one

2. General Ambrose Burnside captured Roanoke Island with a small amphibious force on February 8, 1862, threatening Confederate control of the naval yard at Norfolk, Virginia (Long, *The Civil War Day By Day*, 168).

3. Fort Donelson on the Cumberland River in Tennessee fell to General Grant on February 16, 1862. Both Generals Gideon Pillow and Bushrod Johnson escaped capture (Foote, *Fort Sumter to Perryville*, 212–13).

school house Meeting house Store or Hotell did we see in that whole distance which we might call such comparitively speaking after Vermont. What is the cause is it because she has not the country and the means for making improvement.— no, it is Slavery   place the enterprise of New England husbandry here and see the difference. This beautiful country which lays waist—woul[d] thrive: yea it would surpass New England in Agriculture and commerce   the main object of the planters seems to be traffic of the Slave and as such make it their God, forgetting the cultivation of their soul, and the refinement of their people:

> Yours Respectfuly
> Wm H. Daniels

"it is a dogs life to live"

Private Stephen H. Brockway of St. Johnsbury, Company G, Fourth Vermont Infantry, to his friend Allard, March 2, 1862.[1]

Washington D.C.
Camp Griffin
March 2, 1862

Friend Allard

I received your letter and I now seat myself to answer it. I am well and I hope that these few lines will find you enjoying the same Blessing. I was sorry to hear that your Mother was sick. I hope by the time you Received this that she will be smart again. You wrote that the snow was verry deep. we have not had much out here yet, but good deal of rain   you wrote that Asa had Enlisted   he will find that their is not much fun in it   I advise you as a friend not to enlist as a soldier for it is a dogs life to live. I had [quite?] a time last night. myself and another Boy went of to steal some milk and came verry nigh getting Catched. We milked Eight Canteens full & got back to camp at 4 in the morning we do not get any milk onley what we steal and we steal all that we can get. I saw [David?] about a week ago he was well then and tuff and all the rest of the boys that came from up that way. [Tip Way?] has got as fat as a Hog. Speaking of fat, I guess I will claim a little of that myself for I weigh 165 lbs   I never was so heavy before in my life   Ask for news their is none only that Gen. Banks has cross the river. Harper's Ferry is under our command and Charlestown & Bolivar so we hurd in our camp [Saturday] Night.[2] give my respect to [R   ] and Harriet. tell

1. Stephen H. Brockway Letter, Wendell Lang, Jr., Collection, MHI.

2. "Bolivar" is a reference to Bolivar Heights, a ridge to the west of Harpers Ferry. Charles Town is five miles southwest of Harpers Ferry.

them that I am well at present. so I will close by signing my name. write as Soon as you can. yours truly

Stephen H. Brockway

FIGURE 16. Walter W. Smith. Vermont Historical Society.

1. Walter W. Smith Papers, Duke.

"I dont think we shall move till we have Sharps Rifles"

Sergeant Walter W. Smith of Wilmington, Company H, Second U.S. Sharpshooters, to his sister, March 9, 1862.[1]

Washington March 9th/62

Dear Sister

I suppose you are looking for a letter from me by this time. I received one from you about a week ago. you must have a sweet time there in the snow, there has been no snow here for some time, & the mud is drying up fast, our streets & parade ground are dry & hard, our streets are as hard as a house floor, have to sweep them every morning as regular as you do your kitchen. we have had rather lively times here in Camp for a few days past, last Thursday Orders were read on dress Parade to have every thing in readiness to go over the other side the River, into Gen. Mc.Dowells division, Saturday morning, the Boys got up a petition & sent to certain Senators to have different guns before we were put in to active service. so Friday orders were read temporarily suspending our going, so that is the way we are situated now. I dont think we shall move till we have Sharps Rifles, but we may any day, it made our Regimental officers pretty mad to think that the Privates could defeat their plans when they had got them all laid so nice I have just been to the Post Office & got our Co. Mail I got a letter from Wilmington you had ought to see the Boys huddle round till they get a letter the Reg has a Post master & a Seargent from each Co. gets the Cos. Mail We had pretty thorough inspection this morning we went on the Color line at 10 o. clock & they were two hours in going through the Reg we had to have our rigging all on Church call has just blown & we are to have dress parade at 4 o. clock it has been pleasant here for the last 3 or 4 days I am sitting outside of our tent in the sun writing this warm and pleasant as can be I am tuff as usual there has been no deaths in the Regt. since the last one died in our Co. there is a good many play sick to get rid of doing duty & some feign sick to get their discharge there has been two discharged from our Co & there will be four or five more discharged soon some need to be & some are as well able as they ever were only a little homesick or havent got an office as they expected   the Col. presented us our Colors   it is all silk & a good looking one   we have not been paid off yet   dont know when we shall be   in the course of a fortnight probably   I dont know of much news to write   perhaps there will be more next time

    Yours Truly
    Walter W. Smith

"if it is my fate to die for my country I hope I shall meet it like a Soldier and a Christian"

Private George M. Lanpher of Hyde Park, Company D, Fifth Vermont Infantry, to his family, March 16, 1862.[1]

Alexandria Va   March 16th 1862

    Dear Parents & Sisters   having a few liesure moments I will improve them in penning a line or two to you to let you know that I am alive and so that you kneed not worry about me   our regimint and all the Vt regts are here   we are on our way either to join Burnside or to go to fortress Monroe   I do not know which yet   we are now quarterd in the M E Church in Alexandria the place where Col Ellsworth was shot   it is quite a place and the stars & stripes float proudly in every street   the house where Ellsworth was killed is pretty well riddled the flag staff is still standing on the top of the house where once waved the seceshion flag which the brave Ellsworth tore down with his own hand   it is sunday but it hardly seems like the holy Sabbath   the streets are full of soldiers of all brigades and all sorts of uniforms   the dark blue of the Vt infantry contrast widily from the red pants and blue jackets of the Zouaves and the yellow striped jacket of the dragoons. We have just listind to An adress from our beloved comander in chief Gen Geo B McLellan   he tells us that our days of inactivity are passed and now we are to come into the field of battle   he says he feels like a father to us and will share our dangers and privations hoping that God will be with us   we shall probably take the boats to night or in the morning and continue our way   I want you to write   you will direct the same as you have and they will find us some time   direct to Washington D C Co D fifth Regt Vt Vols   I cant write a great deal more now and perhaps before you get this I shall be on the battle field   you may never get another one but I put my trust in god who doeth all things well   you have probably got the news of Manasses and Bulls

FIGURE 17. George M. Lanpher. Special Collections, University of Vermont.

1. George M. Lanpher Papers, Gertrude Mallary Collection, Bradford, Vermont.

Run being occupied by our troops   the rebels left without firing a gun a few more battles and the Victory is ours and we will return to our homes those of us who are spared   some of us and we do not know how many must fall   if it is my fate to die for my country I hope I shall meet it like a Soldier and a Christian   pray for me ever   good bye for the present and may God grant that if we meet no more on earth we may all meet in a happier and better world where parting is no more this from your afectionate Son & Brother   George M Lanpher

Co D
Fifth Regt
   Vermont
Volunteer Militia

"The Regt is in an awful state"

Lieutenant-Colonel William Y. W. Ripley of Rutland, First U.S. Sharpshooters, to his wife, Kelie, March 19, 1862.[1]

1. William Young Ripley Papers, Duke.

Washington
Mar 19th 1862

My dear Kelie

Your letter of the 16th came to hand this P M—& Kelie dear it was like a blessing to me to get it to day. We have had an awful time to day— I wrote you yesterday that we had marching orders & that the men were to take Colts Rifles for the present. Well this morning I had orders to deliver the guns to the men but no go, the men would not take them. It was thot that if our co took them the others would so I went to C[o.] "F" (Vt) & if ever I talked in my life I talked to them & all but five took the guns—two of these men have since taken them & the others will I think soon. No other Cos would touch them at all. We are going to try a new tack tomorrow—what the result will be I cannot say—I hope it may be satisfactory but I fear the thing will not work The Regt is in an awful state— I will write you when the thing is settled

We march tomorrow any way, if the men will not take the arms they will be sent in without them & set at such work as they can do without guns. I wish I had never heard of the organization in my life— One thing I am thankfull for: Vt is all right on the subject. John was the first man to step out & Lamphear the second—[2] I sent you 100.$ yesterday by express. let me know if you rec it—

I expected to have to leave a good . . . deal of baggag—but I find that

2. John W. Thomas was an orphan brought up by the Ripley family, according to Eisenschiml (*Vermont General*, 13). He enlisted first in Company F of the First Sharpshooters, and later in Edward H. Ripley's Ninth Vermont Infantry, rising to the rank of first lieutenant. "Lamphear" was probably their fellow townsman Chauncey R. Lanphere (Peck, *Revised Roster*, 602, 603, 349).

except my camp furniture I shall have to leave very little—at least I shall take every thing as far as Fort Monroe which is our first destination or at least said to be—

When I packed my things I took the precaution to take your picture with that of Willie & Bessie & two or three sheets of paper & put in my pocket book so that whatever I might be obliged to leave, those pictures would not be among the things—& Kelie dear tho this has been a rough day when ever I thought of your picture near my heart, I felt new courage & energy and my heart felt warm & bright again— I have written this hastily & hardly know what I have written but I can write no more now

   Good bye darling Your aff
    Wm

Since you have gone up town & will get your mail there I think you had better get your Father to get you a box in the post office—other wise your mail will go in Fathers box & you may not get it so soon

   Your aff
    Wm

Chapter 5 Spring 1862

One year after the Civil War began, Vermont soldiers found themselves in the vanguard of the first sustained campaign to defeat the Confederate armed forces in Virginia. The goal of the Peninsula Campaign was to capture Richmond and bring about the collapse of the Confederacy. No efforts were to be spared in this final drive to victory.

The first significant engagement of the campaign took place at Lee's Mill on the Warwick River twenty miles northwest of Fortress Monroe. The rebels had built rifle pits and fortifications along the river, which stretched nearly the width of the ten-mile-wide peninsula from its source near Yorktown to the James River. Dams caused the river to back up into deep pools that would make crossing difficult or impossible. On April 16, acting on orders to stop the enemy's work on fortifications, the Vermont Brigade's General Brooks sent parts of the Third and Fourth Vermont regiments across the river. Under heavy fire, the Vermonters captured some of the rebel works but were forced to retreat for lack of reinforcements. Conferring with General McClellan, division commander William F. Smith decided to attempt another crossing to see if the rebel line could be broken. Soldiers of the Fourth and Sixth regiments stormed into the river but were driven back with heavy losses by the rebels, who were now strongly reinforced.[1]

The Vermonters suffered 192 casualties (65 deaths) to little purpose. Some resentment may have manifested itself in a charge of drunkenness against General Smith. The general's horse had stumbled during the battle, throwing him violently to the ground, and some witnesses mistook his dazed and ruffled appearance for inebriation. A military court soon cleared Smith, but not before he was subjected to a great deal of public scorn.[2]

Despite the loss at Lee's Mill, triumph appeared to favor the Union army. On May 3 the rebels abandoned Yorktown, the northern anchor of the Warwick River defensive line, and the Yankees pursued them over the next two weeks to the outskirts of Richmond. Confederate general Joseph Johnston struck back at Fair Oaks, with little success, on May 30 and June 1. Soldiers of the Vermont Brigade heard but did not participate in the battle. They did, however, witness the ghastly effects of war as they passed by the unburied corpses of enemy soldiers and horses, and saw the waste and destruction of the battlefield.

No large-scale fighting took place for the next three weeks as both sides prepared for a showdown. McClellan's "defensive offensive" strategy called for careful planning and minimal risks.[3] Meanwhile, Robert E. Lee took command of the Army of Northern Virginia, bringing to the Confederate side a leader more than willing to take calculated risks. Part of McClellan's caution derived from his continual overestimation of the enemy's strength. Yet he was justified in complaining that President Lincoln had withheld thousands of troops that he had counted on for the campaign: concerned about the safety of Washington, Lincoln had suspended the transport of fifty thousand soldiers to the peninsula in late April.[4] Lincoln's fears for Washington were the result of Confederate general Stonewall Jackson's victorious campaign against Union general Nathaniel P. Banks in the Shenandoah Valley.

The First Vermont Cavalry, part of General Banks's army in the Shenandoah, learned quickly the perils of war. When Banks was forced into a rapid retreat to avoid capture in late May, the horsemen found themselves cut off from the main body of troops near Middletown. Many were wounded or captured trying to fight through the rebel line, though most managed to gallop to safety around the enemy's flank.[5]

By the time Jackson routed Banks in the Shenandoah, the Vermont cavalry had already lost two colonels. The first, Lemuel B. Platt of Colchester, had resigned in February, and the second, regular army officer Jonas P. Holliday, committed suicide early in April. Charles H. Tompkins, another regular army man, accepted the colonelcy soon after Holliday's death, but resigned in September 1862. Cavalry life was harsh and dangerous, and cavalry leadership required a great deal of skill and courage. Many long months would pass before the First Vermont Cavalry found a man equal to the task.[6]

A thousand miles from Virginia, some ten thousand soldiers in the Gulf Department camped on a strip of sand called Ship Island. Seven miles long and less than a mile wide, the island had only a small grove of trees at one end to break the monotonous horizon of sand and sea. Although grateful to be on land after a harrowing voyage, the Vermont men quickly grew weary of the sandy camps. On May 2, however, news of the fall of New Orleans cheered the troops.[7] Soon thereafter, the Seventh and Eighth Vermont Infantry regiments and the two bat-

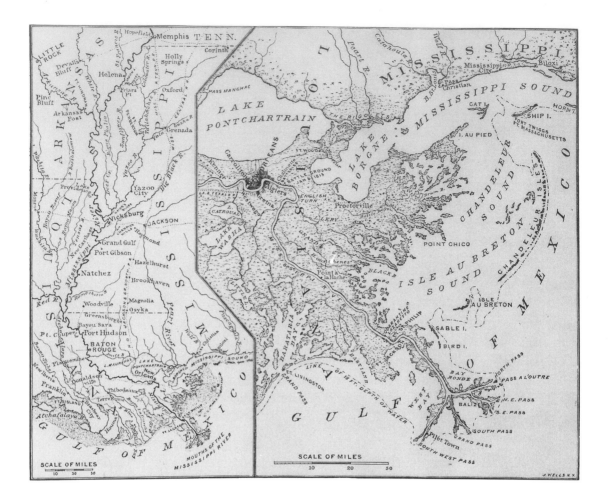

MAP 3. Two maps of the lower Mississippi. Ship Island is in the upper right-hand corner of the right-hand map. *Battles and Leaders of the Civil War,* vol. 2, 25. UVM.

teries of light artillery steamed up the Mississippi River as part of an occupation force.

The end of June found the Vermont Brigade involved in a seven-day series of battles, too busy and tired to write home. In the Gulf Department, the Seventh Vermont Infantry joined an ill-advised expedition to capture Vicksburg, by now the only major obstacle to federal control of the Mississippi River. Both campaigns would take a heavy toll in lives and morale.

Captain William Wells of Waterbury, Company C, First Vermont Cavalry, to his brother, Charles, April 5, 1862.[1]

1. William Wells Papers, carton 1, folder 22, UVM.

Camp Near Woodstock V.A.
April 5th 1862

Bro Chas

I wrote you last from Strasburg Our Regt left Strasburg this morning at 8 AM for this place. this morning we started in the rain, but before we had gone far it stoped & the remainder of the day has been fine. Yestarday it was hot   I felt uncomfortable but the nights are rather cool.

We are now about ten miles from Strasburg. There is a Rail Road that passes through S— to this place, but the Bridges are all burned our forces are re building some of them between Strasburg & Manassas it is the Manassas R.R.   three bridges have been burned between here & Strasburg   they were very large ones. we are about 1 1/2 miles from Woodstock. Our forces are near Edenton 7 miles from here. we are to do Patrol duty, scout a little & forage for the army ahead so says Maj Perkins of Genl Banks Staff. several Capts have been down town. had an introduction to the Genl. I do not think we are to do any fighting, as our force is stronger than the Rebals.

A Scurmish took place about 7 miles from here to day. some of our Infantry tried to cross a ford whare the Rebals had burned the Bridge. the Rebels opened two Batteries on them but soon our Batteries drove the enemy away. They fall back a little every day.

We have our tents pitched and are well situated, Lt Holden is now making up the bed—he is going to retire. I am officer of the day   have got to be up to go the Grand Rounds after 12 M   it is now 10.

To day as the Regt had mooved about one or two miles this way word came forward that the Col. [Jonas P. Holliday] was wounded & had sent for the Surgeon. all was excitement.—it appears that after the Regt. had got well under way that the Col togather with the Orderly Bugler & an orderly from my Co. (Moffitt) rode back towards Camp. the teams had not all passed. he first sent the Bugler for the Ajutant & then his ordely   he rode down from the Road to the River (the Shenandoah) about 5 or 6 Rods from the Road there dismounted hitched his horse took out a Revolver and *shot* himself & fell into the River. he shot himself in the middle of his forehead. the ball did not come out. the Ajutant & my Orderly were within about 40 Rods from him, going towards him. when they got to the River he was just floating away from shore   they pulled him out. the Ajt went for help   he found my

Quarter Master King & Caldwell of Co I. near by, when they all returned to the Col he was breathing   they sent one of my Corpls (Mr Nichols of Northfield) after the Surgeon, but it was to late.

I do not know what the Cause of his committing such an act was. we shall miss him very much.—

Capt Sawy[er] is to take his remains home to Oswego N.Y. I think Capt will go to Hyde Park if he does. when he returns you can send your pictures—

He leaves tomorrow morning. I will send a letter by him. he may not however get to Vt. Capt can tell you more than I can write   I will write a note for him to leave with you so that you may know when he arrives in town—

Let me hear from you often   Direct to Woodstock V.A. Genl Banks Div   we are not *Brigaded*. Love to all. How is Grandmother—

I am well

> Your Bro
> Wm Wells

PS
I will write again in a day or so

> Wid

Mother don't worry about me for we shall not see any fighting

"It looked wicked, but all we had to do was to go ahead"

Corporal Henry E. Dunbar of Newbury, Company C, Third Vermont Infantry, to his wife, Mary, April 17, 1862.[1]

1. Henry E. Dunbar Papers, MHI.

Thurs.y 8 a.m. Apr 17th   My Dear Mary

Thank God I am alive yet & considering the circumstances comparativly well. We went yesterday morn up to within less than 1/4 mile of the enemys works where they had 3 or 4,000 & 2 large Guns mounted & between us & them a creek some 8 to 10 rods wide, from knee to waist deep. Our Reg.t were posted in the woods directly in front of their works & so near that occasionaly a ball from their Rifle pits aimed at our skirmishers would come up quite to us. Our Batterys commenced shelling them about 9 a.m. & continued to do so thru the day & except silencing one of their Guns, appeared not to have much effect. as soon as we got there all but 4 company.s of our Reg.t D, E F & K, were sent off as skirmishers, & continued so thro. the day. these 4 companys & the Color Guard remained perfectly quiet till about

3,p.m. when Col. Hyde came along & told Capt. Harrington of Co. D & Pingrey of Co. F. that they must take their 2 Cos & cross the creek & take the Battery with only Co.s E & K to support them & he said the *Colors* must go too. It looked wicked, but all we had to do was to go ahead, so we threw off our Blankets & all but our Equipments & started   went about 4 rods & come to the water, which we entered & found it about knee deep for the first 4 or 5 rods   then we went into our waists & where some crossed they went in up to their necks. I got in about 6 inches above my waist belt. The bullets began to meet us when we first entered the water but when we got in waist deep & within 5 or 6 rods of their Rifle pits they began to shower the balls into us like hail & our poor fellows began to fall. just as I got in up to my waist & directly behind Heath with the Flag a ball struck me on the left side of my head & partly knocked me down but I put one hand down & happened to hit a stump & kept from falling   it cut the cloth & paste board of my cap rim but didnt go thro. the inside leather   It sort of confused me for 2 or 3 hours & that side of my head is some numb yet but thank God that it didnt come 1/2 inch nearer   about half of us got into their works & drove the Rebels out but couldnt hold it & when Harrington saw how they were cutting us up & that we must all be killed or taken prisoners he ordered us to retreat which we did under a perfect shower of Balls & out of these 4 com.ys there is 22 killed 56 wounded & 5 missing   I crawled back to Camp & Jim built up a good fire & made me some coffee & after drying myself as well as I could I laid down about 10 oclock, & slept some tho. I ached all night & this morn am so lame I can scarcely go, but I am alive & *again* I thank *God*. Our boys all safe. Will write again soon

Aff. *yours* H E Dunbar

"The boys were as cool as tho. shooting at Turkies at home"

Captain George Quimby of Barton, Company D, Fourth Vermont Infantry, to George Tucker, April 25, 1862.[1]

Quimby took over as captain of the company after Tucker resigned in February.

Camp near Yorktown, Va.
April 25th 1862

Friend Tucker—

I will just answer your letter today as everything is quiet and no certainty when I shall have another chance of writing. Things as you may

FIGURE 18. George W. Quimby. U.S. Army Military History Institute Photo Archives.

1. George Quimby Papers, folder 4, UVM.

well beleive are quite different now from what they were when you left. We are here in the woods about 25 miles from Fortress Munroe and about five miles south from Yorktown on the Warwick Creek and not more than 150 rods from that Creek. Our conveniences and accommodations are on a huge scale. Officers are allowed to carry a small valise in which are all their worldly goods, and when we move camp any great distance—that is 4 or 5 miles we have to remain two or three days without anything on account of the superior ability and energy of the Qr. Mr. [Quartermaster]   We are supposed to have two tents for the Line Officers and we have got one and generally get this about the same time we do our other things so that if we happen to move in the rain which the boys say always happens it makes it *agreeable*—

Sunday 27th. I had got thus far when the order or detail came for me to take charge of 33 men on fatigue and come to report to Brig. Hd. Qr. I had to take charge of 100 men, and our business was to carry sand bags holding 3 pecks sand each for protecting Embrasures. You have seen better accounts of the battle or skirmish of Lees Mills in the papers than I should be able to give you. I with the Co. were ordered at the same time to move in another directi[on] within about 30 rods of the Fortifications and fire upon them, while the other Co's. were attempting to cross, so we had a fine opportunity of ascertaining the precise sound or rather whistle of bullets, its a beautiful sound, but more agreeable some distance off. The boys were as cool as tho. shooting at Turkies at home. None were wounded in the Co. and most of those wounded were in Co. I and the two killed also— Capt. Atherton was not severely wounded and is going home on a leave of 30 days.

It is generally considered a blunder I think, or at least looks so to us the un[in]itiated, but that statement of Morrells[2] in the House that the General Comdg. (Smith) was drunk is a lie without doubt, and two Gen's. McClellan and Keyes were both here and approved or as some say ordered it—anyway there has some good resulted from it, we know just where and about how strong th[e]y are which we could not find out before. There have been a good many changes since you left. First I was made Captain just as we moved from Camp Griffin and Lt. Lillie was promoted and put in my Co. and John Curtis Tyler was made 2nd Lt. in Co. E.   that must have been a promotion. Now Capt. Gove has resigned on account of ill health and I suppose Pingree will be made Captain in that Co. then there is the rumor that Hooker will be made Lt. in some co. and Lt. Wheeler promoted to 1st Lt. in some other co. but how it all came about I cant tell. Things in the Co. remain about the same—the boys are healthier, than when in Camp Griffin— there are present in Camp, about 65 men, all but two on duty at present. The boys mention you frequently but take to the new order of things well. Lillie has been in the Co. but little having been in command of Co. I for nearly four weeks. We expect to have some severe

2. U.S. Representative Justin S. Morrill of Vermont sponsored a resolution in Congress asking the president to fire any officer found to be habitually drunk, citing the rumor that the officer in charge at Lee's Mill was so drunk he fell off his horse. The resolution passed (*Burlington Sentinel*, May 2, 1862, p. 2).

fighting, before we break thro. these works, but we are all bound for Richmond and shall go some way without doubt. I would like to hear from you occasionally, tho. I will not promise many in return for to write a letter is some work here— My regards to your wife and Almira— Your friend

> G. W. Quimby

FIGURE 19. Ship Island. *Harper's Pictorial History of the Civil War*, 263. UVM.

"The principal inhabitants of the Isle are alligators snakes and Yankees"

Adjutant Charles E. Parker of Vergennes, Seventh Vermont Infantry, to his father, May 13, 1862.[1]

1. Charles E. Parker Papers, carton 1, folder 10, UVM.

Ship Island Miss
May 13th 1862

My dear Father,

Orders having come last night, to prepare to march immediately, I have just finished my preparation and part of my baggage has gone to the boat, and here I am seated in my tent and writing on a cartridge box cover to acquaint you of our destination. we go I suppose a little above New Orleans where Gen'l Phelps is stationed. Nearly all the troops are to leave the Island and join those already gone. Of our movements from thence I have not the least idea, but will acquaint you as soon as they shall transpire. All are rejoiced at the prospect of leaving the Island and going to some place where they can tread good firm soil. The sand here is so deep that it is exceeding tiresome to walk far, so you can imagine the difficulties under which we labor in our drills. The Island is very low, hardly averaging more than 3 or 5 feet from sea level. fresh water can be had by digging anywhere to the depth of 18 inches to 4 or 5 feet. in my tent I have dug up the sand with my hand to the depth of 18 or 20 inches and found water. I am inclined to think the water sea-water freshened by filtering through the sand for the different levels of the sea seem to make a corresponding difference in the height of water in the wells. We have been having plenty to eat such as ham, beef, potatoes and plenty of soft bread which is baked on the Island. Several buildings have been erected most of them portable ones they have a machine shop which has just been put in operation, and a paper is published here. If the Southerners would visit us we could I think prove to them that Yankee pluck and especially Yank enterprise are no fiction. The principal inhabitants of the Isle are alligators snakes and Yankees   the former do not associate with the latters being at the upper end of the Isle but there are some more beautiful productions than either of the last named which you will find enclosed. We have received no pay yet and do not actually need any as long as we can get trusted for what we need to eat. The men who enlisted from Vergennes are well. Lewis Liberty is at fort Pike with his Co which is there with a few more of our men to garrison the fort. Fred is well and so am I with much love I remain your aff Son

C. E. Parker

"I, in common with the other officers am called <u>Massar Linkum,</u> 20 times a day"

Adjutant John Lester Barstow of Shelburne, Eighth Vermont Infantry, to his parents, May 18, 1862.[1]

Head Quarters 8th Regt. Vt. Vols.
New Orleans   May 18th 1862

I wrote to Laura a few days ago, & supposed that my Letter would leave there the same day that I wrote it—but the steamer that took the mail met with an accident and had to return here for repairs so that I have a chance to write again— We left Ship Island on the 6th & after hardships and privations too numerous to tell off arrived here in 7 days, instead of 2, as we expected— The city had at that time (5 days since) been occupied by Gens. Butler & Phelps and 4000 men, for about 10 or 12 days, and great fears were entertained that either the people here would rise against them, or that Gen. Beuregard would come down by Rail Road from Tennessee and wipe the little army out of existence, and it is Still very much feared that some such attempt will be made. Since I wrote Laura we have changed our Quarters from near the river to a higher & far more pleasant locality   we are now in the Mechanics Institute a large new building, more than 4 times as large as the Town Hall in Burlington and 4 stories high, and also occupy 2 other large buildings adjoining. My office is a front room on the Second floor 25 feet square, and I am infinitely more comfortable than at any other time since I left home. I think I wrote you Something of the high prices of every thing at Ship Island—but I find every thing much higher here— Before we came here there was *no* Flour for sale in the city—now it sells for $30 pr Barrell—Beef steak 60¢ a pound, Eggs 75¢ a dozen and so on—Coffe 80¢ Tea 2.50 a pound—but this cannot last long as ships are coming from Havanna and other places, and the country people—finding that we harm no body, and pay for every thing we want in gold are beginning to come in with chickens etc.— Lettuce, cucumbers, tomatoes and all garden Stuff is plenty—but the owners, are afraid to sell to us for fear that we shall leave the city and then they Say the rebels would kill every one that helped us to any thing. A few Union men visit us at night—but there is *no* open Union feeling in the city, and I do not beleive there is *much* that is genuine, any way— The poor people were actually in a starving condition when Gen. Butler came here—he has given away more than 3000 Bbls. of Salt beef that he captured from the Rebels—to the poor of this city— At first, no officer was allowed to go out of his quarters without being armed, and having an escort—but now two officers are allowed to go out together—carring revolvers and bowie knives— I have been in nearly every part of the city on business, and have met with no trouble worth mentioning—but do not go out after 8-o-clock—in the evening at all.

When we landed the wharves and property that the rebels burnt— was still Smoking and in many places I have walked (with the Regiment) where the ashes of the burnt cotton, was ankle deep. The negros are plenty and of course civil—but seem to be chiefly glad to see us, because they think that provisions will be cheaper— They appear to be as happy and contented as any class of people can be—but, of course, I have no chance of *knowing* any thing about it.— I, in common with the other officers am called *Massar Linkum*, 20 times a day—they Say "God bless you, we're glad you come" etc. If I should write you my experience for a Single day, it would no doubt, prove very interesting, but my office [is] thronged all day, and no one can stand the labor in this hot climate that they can North & when night comes I am tired enough to go to bed— My duties are arduous and responsible but I hope I have proved myself *adequate*— Give my love to all & write often addressing your Letters in addition to what is printed—New Orleans.—

    From your son Lester

1. Parker Family Papers, folder 8, UVM.

"Eliza I have pretty much concluded that I have seen all the rebels all the fighting, war, dead men etc. that I want to see"

Private Moses A. Parker of Concord, Company C, Third Vermont Infantry, to Eliza Hale, May 26, 1862.[1]

May 26th 1862

Friend Eliza

In Compliance with your wishes I now seat myself to employ a few leisure moments to answer your, always very welcome letter which came safely to hand the 12 inst. (I feel somewhat kind of sad and cross today but perhaps will feel better before I get this finished)   We are camped to day 7 miles from that (to the rebels) consecrated city the capital of the southern confederacy; but I fear that before annother week passes over their heads they will be compeled to leave their sacred city or surrender it to McClellan for his innumerable hosts are fast approaching it on all sides   But before it falls into any hands hundreds of brave and noble fellows as our country affords will be streched bleeding and lifeless on the ground

Eliza I have pretty much concluded that I have seen all the rebels all the fighting, war, dead men etc. that I want to see at present that I want to (I would not have [you] think by this that I am growing cowardish for I am no more so than ever)   I saw them at Warwick at Williamsburgh piled in heaps and at various other   It is rather a sickening looking sight although rebels to see a field strewn with dead and dying men   at W——gh in one smal fort there was 50 dead and 104 wounded rebels   But I trust that such writing will neither delight or amuse you so I will cease it   I[n] answer to your question if [I] was one that stole, and what. I will own that I helped kill and dress an ox and brought a quarter into camp but will not own the nigger wench's the privates stole the meat and the officers had to take the scolding from the Gen. We *took* the beef because we *needed* it   we were hungry and had been for the past 8 days for we had to live on half rations about two weeks   Gen. Smith *I say was not* drunk and the state of Vt. has been meddling with that which is none of their business at least until they heard the truth of the story   I like this part of Virginia much better than I did where I was last summer; some parts of it is a splendid country; with some nice plantations; grass is fit for the scythe and the wheat is all headed out   I went through a field yesterday of 500 acres that the heads came as high as my chin. I think after this war is over and I get out of it that I shall come back here and settle down with some pretty darkey gal if I cant get a white one   Eliza I have thought of your advice in the last letter you wrote me a great many times since

I read it warning me to put my trust in Him whose arm is ever able and willing to save those who will seek him   I have a good mother and two sisters at home who are continualy writing me such advices and it has been a subject on my mind for the past 4 months   I have wept hours over their letters pleading with me to throw my cares uppon Lord   I have tried to pray have had others pray for me (and I beseech you to do the same for me) but still I feel myself a sinner but there is one thing that I have broke myself of and that is swearing   I [am] ashamed to own that I ever did but I used to and dare say that you have heard me but I have made a promise to never let another oath pass my lips

"Our retreat and defeat I suppose has caused considerable excitement in the northern states"

Private Henry A. Smith of Royalton, Company E, First Vermont Cavalry, to his family, June 7, 1862.[1]

1. Henry A. Smith Papers (Miscellaneous File 245), VHS.

Williamsport Md June 7, 1862

Dear Mother Sisters and Brothers   I received your letter yesterday and was glad to hear from you   I wrote to you the next day after we got here but I guess you did not get it untill you sent you letter   Our retreat and defeat I suppose has caused considerable excitement in the northern states although we got out of it well considering the situation we were in. Gen McClellan sent a dispach to Gen Banks ordering him to retreat but Banks got it nine hours to late so the enemy had nearly out flanked us and had all the chance they could ask for to capture our little handfull of men numbering only 5000. Our Company have lost twelve men either killed or prisoners   George Dodge was one of the teamsters and was shot in his wagon   Lant Blake and Gene got cut off from the Company and crossed the river with some of the New York Cavalry 20 miles above here and got here two or three days after we did. the morning we were in Winchester a little drummer boy was walking along under a window and an old Secesh woman caught him by his hair and with her revolver blew out his brains   the next moment a ball passed through her head and she hung there across the window case   another woman who was seen fir[ing] out of the house at the Soldiers was shot by an Officer and a great many were seen firing at the Soldiers. They have got their pay now for General Fremont has had a battle with them and is driving them through the Valley   Rosencrans is on the other side of them.[2] When we were in Newton where

2. General John C. Frémont's small army in western Virginia had teamed up with a division under General James Shields to try to corner Stonewall Jackson after Banks's hasty retreat (Foote, *Fort Sumter to Perryville*, 452–59). Private Smith probably meant Shields, not William S. Rosecrans, who had a command much farther to the west.

the battle first commenced the dust was so thick that you could not see one yard   after the dust got cleared of I looked out into the field where the rebels were. up on a knoll above them was a battery throwing shells at us while part of them in the hollow were deployed as Skirmishers and the rest were advancing in line   One regiment I noticed in particular, wore red Shirts green pants light colored broad rimed hats and long flowing hair   most all the others were bare head and bare foot with mixed up raged uniforms   We have got another new Colonel   his name is Tompkins the Lieutenant that led the gallant Charge to Fairfax Court House[3]   he has been to Washington and got a lot of new haversacks canteens and Pistols for the regiment   the rebels did not drive our men across at Harpers Ferry they made a stand there our men left some tents on Bolivar hights and when the rebels came along they all went into the tents then our men threw a hundred and sixty pound Shell over with 200 one ounce balls in it   it struck right among the tents and tore them all to pieces   what fiew men were left scattered in all directions   the rebel regiment with the red Shirts and green pants were called: the Louisanna Tigers. A good many of our sick were left in the Hospital at Strasburg and are probably Prisoners gastin Walker was among them. all our regiments teams and tents were lost encluding the regimental Colors   the road from Winchester was jamed and cramed full of teams Hospital wagons full of our wounded a good many of the wounded that could not help themselves fell victims to the Bayonet and Sword   My hand has got most well and my health is first rate   my paper and envelopes I put in a box to Annapolis with the rest of my stuff. Write soon and tell me how you get along so good by   H A Smith

3. Tompkins had led a company of cavalry charging through enemy-held Fairfax Court House in June 1861, "winning both praise for his gallantry and blame for his rashness" (Benedict, *Vermont in the Civil War*, vol. 2, 556).

FIGURE 21. "A Louisiana 'Tiger.'" *Battles and Leaders of the Civil War*, vol. 1, 196. UVM.

1. Smith Family of St. Albans Papers, carton 1, folder 44, UVM.

"there is no restraint on man here and there seems to be no fear of man or God"

Aldis O. Brainerd of St. Albans to his sister, Ann Eliza Smith, June 13, 1862.[1]

Brainerd resigned as quartermaster of the Fifth Vermont Infantry in May 1862 following an extended illness, but returned to the battlefront as a civilian.

Camp near Richmond Va
June 13th 1862

Dear Sister

    I received your Kind Letter   I found that the hardships of the QM department would be rather hard for me as we were shifting about and in fact I have not been very tuff sence I returned not very smart to day but . . . have been more like my self for the last week than I have before sence I was sick it is now tremendous hot and takes the strength all away I have had a very pleasant time for the last 10 or 12 Days roaming around and seeing and learning what I can I have [been] over the Batle fields but could not find any thing but old Guns & clothes but if we have another big fight I mean to go on the ground as soon as it is over and see what I can find I witnessed the big battles of Saturday & Sunday across the Chicka[hominy] River but we could not help them as there was abt 3/4 Mile marshey land laid between us and them[2] I also have witnessed a battle between the Rebbels on one side & we on the other the Batterys plaid lively for abt 5 or 6 hours without much damage to us I was quite near our Guns not more than 8 or 10 Rods on one side now that we are across the River I take my Glass & by the way I have a verry Good one and can see the Rebbels within Musket Shot they are very bold & they can see us they are throwing their shells over our heads every day but they do not seem to do much harm but they keep it up & for some Reason we do not reply I think our folks are afraid that it would bring on a gen engagement and we are not quite ready they sent over a shell last evening that killed a Cavelery man in the road near our tent there is a tremendous Army here now yesterday there was 30 or 40 thousand crossed over the River and many coming in from all parts of the Army concentrating around R[ichmond] I hardley know what to think about it I sometimes think we shall be in R within 3 or 4 Days and at other times I think it will take a Month I mean to stay buy for some days and see my intentions are to go into R with the rest but if it takes all summer I think I shall go home monday & tuseday I went down to the White House[3] on the carrs with Capt Wetheral the Brigade QM there are 3 Brothers in the comissary & QM department and they are verry likley men are from Boston I am now willing to help what I can without pay from U.S. I am glad that I am free from the Shoulder Strap although I still wear them there are many things about the Army that is verry unpleasant the Society is so degrading I hope that I may soon forget that part I never realized so fulley the want of good morral and refined society as I have since my return there is no restraint on man here and there seems to be no fear of man or God I would not stay in the Army one year longer for any amt I do not speak of any particular part of the Army as there seems to be but little differance the Vtrs are as bad as any do not make this part of my letter public but one thing I will say in the praise of the Vermonters they are as good Soldiers as there are in the Army and I think no braver men than the Vtrs can be found when I shall leave I cannot tell as long as I can make it pleasant for myself without making it unpleasant for others. I have had a good opertunity to see much of human nature sence I have been hear and learnt much one thing I can say that be-

FIGURE 22. Aldis O. Brainerd. St. Albans Historical Museum.

2. These "big battles" were in fact small skirmishes.

3. General McClellan established his headquarters and supply base on the Pamunkey River at White House, the plantation of General Robert E. Lee's son William H. F. "Rooney" Lee.

cause I had Shoulder Straps on it made no differance to me I always treated the Privates as men and when the war is over these same Privates will talk differant than they now do as they are under restraint there is many ruined for life hear   they have plenty of money and make free use of it and have every thing furnished them and what little economy they had will all be lost and when they return to their homes. I called yesterday with Capt Wetheral at one Doct Gaynes Plantation on the other Side of the River and had a verry pleasant time with the Doct & wife   they are Secesh in every respect   they live in the best Style and are quite polite   it is desidely the finest Plantation in every respect that I have seen   the Groves & Fruit & buildings are all fine   they say that all their friends are in the Army or in R. & they would have been in R but we came upon them little to quick   he is under guard which he does not like much   they say that they should be glad if there could be some settlement   we had quite a talk with them and when we left we shook hands & I remarked that I hoped their Friends would all return in safety   they were quite anxious about them   I would not live in this state for the whole [c   ]—it is a contemptable mean state in every respect & I am hartily sick of the sacred soil & shall be glad to see the end of this war   oh what a sacrifice of life   think of the thousands that die from disease & of others that fall from the sword & ball slaughtered in every way. we get hardend to it here & while one is well he can get along but when sick there is but a small chance for comfortable quarters and no Friends to take care of them   it makes but little difference how many Friends he has in the army they cannot go along with the sick. now A.E. [Ann Eliza] I dont think much of this Letter say to J.G.S. [John Gregory Smith, Ann Eliza's husband] I had acted before I received his letter and should have done just as I have & would do so again under the circumstance   those that have not been hear cannot tell any thing about matters & things   sufice it to say that I am sure I have done for the best—and am quite sure of that   write   give my love to all   cannot tell when I shall be at home   I remain with the Army for the present

> your Dear Brother
> Aldis

As long as I feel well in regard to what I have done I hope you will however I thought we should be in R long before this   I cannot stop to correct errors or Read this over as my attention is called another way just now

Summer 1862

Chapter 6

Three months after the Peninsula Campaign began, the Army of the Potomac camped along a line straddling the Chickahominy River a few miles east of Richmond. The Confederate capital appeared to be close to capture. Its outnumbered defenders readied themselves for the imminent siege as the Confederate government prepared to evacuate. Without a capital, many believed, the Confederacy would fracture and the war would soon end in a Southern defeat.

Everything changed during the last week of June. The rebel army, now called the Army of Northern Virginia and led by Robert E. Lee, took the offensive in a seven-day series of attacks against George McClellan's Army of the Potomac, beginning on June 25. Tactical errors, poor execution, and poor coordination frustrated Lee's battle plans. The Northern army won most of the battles. Yet General McClellan, convinced that the smaller rebel army was far larger than his own, retreated after each encounter. McClellan "lost the courage to command," historian Stephen W. Sears wrote. By early July, the Army of the Potomac took refuge at Harrison's Landing on the James River—twenty-five miles from Richmond—where it was protected by the fearful power of the Union gunboat fleet. Strategically, the campaign was a victory for the South.[1]

For the Vermont Brigade, the Seven Days brought moments of glory and tragedy—but mostly, the rapid succession of battles brought exhaustion, hunger, and thirst. Already considered one of the most reliable divisions in the army, William F. Smith's division, to which the Vermont Brigade belonged, served as rear guard throughout much of the Union retreat. Guarding a large train of retreating federal wagons and artillery at Savage's Station on June 29, the Vermonters helped repulse a strong Confederate attack, inflicting heavy casualties. The Fifth Vermont Infantry, caught in a cross-fire, suffered severely, losing 206 men. In Company E, five brothers of the Cummings family of Man-

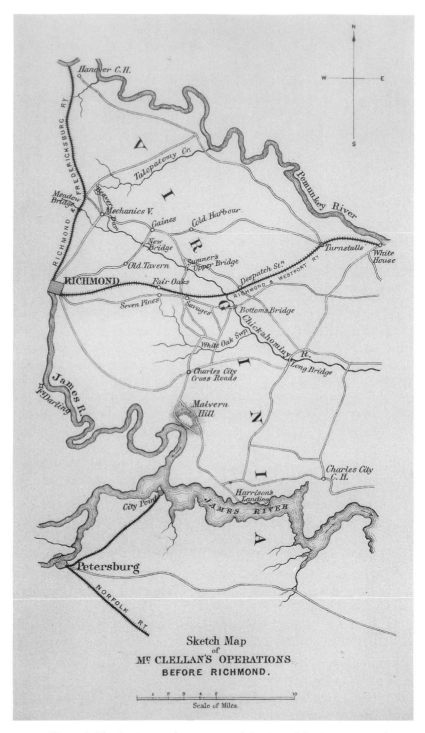

Sketch Map
of
Mc CLELLAN'S OPERATIONS
BEFORE RICHMOND.

Scale of Miles.

MAP 4. Henry C. Fletcher's map shows many of the sites of the Sevens Days' battles: Fair Oaks, Gaines's Mill, Savage's Station, White Oak Swamp, and Malvern Hill. Fletcher, *History of the American War*, vol. 2, 20+. UVM.

chester, a cousin, and a brother-in-law fell in a single blast from a rebel cannon. Only one of the seven survived.[2]

Retreating across White Oak Swamp, the army in near panic, the Vermonters continued to guard the rear. There was little chance to rest and no clean water to drink. Most of the wounded had to be abandoned to the enemy, as were tons of supplies.[3] The last battle of the Seven Days, at Malvern Hill on July 1, was a major defeat for Lee's attacking columns, but just the same the Army of the Potomac withdrew to the safety of Harrison's Landing. The Vermont Brigade saw no action at Malvern Hill but the three companies of Vermont sharpshooters took part in some desperate fighting. Lieutenant-Colonel William Ripley received a serious, disabling leg wound and was nearly left behind as the army retreated. It was to be his last battle.[4]

In the Gulf Department, General Benjamin Butler sent a small brigade, including the Seventh Vermont Infantry, on an expedition up the Mississippi River to Vicksburg, the last rebel stronghold on the great waterway. Butler's plan, to be carried out by Brigadier General Thomas Williams, was to divert the river from Vicksburg's west-facing waterfront by digging a canal across a neck of land where the river began to loop toward the city. River traffic would thus be out of range of

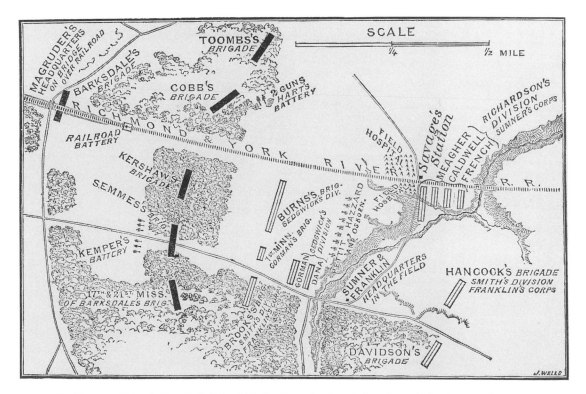

MAP 5. The Vermont Brigade (Brooks's Brigade) helped repulse the rebels at Savage's Station, at a heavy cost to the Fifth Vermont Infantry. *Battles and Leaders of the Civil War*, vol. 2, 374. UVM.

Vicksburg's artillery and the city itself made vulnerable. Unfortunately, the river began falling faster than Butler's men could dig. General Williams, whom Major Holbrook later labelled "a great martinet," insisted on drilling the men in the broiling heat.[5] Camping in the swampy lowlands the Union soldiers grew increasingly sick until few were able to work. Of the nearly eight hundred Vermonters in the expedition fewer than one hundred were fit for duty at the end of July. Hundreds of liberated slaves carried on the work but could not catch up with the dropping river. Finally, General Butler called a halt to the project and ordered Williams's men to return south.[6]

Williams's expeditionary force retreated down the Mississippi greatly weakened. On August 5, a small force of rebels skillfully managed by General John C. Breckinridge attacked the Union camp at Baton Rouge. The rebels came close to breaking the Union lines but were repulsed after several hours of hard fighting. General Williams and Colonel George T. Roberts of the Seventh Vermont Infantry were killed. To make matters worse, General Butler formally censured the Vermont regiment three weeks later, accusing it of retreating in disorder, firing on a neighboring regiment, and refusing to support a nearby Indiana regiment when requested. The charges were inaccurate at best, "wholly unmerited," according to historian George Benedict, and much of the specific evidence upon which they were based was found to be false.[7] To clear the regiment's name, however, would require a political battle against one of the Union's most powerful political generals.

As Butler abandoned the Vicksburg area early in August, the Army of the Potomac began abandoning the Yorktown Peninsula. President Lincoln had put General John Pope in charge of a new army—the Army of Virginia—which was to have attacked Richmond from the north and west in coordination with McClellan. Now, with McClellan going nowhere, Lincoln ordered the withdrawal of the Army of the Potomac, corps by corps, to reinforce the Army of Virginia. Pope, a brash Midwesterner with some success on the battlefield to his credit, had an attitude of unmistakable aggression toward the enemy, and it was President Lincoln's hope that he would succeed where McClellan had failed. Pope's aggression, however, proved to be no match for the tactical skills of Robert E. Lee and the disciplined maneuvers of Lee's best lieutenants, Generals James Longstreet and Thomas "Stonewall" Jackson. On August 29 and 30, on the same ground where the Union army lost its first battle in 1861, Lee routed Pope's army in the second battle of Bull Run. Pope mismanaged his troops, many of whom (including the Vermont Brigade) remained idle throughout the battle.[8] Among the Vermont units only the sharpshooters participated in the battle.

General Lee realized that the thrashing he gave John Pope at Bull Run would count for nothing if the Confederate army simply fell back to a defensive position. He gained the approval of the Confederate

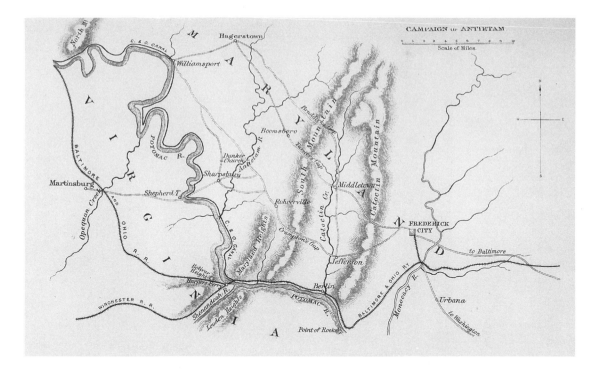

government to bring the war to Northern soil, and in September the Army of Northern Virginia crossed the Potomac River into Maryland. President Lincoln dismissed John Pope and reluctantly brought George McClellan back to lead the reunited Army of the Potomac.

McClellan soon learned that Lee had divided his army into four parts, three of which were to cooperate in an effort to capture Harpers Ferry, and the fourth to occupy Hagerstown far to the north. If he moved quickly, the Union commander might destroy Lee's army piecemeal. On September 14, the Vermont Brigade participated in a battle at Crampton's Gap, a pass through a mountain range that afforded some protection to Lee's divided army. Advancing uphill against the lightly defended pass, the Union soldiers drove their way to the crest, opening a potentially critical gap between the Confederate forces.[9]

Meanwhile, at Harpers Ferry, the garrison of thirteen thousand Union soldiers, which included the newly-arrived Ninth Vermont Infantry, grew increasingly nervous as reports of approaching enemy divisions were received. The Union commander, Colonel Dixon Miles, took a narrow view of his orders to hold the town. He refused to withdraw or to occupy in strength the three heights of land that overlooked the town. Properly deployed, the Harpers Ferry garrison might have held out long enough to be relieved by the Sixth Corps, now just a few miles away after passing through Crampton's Gap. But the feeble force Colonel Miles sent to oppose the Confederates on Maryland Heights was too little, too late, and the Sixth Corps' General William Franklin

MAP 6. The Sixth Corps remained idle to the west of Crampton's Gap as the 13,000-man garrison at Harper's Ferry surrendered. Meanwhile, McClellan established his camp on the east side of Antietam Creek. Fletcher, *History of the American War*, vol. 2, 158+. UVM.

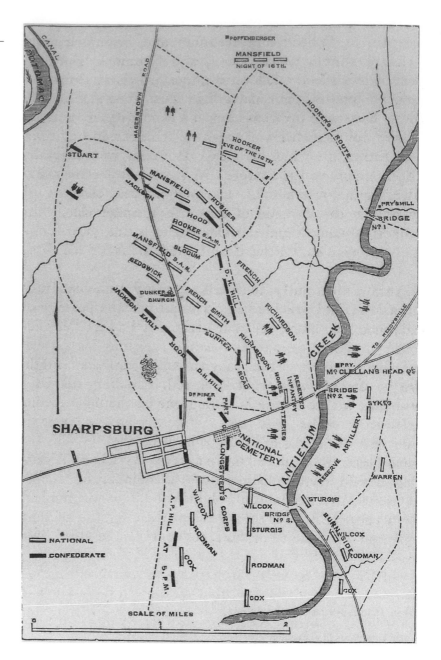

MAP 7. In the day-long battle of Antietam the Vermont Brigade (part of Smith's Division) made one of the last advances from the northeast, and held its position near the sunken road, or "Bloody Lane." Lossing, *Pictorial History of the Civil War in the United States of America*, vol. 2, 482. UVM.

made little effort to advance to the rescue. The rebel forces took control of the heights without much opposition, and the Union garrison surrendered on September 15.[10] Just one month in the field, the Ninth Vermont lay down its muskets, most of them never fired in battle. Stonewall Jackson paroled the entire garrison, releasing them on their pledges not to take up arms until exchanged for Confederate prisoners, and soon the men began a bitter march to Baltimore. The Vermonters would serve their parole at Camp Douglas in Chicago until they could be exchanged for an equal number of rebel prisoners.

McClellan still had an opportunity to inflict major damage on the Army of Northern Virginia. General Lee, with the fourth and largest part of his army, occupied Sharpsburg, Maryland, a village that lay between the Potomac River and Antietam Creek. On the east side of the Antietam, outnumbering Lee by a wide margin, McClellan cautiously deployed his troops, waiting until everything was in near perfect arrangement even as more and more of Lee's troops arrived from the South. McClellan finally launched his attack on September 17. The landmarks of that battle—the Bloody Lane, the Cornfield, Burnside's Bridge—are legendary reminders of the bloodiest day in American history. The two armies fought back and forth, one side gaining the advantage with fresh troops only to be stopped, then driven back by the reinforced enemy. By day's end the Northern army had pushed the rebels a considerable distance from their early position, but had not broken through the Confederate line.[11]

The Vermont Brigade entered the fray late in the day, making the last push that established the Union position near Bloody Lane. The brigade's casualties were light—only one killed and twenty-four wounded —but what the Vermonters saw affected them as nothing had before. Bodies were piled behind fences and lay thick in cornfields, where every stalk of corn had been clipped to the ground. More than thirty-six hundred soldiers lay dead and another seventeen thousand were wounded. Never before or since had so many Americans been killed and wounded in a single day's fighting.[12]

"such a skedadling you never saw in your life—each one for himself and the D——l take the hindermost"

Second Lieutenant Alfred Horton Keith of Sheldon, Company K, Sixth Vermont Infantry, to his friends, July 6, 1862.[1]

In camp near Harrisons Landing
July 6th 1862

My dear Friends

As this is to be an account of our doings for the past week or two I will write to all generally and each individualy— On Thursday the 26th ult [i.e., of the preceding month] I went on pickt at 10 AM Every thing remaining quiet along the line—the Rebs in sight at that though I

FIGURE 23. Alfred H. Keith. Vermont Historical Society.

1. Alfred H. Keith Papers (MSA 82), folder 6, VHS.

had been told on good authority that there was to be an attack and about 3 PM we began to think that the prediction was to be fulfilled for I never heard such cannonading in my life as I heard that day on our right—you may judge what were our feelings expecting every moment to be attacked ourselves, and till 10 PM we remained in ignorance, but then we heard loud cheering and knew that we were victorious and soon the news was confirmed— Well nothing of importance occured the rest of the time I was on picket   We were relieved at 10 AM Friday morning— I went into camp but had not been there long before the enemy commenced shelling us but no harm was done and our batteries of 20 lb & 32 lb guns soon silenced them— About 4 PM however (Friday) the enimy made a vigorous attack on our picket line and the Vt Brgade were ordered out to support them—in fact I believe the division—they were (the Rebs) were soon driven back with great loss—our Regt had 7 wounded that night— We remained out all night, another sleepless one for me to support the picket but were relieved by the 33rd NY at 10 AM   Meantime the rest of the Vt Regts had packed knapsacks and moved off some where and we went in to get paid off— the rest of the Vt Regts having been paid of the day before— We had not been in camp half an hour before the enimy oppened on us all sorts with three or four batteries and the way we Skedaddled was not slow I tell you leaving every thing behind that we had there— You remember I mentioned in a former letter that our baggag had been sent to the rear We went back into the woods—and as soon as the shelling had ceased we went back and took our blankets and such other stuff as we could carry and burying and destroying everything we could not carry— We had two men wounded by shells that day—Fisher—finger cut off and a spent shell hit P D Arsino on the arm bruising it some— We remained that night (Saturday) in the woods back of our camp— Sunday morning we started again and marched about seven or eight miles but had to march back again through a mile or so of woods in line of battle to fight the enimy who had attacked our rear guard— We drove them about a mile—loosing two wounded in our Co—Corp Martin color barrer and Watson Chaney wounded in the hip and left at the hospital which fell in the ha[n]ds of the enimy   Missing James Judd A Richardson Ruben Magoon Mike Mason R Columb and one or two others whose names I do not recollect and who you do not know— I was hit twice with spent balls making me quite lame but I am all right now— by the time we had finished fighting it was quite dark but away we marched about seven miles farther and encamped   Monday morning being the rear guard we had to wait [until] all the rest had gone— When I say we I mean Smiths division   We remained there till about three or four PM when the enemy opened about 40 guns on us at once and such a skedadling you never saw in your life—each one for himself and the D——l take the hindermost— We had two men slightly

FIGURE 24. "The Rear-Guard at White Oak Swamp—Showing General W. F. Smith's Division," by Julian Scott. *Battles and Leaders of the Civil War*, vol. 2, 380. UVM.

wounded that day   We soon rallied however and our batteries commenced trying their skill and soon showed the Rebs that we were not all gone   As was seen by their imatating our Example and moving batteries and all out of sight   We stood in position till about 11 o'clock PM when we commenced one of the hardest marches I ever marched 15 miles in five hours, arriving at our encampment about 2 AM— where we dropped down in our places and had two hours good sleep— Next day we took our position and again as rear guard let all the rest procede us— And Wednesday *we* the honored rear guard came to gaines river throug mud up to our knees—now I am telling you the truth—having lost in our Regt in killed wounded and missing according to the last report 120— the 5th have suffered worse than we The 4th hardly any the 2nd & 3rd a few— The other one missing in our Co is John Clark—but I think he is safe some where here   the rest are with out doubt prisoners— During all our marches I have been with the Regt & Co Gods hand protecting me thus far   Lieut Green moved ahead all the time so has not been with us—is some better to day   I have been out today with 120 men building a brest work and are quite tired   officers are scarce in our Regt   I Received Mothers and Kate['s] letter to day of June 30 with stamps   had received others before—the day before Fathers & Mothers letter   also one to A Richardson which I have laid one side— Tell his folks not to feel allarmed about him as I think he is all right though a prisoner— And now while closeing let me give one peice of advice to Father, do not you stir from

Vt one mile to come out here in any capacity less than a Genl—it would kill you sure—it is as much as I want to do to keep up—and I feel every day that one year here is shorting my life two any way an undermining of the system

I can not write more now

Affect Son
Horton

Tell Mr. Hubbell he can not think how thankfully his papers are received

FIGURE 25. Jonathan Remington. Special Collections, University of Vermont.

1. Jonathan Remington Papers, Manuscript Files, UVM.

"I can not discribe it but the Air was full of iron and lead"

Musician Jonathan Remington of Arlington, Company E, Fifth Vermont Infantry, to his friend Thell, July 9, 1862.[1]

Camp in the fieald July 9th 1862

Old Friend thell

I thought I would spend a Few moments in writing to you it is rather lonsome for ous the most of our company is killed and wounded and taken prisoners those that was taken they was wounded there Was forty six that was killed and wounded Wm F Bryant wounded and prisoner and Joseph Lasard wounded and prisoner our Redgement Fought three redgments of rebels and whiped them dam them and they will take another Drubbing in a short time there is ninteen of ous all in the company it was hard fighting on bouth sides you will get the news the shot and shells flew like Hale it beat all I ever saw I can not discribe it but the Air was full of iron and lead I am alive and Well and happy Thank god (and dont fraid Easy) Mat is wounded and a prisoner tell Marke that His Brother Duane is Dead he [was] Kill[ed] instantly on the fieald A brave boy and a good soldier he would been second sargent in a day or to)

I will send you twenty five dollars this time for the next pay Day I cant send you mutch for the boys that was killed oad Me Eight or nine dollars and that is lost I want you to send the watch and chane that [I] rote to you for and the Box with the gin and tobacco did you ricive that order on Dr Hulett I sent you

I dont know as you can read this I will write agane in afew days give my respects to all good by

yours Truley
Jonathan Remington

"We have been laying here in front of Vicksburg over a fortnight & nothing Done yet towards taking the place"

Sergeant Rollin M. Green of Poultney, Company I, Seventh Vermont Infantry, to his friend King, July 12, 1862.[1]

Encampment Oppisite Vicksburg
July 12th 1862

My friend King

I have not written to you as I agreed to Do when I saw you last— In fact I have not written to any one except my own folks. I have written a good many letters to them & have recd only three letters in answer— I should like above all things to Drop Down in Vermont too Day & get something good to eat & Drink more especialy some good Vermont water (not whiskey)   We have to Drink Missisippi River water & it is muddy & nasty but I Don't think it is very unhealthy— We Draw two or three Barrells full & let it settle & it becomes somewhat clear after a while. The Reg't is quite sickly at present. we are in an unhealthy spot now. We have not got our tents with us—left them at Carrolton nine miles this side of New Orleans   So that we have to live on the Boats We Do our cooking ashore & I am writing in [a] nice little arbor built out of bows & I have been putting up a bed in it too Day—it is about two feet from the ground—four stakes Driven in the ground with a crotch at top—two side peices laid on—then I took Barrell Staves & laid on—so that makes it hollow enough so that I shant roll out of bed you see—but to tell you the truth it is the best bed I have slept in—in a long time. To tell the truth King this soldiering is Devilish poor Buis . . . The way this war is conducted is enough to Discourge any man or Soldier here   we have been laying here in front of Vicksburg over a fortnight & nothing Done yet towards taking the place & the Mortar fleet has gone back Down the River after firing away occasionaly for several Days   There is four Regts here & two Batteries under Gen. Williams. They are Digging a *canal* across the Point so that they can navigate the River without having to take Vicksburg—have got about one thousand niggers to work on it & besides they detailed about one third of the Reg't for awhile until the boys got sick so many of them that there wasn't enough left to Do guard Duty.

But I think it is going to prove a failure for the River is lowering every Day—if they had taken it when the water was high they could have Done it   I have been sick for the last two or three Days but feel quite like myself again to Day. Jud. Howard has been sick for some time but is all right now. He is first Serg't. now. Lon. Reed is Down to Carrolton waiting for his Discharge fat & tough as a bear, tho' I sup-

FIGURE 26. Rollin M. Green. Vermont Historical Society.

1. Rollin M. Green Papers (MSS 27-59), VHS.

pose he writes home that he is feeble—but you musn't say a word that I have said to you. If you hear any of my friends talking of enlisting tell them not to Do it—not even if they could get a Lieutenants berth   I must close or I shall lose the chance of sending by this mail

>Yours Truly
>R W Green

"For five successive days and nights I never for a moment had my belts off, and did not get ten hours sleep in all"

Sergeant John F. Cook of Hardwick, Company I, Third Vermont Infantry, to Olin H. Harvey, July 18, 1862.[1]

1. John F. Cook Letter (Miscellaneous File 235), VHS.

Harrisons Landing, Va.   July 18th 1862.

Friend Olin:

Your wellcome letter, wich bears for its date the 13 inst., I recieved by this mornings mail. As you mention nothing in particular of your folks, I take it for granted, that all are in the enjoyment of good health.

Your papers, you say state, that we had quite a hard time before Richmond. Well my friend I can assure you, that a hard time it was indeed   It would be useless perhaps, for me to give many particulars, as no doubt you are ere this pretty well informed of all principle events of the bloody "seven days" fighting, but after all, the papers do not verry often, say or know much about the thousand little accidents, dangers, and hairbreath escapes, that happen and are only known in fact to those, who are actually engaged in the carnage of the battlefield. Perhaps it will prove interresting to you, if I should mention to you, *afew* in this letter. For two days the battle raged in all its fury on the east side of the Chickahominy, there on the 26th of June the battle of *Mechanicsville* was fought, and on the following day that of *Gaines Mills*, our Division, (Smiths) was quartered on the west side of that river, directly opposite of Gaines Mills, and while all day in line of battle, momentarely expecting an attack on our possition, we wittnessed the whole of that days terrible work. During the night, while our forces fell back, the rebels placed batteries into possition and on the next morning opened on our camps. They done but little damage, and while most of our artillery, during the privious night, has been removed to the rear, we slowly fell back out of their range, into the woods. The rebels however knew, by lessons we had learned them in the past, that Smith's Div. was a rather saucy one to deal with, and consequently they deemed it not prudent to follow us very rapidly. In fact, nothing was again seen of the *devils*, untill in the afternoon of Sunday, at Savages's Station. This is a railroad Station in a large field, surrounded on three sides by woods, in the oppening on the fourth side, 20 pieces of our artillery were placed in line, all masked with bushes exepting two of them, wich boldly stood out, glittering in the sun. Behind these, lay our infantry on their faces, invisible to the foe. At three oclock P.M. the rebel skirmishers advanced from the woods on the oppside side of the field, and soon after their black columns came on, at double quick, yelling like demons, intending to take our guns. Not a shot came from our side, untill the rebels were to within about 100 yards or our batteries. Quicker than lightning, our guns were unmasked, and each laden with a double charge of canister, they opened on their lines. Great God! Olin, what a sight! They fell in heaps, and the way they put back to the woods, was a caution to see. But soon a heavier force came on again, but the same fate awaited them. For the third time they came on, fairly covering the field with their hordes, but this time they fared worse than before, fearfull was the slaughter wich our canister made in their crowded ranks, but as soon as they got up allmost to the mouths of our guns, up rose our infantry and more than 10,000 rifles, were emptied into their allready thined ranks. In terrible confussion they broke and run, and with fixed bayonets, and a yell that seemed to shake the verry sky, our boys charged after them. At this time the rebels appeared in the woods on our left flank, the Vermont brigade was immedeatly ordered in, and in afew minutes we were engaged. It was now nearly sunset. But by the time it was dusk, we had whipped the rebels completly of the field. Our Capt. (Thos. Nelson) had three toes shot off his left foot, early in the fight, but he stood through the whole of it, like a hero. Six more were wounded in our *Co.* and one killed. I am unable to give you a full list of the cassuallities in our Regt or brigade, no doubt you will get it in some of your papers. The loss of the 5th Regt. was heavy. The loss in our Regt. would have been severer, but as we mostly laid down, loading while lying on our backs, and then rolling over and firing, the rebels shot over us. Fortunate for me, I did not get hurt. One ball went accross my breast, and as it passed through my breast pocket of my shirt, it tore to pieces one half of a picturecase, I had in my pocket, hurting however neither myself, nor even the face of the picture. Quite a close call, I thought. I could tell you of many more instances, like or similar to the above, but I have no room here. During the following night, we marched all night, and on Monday morning arrived on the other side of *White Oak* swamp. In the afternoon the rebels attackted us again, but they got another trashing. And so it has been all along; in the day time, we fought, and at night we marched, untill at length on the evening of the second of July, we arrived on the James River, weary, tired and worn out. For five successive days and nights I never for a moment had my belts off, and did not get ten hours sleep in all. I leave it for you to judge, wether this would be called a hard time. A great many fell out on the road; some have since come in, others no doubt have been captured by the enemy.s cavalry. Our camp is now, some four miles from the river, on high ground, and we are allready strongly entrenched. We have a splendid possition, and the rebels, will get a warm reception, should they attack here. Our old possition had a front of some 30 miles; in order to hold it, we ought to have had, three times our number. But as there was no prospects of getting reinforcments, our Gen. knew that it would be useless to try to hold it: consequently we fell back. In what stile we accomplished our change, and reached our new base of opperation, history will tell, all I have to say is: "I am proud that I belong to the Army of the Potomac."

After the battle at *Savage.s Station*, I went for afew minutes over the battlefield. The rebels lay there in rows, in some places three and four thick, legs and arms lay scattered in every way and the wounded lay groaning, covered with the dead, and unable to get out. There was a strong smell of rum, and on picking up some of their canteens, I found that in most of them, was some rottgutt. The fact is Olin, they were nearly all drunk, and this accounts for their boldness in walking up all-most to the cannons mouth. Give me however a sober man to fight; liquor may deaden a mans senses to danger, but when you come up to hand to hand work, a drunken man can do no execution; he'll do verry well to be shot down. I have since seen from the Richmond papers, that they themselves admit a loss of 8000 in that battle. I know it was much larger, while we did not loose one sixth part of that number in killed and wounded. My friend, I could write a dozen more sheets over, and then not get half through, but as my letter is allready quite lengthy, I will close. I hope the states will answer promptly to the late call for more troops, and then this rebellion will soon end. I see by the papers that Vt. leads the van, and I am glad to hear it. I have been unwell for afew days back, but to day I am somewhat better. Our Captain has gone home. It has been verry hot of late, and quite sickly, but the health of the boys is rappidly improving.

Give my best respects to all of your folks as well as all inquiring friends.

Hoping you will answer as soon as possible I will close, while I re-main as ever

> Your true friend
> John.

Sergt. John F. Cook
   3rd Vt. Regt. Co. I.
Smith.s Divission
   Army of Potomac

"On the whole they met with a severe rebuff"

Major William C. Holbrook of Brattleboro, Seventh Vermont
Infantry, to his father, Governor Frederick Holbrook, August 8,
1862.[1]

1. William C. Holbrook
Papers, folder 13, UVM.

Hd. Qrs. 7th Vt. Regt.
Baton Rouge Aug. 8th. /62

Dear Father

You will doubtless hear before this reaches you that we have had a
severe battle at this place of which you will be anxious for particulars

It was on the morning of the 5th Aug. about 3 o'clck that the enemy
made their appearance in force directly in front of our centre. I was
Field Officer of the Day & had command of the pickets, consequently
had the honor of opening the engagement. the rebels rushed on with
loud cheers. my pickets I deployed as skirmishers & advanced to meet
them   they opened with a brisk fire which we answered. they soon
drove in the pickets however, on our centre & left flank. in the meantime the regts. & batteries had taken positions & the battle commenced in earnest. at this time I was obliged to go to my pickets on the
right flank & on the extreme left flank. neither were attacked as they
were covered by the gun boats & I suppose the rebels did not deem it
advisable to expose their men to the galling fire they would have met
with had they attempted it. on account of my being Field Officer of the
Day I was necessarily absent from the regt. the most of the day. the
regt. acted finely although exposed for sometime to a severe cross fire
from our own troops & the enemy. it is with much pain & regret that
I must mention (soon after this at a change of position) that Col.
Roberts fell mortally wounded. he was cheering his men on bravely,
when a ball struck him on the back of the neck near the spinal chord &
another in the thigh. he appeared very cheerful & looked bright until
last evening he suddenly grew worse & began to fail rapidly   he has
not been sensible since. I have just returned from the hospital & I think
he must be dead by this time as it is impossible for him to live long. his
loss *will* be *deeply felt* by all the regt. & his many friends. a *braver* man
never stood. he was humane & kind to his men & was *much loved* &
respected by them. I will detain this letter a short time hoping something definate about him will occur in the meantime, I trust his life will
[not?] be spared. the Lt. Col. here took command of the regt. the enemy were pushing us at this stage but we gradually turned the tide &
drove them back to the spot they started from in the morning. Gen.
Williams our commander was killed early in the fight. after pushing the
enemy back we fell back farther into town to a strong position where

we could sweep the approaches with our artillery, but the enemy were so terribly cut up that they made no further demonstrations; they are now some ten or twelve miles back. Gen. Breckenridge commanded them. their loss must have been great. they were misinformed as to our strength   it had been reported to them that our men were all sick & so much reduced by the expedition to Vicksburg that we could be easily driven out. our artillery made terrible havoc in their ranks. it was a part of their plan that the famous "ram Arkansaw" (which made such a dash at V——) should come down the river & attack our gunboats, but fortunately it did not make it[s] appearance until yesterday noon when our gun boats engaged it & blew it up.[2] with this their last hopes must have exploded. on the whole they met with a severe rebuff. our regt. had 12 wounded although this may not be authentic as it is impossible to get an accurate return so soon after the engagement.

I did not receive a scratch   my escape was providential & I have reason to return thanks to Him who rules the destinies of battle. no other officers was wounded.

I have just rec intelligence that our beloved Col. is no more. We shall send his body to Gen. Baxter. all is quiet   I do not think we shall be attacked again at present. we have a very strong position & will make a more desperate fight than before, if necessary.

Will write again in a few days. Much love to all at home. do not be anxious about me.

Your aff son
W. C. Holbrook

2. The crew of the rebel gunboat "Arkansas" blew her up to avoid capture after her engines failed (Foote, *Fort Sumter to Perryville*, 580–81).

FIGURE 27. John Q. Dickinson. Vermont Historical Society.

1. Stewart Family Papers, Sheldon Museum.

"We have been disgraced deliberately as you see, and <u>falsely</u> as I pledge my honor to show"

Second Lieutenant John Q. Dickinson of Benson, Company C, Seventh Vermont Infantry, to Dugald Stewart, September 1, 1862.[1]

Stewart, of Middlebury, was the state of Vermont's auditor of accounts.

"Camp Williams" Near Carrollton La.
September 1st 1862

Dear Sir—   I enclose two General orders of the head of this Department which I trust will make a good preface to this note— We have been disgraced deliberately as you see, and *falsely* as I pledge my honor to show if ever the opportunity is given.

Gen. Butler's opinion or that of any other man as to our bravery I cannot promise to control; but every tangible proposition that order No. 62 lays down to our discredit can be disproven—

Some *facts* are as follows— Col. Roberts did not fall "rallying his men." His regiment was unbroken excepting where one and another were dropped by the enemy's bullets. He had no occasion to rally them. They were eager to be led on. They had stood in line for two hours and a half under orders to "await orders." The fog and smoke was so thick that you could not see 15 rods. *Gen. Williams* thinking the Indiana regiment was formed farther to the right *ordered the regiment to "Fire, and fire as fast as you can."* They did so until a Lieutenant came dashing back through the smoke informing the Colonel that his right was firing into a few files of the Indiana left. The last command Col. Roberts gave was "Cease firing." Almost at the same instant he was shot through the neck and 3 from our company fell at the same time. The bullets were flying thick and fast—they were forbidden to return the fire—the Lieut. Col. was sent away on business—the Major was Field Officer of the Day and was necessarily absent. The Adjutant and two Senior Captains were Still sick from the effects of that awful campaign at Vicksburg. There were three or four minutes in which there was no leader, during which time the regiment fell back in some confusion about 150 feet. Capt. Porter soon found himself in command—rallied the regiment—led it back where it came from—reported the state of the regiment to Gen. Williams who *himself ordered Capt. Porter* to march a little to the left and a little to the rear to "await orders" again, which was done. They obeyed every order that was given them on that day and Showed no signs of flinching excepting what I have mentioned. It is *false* that they were ordered, or requested to go to the rescue of Indiana or anybody else—this was what they were eager for— *Something to do*, and nothing seemed offered them except to Shoot Indianians. Are they to be blamed for obeying Gen. Williams' order? Absurd!

Again, the 7th Vt. Saved their own colors. The U.S. colors were borne through the fight and never so much as changed hands. The *State* colors too were not disgraced. They were not borne in the fight but Sergeant Ross of Co. B. presented them and *John Donaghue* never had either of them in his hands—'Tis a *Damnable Lie*[2]

Sir, you may think it strange I write to you about all this trouble we are in, but I remember you have helped me out of more than one foolish scrape and given me many a friendly lift. Besides, I know you will feel that the State is disgraced and would be glad to know that the matter is not so bad as represented. Major Holbrook now in command of the regiment has demanded a Court of Enquiry of the War Department and we are told here that Gen. Butler is doing all he can to prevent our having it—Isn't that Devilish! In view of these facts we wish the men of

2. John Donaghue of the Fourth Massachusetts Battery claimed to have rescued the regiment's flags but apparently what he "rescued" were the guidon flags used to mark the boundaries of the regiment's camp (Holbrook, *Narrative*, 74).

Vermont to know what our Side of the story is, and we will establish its truth even in the face of the illegal disadvantage of being obliged to *prove our own bravery*—if only we can obtain a Court of Enquiry. This is what I feel that the men of influence in Vermont Should secure for us. I feel that you will be inclined to interest yourself for this purpose especially as Middlebury is compromised in Sending a Color Company that drop their colors and incontinently run.

You doubtless think it strange that such an order Should issue from so high a source with so little truth for its base. It is strange—'tis passing strange, but I may give you some clue. Gen. Butler desired the monopoly of recruiting in New England and expected the Governor of Vermont to become simply his clerk in the business there. The State did not see fit to have him so employed. He remarked when we landed at Ship Island that he would rather see 300 barrels of Pork rolled ashore. The difference in the treatment of the 8th and us is glaring. That regiment has been petted and we have been snubbed at every opportunity. It was more than a fortnight after the battle that any one was heard to say aught but what was complimentary of our action there and how the information on which the order was based reached him except it originated in his brain, God only knows— There are officers and men in our regiment that deserve especial praise for gallant combat in the fight but no mention is made among the Bosh of No. 62 of such *cowards*. But I have no room and you no patience. Please remember me to Mrs. Stewart, Mr. Battell, and all my friends. My love to Joe when you write

Very Respectfully Yours
J. Q. Dickinson

"I do not care to risk my life under such a block head as he is"

Second Lieutenant Avery B. Cain of Rutland, Fourth U.S. Infantry, to his father, September 4, 1862.[1]

Camp near Hall Hill
7 miles from Washington
September 4, 1862

Dear Father

I wrote to you Sunday from Centerville— We left that Tuesday morning and arrived here yesterday morning—all of Fitz John Porters corps are here. We are one mile from Chain bridge & about seven from Alexandria— Sykes division was engaged in the fight all day Saturday

—our loss was very large. I have not learned how many. the Regulars fought splendidly. Gen Mc Dowell said we saved the whole army— nearly all the volunteers broke and ran especially those belonging to Mc Dowells corps— They had not a particle of confidence in him, either officers or men. If Gen Mc Clellan had been in command we would have whipped the rebels easily— The battle took place on the old Bull Run battle field— The rebels had every advantage in the world, they being in the woods and we outside— Our Infantry suffered terribly— Our artillery did not amount to anything as we had but a few batteries engaged, though we had a plenty that was not ordered into the fight at all, and those batteries that were engaged were not placed in the right places— The rebel artillery did splendidly. They seemed to have a correct range of every position we took and they poured the shell and ball into us like rain. You ought to have seen the Regulars march in line of battle under a heavy fire of musketry & artillery from the enemy. I will not undertake to tell you the number of times that pieces of shell cannon balls & bullets came within two or three inches of my head. I was struck twice by bullets, once in the leg and again in the arm but neither hurt me any. I was hit in the leg by a ball that bounded from the ground— The ball that hit me in the arm had come a great distance and as there was but little force to it I only rec'd a black & blue spot about the size of a half dollar— Capt Collins commanding 4th Infantry was wounded slightly— He has been sent to Washington— Capt Durgin is now in command of the regiment. He is the only captain with the regiment   Our Senior 1st Lieut is acting as Lieut Col. I was very confident the morning of the battle that we would be defeated and told the officers so— there are not fifty men in the army that have any confidence in Mc Dowell as a General. It is said that Gen Sigel shook his sword in Mc Dowells face the day of the fight. He was very angry at him— I will resign before I will fight again under Gen Mc Dowell. I do not care to risk my life under such a block head as he is— We have had a pretty hard time since leaving Harrison Landing— We left there Aug 14 and marched all the way to Newport News. We embarked there for Aquia Creek. I wrote from camp near Fredericksburg on the 23rd. Stone wall Jackson is a *great General*— He made a bold dash when he destroyed a rail road bridge and several miles of track and a great many cars of the Orange & Alexandria R.R.— He went to Gen Popes head quarters and took all of his papers & clothing— Then Pope thought he would cut Jackson off and take him & his whole army prisoners but he was not smart enough to do it— Jackson knew what he was about when he made that dash into Popes lines but Pope didn't—

Gen Mc Clellan turned his whole army over to Gen Pope when he left the peninsula except Gen Keyes Corps— Mc Clellans enemies were much delighted then, but now he is all right. I heard hundreds of men on the day of the battle belonging to both Popes & Mc Dowells commands say they wished Mc Clellan was in command and then all would be right— Tuesday evening when we arrived at Lewinsville near "Langleys" (William knows where it is) we saw Gen Mc Clellan and learned he was in command of us again. The regulars gave him three cheers. He rode along our lines and said, "I have got you back again"—. I tell you the men felt delighted to see him and to hear he was again to command them. I might write forty pages . . . and then not tell you half that has occured since we came into Popes army. I will remember all and when I come home will tell you all that I know and alittle more. I hope we will be ordered to Washington but think it very doubtful. Fitz John Porters corps has seen the hardest service of any in the army. We will leave here pretty soon and go to some fort near here— I suppose you all were very anxious to hear whether I came out of the fight safe. Mother must have worried a good deal about me— I will write to William in a day or two. I wish Mother would have some shirts & drawers made for me and a few pocket handkerchiefs and some good woolen stockings— I have lost nearly everything I had— Everything I buy is very dear and not good for much   Love to Mrs. Marsh, Ellen Mary & Lucy and all our family—

> Your affec Son
> Avery

"there was an awful slaughter"

1. Walter W. Smith Papers, Duke.

Sergeant Walter W. Smith of Wilmington, Company H, Second U.S. Sharpshooters, to family, September 15–18, 1862.[1]

Stop beside the road in the range of the Alleghana between the Potomac & the Monocrasy, M.D. Sept 15th/1862

Dear Parents Brother and Sisters   Well we have been through another Fight & I am all right yet   can tell some large stories when I get home but havent time now enough to say we have whiped the Rebs here for one pretty thoroughly I think, our Regt. are stoped beside the road guarding Secesh Prisoners   we have some 30 or 40 here which is a small part of what we have taken   most of them appear to be well pleased with their luck   There was none killed out of our Regt. & but few wounded   How many were kill[ed] on either side I have no means of knowing except those that I saw there were mostly all Rebbels   they had a first rate Position but they couldent stand the Pressure

FIGURE 29. William F. Smith's division in action at Antietam. *Battles and Leaders of the Civil War*, vol. 2, 646. UVM.

Sept 16th when I stoped writing yesterday we had orders to march & we have followed the Rebs to this place & two or three miles south of Boonesboro M.D. we got here about 3 o.clock the Rebs have made a stand there they are the other side of a stream I dont know the name of it & we are on this it is about 4 o. clock A.M. & the cannon are going lively fireing commenced about half an hour ago what is to be done I dont know but a great Battle is to be fought I expect & I hope it may terminat favorably for us I have seen all the fighting I care about for the present. if we whip them here seems if they must give up their ship & so with our side I hope it will turn out for the best I fear for our side though the report here this morning is that the enemy have got Harpers Ferry if so they have got their rein-forcements I must stop for we expect to march every minute dont know as I can send this but if I do you will know that I am well at the present time though we cant tell what will happen in the future we must hope for the best

   Yours in Love & haste
   Walter W. Smith

Sept 18th Since writing the above we have done some work we lay near where I was when I wrote before till after noon when we crossed the stream had to ford it & as soon as we were across there was two or 3 shots fired at our Colonel our Brigade & one more was all that had crossed then. Our Regt. were Deployed & we advanced to the wood where the fireing came from they were not in force & we were ordered back one man wounded in our Regt. We then marched in column with the rest as I should judge on a line at right angles with the

former line of Battle that is the line turned a square corner on the right
& changed Front   we marched till 10 or 11 o clock at night & then
lay on our arms till about daylight when the enemy commenced the
fight (there had been some fighting near where we were the night before)   We got into line & went up to the front   Shot & Shell were flying thick   I think there were two or 3 wounded before we got into
position   we were brought up within 50 yards of the enemy & we
went at it   you musent think our Regt was alone for there were troops
on each side of us   we made one Brigade of . . . the Rebs run but another came onto a Wisconsin Regt on our left & they fell back & we
were advancing so the Rebs had a good chance at us   they cut our
Boys down like grass & we them till we were ordered to fall back   Our
Colonel was wounded & most of the officers in the Regt. I believe
there is one Capt. left   1st Sergent was the highest officer we had in
our Co. when we went into the fight & about 10 men when we were
ordered to fall Back   I helped off one of our Boys that was wounded I
think mortally   we got him Back to the Hospital & other troops took
our place   as for myself I was played out   had had no Breakfast nor
supper the night before so I have not been Back to the Regt so I cant
tell how many there are left   I am going back as soon as I get rested a
little more   there has been no fighting this morning   may get at it
afternoon   if they do I want to be there   I cant tell who got the best
of the fight but I think we did   cant tell anything by what we hear
some say we have whiped them hard & some think not   I think it
was [   ]

I must stop & go to my Regt   I have writen this sheet about full but
dont know when I shall have a chance to send it

Walter W. Smith

I will send this to show you how hard up the Rebs are for paper etc.
Sept 20th Keedyville I joined the Regt yesterday   they [have   ] advanced nigh the river   the enemy have gone across but have lost terribly   I went across the Battle field   there was an awful slaughter   the
Rebs lay thick all over the ground had not been buryed & our men had
not got our own buried yet   they were an awful sight hundreds of
them piled up together   we must have given them an awful whipping
I was ordered back here to the Hospital with 14 others from our Regt
I am not sick but about tuckered out   shall go back to the Regt. in a
few days   Yours Truly

Walter W. Smith

"I never had such feelings come over me as at that time and I could hardly surpress the tears"

Captain Valentine G. Barney of Swanton, Company A, Ninth Vermont Infantry, to his wife, Maria, September 22, 1862.[1]

A year after the First Vermont Infantry mustered out of service, Barney received a captain's commission in the Ninth.

1. Valentine G. Barney Papers (MS 104), folder 1, VHS.

Camp Parole near
Annapolis Sept 22d, 1862

Dear Wife

I arrived here last eve with my co after a fatiguing march   we came over 20 miles yesterday and when we got here I had but 25 men in the co and I left Hap Ferry with 96. I found the rest of them here for as they fell out they were put on board the cars and got here before us We have had a very hard march and had I not been very tough I could not have stood it but I am here safe and feel finely this morning Sitting in the warm sun, with Sartwell on one side and Lester Green on the other and a stump for my Table and knapsack for my chair   I found 3 of my men here who were left at Winchester   one of them is C. Walker   the rest are there yet and I have heard nothing from them yet, but I hope soon to see one of my Lieuts here before long for I am kept so clost to my company. It is thought that we were sold at H. Ferry and I am inclined to the same opinion, but what they will do with us I cant tell   Some say we are to be sent west to fight the Indians and others that we are to be Sent to our own State but what to believe I cant decide   I am perfectly reconciled to any thing that comes and if we are ordered to Cape Horn I am willing to obey though I would much prefer to be exchanged and fight the Rebels for a while. I will give you a little account of the part I took in the engagement at H. Ferry   Well after the Rebels had driven our forces from Maryland Hights and were planting Batteries there as well as on Loudon Hights I was at about noon of Sunday ordered out with my Co to Reinforce the Pickets as there was fear of their being driven in   So off we started and while on the way out the Rebs opened fire on our camp from 4 different points our Batteries returning the fire   After I arrived at my post I stationed a part of my men in the edge of the woods to watch the movements of the Enemy and their pickets could be seen just across a field and near enough so our boys might have Shot some of them but the orders were not to fire but to keep watch of the moves and report often   I kept the rest in the rear of the woods as a reserve. this was hardly done when a Battery opened fire on us from the opposite woods and our guns opened on them but as they did not elevate their pieces enough we were exposed to both fires   I changed our position quite often and thereby kept out of range of their Shells though many came very near to us but lucky for us none were hit   at about 5 oc. a column of Rebels advanced on our left and as we were in danger of being cut off from camp we fell back to a cross roads and remained there till the fight was over the next morning   at dark the canonading ceased, and all night it was no very pleasant Job to be around Stationing men at different points as often to be abandoned by them by some appearance of rebel scirmishers   at day light we got orders to return to camp but after about 1/2 of our men had gone in with a Lieut the order was countermanded and I remained   very soon the ball opened and with 7 Rebel Batteries and ours together the Shells flew pretty thick and kept up a continual roar till about 9 oc when after the Ohio pickets abandoned their posts and the Rebel Scirmishers advanced to our rear and fired on us I then had my men fall back towards camp to keep from being flanked but in a good line well spread   we had not gone far when the white flag was raised to my great Surprise and cheer after cheer went up from the rebels. we went into camp and though not many were killed it was an awful sight to see a few dead who were struck by shells and lay in the ditch   Some of the rebel Batteries continued Shelling us for some time after the flag was raised as they could not see it for smoke. I never had such feelings come over me as at that time and I could hardly surpress the tears. I expected to have to go to Richmond after giving up my side arms and many threw away their revolvers and swords, and many of the boys broke their guns over Stumps but happy for us the terms of Surrender were to parole all and respect private property. Shortly in came Gen Hill and Staff and met Gen White and soon the whole camp was alive with rebel Soldiers and among them Gen Jackson   I saw him twice—   before an hour rebel & Union Soldiers were all mixed up together and in conversation and telling Jokes, swaping canteens etc etc but it was eazy telling them apart as the rebels are the rustyest looking set I ever saw. well we remained there till next morning and just before noon came away   I tried to bring a negro who had been cooking for the Co but did not succeed. I will close now and write again Soon

   Love to all

      Your aff Hus
      Val G Barney

I have not heard from you for one month

Autumn 1862

Chapter 7

The battle of Antietam gave Northerners some reason to celebrate, despite its horrible cost in lost and shattered lives. The rebel invasion had failed to rouse secession sympathizers in Maryland and the Confederates were forced to retreat with heavy losses. The British Parliament reacted to Antietam by postponing any decision on official recognition of the Confederacy. The Maryland campaign was perhaps more of a Confederate failure than a Union success, but nevertheless Washington and the Northern newspapers hailed Antietam as a Union victory. President Lincoln took the opportunity to announce the Emancipation Proclamation, which —symbolically, if not in fact—would free the slaves in the rebellious states beginning on January 1, 1863.[1]

Victory or not, the battle at Sharpsburg did little to improve President Lincoln's opinion of George McClellan. The Union general had not crippled Lee's army as he might have done, nor did he pursue the retreating rebels once the battle ended. In early November Lincoln relieved McClellan of his command once and for all, and appointed Major General Ambrose Burnside to lead the Army of the Potomac. Burnside protested that he was unfit for the command. He had turned down the post before, but this time Lincoln persuaded him that no one was better qualified, and the country needed him to lead. The reluctant commander soon led his army on a rapid march south toward Richmond.[2]

The Seventh Vermont Infantry took some satisfaction in seeing Benjamin Butler transferred out of the Gulf Department in the fall of 1862. Still suffering a high rate of sickness, the regiment moved to Pensacola, Florida, in November, and then to nearby Santa Rosa Island. The men found Florida's climate more to their liking and the sick list soon began to shorten.[3]

Since early July, when Lincoln issued a call for three hundred thousand more troops, Governor Holbrook of Vermont had labored to raise two new regiments of infantry. The Tenth Vermont Infantry took the field in September and spent the next ten months guarding the far right wing of Washington's outer defenses along the upper Potomac River. The Eleventh, though recruited as infantry, was converted to a heavy artillery regiment late in 1862 and took its place in the forts on the northern outskirts of Washington.

The government also called the state militias to federal service for a term of nine months, under the Militia Act of July 1862. Vermont's share of this call was five regiments. The militia, in theory, comprised all the able-bodied men of military age in each state, but Vermont, like most of the Northern states, had abandoned active militia training long before the war. Nevertheless, the nine-months regiments filled up quickly with men who wanted to do their duty—and perhaps avoid conscription—in something less than a three-year commitment. Business and professional men could enlist with minimal disruption to their livelihoods. Of the five thousand Vermonters recruited under the Militia Act, George Benedict wrote, there was "an unusual proportion of men of liberal education and recognized standing."[4]

The five regiments raised in Vermont under the Militia Act—the Twelfth, Thirteenth, Fourteenth, Fifteenth, and Sixteenth Infantry regiments—were brigaded together in Washington in October. Soon, the Second Vermont Brigade marched from its camp on Capitol Hill to the vicinity of Fairfax Court House, about fifteen miles southwest of the capital. Edwin H. Stoughton, formerly colonel of the Fourth Vermont Infantry, assumed command of the brigade in November. Stoughton, at age twenty-three, was the youngest brigadier general in the Union army, though his commission had not yet been confirmed by the Senate.[5] The brigade's mission, to guard several key approaches to Washington, involved strenuous but relatively quiet picket and guard duty in the Washington defenses.

It did not stay quiet for long. On the night of December 28, brigade headquarters received reports of enemy cavalry in the area, and the Vermonters marched out to confront them. Jeb Stuart with eighteen hundred Confederate cavalry had slipped through the defenses and commandeered a railroad telegraph office at Burke's Station. Stuart's intentions were to gather information on Union deployments, disrupt rail and telegraph communications, and capture or destroy supplies and equipment if possible. After intercepting telegraph messages and failing to lure a train full of supplies into his hands, Stuart and his cavalry left Burke's Station and rode west, hoping to capture Union stores at Fairfax Station. They found the turnpike blocked by the Twelfth Vermont Infantry, which fired a volley into the cavalry vanguard, forcing the horsemen into a long detour to escape further harm.[6]

Some of the Second Vermont Brigade soldiers had heard the distant rumble of cannon on December 13. At Fredericksburg, Virginia, half-way between Washington and Richmond, General Burnside launched

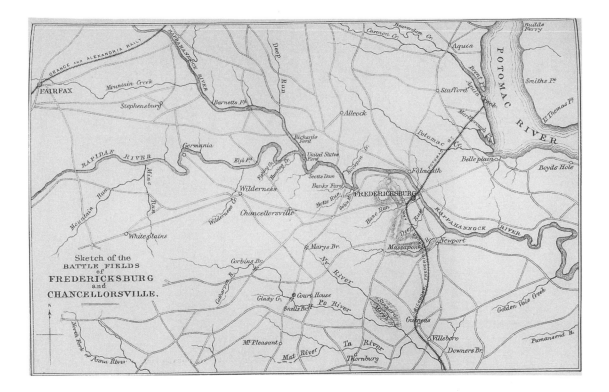

an attack on two fronts against General Lee's Army of Northern Virginia. The Union soldiers crossed pontoon bridges over the Rappahannock River on December 11 and drove the rebels out of Fredericksburg. Behind the city the land rose in a series of hills roughly parallel to the river. The main attack on December 13 was supposed to be to the south of Fredericksburg, on the Union left, where General William B. Franklin had orders to take the heights in his front and turn north, outflanking the strongly entrenched rebels directly behind the city. The right wing of the army would hold these rebels in place through a series of head-on attacks against Marye's Heights.[7]

The First Vermont Brigade, as part of the Sixth Corps, occupied a skirmish line in the center of the Union front close to Franklin's left wing. On December 13, a constant fire was kept up with rebel skirmishers, and the Vermonters helped repulse several counterattacks. Although General Franklin could have used the Sixth Corps to try to overwhelm the rebels on the Union left, he chose not to. Despite some heavy fighting, Franklin never pressed the attack, and the flanking movement never materialized. It was on the right wing where the heaviest and deadliest fighting took place. Here, across a half-mile-wide field, the Yankees faced ranks of enemy infantry protected by a stone wall, while the rebel artillery roared freely from Marye's Heights just beyond. Brigade after brigade of Union soldiers charged across the field that afternoon. Not one man got within fifty yards of the rebel

MAP 8. The battlefields of Fredericksburg and Chancellorsville. Fletcher, *History of the American War*, vol. 2, 246+. UVM.

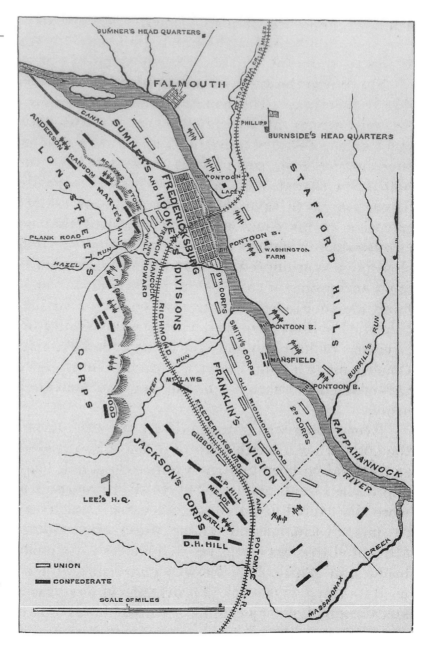

MAP 9. William F. Smith's corps fought in the center of the Union line at Fredericksburg, while the bloodiest fighting took place west of the town, near the stone wall. Lossing, *Pictorial History of the Civil War in the United States of America,* vol. 2, 495. UVM.

lines. The First Vermont Brigade's 148 casualties would have seemed heavy earlier in the war, but they were insignificant compared to the carnage in front of Marye's Heights. In all, nearly 13,000 Union soldiers fell at Fredericksburg.[8]

In what was becoming a routine of heavy battle casualties, the struggle at Fredericksburg seemed to add an element of senselessness. Burnside's frontal assault against a strongly-held hillside protected by well-placed artillery was doomed to failure. In most of the previous battles the men of the Army of the Potomac could claim to have fought well regardless of the circumstances, but at Fredericksburg they never had a chance. As 1862 drew to a close, morale sank to a new low, and both soldiers and civilians began to wonder whether the North could win the war.

"Their love of Whiskey is seconded only by their insane hatred of the yankies"

Corporal George J. Howard of Mount Holly, Company G, Fifth Vermont Infantry, to his family, October 17, 1862.[1]

1. George J. Howard Papers (Miscellaneous File 692), VHS.

Camp Near Hagerstown M.D. Oct 17th 62

My Dears

I am well & strong   we got back yesturday from our expidition without getting into battle. The enemy left Some places mighty hastily leaving in some instances numerous swords Belts & trapings the real *sec* [secessionist] having the C.S. [Confederate States] upon them Canteens different articles of clothing Knapsacks Haversacks pipes and other things to numerous to mention. They probably got a handling before they got out of our lines   A multitude of Stories and reports are extant in relation to Stewart and Lees (Lee was with them) Cavalry raid into P.A.[2] I will not attempt to correct my [mistakes] at present   the press will probaly do its work   yet one fact among the many interesting particulars I cant refrain from mentioning   a fine Stallion valued at $16.00 owned by a man living in Chambersburg was bought back by its owner after being siezed by a Rebel for a *Botle of Whiskey* after refusing $200, in cash   Their love of Whiskey is seconded only by their insane hatred of the yankies   Many of the boys are quite unwell and some get homesick   The 2 Frost boys I am told are in the Hospital   I have not seen Sumner Lincoln yet   The Reg composing this Brigade are all here but I have not had time to look around much yet. I have been treated very kindly by both Officers & men Since leaving Vt   I send you a couple of papers to day   I sent you some new music from Alexandria did you get it   if so I want Addie to tell me how many little Girls besides herself is able to Sing those peices

You asked me in yours what I thot about the war being soon closed up   I think it is an event not clearly seen by any as yet   I have seen rebel prisoners privates and conversed with them in relation to this

2. Jeb Stuart's Confederate cavalry raided Pennsylvania in mid-October and returned safely with twelve hundred Yankee horses (McPherson, *Battle Cry of Freedom*, 561).

war. Thier outer clothes when they have any are generally what I have seen made of what we call at the north Peter sham cloth   The Cavelry brot one in the other day a teamster with his team captured in Virginia his team consisted of four mules attatched to a well built waggon (but not so heavy as the waggons used in our army) bearing the CSA   Mr *Sec* was a man about the size of Grandpa Jackson with a sour determined looking face in spite of his endeavers to be aggreeable   he conversed freely   he expressed deep regret that the country was in such a state of war and Blood shed   he Stoutly laid the cause of the present state of affairs in this country to the "little State of South Carolina" Seceding and dragging the other states along with it against the wishes of the people and if the Soldiers could have their way about it, it would be settled up right smart   there would be no more fighting   he said he lived when at home six miles out of Richmond   was a Carpenter by trade had a wife and four Children   was an enlisted man   did not expect when he enlisted that the war would last long   was told that it would be settled right up. His term of enlistment would expire on the 16th of this mo and did not care to take the oath of allegiance and remain with us as he was over 35 years old and would not have to serve again in ther army   would soon be exchanged "I recon" and then he could return to his family   They had gone into making salt themselves and was Short of nothing but Shoes and Coffee   thought the Officers would carry on the war with the utmost power of the Southern States He did not expect to be treated so kindly by the yankies, if the Soldiers only knew how well they would be treated here they would fast give themselves up without fighting but they are grossly decieved by their leaders   Stone Wall Jackson was desc[r]ibed to me whilest at Sharpsburg as being a small dirty man wearing a black Hat a black coat out at both elbows, and dark Pants and no mark of rank save a leather belt in which was stuck a Saber Bayonet at his side   The appearance of their dead is said to be (with one exception) bearing on their faces a fearful repulsive Hideous and demoniac grin wh[il]st their corps turn to a negro blackness in a few hours   Whilest the dead of our army universally wear a pleasant smile as they fall in defence of our country and remain a much longer time without the action of decomposition taking effect   We have a desperate foe to contend with who comes at us in taters and rags with a miscellaneous multitude of weapons and fight as expressed at Antietam Battle "like Devils from Hell" yet we shall firmly meet them with our Steel until we conquer a piece that shall be worthy of our deeds   We are now about to cross over into V.A. very soon   what our reception will be I know not   And now my dears the Treasure of my heart Should I fall in the mighty Struggle which is before us may this be ever your protecting Shield your glorious and divine Halo your consolation and your Staff that you un[murmur]ingly gave your willing sacrifice and best efforts in the defence of that Liberty which the untold millions yet unborn will arise to call us Blessed

I found Don very destitute upon my arrival here being bare foot dirty ragged and I advanced him some money from my small stock and took an order from him for [one] mos state pay which you may draw with mine   I think you can draw every month   I shall probably send you more   you may send me by return mail if convenient $5.00 or $6.00 or ten just as you can spare

Oct 18th We were very happily surprised to day by the appearance amongst us of L Curtis safe and sound   he was not killed   it was another man   you will please correct   I found S—— Lincoln today   I had seen him before since being here but did not recognize him he has altered in his looks so   he is quite lame from a hurt [by a horse?]; walks with a cane   I Also saw Lieut Phillip Chase and G Martin to day both well   Phillip enquired about uncle David Coles Girls   are any of them in Mt Holly now   Joel Martin is in Pensylvania Getting well

to Gertrude & addie

    Yours Truly
    Geo J Howard

Co C 5 Vt Vol Washington D C

19th   I saw L Kellogg to day   he is well has gained 53 lbs flesh he says   Sends you his best respects   G J H

"we have some Surgens that have no more feeling for us then the Hogs that run around here"

Private Willard M. Thayer of Warren, Company B, Tenth Vermont Infantry, to his wife, Esther, and his children, October 17, 1862.[1]

1. Esther M. Thayer Correspondence (MSA 84), folder 1, VHS.

Camp on the Potomac
Neare Seneca Mills Oct 17th/62

Most Affectionate Wife and Children

I sete myself this evening in my tent to answer your kind letter that I received to day riten the 6th of Oct and numbered one and write glad I was to here from you   I have riten two letters that are on the way unless you have got them   I presume you have before this time at any

rate I hope you have   I have not much news to write and I hardly
know what to write   I am well and tuff as a not and I hope when these
lines reach you they will· find you the same   I cannot think of any
thing to write for the two Georg are here and boath of them are a writing and asking questions so that it disturbs me very much so if I make
mistakes you must excuse them   well to day I have experanced one of
the most solom senes that I have seence I have been in the servis   the
14th at nite one died in Co. H and the 15th in the nite one other in Co
G. died   he was burried here to day acording to military stile   the
first one that died or the one that died the 14th was sent home   his
home was in Ludlo and was a young fellow just married   the one that
was burried here his foalks live in the north part of the State   the Co
could not rase money enough to send him thare   he had a brother in
the same Co   O he felt bad I tell you and who wouldent and I tell you
we have some Surgens that have no more feeling for us then the Hogs
that run around here   the one that died the 14th the Surgen told him
that same day that he must go a way from the Hospital and would give
him five minuets to leve in   he did not start and he kicked him away
once before this one other fellow went thare   they told him he was
well enough   he started to go away and before he got but a few rods
he fell down and he was helped to his Co so you can see how much care
we have   well I presume this is all you will want to here about such
tell Elieh that George is better   I guess he will com out all rite yet
the Surgen Doctered him till they told him that nothing alded [ailed]
him and our Ordly is a fixing him up   I think that we have got some
grand good Oficers in our Co. untill we get to some of the sargents
some of them are pretty Hard chaps and ugly but we have to put up
with it the best that we can   I shall dred to see them come in Ordly
but just as soon as thar is a vacancy Our Ordly will be promoted   well
enough of this   you wanted that I should say what I thought about
you going up to Jeds   I have said do as you thinks best   if Walters
family is thare you cannot take so much comfort thare as you could if
they was not but I do not know but that you will do as well to go thare
but I want that you should take care of the money if you have more
than . . . you want to use but use what you want for I tell you that I
have to go through with a good deal her[e] and what can be saved will
come handy if I live to come home   Well Et our tents come day before
yestaday and I tell you we put them up quick   our log Pigpen was just
rite to put the tent on so you see we was all rite   thar my Ink is so
thick or something else   well good by with this sheet of paper for I
think that is the trouble and I will try another sheet

W

"it was a splendid sight to see those five thousand stalwart sons of old Vermont marching down Pennsylvania avenue"

Private Richard J. Irwin of Burlington, Company C, Twelth Vermont Infantry, to his mother and sister, November 1, 1862.[1]

FIGURE 30. Richard J. Irwin. Special Collections, University of Vermont.

Fairfax Virginia   Nov 1st/62

Dear Mother & Sister

You will see by the heading of my letter whare we are now, last Monday we were formed in a brigade with the 13, 14, 15, & 16th Vermont Regts and supposed that we would stay in Washington some time if not all winter so we went to work and fixed our tents up so that they were verey comfortable   some of the men spent four or five dollars in fixing them and all went merry as a marriage bell. but Oh the uncertinty of war   Wednesday evening about 8 O clock we were notified to have knapsacks packed canteens filled with water and one days rations in our haver-sacks and to start at half past 7 next morning for —the Lord onle knew whare we did not. well time came and we were ready the whole brigade started down by the Capitol and through the city and I tell you it was a splendid sight to see those five thousand stalwart sons of old Vermont marching down Pennsylvania avenue. we marched down to the Potomac crossed the long bridge and at nine O clock we were all over the bridge and invaded the sacred soil of Virginia. we marched into the rebel Gen Lee's plantation which was the Battle field of Balls Bluff on the direct road to Bull run[2]   the boys pick up cannon balls and peices of shell in any quantity   we are encamped in the woods in the prettiest place that we have had yet. plenty of wood and water. you would be surprised to know how warm the weather is here   it is now half past 8 in the evening and the boys are sitting in thier tents in thier shirt-sleeves and stocking feet. we have all been verey healthy in our Co so far. we have had but one death in our Co Geo Collamer from Shelburn   he went with me and two others about two miles down in the City after mules and one of them kicked him and he was sick from that time till he died he was a fine fellow and we miss him verey mutch. If you want to hear from the Regt get a copy of the Free Press when you can as Mr Benedicts letters are verey interesting and they tell the thing just as it is   if you can get a copy of the free press of Oct 22d you will see how we got the mules into camp   I have received two letters from you and am very glad to hear that you are getting along so well and I hope that it will continue to be so with you. As for me trust to dick   It is getting late and I must bid you good night
   Please accept this from the boy

   Dick Irwin

1. Richard Irwin Papers, Manuscript Files, UVM.

2. Irwin was mistaken; Ball's Bluff was far to the northwest of Washington on the Potomac River. The brigade did march past Robert E. Lee's Arlington estate, soon to be converted into Arlington National Cemetery.

FIGURE 31. George G. Benedict. Special Collections, University of Vermont.

P S I bought a very pretty knit wool cap to sleep in for half a dollar   it is made of the material whitch I send you a sample of

R J I

"we hope you will ever be found a <u>modle soldier</u>, refusing to . . . take the rations that are being dealt out in <u>gill measures</u>"

Asahel Hubbard of Whiting to his brother, Frank, November 9, 1862.[1]

Asahel managed the family sheep farm while Frank served as a musician in the Second Vermont Light Artillery.

1. Hubbard Family Papers, folder 6, UVM.

2. Perry Baker, a sergeant from Whiting who served in the Second Vermont Light Artillery. See his letter of August 4, 1863, p. 178.

Whiting Nov. 9th 1862.

Dear Brother Frank

We have just received a letter from you bearing date Oct 21st. Were right glad to hear from you, but I must say I was sorry to hear some things you wrote, but we hope you will ever be found a *modle soldier*, refusing to . . . take the rations that are being dealt out in *gill measures* & some other habits spoken of in your letters. I hope you will not practice such things as I am sorry to hear from Perry[2]   Frank I do not know as I ought to say anything about this in a letter to you, for fear Perry may hear of it & think you have been writing home about his conduct, but I cannot help it, you must not let him see the letter & say nothing about it, But I will say no more about it, if he should see this & blame you for writing anything about him write me about it. Frank I want to ask you a few questions   I see by the papers you have not been paid off yet   if so are you in want of money   if so let me know it. & I hear you are not bugler now, if this is so why not   write us about it & let us know what you are doing, & why you changed your position in the Battery. I think by your writing you are a Gunner now are you not. please write me about your situation, will you not. I wish you would immediately after receiving this sit down the first oppertunity you have & write me all about your self & your position. you know you never say anything about it in your letters & we are all anxious to know why you have made the change.

Perhaps you would like to know what is going on at home. I will tell you what has been doing to day, you will see by this date it is Sabbath day & you know what my business is such days generally but to day it has been different   my boy & I have been at work all day taking care of the stock as it has been a very bad day   it has been snowing & blowing very hard all day   snow has fallen almost one foot deep within the last two days   we have to fodder all our stock & it has been so dry there is no water for stock   to day we took 29 head of cattle & our horses all in one drove, down to the old pump well to water as there is none nearer. the Pratt well is almost dry, the sheep have not had any water for some time. though we are in hops this snow will go off and make some water, the snow has come so quick that no one was ready for it   I have not got my plowing done it is so dry I cannot plow. the house is not banked & some other work that is not ready for winter. you wanted to know some time ago how the beef cattle sold this fall & I could not tell you then for I had not sold I believe   I have sold now for 284 dollars 11 [head]. I have sold the sheep down to 110. I have got 55 breeding ews that look well   the best we ever had. But I must close Ann & Mother will write some. I do not know but I have sold my share of the Lane Buck for 50 dollars to H E Mac

Write soon & be sure & tell me all about yourself from your Brother Asahel

Mr Ellsworth is very dangerously sick with fever

"No chaplain that I have talked with feels certain at all times that it is of any use for chaplains to be here"

Chaplain Edward P. Stone of Berlin, Sixth Vermont Infantry, to his family, November 15, 1862.[1]

FIGURE 32. Edward P. Stone. Vermont Historical Society.

1. Edward P. Stone Papers (MSS 25-72), VHS.

Camp near New Baltimore, Va.
Saturday night, Nov. 15, 1862

Dear Home,

I am peculiarly happy this evening in getting two good letters from home in one envelope, one from father and the other from Minnie. If they had been one day later, I might not have got them for some time, as we have orders to move in the morning   It is very sad and discouraging to us chaplains that nearly all our sabbaths are spent in this way. Last Sunday and Sunday before last we were on the march and I hardly had an opportunity to look at my Bible.

It wd not do any good I suppose, for me to try to tell you how little there is to encourage me here in the army. No chaplain that I have talked with feels certain at all times that it is of any use for chaplains to be here. Some of them have been here for a month or two without an opportunity to hold a single meeting of any kind or do anything else as a minister. but they are compelled constantly to listen to such profanity and obscenity from both officers and men as no one ever hears at home except from drunken men. We can do nothing but pray. Do we have the prayers of the churches at home to help us as we ought?

I did not intend to write a complaining letter, but only to tell you that I am well and that there is but little sickness or suffering among the men as yet. Love to all from

Edward

P.S. It will not do to print such a letter as this, but you have opportunity to call attention to such things in other ways

"What a finale to Burnside's grand advance! Fifteen thousand as brave men as ever lived, are no more numbered in Lincoln's Invincible Army!"

Sergeant William B. Stevens of East Montpelier, Company G, Fourth Vermont Infantry, to his sister Ann, December 22, 1862.[1]

Stevens was promoted to sergeant in October 1862.

1. Rokeby Museum, Robinson Family Papers, box 15, folder 5, Sheldon.

Camp of the Vt. Vols . . Dec. 22d 1862

My dear Sister:

As I suppose thee is enjoying thyself at home now, I will give thee some notice of my whereabouts. Before reading this, thee will have seen mine to Mother of one week ago to-day & seen by the papers, if they give a *true* account, which they seldom do, at *first* the news of Burnside's glorious advance & inglorious defeat & retreat across the River. Of these things, then, I need make no more mention, as, I suppose northern Editors & Politicians are more able to write & argue of these things than I am. I little thought when I sent that letter over the River & got supper and then rolled up in my blanket, (*alone* now) to sleep that one hour more, would see us crossing the Pontoon Bridge, *double quick*. When the order "Fall in, rapidly," came I could not believe we were to retreat, but other orders and our direction of march soon taught us all the truth. What a finale to Burnside's grand *advance*! Fifteen thousand as brave men as ever lived, are no more numbered in

Lincoln's Invincible Army! Viewed as a subject for history, or an exhibition of the firmness of men, that Saturdays sights were *sublime*; as a blunder of Generals, it was — search Worcester's [dictionary], and *fail*, for the proper word! Kearney's old Division, now commanded by Stoneman was on the left of ours, suffered probably *more severely*. Our Regt. only of Vt. was ordered to the Front at first & Co's "G" & "H" of that, were not sent to the *extreme* front for a long time after the engagement became general. Though the Minnie Balls made constant music over our heads and made an increasing chuck! chuck! chucking, in the soft ground among us and we were ordered to hug the turf closely, hardly a man was there, who did not lose his fear of Minnie's in his admiration of the same. Our Regt. in front some one fourth of a mile, at a distance of five paces from man to man, was maintaining as firm a line, before a line of battle & two pieces of Artillery, opposing them as I ever saw, & when Kearneys old Division was ordered to *"charge"* & Battalion after Battalion marched in solid column, with Colors waving, towards those woods, so full of death to them, the sight was grand, but now came orders for us to go out to strengthen the skirmish line & we left off looking at others, to act our part. The result I have written before, so I need not repeat it here, as I have some confessions of another kind to make. First; these last lines are being written on Saturday instead of Monday, as I was taken unwell & have not felt able to finish sooner. Though nothing very serious has been the matter with me, as usual I have felt miserably & laid in bed most of the time. I am much better now & hope to be on duty again soon. Our Chaplain who went to Washington with the wounded boys, has returned & reports favorably, with a few exceptions. Kent of our Co. who had his foot amputated, above the ankle, has since died. This makes three from our Co. [Henry] Mc[Allister] was doing well & the other two were rather nominal affairs at most. I hope Mc.. will be sent to the Hospital in Phila. as the Patent Office at Washington, offers few comforts for a sick soldier. We are now encamped about five ms. from Fredricksburg and three & 1/2 from Belle Plain, but have no assurance of staying here any length of time. Most of the boys are getting Log huts built, so that they are becoming more & more comfortable.

1st day afternoon, I will try to finish this. I am much better to-day & have some appetite. My Box came the fore part of the week & everything was in as nice shape as could be. I got thy letter yesterday & one from Mary the day before. I am glad to hear from you so often. I have not heard directly from Mc.. since he went to Washington   I was in hopes of a letter from him yesterday, but it did not come. I am much in hopes that his injury will not result in a permanent lameness, but we cannot tell in the Army how such things will be   I saw Cyril Wheeler after he was wounded, on the field & though his head was cut severely, he was able to walk to the Hospital & I have not seen him since. I shall think of you some at "New Year's," but I guess not enough to make me homesick much, however. Have just as good a time as you can. My turn will come sometime I reckon.

With love to all, as ever.

> Thy Brother
> W. B. Stevens

To Ann Stevens

"We enjoyed another good defeat to Fredericksburg as usual"

Private James W. Bromley of Danby, Company B, Second Vermont Infantry, to his brother and sister, December 25, 1862.[1]

1. James W. Bromley Papers (MSC 5-18), VHS.

Camp near Bell plains Virginia
Dec the 25— 1862

Dear brother and sister   I now have a few moments of leasure in which I will occupy in writing to you   I received a letter from you about ten days ago and have not had time to answer it until now   we are having a holiday here to day   this is what we used to call Christmast when I was in Vermont   I should like to step in and take supper with you but I guess I will not to night as things is now and I am to work for uncle sam and get my bord where I do my work   I am well and tough this winter and enjoying myself as well as can be expected considering the circumstances   we enjoyed another good defeat to Fredricksburg as usual   if we did not get whiped perhaps we would whip somebody but it is our luck to get defeated about evry time but I guess that I can stand the press my time out and then the union may go to the Devil for all I care   there is somebody that is to blame a most damdly about this and who is it   I think it is the secretary of war and our Congress men and old abe   they can sit there in Washington and say go ahead and they dont have the least idea how things is comming out   our Generals knew before we crossed the Rapihanoc that we could not drive the rebs out of their position they had got so strongly fortified but them men to Washington must have them advance   wal we did advance and what did we gain by it   O we only lost about fifteen thousand men and used about three millions worth of amnition and got a damd good whiping but that is nothing   let them work we have got men to be kill[ed] by the thousand and money to spend by the million   this thing never will be settled by fighting that is plain to

FIGURE 33. Destroyed bridge over the Rappahannock River at Fredericksburg. Lossing, *Pictorial History of the Civil War in the United States of America*, vol. 3, 18. UVM.

be seen now and the taking of Richmond is plaid out but I think that our men are a sparing for another battle soon but let it come the sooner the better   in the first place we hant got a man that is capable of Commanding so large an army as we have got here   little mc came the nearest to perfection of any general and the secritary of war see it and he must then have him removed   But old Burney is a good general and I think that he will be removed now and somebody else must be commander in Chief of the army of the potomac   those generals must all have their turns in Commanding the army of the potomac and then there will be somthing done about settling   I think that the south will gain their independance   I think that they will be recognised by the foreign powers now   I hope so for one   the way this thing has been carried on it has not been anything but a speculation so far as you can see it   I will send you a paper that has got old Burneys plans in and so forth   I guess that this is about enough for this time and I will save the other part of the sheet to write another letter on   I received a pair of gloves from P holton and I sent him one dollar and fifty cts to pay for them   you write if he gets it

Stephen Woods is sick in the Hospital yet

I will close now by wishing you a happy new year   perhaps you will get this about new years day   Yours etc   write soon

    J W B

"I am sick sick Heart sick, of this War, and I want my Son out of it"

1. Charles E. Parker Papers, carton 1, folder 14, UVM.

Henrietta M. Parker of Vergennes to her son, Captain Charles E. Parker, Company E, Seventh Vermont Infantry, December 25, 1862.[1]

Charles had gone home on a furlough during the summer, because of sickness, and returned to the regiment after the battle of Baton Rouge. Formerly the adjutant, he was promoted to captain in early December.

Vergennes Dec 25th 1862

My Dear Son,

Yours of the 9th has just reached us, I did not expect to receive another letter from Pensacola unles it were to tell us—that you were about to sail for the North—and I assure you I am disappointed that you have not yet received orders for your return   We do so long to see you home, yet it is a bad season for the voige and since you are so comfortably situated it may be as well for you to remain there awhile longer, We are rejoiced that your health is good and that you are so nicely situated, I do hope and pray that you may remain so and speedily as may be, return to your home, and to the loveing ones so impatient to see you, You do not speak of resigning but I *do hope it* is your intention to do so, I cannot feel willing that you should remain longer in a service that promises so little. Managed as things now are, the enemy have and will have the advantage, I am sick sick Heart sick, of this War, and I want my Son out of it and I must have you out of it, Do my dear Charlie make this your decision that when your Reg comes North, you *will resign*, I cannot sacrifice you to this Unholy War, They accomplish nothing but the slaughtering of thousands, and to all appearances it is all they will accomplish,

This is Christmas day   you have been much missed at home and at Church, Ellen and Charles dined with us, George also—he came from Burlington this morning, returned this eve, The children have had a happy time with their presents today. This evening Ellen and Lizzie with the Stevens families are at Mr Woodbridges, where they were invited to see the Christmas tree, Ellen has been very unwell all winter, but is much better now,

You speak of our being surrounded with deep snow, you are quite mistaken for once, our streets are as bare, as free from snow as in June We had, the first of this month a little sleighing for a few days, it soon disappeared and we have had none since   We had a few *very* cold days, today has rained a little, Business is good, your Father says, their business has never been better. I should have written you again before this but I thought you we[r]e probly on your way home, Now my dear

Son, do write me that you will resign and come home, I will not speak of it to any one before you arrive, (*But* you must *Resign*)

You see I have a large sheet, for the reason that I had not a small one, but I do not intend to fill it. Why should I, when you but half fill a small one, Do please try to give us longer letters   I am sure you may have time enough now,

How do you like your new position   Dont let one Steamer leave without a letter. you know not our anxiety to hear from you.

Now my dear Son as soon as you receive this just take your pen, and answer all my questions and write a long letter and have it ready to send by the first mail, adding to it the day of leaving

It is nearly ten oc and I can write no more

>With Much love
>Your Affct. Mother
>   H M. Parker

P.S. We have a nice pair of Boots here awaiting your return,

"Mary thinks she is seeing enough of war"

Lieutenant Colonel Roswell Farnham of Bradford, Twelfth Vermont Infantry, to his sister, Laura, December 31, 1862.[1]

Farnham's wife, Mary, and the wives of several other Second Vermont Brigade officers paid long visits to their husbands during what was supposed to be the quiet season of winter.

Camp of Vermont 12th Regt.
Near Fairfax Ct. House Va.
Dec. 31st 1862—

Sister Laura:

Your letter mailed the 28th was rec'd tonight. We are still in our camp here but how long we shall be I dont know for we have been threatend by the rebels for the last three or four days & are now under orders to be ready to march at a moments notice with two days rations— My trunks are all packed & every thing lies ready for moving instantly—

Mary is still boarding at Mr. Whaley's— She has not yet stopped in Camp as it is hardly safe & it will not do for me to be absent for we are liable to be called out at any time—

We had quite an excitement & a little fight the other night about a mile from here— Mary did not sleep much thro' the night I reckon.

FIGURE 34. Roswell Farnham. Vermont Historical Society.

1. Roswell Farnham Papers, box 20, volume 37, UVM.

Our Regt. was ordered out Sunday evening while Mary was here, & we left while she was still in camp. Col. Blunt was gone to Fairfax Seminary about eighteen miles from here & the command of the Regt. devolved upon me— We marched up to the Court House & then took the road to Washington till we came to a redoubt & some rifle pits about a mile beyond the Ct. House— Just before we were posted I learned for the first time that a large force of rebel cavalry was expected down the road toward us— A battery of artillery was posted in the road, the 12th Regt. on the right, the 13th on the left & the 14th in the rear— Two companies of the 12th were thrown forward as skirmishers— Cos. B. & G. from Woodstock & Brandon— It was a beautiful night but rather cold. The boys were as calm as you please— There was a great deal of riding backwards & forwards by aids & orderlies—just enough going on to keep the boys rather excited when some scouts came rushing in saying that they had been chased by the rebels. The command was given at once to load— But before the men had loaded their pieces we heard a yell & then a volley in the woods where the skirmishers were stationed— A body of rebel cavalry had charged upon the picket set in the road by the skirmishers— As the rebels started the boys run into the woods & at the same moment our men fired. The rebels took themselves out of the way as fast as possible. They left two dead horses in the road & we have since learned that quite a number were wounded   Of course we expected the full force upon us at once— The boys were still & finished their loading— The main body came up to within about three quarters of a mile of us & set the woods on fire— Genl. Stoughton ordered some men to go out & reconnoitre— A sergeant & a few men started from Co. G. of the 12th & the sergt. tied his handkerchief to his gun & walked boldly into the rebel camp— They asked him who he was & what he wanted— He told them he was a Union soldier & wanted to know whether they were friends or foes— After conferring with their higher officers the Segt. was told that the Genl. would communicate with our forces in the morning— Stoughton concluded not to wait till morning but threw a few shells among them & they moved—

We remained in our position a couple of hours longer when I was ordered to take the 12th on the double quick thro' the town to the Chantilly road. The boys hurried down to the Ct. House— I reported to the Genl. & he told me that he had heard from the enemy between them & Chantilly—the latter place is only four miles from the Ct. House—and directed me to post the 12th so as to command the road— We moved out beyond the village, a battery accompanying us, and posted ourselves in a position to control the road completely & at the same time we were almost entirely safe from a cavalry charge— We waited there rather impatiently till morning—& marched into camp about six o'clock—

I went over to see Mary & took breakfast with her— She & Mrs. Blunt had not slept much— The firing had caused them a great deal of anxiety. Mary thinks she is seeing enough of war—

The Cavalry was under Genl. Stuart & was two or three thousand strong— They passed around us, but we, not having any cavalry, could do nothing with them— They have gone up toward Harpers Ferry, it is said— Since I have commenced writing here I learn that Jackson with twelve thousand men is on the way here— He crossed the Occoquan 20 miles from here at 11 o'clk today— I expected that the Rebels would make some demonstration about New Years to offset the President's Proclamation.[2]

We may have an engagement tomorrow or next day & it may be that Jackson is only making a feint & intends to move in some other direction—

Tell Charlie Harding that I have written him one or two letters since I have heard from him— I had a letter from Col. Andross last night— I intended to write a long letter to Charlie about our affair the other night but have not had time— I should have added that the Rebs. run the telegraph at Burks Station two or three hours & arranged some matters to suit themselves. We were cut off from Washington about 18 hours— Col. Blunt got home safly the next day—

Remember me to all who enquire—

Write to Mary again & direct to me—

Yours truly
Roswell Farnham

2. The Emancipation Proclamation took effect on January 1, 1863, but fears of a Confederate military response proved groundless. The report of Jackson crossing the Occoquan River was false.

Chapter 8 Winter 1863

After the battle of Fredericksburg the friends and families of Union soldiers once more scanned the casualty lists and waited impatiently for letters from the front. Some grieved to find familiar names among the dead and many others were thrown into a state of terrified suspense until the condition of the wounded could be confirmed. This dismal holiday season held few consolations.

General Burnside was not through with the rebels. Despite the loss of men and the damaged morale, the Army of the Potomac still outnumbered the Confederates and Burnside still held the advantage against an enemy forced to maintain a defensive position. The Union commander drew up a plan to assault the rebels holding the hills behind Fredericksburg by crossing the Rappahannock River a few miles to the west and descending upon General Lee's left flank—on more advantageous terrain than the Yankees had faced a month before. The army started moving on the cold, sunny morning of January 20. Later in the day, however, a steady rain began falling, and as the cold earth thawed, thousands of feet and wheels churned the road into mud. By the next day the wagons, cannon, caissons, and pontoons had sunk so deeply in the mud that entire companies were detailed to pull them out. The rain continued, and rebels on the far side of the river, now fully aware of Burnside's intentions, jeered at the mired Army of the Potomac. Burnside finally called a halt to the "Mud March" late on the 21st and the soldiers plodded back to camp, wet, exhausted, and hungry, because rations could not be brought forward on the muddy roads.[1]

This inauspicious start to 1863 gave way to a season of general rest and recuperation. Burnside resigned, to be replaced by Joseph Hooker, an energetic corps commander with a talent for organization. Hooker immediately set out to reform the army's command structure. Several general officers were dismissed, including the Sixth Corps' General

William F. Smith. Hooker clamped down on desertion, which had reached epidemic proportions after the Fredericksburg fight, liberalized the furlough system, and brought a greater sense of order to the army.[2] "Fighting Joe" inspired confidence in the troops, an element in short supply since the Fredericksburg disaster.

The First Vermont Brigade settled into winter camp at White Oak Church under a new commander, Brigadier General Lewis A. Grant, formerly colonel of the Fifth Vermont Infantry. Perhaps the most memorable event of the winter was a snowball fight pitting the Third and Fifth regiments against the Twenty-Sixth New Jersey, a nine-months regiment attached to the First Vermont Brigade since October 1862. The Vermonters disdained the Jersey men, whose bravery and honesty they doubted. The men of the Twenty-Sixth thought themselves superior in the art of snowballing and challenged the two Vermont regiments to a good-natured battle. Roughly equal in overall strength, the two sides met in mock combat on February 25, and the Vermonters won a resounding victory.[3]

For the Second Vermont Brigade, the hard work of picket duty in the outer defenses of Washington continued throughout the winter. General Edwin Stoughton aspired to lead his troops in battle, not to be left with the inglorious task of protecting the capital from largely imaginary threats. He showed a rash bravado by choosing for his headquarters a comfortable house in Fairfax Court House, miles from the nearest regimental camp, protected by only a small guard detachment.

After Stuart's raid at the end of December, no large-scale incursions of enemy troops threatened the Second Brigade's picket line. But increasingly the pickets were subjected to guerilla raids, principally by the irregular cavalry of Captain John S. Mosby. On the dark night of March 8, Mosby and thirty men quietly surrounded General Stoughton's headquarters at Fairfax Court House, and took the general prisoner. As a result of this humiliation President Lincoln withdrew Stoughton's still-pending nomination for brigadier general, and when he was exchanged in May, Stoughton found his army career at an end.[4]

The First Vermont Cavalry also had picket duty during the winter of 1863, and also found its pickets vulnerable to Mosby's raids. The regiment was poorly coordinated with the other cavalry units along the picket line. Twenty-five men of the First Vermont were captured at Herndon Station in broad daylight on March 12 when they mistook an approaching column of Mosby's cavalry for their own picket relief. Captain William Wells and three other officers were also captured. Mosby paroled the soldiers but sent the officers to Libby Prison in Richmond.[5]

Meanwhile, the Ninth Vermont Infantry, captured and paroled the previous September at Harpers Ferry, languished at Chicago's Camp Douglas. The conditions of parole prohibited them from fighting or filling any positions that would free others to fight. Instead, they waited at Camp Douglas, camping under conditions little better than those provided for enemy prisoners, until an exchange for a like number of rebel prisoners could be arranged. When the exchange finally came through in early January, the men learned to their dismay that they were to remain at Camp Douglas to guard rebel prisoners recently captured in the western theater. "It is not a particularly chivalrous career," wrote Captain Edward H. Ripley, "to lie here with our heels on the necks of a few worn out, diseased and dirty rebels."[6] Not until early April would the regiment return to active service, on the Yorktown peninsula. By the end of winter, Colonel George J. Stannard won a brigadier's commission and left the Ninth to become the new commander of the Second Vermont Brigade.

Vermont's veteran soldiers were fully aware, during the winter respite, that the war was far from over. The optimism of March 1862 was replaced a year later by a realization that much hard work and suffering lay ahead. The nature of the war had also changed. The Emancipation Proclamation made the war a struggle for liberty. Even if many Union soldiers, Vermonters among them, were ambivalent about extending freedom to slaves, they supported the proclamation as a means of weakening the Confederacy.[7] The winter also brought to Capitol Hill a bill to create a federal draft to raise more troops for the Union war effort. Passed in March, the Enrollment Act boosted the hopes of fighting men from the north that more help would soon be sent to turn the tide of war.[8] With this sign of determination from Washington, and Hooker's efforts to reform the army, the winter that had begun so discouragingly ended with renewed hope and commitment to the cause.

"All my aspirations are just as high as ever—"

1. Rokeby Museum, Robinson Family Papers, box 15, folder 5, Sheldon.

Sergeant Henry McAllister of Stowe, Company G, Fourth Vermont Infantry, to Ann Stevens, January 8, 1863.[1]

McAllister was promoted to sergeant (as was his friend William B. Stevens) in the fall of 1862.

Harewood Hospital
Washington D.C. Jan 8/63

My Friend Ann—

You have heard long before this that I was wounded in the battle of Fredericksburg. I received a bad wound there, but that is not the worst phase of the case. My leg has since been amputated. My right leg, just above the knee. I am getting along finely—taking the lead of the amputated cases   I shall bee weell in a few weeks. I do not suffer much pain. We have good surgical attendance. Our nurses are Soldiers.

I have sustained a great loss but it might have been worse   I had rather lose a leg than an Arm   I can so shape my course of life that it will be of but little inconvenience. I can get a wooden leg on which I can get round nearly as well as on my old one. All my aspirations are just as high as ever— You must write me at once. I have not strength to write more. Direct Harewood Hospital Barrack "B" Washington D.C. Please remember me to Mr & Mrs Orcutt & Nancie

With many kind wishes for your welfare,

> I am
> Your Friend
>   Henry—

"when i git nurvos then semes if I coldent stand it till I hear from you"

Esther Thayer of Warren to her husband, Willard M. Thayer, Company B, Tenth Vermont Infantry, January 23, 1863.[1]

The Thayers had three small children.

1. Esther M. Thayer Correspondence (MSA 84), folder 5, VHS.

Warren Jen 23 1863

Dear Husbin mine

It is with plesure that I sete mi self to answer your kind leter that i haint gott yet but hope that i shal some time   i haint got eny senc i wrote to you but if I git one once a week I try not to find falt only when i git nurvos then semes if I coldent stand it till I hear from you   But we dont trust in the Lord   uncle Jo Wickry wod say a nuf of such stuf Sarys man ses if he lives to see another new year he shall see pees dclard Oh i pray he will with out eny more lives lost   I am agoin to put in a paper and a shet of paper and envelops in it but i dont no as I shall be able to git a stamp to send to you   I shant sele it up till i see if I Can git one   Mother is a goin down and i hope she will git so[m]   I sent down by asy and gorg woldent let him have eny but i gues that she will I ame wating for the 7 seven dolars and to hear from you to send a box[2]   i hant got eny but three times   tha say that tha send it to me as son as tha git it   i am agoin to git Sister a litle Chare   I dont no but you will think it is folish but she takes so much confort when she is to

2. The seven dollars was the monthly state pay awarded to each soldier's designated dependent.

Reubins that i thout that i would git one   Jed thinks that the war will end soon   I dont think of eny thing to write   Sister fedes her self to the table   Wille and Libby are runing and holring as loud as tha Can Burty is at scool   Willy ses tell Father to send a leter and a Kiss to him he kiss this for Father   so good by for this time

       Esther Thayer

"if this is the way the war is to be carried on I think the sooner we are divided the better"

Sergeant Frederick Godfrey of Bennington, Company A, Fourth Vermont Infantry, to his friend Sophia, January 29, 1863.[1]

1. Frederick Godfrey Papers, Park-McCullough House, North Bennington, Vermont.

Camp near White Oak Church
Jan 29th   63

Dear Sophia

I received your kind letter which contained a short note from Dora a few days since. I shall grant you a full pardon for disobeying my orders in this particular case, and you will please accept my sincere thanks for your kindness as it all turned out for the best. I wrote to Dora the same day that I received your letter, and she has probaly received it ere this. I presume you have seen an account of our second attempt to cross the river or perhaps the papers will not harp about this affair as it proved to be an entire failure. We had been under marching orders for several days when the order came to be ready to march the next morning which was the 21st with three days rations, and 20 rounds extra cartridges   The next morning we broke up camp bright, and early never dreaming but what we should see Richmond before we should visit our old camp ground again. It commenced to rain soon after we started but the bands played some lively tunes, and we minded nothing about it. we marched some ten miles above Fredricksburg, and camped in the woods   we were completely wet through, and we had just got our tents pitched when the orders came to pack up ameadeatly, and be ready to march. It was not long before we were on the road again but the mud was so deep that it was very slow, and tedious getting along   we had marched some three or four miles when we came to the Pontoon bridges stuck fast in the mud   we stacked arms, and waded in with ropes, and helped to pull them out which we accomplished about 11 oclock at night, and then were marched back to camp wett and cold, and covered with mud from head to foot   If we ever thought of home, and all its pleasures it was then. Several were run over by the pontoon wagons, and injured very badly   Wallace Kendal of our company had both legs run over but the mud was so deep that it saved them from being crushed   he is in the Hospital now, and doing well. I dont know that I ever saw the troops so worn out, and discouraged before in my life. 20 deserted out of one battery that went with us in one night. They made an attempt to lay the bridges in the morning but the rebels were well prepared for us   we could count 60 peices of artillery down near the river, and the opisite bank was lined with rifle pits   four of the bridges were laid down, and as soon knocked to pecies by rebel artillery. It still continued to rain, and we were out of rations and it was impossible for the teams to get where we were so we were marched back to our old camp   Burnside is superseded, and Hooker is to take command now   if this is the way the war is to be carried on I think the sooner we are divided the better   It is to bad if we are to be made tools of for men to practice with that are no more fit to take command than an eight[h] corporal   if the people of the north will suffer this thing to go on this way the soldiers wont   they are getting disgusted with it, and it is nothing uncomon for a Capt to get up in the morning and find half of his company gone   It is certainly to bad but it is a fact that cannot be denied. Last night it snowed to the depth of three or 4 inches, and the weather is very chilly this morning. If you chance to see any of our folks please remind them that neither Georg nor I have received a letter from home for a long time.

Remember me to all and accept from your true friend

Fred

"O! if I could but have the privilege of taking care of you myself how <u>happy</u> I should be"

Franky Brown of Craftsbury to her brother, Elijah S. Brown, Company F, Second Vermont Infantry, February 8, 1863.[1]

1. Brown Family Papers (Miscellaneous File Additions), VHS. See Elijah's letter to Franky, July 26, 1861, p. 38.

Sunday eve Feb 8th/63 Craftsbury Vermont

My *own dear brother*,

Words cannot describe my gratitude when last Tuesday I learned that my dear soldier brother was yet in the land of the living—although very much grieved that you so poorly remain yet I do sincerely hope that through divine mercy and goodness you may ere long be restored to health.

I suppose you want all the news—The article is very scarce in this vicinity—nothing of any importance going on, but if I could converse with you face to face I can assure you I could find enough to keep my jaws wagging *right merrily*. O! my dear brother I think of you *many* Yea *very many* times and *long* so much to see you— cousin Moses wrote me that he saw you start for Providence RI and that you promised to write him immediately after reaching said place but he had heard not a word from you   I felt quite encouraged when I learned that you had come to "Old New England" hoping that a change of climate might serve to revive you. But week after week went by and all my watching for a line (from you) had proved vain. I was unable to endure the suspence any longer. consequently I wrote you a line and directed it in such a manner that I thought it quite possible you might receive it if you had remained in afore-said-place. on went the weeks and still no letter from you. I can truly say that I was *well nigh weary with watching*. and not until last week did the *long-looked-for* missive arrive. *My dear brother "my joy knew no bounds"*   I thanked God in my inmost heart that you were yet spared. Who takes care of you? and do you have good care? and things to make you comfortable? O! if I could but have the privilege of taking care of you myself how *happy* I should be—but I *cannot* go to you. *alas*—the disadvantages that attend the children of poverty. I am lonesome as any *old maid* in Christendom this winter—not a *bean* to lay my jaws *too*. perhaps you did not know that the "Doctor" and *I* had dissolved partner-ship—well— we have—we fell out yes right out [ker]-flop—(and I tell you) there was considerable bluster about it too. But *woe* be to the man that attempts to deceive *me*—I would not trust him as far as "I could throw a dog by his tail"

The brothers and sisters were well the last I heard from them. Who is the kind Friend that *troubled* himself to write for you. I hope you may be able to *return* the kindness in some way. My *unbounded thanks* to him   Uncle's people all wished me to remember them with love to you   The door-bell has just rung and Auntie informs me that there is company in the Parlor waiting to see me   Hoping I may be able to hear from you again soon I am as ever your loving

     Siss

My very best love and good wishes for your health and happiness Good night[2]

2. This letter was returned to Craftsbury two months later with a short note written on the back of the envelope: "Said to be *dead*."

"if they die off as fast as they have since they first arrived for a month or two there will be none left to guard"

Captain Valentine G. Barney of Swanton, Company A, Ninth Vermont Infantry, to his wife, Maria, February 10, 1863.[1]

Camp Douglas
Chicago Ill Feby 10th 63

My dear Maria

FIGURE 35. Valentine G. Barney. Vermont Historical Society.

1. Valentine G. Barney Papers (MS 104), folder 2, VHS.

"I now take my pen in hand to let you know that I am well and hope these few lines will find you in the enjoyment of the same great blessing" It is now Tuesday and I should have written to you last Sunday but as Mr E B Rounds arrived here on his way from Wis— to Vert. I went down to the city and attended church with him & wife After church we went back to his nephews and had dinner and Mr Rounds came up to camp with me but I could not succeed in getting him passed in to see the Rebels but he got a sight at them through the cracks in the fence. he intended to start for Vt. that night and perhaps he will call and see you when he gets home He was somewhat disappointed in not getting inside but the rules are very strict and no citizen is allowed inside except in case of sickness To day is a very pleasant day and the sun shines out brightly. we have had a very hard rain storm for a few days past and it seems good to once more see the sky unclouded. I am now in command of the company again for a few days as we have adjourned for one week and I have made some alterations to day I have reduced our corporal on account of bad conduct and appointed one in his stead I have also confined one boy for trying to get others to desert with him and I am afraid he will see hard times before he gets through with it

We expect Col. Stannard here evry day also Maj Stowell, the report is that Col is promoted to Brig. Gen. I hope it is not so for I dont want to loose him from our Regt but perhaps I should not be selfish, if he has been promoted I presume Col. Andross will be made Col & Maj Stowell Lt Col and Capt Ripley made Major as he is a particular friend of the Majors and has worked in many ways to secure a place in case there was a vacancy and there is not much doubt but that he will get it. We are having pleanty to do now days guarding the rebels it takes a whole Reg. evry day so we come out evry three days but if they die off as fast as they have since they first arrived for a month or two there will be none left to guard. Ab[o]ut 10 have died per day and last night 33 died and it keeps the undertakers full of business. Night before last the 65th Ill Regt got offended at their Sutler and tore down his store and robbed him of evry thing he had and they thinking it so much fun commenced on ours but they had hardly got the window broken in when Lieut Bascom [of] Burlington Co shot his revolver amongst them twice and they scattered like sheep. they got together again and were getting ready to make another desent on the Store when the guard were ordered out and made a charge on them and dispersed them. they declare they will tear evry Sutlers store in camp if they are not allowed to trade with an old lady who lives so close to the fence that she would cut holes through and sell stuff to the boys but the hole is stoped and we expect a row evry night. If the officers of that Regt would stay with their men I think there would be no trouble but they are all away almost evry night and the men do as they please. it is a wonder all the blame was not laid on the 9th Vt but for once the papers dont mention us—but speak of the 65th as brave boys and say if they only charge on the enemy as they do on Sutlers Stores, they will risk them any where We all continue in very good health and my Co I think are the healthyest of . . . any in the Regt. I succeeded in getting back four of those men who enlisted in the Regulars and have sent on a list of the names of all deserters to have them arrested if they can be found, I had a letter from Elisha a few days since   he was well— Well Maria I will close this by wishing that this war may soon come to a close and I permitted to again return to my little family. I look forward to that time with pleasure and may God speed the time when it will so be   Kiss the children and allways bear in mind that I am your devoted husband and that you have the warmest affections of my heart— I will try and write a more interesting letter next time

Good Bye   Val G B—

"an affair which has for the last few days afforded us an incalculable amount of merriment"

Corporal George J. Howard of Mount Holly, Company G, Fifth Vermont Infantry, to his wife, Gertrude, February 13, 1863.[1]

1. George J. Howard Papers (Miscellaneous File 692), VHS.

Camp Near White Oak Church V.A.
Feb 13th 1863

My Dear Wife   are you well   how is my darling Girl   is She not better   it gives me great uneasiness to think she is sick   I am quite well and sound again   that Rhumatict attact was pretty severe but I have quite drove it away   I am glad to hear that Dr Richardson has got up again and is coming back into the Mill again   I trust there will be something done in it now and since he is an old Soldier and knows how Soon Soldiers learn how to steal after coming out here I will venture in a few words to tell how the 26th N.J. Vol. (a reg of 9 month men wich is attached to our Brigade & which I have before spoken of) placed themselves on a night last week in a disgusting attitude and Subjected themselves to the keenest Sarcasm and good natured ridicule (which I will assure you they are recieving to the full extent)   Comisary Sargent Lincoln (Mrs J. Goodells Brother) wishing to use the Hide of a large new found land Dog which he had, to put upon the Saddle of his Horse Secured the servises of a Butcher to kill and skin his dog which is done in due time   The 3d reg Vt Vol being an old reg and something smarter than them 9 months gatherings Secures the dead boddy of this dog and dressing it properly place it in an apparantly Secure place but within reach of the 26th N.J. reg   Sure as fate they discover the prize   they sieze the bait take it to their reg make a feast and 5 Cos. of them partake of this interesting Pot to go out in the morning and boast to this (rogue of a reg.t) the 3d that they had a d——d good meal of mutton last night   to this interesting piece of information the Jerseys recieve the incouraging congratulations of the 3d boys dispencd to them in the character of a sharp whistle as if calling a Dog mingled with which is loud calls from others of, [Sit] boy, get out, here, here, etc. The Jerseys See they are sold very properly laugh off an affair which has for the last few days afforded us an incalcuble amount of merriment

I have not time to answer your letter in detail this morn but will attend to it directly   Inclosed I send an order from Mr Lambert for you to endorse & present for payment for the $32 00 due him   You can write your name on the back of it & send by express to Mr Page for [discount]   please collect immediately and forward me the $48 00 order as soon as possible after you get payment on this and he will pay me the bal here. You will please not delay in this matter and we will see whether or no we can collect our dues   yours in haste

     Geo J. Howard

G. B. Howard

"a good many of them got bludy noses and black Eyes   it was the most fun that I have had for a good while"

Private Peter M. Abbott of Barnet, Company K, Third Vermont Infantry, to his family, February 28, 1863.[1]

1. Peter M. Abbott Papers (MSS 17-2), VHS.

Camp near Falmouth, Va
Feb 28th/63

Friends at Home

    I now seat myself to write you a few lines to let you know that I am well and I hope that these few lines will find you the same   the rest of the boys are all well. I recieved a paper from you to day with a plug of Tobaco in it, that will cum very handy, we was mustered in to day for 4 months pay   I dont know when we will get it but I hope it will cum before long, Walter Harvey has been promoted from Corporal to 5th Sargant & Harvey Fullar has been promoted to Corporal   we had a fine time snow Balling the 25th   the 3d regiment & the 5th had been snow Balling the 26th New jersy and had always drove them   that they did not like very well for they have more men than both 3d & 5th, so the Col of the 26th sent a chahalange [challenge] to our Col. and the Col of the 5th to snow Ball with them   so they picked out the ground, it was conducted the same as a regular pitched battle   they threw out a line of skirmishers in front of their men and our men threw out a line Company K and G, was deployed out as skirmishers so we had to lead the first figure   then the Coln give the comand to comence fireing and we comenced pluging snow balls into wone another full drive   then the Coln give the comand to charg and the rest of the regiment all rushed on to them   we toock about 1/2 of them prisoners, we toock their Col and Major . . . off their Horses and toock them prisoners and drove the rest of them back into their camps   their was a good many of them got bludy noses and black Eyes   it was the most fun that I have had for a good while   their Col give up beat and told our Col that he guessed they would go and take a drink, I guess the most of the oficers got tight that night, Walter Harvey has recieved $75 to send Hirams body home but he has not Concluded what it is best to do yet, I cant think of anything more to write this time   write as soon as you get this and tell me all the news   give my respects to all the folks
    no more at presant

      From your son
      Peter M. Abbott

Washington D.C.

"It was a most complete surprise and was a brilliant exploit"

1. Charles Cummings Papers (MSA 28), folder 3, VHS.

Lieutenant Colonel Charles Cummings of Brattleboro, Sixteenth Vermont Infantry, to his wife, Elizabeth, March 9, 1863.[1]

Fairfax Station   March 9th 1863

Dear Wife

Your letter of Feb. 15th was received Feb. 28th and yours of Feb. 25th and March 1st came to hand in due course of mail. Since then I have not received any letter from you. I wrote you last Saturday & sent the letter by Capt. Clarke who then said that he should be at home Tuesday, but who, I apprehend did not "fetch around" at that time. I also sent home the sword presented me.

Last night was an exciting time in this vicinity. It was one of the darkest, rainiest and muddiest nights that was ever felt—it could not be seen. In the night Fitzhugh Lee's cavalry made a raid into Fairfax C.H. from the direction of Falls Church, and captured Gen. Stoughton, all of his horses and about a hundred men. They surrounded the house, barn and other houses where Col. Wyndham and Col Johnson's headquarters were.[2] An officer rode up & knocked at the door of Stoughton's house. John Martin asked "Who's there." The reply was "a friend who wishes to see Gen Stoughton—open the door." John opened the door when the officer and others entered and putting a pistol to John's head demanded to be shown to the General's room. John said that the General was at Fairfax Station. One of the party replied that "he knew better as he had seen the General at the Court House late in the afternoon." John then showed them to his own room where [blank space] was sleeping. But further threatening on the part of the rebels led him to show them to the General's room. The officer entered, and waked the General and told him that Fitzhugh Lee commanded the place and that he (the General) was his prisoner. So Stoughton got up, dressed and followed his captors without more ado. Col Wyndham was in Washington so he was not captured, and Col. Johnson of the 5th N.Y. Cavalry, who is with his wife and children making his headquarters in the village, escaped by jumping from his window in his shirt and secreting himself under a barn floor not ten feet from where a rebel guard was stationd. Some of the men taken belonged to the 16th Regiment and two of them to Co. B. to wit: Putty Baker and [blank space][3]   I do not learn that even a gun was fired by our guards. It was a most complete surprise and was a brilliant exploit. Gen. Fitzhugh Lee used to live close to here. He owned the ground on which our camps now are. Nearly all his cavalry were raised in this country and they know every road, lane, path, stream and house intimately. Besides there is good reason for believing that they have spies in at Fairfax C.H. nearly every day.

I had a narrow escape. I went up to the Court House after dinner yesterday. It got to be dark before I got through supper at Spencer Jackson's—where I boarded while I was Provost Marshal—and they wanted I should stay all night it was so dark and rainy. I was also urged

2. The rebel raider was John S. Mosby, not Fitzhugh Lee, but Mosby delivered Stoughton to Lee. Colonel Percy Wyndham of the First New Jersey Cavalry and Lieutenant Colonel Robert Johnstone commanding the Fifth New York Cavalry also made their headquarters at Fairfax Court House (Benedict, *Vermont in the Civil War*, vol. 2, 427).

3. Barney F. Pratt and Ornam Prescott Jr. of Company B were also captured (Peck, *Revised Roster*, 552).

to stay at headquarters. My horse was put up in the General's barn. I waited until it was time for the moon to rise—say half past nine—and then got my horse & started for camp. Up to this time it had not rained & although rainy in the morning, the sun had set in a tolerably clear sky. I had hardly mounted my horse when the rain began to fall— slowly at first. My path was across lots, through woods, brush and mud, & I could not see a rod before me to discern anything. The sky was a pitchy black and the rain increasing. I rode on about two miles until I came to the house of a good Union man where some of our sick soldiers are quartered, and as the rain was then falling in torrents and I had a stream to ford I concluded to stay for the night. This morning I was in camp before breakfast. It is proper to remark that at two o'clock it nearly cleared off, and the moon shone out. I was away from the Court House about an hour and a half before the raid. Had I staid all night my horse & saddle would have been captured & I should have been on my way to Richmond— As it is I am here, and very well.

Love to all

Your affectionate husband
Charles

Mrs. Stoughton the Gen's mother and her two daughters are at the C.H. and were stopping in a neighboring house. It is not necessary to say that their feelings are painful in the extreme. Gen Lee who captured Stoughton was a class mate of his at West Point.

FIGURE 36. William Wells. Special Collections, University of Vermont.

1. William Wells Papers, carton 1, folder 26, UVM.

"We are on the road to Richmond"

Major William Wells of Waterbury, First Vermont Cavalry, to his brother, Charles, March 17, 1863.[1]

Wells won promotion to major in November, 1862. Charles was visiting in the cavalry camp.

On Road to Richmond
March 17 1863   10 PM.

Bro Charles

To day about 1 P.M. Cap Scofield Co F Lt Cheny Co C & myself started to visit pickets at Hernden. just as we got ready to leave Mr Hanna offered to give us some Dinner. just as we got through eating we heard a yell & pistol shots   upon looking out the window we saw about 50 men   Confederates   Mosby   we are on the road to Rich-

FIGURE 37. Libby Prison.
Lossing, *Pictorial History
of the Civil War in the
United States of America*,
vol. 3, 46. UVM.

mond   they let us ride our horses thus far, guess they will as far as
Culpeper whare we take the Cars. *We have been well treated.*

You can collect $42 from Dr Edson $40 from Farnan $10 from Qr M
Sabin & if you want any [more] get it of Col   he owes me $50   you
can leave my things with some one in Washington, C R Clements   Col
will tell you whare he is   leave my horse with Co C.   tell them to
take good care of him untill I return. I guess [Norse] will take him.

You had better go home, perhaps you can get to see Ned. go to the
Col to get you a pass

Lt Watson had only 18 men at Post—

"I think Moseby is doing a big thing—he has taken a good many of our men"

Commissary Sergeant Lorentio H. King of Northfield, First Vermont Cavalry, to his aunt, March 20, 1863.[1]

FIGURE 38. Lorentio H.
King. Special Collections,
University of Vermont.

Hd Quarters 1st Vt Cavalry
Camp near Ft Scott Va March 20th 1863

My dear Aunt

It has been a long time since I heard from you—so thought I would
write you agan to se what the reason is, that I dont hear from you—
Probably you have heard that Major Wells is captured. The Maj: Capt
Scofield: Lieuts Cheney (Co C) & Watso[n] (Co L) were all captured
on the 19th Inst   They were about four (4) miles from Dranesville at

1. Lorentio King Papers,
Manuscript Files, UVM.

a *Picket Post* with thirty or forty (30 or 40) men about (25) twenty five of the men wer taken with them— I understand the officers wer in a house taking dinner: it was about time for the relief to come, & the Rebs came the same way, and they thought it was our men—coming to relieve them—but it proved to be Rebels, under command of Capt Moseby—so they just took them all: and sent them on the way to Richmond   Charlie is at Drainesville—think he is coming to camp soon—

I have been trying to get a furlough to go home a short time—am afraid I will not succeed—it is pretty hard to get furlough—but if I can get one you will see me in Vermont again— My health is all right: never felt better in my life   I was at Fairfax just one week before Gen Stoughton and his gang were taken to Richmond:— I think Moseby is doing a big thing—he has taken a good many of our men: he has got six (6) officers, and a good chance to get more of them

I suppose there will be a big time soon as they commence drafting— I hope they will go in big. I want to see men enough out here to eat all the Rebs, and do it up quick when we get at it— Caldwell is all right— has gone to Washington to night   is going to the Theater—I dont go very often: have to go once in while: had an invitation to go to nig[h]t —but thought I would not go.

Henry Phillips is at Drainesville   was all "ok" the last I saw him— I think all the Waterbury boys are well.

I am afraid I should be homesick to be in Northfield now—the boys are all gone and some of the gals—reckon I could find some that I used to sell Calico to when I was doing business on my own hook. I like that about as well as I do to work for *Uncle Samuel*—although I think Uncle Sam is about as good pay master as I can find in these hard times—

I wrote Julia some time since—but have not receive[d] any answer— am looking for a letter every day

I am going to send in a furlough to morrow—dont think it will do any good though— I cant get up an excuse large enough unless I strech the truth a little—would not mind a little: but dont want to go it to big I recd a letter from Nathanael this evening—he seemes to enjoy life— I have not heard from Jennie for nearly two (2) weeks— Nat wrote that they had bought a farm—so it seemes they are going to farming— they dont fool me that way: I rather work for Uncl Sam— I did my farm work when I was a boy— I rather sell *Tape* to the old Ladies—and dont mind if their are some that are not so old

I keep the same horse I had in Burlington.—I guess she is a good fighting one—she kicked a Nigger over the other day in Washington— reckon she hates them as much as I do— If she lives, and I dont stop *breathing*—I reckon she will go to Vt with me—I can then show you a *war* horse—*which is a horse*

I wrote to Aunt Martha a few weeks since but have not recd any answer   I dont seem to be very fortunate in writing to her   have written a number of times—but think she has not recd them: if she has I guess she think they are not worth answering: and I am of the sam opinion— It is getting very late, and my fire has all gone out—have not had any this eav[en]ing—and it is quite cold, so reckon I had better make my bed, and tumble intoo it—

Please remember me to all friends   I hope to hear from you soon—

Perhaps I may be home so as to fool you the 1st day of April—but dont believe I will though—

> Good night—
> I remain you aff nephew
> > Lorentio H King
> > Commissary Sergt
> > 1st Vt Cavalry

Always direct to
Washington

March 21st

Prisoners that were captured with Major Wells—returned last night: the Maj has gone to Richmond: he was not eating dinner, as reported: had just arrived—was visiting picket post. All the officers went with him

Chapter 9 · Spring 1863

With the coming of spring, General Joseph Hooker launched his own campaign to defeat the Confederate army camped on the heights west of Fredericksburg. Beginning on April 27, with surprising speed and unprecedented secrecy, Hooker marched three corps northwest of the Union camps near Falmouth and across the Rappahannock River. The Sixth Corps and other troops remained behind, across the river from Fredericksburg, ready to strike when the opportunity arose. Once over the river, Hooker turned south and occupied a position to the left and rear of Robert E. Lee's Army of Northern Virginia. Here the terrain was much more suitable for an attacking army than the hills behind Fredericksburg, where so many Yankees' lives had been wasted in December. By May 1 Hooker had established a battle line centered on a crossroads clearing in the midst of a dense forest called the Wilderness. The lone house at this crossroads, belonging to the Chancellor family, gave it the name of Chancellorsville.[1]

Hooker knew that Lee must attack him or retreat. The Confederate general could not mount an adequate defense against the federals in his rear without weakening the heights overlooking Fredericksburg, and he had little idea how strong the Union army on his Fredericksburg front was. With two of his divisions detached for service far to the south, Lee faced long odds. The safer choice was to abandon the position and retreat to the south or southwest.

Robert E. Lee was not one to take safe choices. Feigning a retreat, he sent Stonewall Jackson's corps west on May 2 along a route roughly parallel to Hooker's Chancellorsville line. Once past the Union line and out of sight, Jackson halted his troops and arranged them for battle. Late in the afternoon the Confederate corps swept down upon the unsuspecting right flank of Hooker's army, held by the Eleventh Corps, driving it in utter confusion for more than a mile. In a short time twenty-four hundred federal troops were killed, wounded, or captured. Thousands more, driven in panic toward the center of the Union line, threatened to stampede the whole army. Only darkness halted Jackson's drive, which might otherwise have thrown the whole Union army into chaos.

Hooker's plan called for the Sixth Corps to cross the Rappahannock at Fredericksburg and capture the heights behind, then fall upon Lee's right flank eight miles beyond. The main army, meanwhile, would attack from the Chancellorsville line, crushing the rebels between. Despite the shattering of the Eleventh Corps on May 2, Hooker's superior numbers made the plan still feasible. But tactical errors on May 3 doomed the effort. After intense fighting that Sunday morning, the Union troops near Chancellorsville fell back to a previously-prepared defensive position well to the rear.

Hooker's expectations of support from the Sixth Corps were frustrated by faulty communications and the reluctance of Corps commander John Sedgwick to assault the Fredericksburg Heights.[2] Sedgwick finally received explicit orders to advance late on May 2, and crossed the Rappahannock with the First Vermont Brigade and the rest of the Sixth Corps. The next day, where thousands of Yankees had died in December in a hopeless attempt to take Marye's Heights, the First Vermont Brigade participated in the charge against the depleted defenders.[3] The heights were soon captured and the Sixth Corps advanced against what had been Lee's front, but now was effectively his rear. As the corps advanced toward Salem Church on the road to Chancellorsville it ran into more and more resistance. With Hooker on the defensive, Lee sent additional reinforcements against the force in his rear.

The Sixth Corps slept nervously that Sunday night, and awoke May 4 to find itself outnumbered and opposed on three sides, its route of advance cut off as a means of escape. In one of its proudest moments, the First Vermont Brigade that afternoon shattered an attack by three rebel brigades that threatened to capture or destroy the entire Sixth Corps. During the night, the Union troops quietly withdrew and crossed the Rappahannock at Banks's Ford, several miles west of Fredericksburg.[4]

Chancellorsville was a brilliant victory for Lee, and it marked the high point of Confederate fortunes. Yet it was a costly victory, for Stonewall Jackson received gunshot wounds on the night of May 2 that cost him his life eight days later.[5] Moreover, the Army of the Potomac remained intact, despite the loss of sixteen thousand men, and remained far superior in men, equipment, and supplies. Nor did the defeat affect morale as profoundly as the Fredericksburg disaster had. The Vermonters, in fact, would consider their effort nothing less than a victory. The brigade emerged from the Chancellorsville campaign with the prestige of a "fighting brigade."[6]

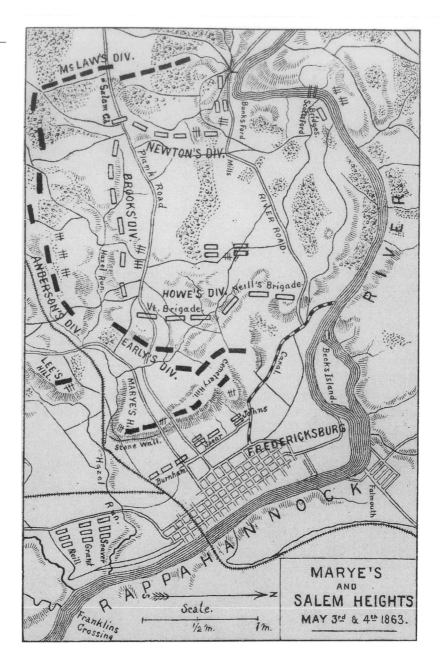

MAP 10. The Vermont
Brigade shattered a rebel
attack by Early's division
on May 4, saving the three
divisions of the Sixth
Corps. Benedict, *Vermont
in the Civil War*, vol. 1,
368+. UVM.

In the Gulf Department, the Eighth Vermont Infantry and the two
batteries of light artillery joined an expedition in May against Port Hudson, one hundred miles south of Vicksburg on the Mississippi River.
The rebels had occupied Port Hudson in force after the failure and retreat of Butler's Vicksburg canal-diggers the previous summer. Port
Hudson was protected on the river side by a battery on a high bluff,
while rough terrain and tangled woods obstructed the land approaches
to the strong fortifications. Colonel Stephen Thomas of the Eighth Ver-

mont, commanding a brigade in General Godfrey Weitzel's division, led an assault against the northern fortifications on May 27. Thomas struggled to within seventy-five yards of the main works, taking heavy casualties, but could go no further. The Eighth Vermont lost eighty-eight men. In a second unsuccessful assault on June 14, the Eighth lost another ninety-six men. The armies settled in a for a siege, and those Vermonters learned the miseries of trench warfare.[7]

The coming of summer was anticipated joyfully by the men of the Second Vermont Brigade, whose nine-month terms would expire in July. Speculation abounded as to the dates of mustering out, the routes to be taken home, and the summer work that might still be accomplished when the men returned. The brigade continued to man the outer defenses of Washington throughout the spring of 1863, sparring on occasion with John S. Mosby's guerrillas. George J. Stannard, lately colonel of the Ninth Vermont Infantry, assumed command of the brigade on April 20. His plain dress and no-nonsense style of leadership quickly won the respect, if not the love, of his men.[8]

By mid-June it was evident to even the least-informed soldiers that a massive military movement was underway. Miles-long columns of Union soldiers marched past the Second Brigade's camps, heading

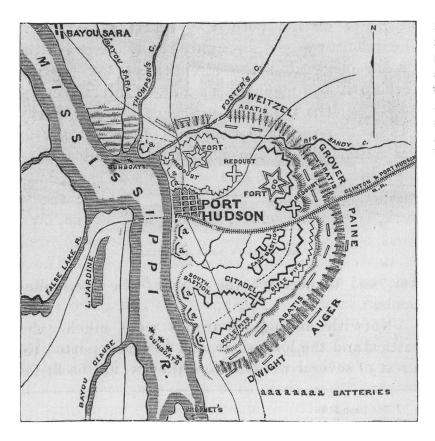

MAP 11. The Eighth Vermont Infantry participated in the siege of Port Hudson as part of Godfrey Weitzel's division. Lossing, *Pictorial History of the Civil War in the United States of America*, vol. 2, 631. UVM.

north. The First Vermont Brigade passed by on June 16 and old friends in the two brigades exchanged greetings. On June 23, orders arrived for the men of the Second Brigade: they had been transferred from the Washington defenses to the Third Division of the First Corps, and were to join the rest of the corps near the head of the huge marching machine.

Brigadier General George Stannard pushed his men to the point of exhaustion, forbidding them at times to fall out of column to fill canteens. As a point of pride the men of the Second Brigade pressed on, aware of the mockery directed against them by battle veterans who thought picket duty an easy way to pass nine months of service. Stannard's brigade marched 120 miles in six days.[9] Late on July 1 they joined what now remained of the First Corps, battered by a day of severe fighting at Gettysburg, Pennsylvania.

FIGURE 39. William C. Holbrook. Vermont Historical Society.

1. John W. Phelps Papers, Manuscript Files, UVM.

"It was a very unequal contest, an old and professional politician pitted against a mere fledgling"

Colonel William C. Holbrook of Brattleboro, Seventh Vermont Infantry, to General John Wolcott Phelps, April 18, 1863.[1]

Holbrook had succeeded to the colonelcy after the death of Colonel George Roberts at the battle of Baton Rouge in August 1862.

Fort Pickens Florida
April 18th 1863.

Gen'l. J. W. Phelps

Dear Sir,

A long time since I received your letters, and although I have made several attempts to answer them, I have always failed. My time since you left New Orleans has been very much occupied. Courts of Inquiry and Courts Martial in addition to my other duties have kept me pretty busy.

The proceedings of the Court of Inquiry convened by Gen. Butler to investigate the part taken by the 7th Vermont Regt. in the battle of Baton Rouge, you doubtless have seen.

The revision and comments by Gen. B—— are somewhat unfair, but they are characteristic of the man. On the other hand the finding or opinion of the Court, and the proceedings are, I consider very favorable to the Regt.

I have written to Father to have the proceedings published in a pamphlet form, that the officers may each have a copy.

I am conscious that we received but a small part of our just due, but I feel that I done the best I could under the circumstances. It was a very unequal contest, an old and professional politician pitted against a mere fledgling

You suggested that I should have preferred charges against Gen. Butler. I thought the matter over very seriously and I should have done so had I felt sure of gaining decisive results. With the experience, knowledge and "wire pulling" disposition of an expert politician, I might have brought out important and advantageous features. I fully realized my delicate and responsible position, and felt that it should have been managed by more skillful and older heads, but it devolved on me alone to extricate the Regt. and the reputation of the state. I done the best I could under the circumstances.

The Regt. is improveing fast in morale and efficiency. the health of the men is also improveing.

We live here very quietly, there is but little going on to relieve the monotony of garrison duty.

There seems to be a good deal of marching and countermarching in the vicinity of Baton Rouge, Port Hudson and Berwicks Bay, but what it means I am at a loss to know.

Capt. Hitchcock is well.

> I am sir,
> With much respect
> Your obt. Serv.
> W. C. Holbrook

"they seem to think that as long as we recd large bountys for coming here, we have not any right to come home alive"

Lieutenant Joseph Spafford of Weathersfield, Company E, Sixteenth Vermont Infantry, to his sister, April 19, 1863.[1]

Camp at Union Mills Va.
Sunday Apr. 19th 1863.

Dear Sister

I recd a letter from you to day so will answer this evening tho' I have nothing in particular to write only that we are still at our old Camp & likely to remain here for the present. It seems from what we can learn that at the time we expected to move, they intended to send us to Suffolk Va. but finally concluded to take Regts from nearer Washington. We have got our tents back & are *living* again.

I'm not yet as black as I was last summer when I came home, but

FIGURE 40. Joseph Spafford. Vermont Historical Society.

1. Joseph Spafford Papers (MSC 9), VHS.

when I *do* come home this time I'll bet I'll show you a *black* Jo, for the weather is getting warm & the sun just beginning to tan

When I go into W—— again I'll get you some photographs; Stought[on] if I can find one, McC & lady, Hentzelmen, the Washington beauties, (the Misses Hales) & any ones I think you will care for, I can get some pretty ones. I probably shall not go to town until we are paid off as I'm thinking my funds would not hold out under existing circumstances. I do wish there was some sort of regularity in regard to pay days, a fellow dont know . . . what calculation to make, you see as yet (& six months are nearly gone) we have only recd what we ought to, before we left Brattleboro. We have got a new Brigadier, Col Stanard formally [formerly], of the 9th Vt, now Gen Stanard of the 2d Vt Brigade. We have also got a new Div. Gen in place of Casey. Gen Abercrombie (if not spelt right, it is spelt so you cant fail to pronounce it)

I was very much astonished to hear that Geo Dodge & Augusta were married; had'nt thought of such a thing, wonder if [Hyren] was reconciled, or was it with him, "What can't be cured must be endured." reckon thats about as near the way as we can conveniently *guess.*—

I notice that all the three years men, & in fact many who are neither 3 years or 9 mos. men, but have staid at home, seem to have a kind of a spite against the 9 mos. men. Where have you or any one else ever heard a good word spoken for them? The 3 years men say they have no patriotism, were *bought*; call them the *Pick Nic* party etc. Even many at home think this Brigade is good for nothing & blame them because they have not been in a fight every other day since they left Vt. etc. I suppose they would be perfectly satisfied if half of us could manage to get killed before our time is over; they seem to think that as long as we recd large bountys for coming here, we have not any right to come home alive, etc. etc. All I have to say is that so far we have gone wherever we have been *ordered* & that hereafter we *shall* go where we are ordered, & different from that we can not do if we would. *They* all seem to think we have rather got the whip now; thats whats the matter, we think the same perhaps. I notice the Tribune speaks of the "9 month *beauties*, who brought neither health or patriotism with them into the army" etc.— I think if this Brigade were placed alongside the 1st Vt Brigade we would fight each other like dogs & cats.

I will write no more to night for its nearly bed time.

Love to all—

Your Aff Brother
Joseph Spafford

P.S. Poor "Ned", bad off aint he? got in a place where he cant tell the truth, wonder if he was ever in a place where he *could*.

Corporal Dan Mason of Glover, Company D, Sixth Vermont Infantry, to Harriet, May 7, 1863.[1]

1. Dan Mason Papers (MSA 89), folder 4, VHS.

Camp in field 2 miles above Falmouth
Va   May 7th 1862 [1863]

Dear Harriet

As the 6th Vt Regt has done some right smart fighting within a few days for which we receive much praise & thinking you might feel anxious to hear from me I seat myself in my little shelter tent for the purpose of giving you a few particulars in regard to the Battle . . April 28th we marched toward Falmouth with 8 days rations in Haversack & Knapsack which with blankets under clothing guns & acoutriments etc made a heavy load   we encamped about a mile from the Rappahannock just below F——burg . . we were ordered to build no fires . . during the night the Pontoon Bridges were carried down to the river by hand so as to not give the enemy notice of our approach   about daylight one Brigade was carried across in the Pontoon Boats & charged on the rebel Pickets taking 150 prisoners 1 Major 1 Lieut   it was a perfect surprise . . The Engineer Corps then proceeded to lay across the Pontoon Bridges the same place that we crossed last Dec . . the Bridges were soon completed & Gen Brooks Divis crossed over the remaining 2 Divis remained this side . . Brooks is the 1st & ours the 2 Divis . . Gen Hooker took the rest of the army several miles up the river leaving only the 6th Corps & 3d Divis of the 2d Corps (we are in the 6th Corps) at this crossing . . we did not cross until Saturday night . . Sunday morning we were routed up & fell in expecting to charge on the heights under cover of darkness   we did not move until daylight   we then marched up toward F——burg when within half mile of the city we halted in the road & laid until about noon   our cannon was constantly playing shell on to their earth works   the enemy returned the compliments with much spirit . . about noon we were suddenly called into line & ordered to unsling knapsacks & pile them up, we then charged on the earth works back of the city   we had to march about a mile across an open field   the enemies cannon rained a shower of shell on us as they burst all around us wounding 8 men & killing Lt Col Hales horse under him (our former Capt)   the reason of our loss being so small was we kept closed up & in good line   many other Regts suffered much more because they scattered so thereby covering much more space . . still we pressed on not a man faltered   the 6th Regt was the 2d one to place its colors on the breast work   we took . . 5 . . cannon at this place & on our left they took 10 more   it was a brilliant affair   the boys felt well . . as I have not time nor space to give many particulars . . our co had but 2 slightly wounded Geo Partridge & Wm Mitchell the one that used to work for your father . . Mon near night the rebs having been reinforced made a desparate attack in front of our Brig . . our regt was placed on the left of a Battery to support it   we laid behind a swell of ground hid from the rebs view   several regts were in front of us & fought bravely for a while but the rebs came on in such force that they were obliged to give away   some however broke & disgraced themselves more scart than hurt the 26th New Jersey in particular 9 mos men who were connected with our Brigade at Hagerstown . . they broke & run like sheep over our regt . . on came the masses of Gray backs sure of victory   they intended to take the Battery which we were supporting . . we were ordered to lay low until they were close on to us then rise fire a volley & charge bayonet . . just as they came over the brow of the hill waving their Battle flag triumphantly when they got within about . . 4 . . rods we rise & poured into them then charged on them yelling hideously   they broke & run for dear life   we pursued them about 100 rods loading & firing into them fast as we could after charging until the enemy was fairly broken . . we took 200 prisoners among which was 21 officers 1 Brig Gen 3 Cols 1 Maj . . this was just what the 6th did . . the other Vt Regts took some prisoners . . our co lost 1–2 wounded none killed   Hobert Bliss was severely wounded in left shoulder . . soon as it was dark our whole force fell back to the river . . Our Pioneers brought Hobert far as they could & left him as the reb skirmishers were close on to them   I fear he is mortaly wounded but hope he will turn up all right some time[2] It seemed hard to leave him in the hands of the enemy but such is war . . our Corps crossed the river safely during the night . . our Regt has the praise of saving the whole Corps   if our regt had broke the whole of us would have been driven to the river & captured   I must now close   I should be glad to write more

> from your lover Dan
> write soon

The reason of our army falling back was that the rebs had heavy reinforcements . . today we marched back to old camp near Bell Plain Hookers whole army fell back the next day after we did

2. Hobart Bliss of Barton was captured May 4 and paroled twelve days later. He survived the ordeal but was transferred to the Veteran Reserve Corps in January 1864, presumably because of his wound (Peck, *Revised Roster*, 193).

"the Vermont Brigade gained all that was gained in the hole fite"

1. Parker Family Papers, folder 10, UVM.

Private Hosea B. Williams of Concord, Company C, Third Vermont Infantry, to Moses A. Parker, May 10, 1863.[1]

Friend Moses A. Parker

I will try to answer your letter that I got last night   I was very glad
to hear from you and to hear that you wer well   I am well and so are
all the Concord boys but Daniel he is sick and in the hospital   he is
not dangerslee sick   I have not heard from him since the battle   it
is pleasant weather hear now and looks likely to be for a few days
We have bin having som very hard fiting and the Vermont Brigade
gained all that was gained in the hole fite   one weak a go to day the
fite comence   we cross the river the night before and took our pursi-
sion in the senter of the Corps and at daylight our batter[ie]s comence
firing upon their works and at nine oclock we had orders to charge on
their forts which we did at a moment notic and hard fiting comence but
we cared the pits with grate Slater killing and wounding as we went
their rifle pits wer filled with their dead and wounded but the grape flue
like hale on the day that the hale Storm was in Vermont   it is death to
all that chitch [catch] it in the head   we folard them dam reabels and
over took them a bout five miles from the pits and a fias [fierce?] action
took place   they had bin reinforst by Longstreet but we drove them
that night and in the night they reinfoarst their army by sending Stone
Wall Jackson   Monday Morning the battle comence in good stile
now I tell you they comence shelling us at long rang but they did not
like the fun for our batte[ri]es comence the same work on them and
they stoped that play and laid their plans for a charge   they wer suar
that they had gut our Corps and at four oclock reabels comence their
dam work   Jackson mased his men and charged on our column
they com kalling and firing like hell and drove our first line and com to
the next line and drove that and at that time the hole Corps was in and
on the run but the Vermont Brigade and three batter[ie]s one was Ay-
ers and the first Marland and Rickets batter[ie]s they fort like heroes
they give them shell and grape like and the deavel   all the this time the
Vermont Brigade laid behind theas batter[ie]s an the reabals com and
had drove all the rest of the Corps and happy boys they reabels wer
on they com   in an instant we rose up and fired on them and then
charge with our baynets fixed and the way we fort was a cau[t]ion to
white men   we had them at cross baynetts and in a few minets the[y]
wer compell to leave their ground and flea for their lives   thousand of
men wer killed in a few minets   we soon had orders to march to
bank's ford and recross the river so that the dam reabals cold not take
us prisoners for they wood if we had staid till morning and good thing
for us for if we had not com over we shoud had to go to Richmon for
they had five men to our one   the hole of the troops that we fort wer
Geogieans and Lou and Miss Jacksons ironsides as they called them

selvs   we took five hundred men and Seventeen oficers all the field oficers in the 9th Lou and three more Majors and three Lieut Cornals and
two Cornals   theas wer taken in the chace that the Vermont Brigade
made on monday night   we are now in camp som miles from our old
camp and all quiet as ever   we had five wounded and one killed
Corp John Crossan killed and Charles Meader and Langmade and
John Flanders and my Self Wounded   I was wounded in the leag but
not so to leave the field   Flanders was wounded in the rist but not so
as to leave the field   Flanders is a recrute come last fall   Crossan and
Langmade came at Lees Mill   Meader was wounded in the leag and
Langmade in the fot   the dam reabels must [   ] me I guess but they
shot to low for it but they worked a good hole for a [   ] now I tell you
and it is a damn Soar thing now I tell you [Thain?] Reed is a gonter
start for home to morrow   Robert Cowan has started for home to
day and if [I] Can get a chance to come I shall   it is as hott as hell hear
to day and if you write me as lame letter as this I will say nothing
write soon as you can   this is from Hosea B Williams Co C Third
Regt Vt Vols Ma Washington D C   give my love to all and tell them
conscrip that their is a grate Chance for them to come out hear to fite
for their Country

"I would like to know how much mony they have got to have if all are taxed as I am"

Asahel Hubbard of Whiting to his brother, Frank, Second Vermont Light Artillery, May 24, 1863.[1]

1. Hubbard Family Papers, folder 8, UVM.

Whiting, May 24th 1863.

Brother Frank,

But a few days ago I received a letter from you saying you had sent
some money   I have been to Brandon for it & sent once besides & did
not find it but last night to my astonishment it came to Whiting Post
Office so it is all safe. Last night we received another letter from you to
Ann. we are glad to get letters from you while so far from home, but I
do not suppose we feel any more anxious to hear from you than you do
to hear from home. Frank it is a very dull time in Whiting   there is not
much to influence one to stay in W—— is there, but after all I do not
know but it is about as good a place as there is for you know I have not
had a very good opportunity to know about any other place. (*you
know John has traveled*) but I have not have I. come to think of it I

have been pretty steady for the past 29 years, do you not think so Frank. possible I may have a chance to try it yet, there is a good deal of talk of a draft & I expect there will be one within six weeks & you know if there [is] a man drafted from W——— it will be me of course for you know my luck is allways of that kind.

I will tell you about my good luck yesterday   I expected Justin Goodrich to plow for me but you know when he is wanted most he can not be had at all, that is the way generally I mean. well he did not come so I took up the old oxen about one half past three o'clock in the morning & went to work but it soon got so hot I was obliged [to] adjourn untill just at night when I got them up & worked as long as I could see. Well in the course of the day the [R.S.?] income tax collector called on me for my List of income for the past year upon which I have to pay 3 per cent tax for Government expences.[2] this tax amounted to between Fifteen & Sixteen Dollars so much more with my State tax of Fifty Six Dollars makes a good smart War tax & then count the fifty Dollars I paid last fall for town bounty. I would like to know how much mony they have got to have if all are taxed as I am, but I am willing to give one half my income if they will let me stay at home.

Well to finish out the day, (you know four years ago I was called to Middlebury as juror   was there two weeks.) & to day I have been notified by the County Sheriff to appear in Middlebury the first Tuesday in June as juror from the town of Whiting. was it not a day of good luck to me yesterday   the time I went I did not mind it much for you were here to go along with things but now I have no help but the boy I have for the season   15 years old   I do not know what I shall do. Sunday morn 31st. Frank you see by the date of this note it has been some time since I commenced writing you. expected to write some every day untill I finished the sheet but have [been] so very busy I have failed to do so. It has been very good weather for getting in crops the last week. I have been very fortunate I have finished all but that piece on the creek where that wood was pilled & got daisies in it   I broke it last spring. shall have to leave it with the boys to do. I have got Henry Simonds to stay here while I am at Middlebury   I have only tomorrow to work   next day have got to go to M———. Oh! Frank what will you think when I tell you I sold the old oxen last Thursday for $175.00. they so big & heavy I could not do much with them on plowed ground. I expect to get another pair before haying. I guess we shall have a good crop of hay to cut   grass looks well now   grain looks well only it is late   I planted my corn yesterday & Thursday so you see it is very late, but it is a very growing time. think it will be out of the ground in four or five days more   I have not planted but a little over two acres of corn & I guess we shall have to go to haying before we can get that hoed. You asked how the grass was looking on the L. piece   it will be big, I think it will want cutting in two or three weeks. It has been very

2. The federal income tax of 3 percent, passed by Congress as a war measure in 1861, was imposed on those who earned more than eight hundred dollars annually (McPherson, *Battle Cry of Freedom*, 443). Vermont did not impose an income tax, relying instead on huge increases in the statewide property tax to pay its war expenses.

warm for some time & yesterday & last night we had a fine rain which makes things grow very fast. The mare I got for the sorrell one had a colt two or three days ago   it is a good one so you see I have quite a horse dairy.

I went last to Cornwall to look at another yoke of oxen but did not buy them   such cattle are very high just now   I shall have to waite a little while longer. Oh! Frank Taylor & one Mr. Powers came home a few days ago   have not seen them. I should like to. It seems next to seeing you to see some one right from where you are. We heard you were promoted to a cheif bugler   is it so if so wright me about it what your duties are & what pay you get— I am glad you sent me that money   I will not be obliged to sell my wool now untill I think best it is going down some now but think it will be all right again before snow comes   but I must close   write soon & often   From your Brother Asahel

"we didn't think a week ago that Joe Hooker wo'd fall back behind the 14th Vt. for safety"

Private Royal D. King of Benson, Company D, Fourteenth Vermont Infantry, to his sister, June 16, 1863.[1]

1. Royal D. King Papers, The Bennington Museum, Bennington, Vermont.

Wolf Run Shoals Va
June 16th 1863

Dear Sister—

We have been having lively times here for a day or two & I will write you something about matters here. I told you in my last that there was movement of the army of the Potomac, rearward. It commenced passing here sunday a little before sundown. There has been a constant stream of trains & troops going towards the Court House and Station ever since. They, the trains, move all night. It is said the train would reach sixty five miles on the road. I should [think] it would myself. Three army corps have crossed at this Ford: the 12th yesterday, the 6th this afternoon—& 2nd is crossing tonight. The 1st Vt Brigade is in the 6th Corps— They halted here 3 or 4 hours—I saw those in it from Benson. There was a sort of general visitation, carried on between that brigade & this Reg't this afternoon. The roads are very dusty & they were completely coverd over with it. I[t] seemed to do them good to, rest & wash off some of the dirt. Besides they were glad to see us if we are nine months men. Many of . . . the men died on the march from Falmouth here, from sunstroke. The Vt Reg'ts lost 7 from that cause. It is a forced march & they hurried them forward, as rapidly as possible. The vermonters looked the best & seemed least fagged out of any troops I have seen. I can't tell the exact number, but thousands, both of teams & men have passed here since Sunday night, & it is now Tuesday night— I saw Henry Dedrick and Wrangham yesterday— They were both well. They are in the 12th, slocums corps.[2] I never knew before, what it was to move a large army, nor the cost of it. If the folks in Benson could see what we have seen for two days past they would not wonder at the slowness of the movements of the army. I presume you have heard of Lee's movement into Maryland Penn, This movement of Hooker is caused by Lee's movement. We do not know what they will think of doing with us. Perhaps we shall stay here to keep up the picket line. I expect to go out morrow. We didn't think a week ago that Joe Hooker wo'd fall back behind the 14th Vt. for safety. We are on the front now. I presume Hooker intends to cross into Maryland to head off lee. I should think from the papers today that [the] North was pretty thoroughly wroused. I think we shall remain here a while longer now. I am too sleepy to write more to night

> Yours
> R. D. King

2. Major General Henry W. Slocum commanded the Twelfth Corps.

"what of us got through without being hurt have reason to thank God and not men."

Private Justus F. Gale of Elmore, Company A, Eighth Vermont Infantry, to his sister, Almeda, June 19, 1863.[1]

1. Gale and Morse Family Papers (MSA 50), folder 8, VHS.

8th Regt. Vt. Vols. Co. A
June 19th 1863

Dear Sister Almeda,

I will endeavor this morning to write a few lines to let you know that I am yet alive and enjoying verry good health. We are stil in the rear of Port Hudson and stil pecking away at the rebels—but have not gained much ground since the day we drove them out of the woods. Last Sunday we were ordered to make a charge on their Entrenchments; this was done some ways further to the left of the line than what our brigade are stationed   of course General Weitzels brigade must go ahead; our brigade consists of the 8th Vt. 12th Conn. 75th 114th & 160th N. York regts. to get up to the rebs we had to go over a peice of ground that is cut into 10,000 little hill and ravines—all covered with fell timber crossed up in all directions; we got over most of this before they opened fire upon us much; but when we got up in good range of them they sent ball buck shot and cold led among us like a hail storm, and we were obliged to fall behind the hill logs and stumps to save our bacon; or rather we were ordered to do so, we held our position through the day and when night came our brigade went back to the place whare we started from in the morning—and other troops were left to hold the ground that we gained by the charge. our loss was heavy; our regt went on to the ground with some over 300 men—and out of them we had 12 killed and 69 wounded and some few are missing; our brigade lost more than most of them because we were ahead. our Company was verry lucky we had only one man hurt he was shot through the arm, our ajutant was killed and 2 or 3 commisioned officers wounded; Lieut Col. Dillingham had two balls put through his hat and several through his coat and pants. what of us got through without being hurt have reason to thank God and not men.

The Elmore boys are all well only Wesley he has been sick—but the last I heard from him he was getting better, I wrote a letter to Mr Chase the other day but I have heard that the garillas took the man prisoner when he was going to the boat with it; if the rebs got hold of it he will get cheated out of his letter, I have recd your letters up to the 26th of May; you wrote that you hadent heard from me for some time and began to worry about me; it isent any use to worry about these things —we given up all such idears as that and concluded to let things come but end foremost or any other way that they see fit to let it come, another thing when we are on the march we dont have a chance to write every day, Tell Mother that the day she went out to Morrisville after Samanthas bonnet I was hunting graybacks in the woods; and thank God some of us caught some of them—some of them we took alive and some of them we took their hearts blood from them; and others run so that a pigeon couldent begin to keep up with them I hope Mother had a pleasant ride and got Samantha her new bonnet and all things nice;

I suppose it makes it bad for you that are at home and for Lyman— my being gone, but you may think your selves pretty well of in Vermont if you have neither friends nor money—what those are that are in the army, but by saying this I dont wish to have you think that I am complaining at all of a soldiers lot I have seen much better fare most of the time than I expected; I never have seen the time yet when I have suffered for any thing to eat or drink; I dont think there ever was a army better provided for than ours; the most of the complaints we hear as you hear at home about food and hard times are made by those who thought they were coming out here to have a good Easy time out of it —and are some what disappointed and are homesick and cant find any thing else to grumble about; fact they were never weaned til they come out here—but I guess they will get weaned before they get home again,

I guess I can write a little more now—Steph and I have just eat our lunch of melted sugar and crackers and I bought a bottle of pickles this morning so we have quite a change to day, the pickles taste nice I tel you for they are something new   What has Father done with his horse and cow   does he keep them to Lymans or what has become of them. I havent had a letter from Lyman since the 26th of April; I suppose he is so busy sawing that he hasent much time to write. I should like to have him send me little Herberts picture,   I suppose he is growing so fast that I shouldent know him if I dont see his picture once in a while; I should like to have all your pictures but I know you havent money to spare nor a chance to get them taken. Oh can it be if I should live to get home that there will be no *dear Charlie* thare that I antisipated of taking so much comfort with on the old place; but a most every letter I get whether from home or from other friends—they speak of *Dear Charlies* death[2]—and I am obliged to believe that it is so. We have had some showers lately but to day it is verry pleasant and warm; they boys stand out door & woods life much better than I should suppose they could; how much longer it will be before we get around to our tents and into camp again is yet to be told, I recd. a letter from Brother Cooper the other day   they were well and appeared to like well; do you hear any thing from Emma Gale—and whare is she; does Orrison ever call on you since he moved to Hyde Park,   I must close for this time; please write often   oblige your far of Brother; give my love and best wishes to Mother & Samantha and all the rest, and except the same your Self; yours respectfully

J. F. Gale

"Gen. Stannard puts us through awfully"

**Lieutenant Colonel William D. Munson of Colchester,
Thirteenth Vermont Infantry, to his wife, June 29, 1863.[1]**

Frederick-town Maryland
    June 29 -1863-
        1 o'clock P.M.

Only 4 1/2 days march yet. Whole brigade completely worn out. We are resting now in a wheat field for a train of Army wagons 2 miles long to pass us. Rained all day. We are going to *Gettys-burgh* Penn. where Lee now is with his whole force. Where he will be when we get

2. Gale's brother Charles died on August 31, 1862 (genealogical chart, Gale and Morse Family Papers, folder 1). See letter of Justus to Charley, February 7, 1862, p. 60.

FIGURE 41. William D. Munson. Vermont Historical Society.

1. Walter C. Munson Family Collection, Colchester, Vermont.

there remains to be seen. Gen. Stannard puts us through awfully. Start at 5 o'clock in [the] morning—camp at 8 o'clock [in] the evening. Sleep out under [the stars] every night. Nothing to [eat but] hard crackers. Never [have felt so] well since I came out as I have for the past week. I think the boys are much healthier when they have hard work to do. but they are all worn out now. We are marching as hard as we can to report to Gen Reynolds[2] who is several hours in advance and marching nearly as fast as we are. We have marched over 10 miles this morning. Camped last night near Point of Rocks   The boys have thrown away almost every thing, knapsacks and blankets, and burnt [them] up. I think I can send [no] *letter* from here, but it [will go out] the very first opportunity [I] have. I am writing on my saddle which I have taken off to let my horse eat wheat. If you can find me, let me hear from you soon. Kiss darling Willie for me, and love to all. and remember you are my own precious dearest wife and I hope to see you very soon.

    In haste
    Your own
    Will

Summer 1863

Chapter 10

Joseph Hooker pursued Robert E. Lee's Army of Northern Virginia into Maryland and Pennsylvania vigorously, but when the march ended at Gettysburg, Hooker no longer commanded the Army of the Potomac. On June 28 President Lincoln had replaced Hooker, who had lost the confidence of his corps commanders and the administration, with one of his lieutenants, General George G. Meade of the Fifth Corps.[1]

The two armies met on July 1, Lee with 75,000 men approaching from the north and northwest, and Meade, with 93,500, from the south.[2] General John Buford and his two cavalry brigades were the first to make contact with the enemy, holding off General A. P. Hill's Confederate divisions northwest of Gettysburg for two hours in the morning. The Union First Corps, minus its newly assigned brigade of Vermonters under General George Stannard, bolstered the cavalry and held the line while the Eleventh and Third Corps approached the scene. In the afternoon, though, new rebel divisions attacked from the north, and the Union troops were forced to abandon their lines north and west of Gettysburg. In considerable disorder they fell back through the village, but soon reformed on Cemetery Hill to the south and nearby Culp's Hill, to the east of Cemetery Hill. The two hills, connected by high ground, provided an easily defensible front facing north, while a ridge extending from Cemetery Hill southward gave the Yankees a strong position facing west.

The Second Vermont Brigade reported for duty that night. The long and rapid march had taken a heavy toll on the brigade, but at least some of the men were pleased to be where they might at last take part in something more exciting than picket duty. The Twelfth and Fifteenth regiments, though, would sit out the battle as guards to the Corps wagon train several miles away. Enlistments were due to expire for the Twelfth on July 4, and for the other four regiments over the next several weeks.

The afternoon of July 2 brought a renewal of the first day's fierce combat. The Union line now stretched three miles, from Cemetery Hill south along the diminishing Cemetery Ridge, to a pair of hills called Little Round Top and, just to its south, Round Top. Late in the afternoon the Confederate corps of James Longstreet attacked the southern half of the Union line in echelon, each wave of attackers striking progressively to the north of the last wave. While Colonel Joshua Lawrence Chamberlain and his Twentieth Maine valiantly held the extreme southern flank of the line on Little Round Top, Longstreet's men struck General Dan Sickles's Third Corps to the north. Sickles had made a dangerous salient in the Union line by advancing his troops well beyond their assigned position. Longstreet's troops tore into the Third Corps, driving it back through "Devil's Den," "the Wheatfield," and "the Peach Orchard"—names that ever since have been synonymous with desperate, bloody battle.

Sickles's advance had left a gap in the Union line to his north. As the Third Corps fell back, to be reinforced by the Second and Fifth Corps, the next wave of Longstreet's attack discovered the gap and threatened to split the Union forces in two. Among the troops nearby, the Second Vermont Brigade was summoned urgently to help plug the hole. The Confederate advance began to falter even as the Vermonters, marching with parade-ground precision to their first engagement, took up their position. Five companies of the Thirteenth Vermont Infantry recaptured some cannon that the rebels had taken, along with numerous prisoners. Lacking reinforcements, the Confederates abandoned the attack.[3]

None would forget the night that followed. The men rested in position on the field, trying to sleep through the horrible serenade of the wounded. Parties of soldiers on both sides worked throughout the dark hours to remove those who could be saved and comfort those who could not. "I was stopped hundreds of times by wounded men," Lieutenant George Benedict wrote, "to be asked in faint tones the way to the hospital of their division, till the accumulated sense of the bloodshed and suffering of the day became absolutely appalling."[4] It was a harsh night for the Vermonters of the Second Brigade, no longer green but not yet hardened to battle.

Having failed to achieve a breakthrough on the north or the south, Robert E. Lee turned his attention on July 3 to the Union center on Cemetery Ridge. Early in the afternoon the Confederate artillery began a massive bombardment focusing on the center. For two hours the cannon blazed away, striking fear but little panic in the hearts of the Union soldiers. The men of the Second Vermont Brigade lay flat on the ground in the most advanced portion of the line, where they had lain since the repulse of Longstreet the previous evening. Some of the balls and shells fell among them, killing and wounding dozens of men, but most of the

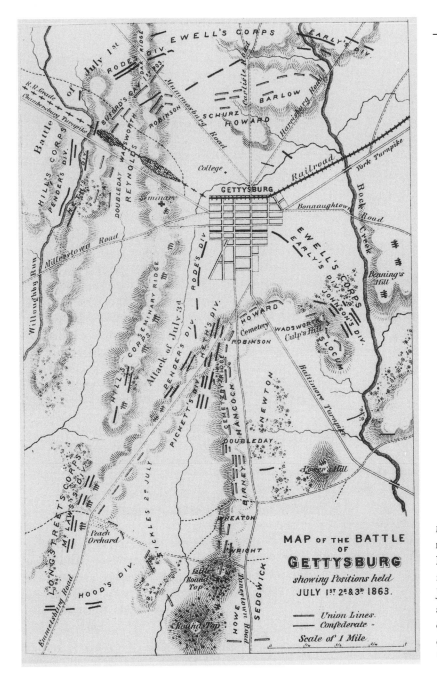

MAP 12. The Second Vermont Brigade fought off Longstreet's assault on July 2 and Pickett's charge on July 3. Farnsworth's cavalry charge took place west of the Round Tops. Benedict, *Vermont in the Civil War*, vol. 2, 448+. UVM.

barrage passed overhead. When the bombardment ceased, the Vermonters rose to find themselves in the path of advancing rebel infantry, nearly thirteen thousand soldiers led by General George Pickett's division of Virginians.

As Pickett's men closed in on the line of Vermonters, the rebels suddenly shifted direction to the north. Soon a portion of the rebel force to the north of the Vermonters broke through and fought hand to hand with the Yankee defenders. Meanwhile, the unexpected shift of direction left the rebel right flank exposed. Second Corps commander General Winfield S. Hancock and Second Vermont Brigade commander General George Stannard saw the opportunity, and the Second Vermont Brigade was ordered to change face from west to north. The brigade swung out to the right until it extended far into the field. The Green Mountain soldiers then marched steadily toward Pickett's flank, pouring a deadly fire into the rebel ranks. This blow, along with the collapse of the rebel breakthrough to the north, brought Pickett's charge to an end. The Vermonters, now dangerously exposed in a long line perpendicular to the Union front, nevertheless beat back rebel troops who arrived belatedly from the southwest to support Pickett.[5]

The First Vermont Cavalry also found itself in the thick of the fighting on July 3. On the southern end of the Gettysburg line near the Round Tops, General Judson Kilpatrick kept one of his cavalry brigades actively skirmishing throughout the day. When Pickett's charge collapsed, Kilpatrick decided to throw the cavalry against the rebel right, hoping to create panic there at an opportune time. The brigade commander, General Elon Farnsworth, led the assault under protest: the charge would take the Vermonters through rocky, wooded terrain, against an enemy of unknown strength and disposition. Before long, Confederate infantry boxed in the horsemen, who were soon "ricocheting from cluster to cluster of whooping rebels" looking for an escape.[6] Captain William Wells and Major Addison Preston managed to lead most of the cavalry to safety, but scores were killed, wounded, or captured. Among the casualties was the young General Farnsworth, killed at the head of the charge.

The battle of Gettysburg was over, and by every measure it was a major defeat for Robert E. Lee. With a third of his troops killed, wounded, or missing, Lee had no choice but to withdraw. As word of the Union victory at Gettysburg spread through the North on July 4, more good news arrived from the west: first Vicksburg, then Port Hudson had surrendered. The Mississippi River at last lay free of rebel obstructions, and the Confederacy lay divided. Northerners greeted these tidings of victory with cautious celebration, for the casualty lists from Gettysburg were slow to arrive. The three days of fighting set a new record for casualties in a single battle. Lee reported more than fifteen thousand killed or wounded and more than five thousand missing or captured, but these figures understated his loss by at least five thousand. Union losses totaled twenty-three thousand.[7]

Lee's retreat from Gettysburg began late on July 4 in a race for the strategic and symbolic safety of the far side of the Potomac River. General Meade, who had won a great victory on the defensive, was reluctant to attack, and made little effort to cut off Lee's retreat. The

Vermont Cavalry participated in a heavy skirmish on July 6, losing another seventy-five men. The Sixth Corps, held mostly in reserve throughout the Gettysburg battles, followed the enemy closely. On July 10 the First Vermont Brigade ran into a brigade of Georgians shielding the rebel retreat near Funkstown, Maryland. The Vermonters repulsed three attacks and suffered seventy-five casualties, but held their ground.[8]

As the men of the Second Vermont Brigade finished their terms of enlistment and headed home, a new brand of soldier—the conscript—began to fill the Union ranks. In Vermont, the call to duty, and substantial enlistment bounties, allowed most Vermont towns to fill their quotas without conscription. The handful of Vermont men drafted in the summer of 1863 joined hundreds of conscripts from other states in distribution camps, where they waited for transportation to their assigned units.

Not all of the draftees went without a struggle, and in New York City, particularly, widespread rioting disrupted conscription efforts in July. The First Vermont Brigade was one of several veteran units sent to New York in August to prevent further rioting. It was a welcome break from the scenes of battle, and the presence of thousands of veterans camping in the public squares cooled the anti-draft fever wonderfully.

As summer ended, the military situation in the East remained little changed from the stalemate of the past two years. The Confederate army, though weakened by the loss of men and officers at Chancellorsville and Gettysburg, remained a formidable force. The Northern optimism brought by the Gettysburg victory began to fade as soon as Lee successfully retreated across the Potomac into Virginia. The Army of the Potomac, now under its fifth commander in two years, seemed once again unable to move.

FIGURE 42. Charles Cummings. Vermont Historical Society.

"We were asked if we could charge. One terriffic yell from our men was the response and then we were after the 'greybacks'"

Lieutenant Colonel Charles Cummings of Brattleboro, Sixteenth Vermont Infantry, to his wife Elizabeth, July 6, 1863.[1]

Gettysburg, July 6th 1863

My Dear Wife,

During the last ten days I have not been very well, owing to the privations of a march added to a not perfectly healthy condition of the

1. Charles Cummings Papers (MSA 28), folder 3, VHS.

system when I started. Thursday the 25th of June we started from Union Mills for, as we subsequently learned, this place. It was that day that I received the last letter from you that has come to hand. When I shall get another—I do not know. I wrote you at Poolesville, Md., Sunday June 28th. That night we encamped near Adamstown, Monday night we encamped I do not now recollect where, but northerly of Fredericktown Md., Tuesday night at Emmettsburg, Md., where there is a Catholic College, and a splendid institution of the Sister's of Charity, the oldest & parent of all in the United States. Wednesday night we came to within two miles of Gettysburg. When within six miles of the place we came in sight of the smoke & heard the cannonading of the first days battle, which was between Gen. John F. Reynold's (the 1st Corps) and the rebels to the number of 25,000. Reynolds was killed & our troops, after splendid fighting, were driven back from the other side through the town to near where we lay. That night we reported to the 1st Corps, Gen. Newton cmd'g. and were assigned to Gen. Abner Doubleday's Division. The next morning our Brigade, consisting of the 13th 14th and 16th Regiments—the other two being at Westminster Md, 20 miles Southeast guarding the Corps trains—prepared for action. We were in position all the morning until about 4 o'clock when the rebels opened their batteries, one having been playing since noon. Within five minutes thereafter a shell fell within six feet of the rear of my horse & exploded without doing me any damage. Soon the field officers dismounted & our Brigade advanced to support our batteries. We were then in rear of the crest on which they were placed & thus so protected that not a man was hit to hurt, although their shells passed just above our heads, and exploded from a few feet to one or two hundred yards beyond us. This music was not at all agreeable. Just before sundown we were advanced up another hill a little to the left and deployed in line, amidst the bursting of hundreds of shells. One came through the ranks about four feet to my right killing two men; one or two others were wounded. Up the hill we went & when on top the firing in that section had nearly ceased. We were near the center, & not in the advance line, There had been fighting on the very ground where we were and two of our batteries had been taken & retaken. Our left had advanced & driven the rebels & they in turn had repulsed our advance with masked batteries and driven us back. Between the rebs & us was a depressed basin through which ran a ravine well protected by bushes & rocks. I was made officer of the picket and then went out and placed three companies as pickets therein, two as support & the balance of the regiment behind a clump of small trees as a reserve. I was on the line all night. After taking care that my line was right I looked around & found this ravine full of dead & wounded soldiers about two rebs to one Union. Stretchers & ambulances were running all night & by morning nearly all had been removed. Between the Union & rebel picket lines parties of both were by a tacit understanding engaged in hunting up their dead & wounded comrades & friends without molestation. I assisted in bringing within our lines in a dying condition the rebel Gen. Barksdale—who was notorious as a noisy member of Congress from Mississippi.[2] I could fill sheets with interesting descriptions of the scenes of that night. The groans of the wounded were mournful & sad in the extreme. Added to this was the confidence that in the morning the terrible conflict would be renewed, and you can well imagine that I was thoughtful. The ground I occupied with my picket was the place where a great assault would in all probability be made.

At half past four [a.m.] skirmishing commenced on my left. I immediately went out to that point to order Co. I, there as reserves[,] to deploy as skirmishers & connect with the line in the ravine at an angle back to woods on the extreme left of the center. While going out there & while on a little eminence about twenty to thirty reb. skirmishers & sharpshooters blazed at me at a distance of 400 yards. The balls fell about me like hail & I felt as if my head was in a hornet's nest, but I was not touched. I accomplished my purpose & then returned by a more protected route. The situation of this part of the battlefield was something like this [fig. 43.] This sketch is rude enough, but from it you can see that we lay between the fires of the two lines of batteries. Of course our shells went over our heads but some of the reb shells burst near us & their grape & canister whistled well. We got on an average all the forenoon about two guns in five minutes, yet not more than four or five men were wounded, but there were many hairbreadth escapes. All this while we lay on our faces. We had had no supper, breakfast, nor did we get any dinner, except some had an occasional moment to nibble on a hardtack. The 16th was in the advance of the whole line as the center was the outer arc of a small curve & the pickets on either side fell back in an oblique direction. During the forenoon we did not feel in great danger, but we expected something ominous in the afternoon.

About 2 o'clock the Rebs opened the most terrific cannonading I have ever heard, & Gen. Doubleday, an old Artillery officer says he never before heard any thing like it. From 75 to 100 guns were in position and full 20 shells per minute passed over our heads and around & among us during the next two hours. Their guns were served with a precision I never thought possible. A great tree around whose base we were lying, as big as one of the largest oaks in Judge Kellogg's yard was so cut up that not a single branch, nothing but the stump remained. But I cannot describe it. Our batteries did not reply so actively for it was apprehended that this teriffic cannonading was a feint, & the infantry attack would be made elsewhere, so they were held in readiness for other service. The line of battle was three miles long, & there was cannonading the whole length, but on the center where we were it cul-

2. General William Barksdale died during the night.

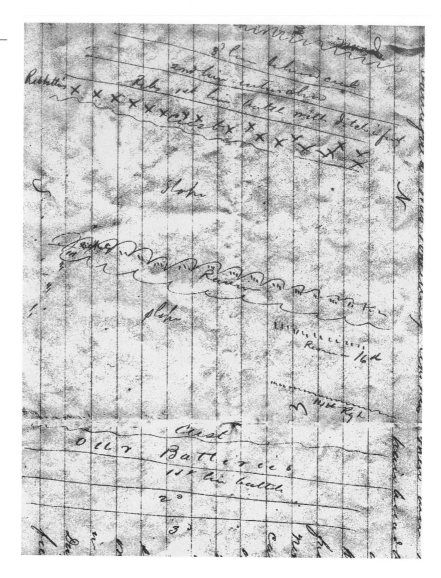

FIGURE 43. Detail from
Charles Cummings's letter
of July 6, 1863. Vermont
Historical Society.

minated. About 4.30 P.M., a large column of infantry was seen to
steadily advance from between the batteries, & right glad were we to
see them. They came out in front, protected by their shells which being
a little above them came over their heads, and deployed handsomely in
line. On they came directly towards my picket line, but the grape &
cannister from our batteries & the fine shots from my pickets, now acting as skirmishers, warned them of the hazard of that route. They then
turned & marched by their left flank. At that moment our bugle
sounded, our pickets came in, we formed a line & with the 13th &
14th rushed in. We were asked if we could charge. One terriffic yell
from our men was the response and then we were after the "grey-
backs." In fifteen minutes the results could be counted thus—300 rebs
dead & wounded on the field and over a thousand prisoners taken, &

2 stand of colors. Of these the 16th took full 400 prisoners & in a 2nd & separate charge made only by themselves they took these two stand of colors, the 2nd Florida & 8th Va., and over a hundred more prisoners. Except some work done by a few sharpshooters the battle in that part of the field was ended.

Our men behaved as steady as veterans. Gen. Doubleday, knowing that we were green 9 months men hesitated to let us charge but Gen. Stannard said he would risk it. While we were at it he asked Stannard if he had instructed us to go through with the manual of battalion drill on the field of battle, for he had never seen such perfect lines before. Our prisoners passed by the old Vt Brigade & they cheered most lustily for us. The Colonel cmd'g the rebel Brigade, now wounded & a prisoner, said that when advancing his line he was sure he should have our batteries in five minutes, for he did not believe there were more than a few straglers in his way as no troops however old could remain undemoralized under such an artillery fire. He never was so astonished in his life before as he was to see those regiments come up so steadily. There is no Corps that saw us that has not cheered us. The next morning Gen. Doubleday issued & sent us a special order complimenting the Vt. Brigade for the brilliant manner in which in the most advanced front line of battle we had withstood the fire of 75 to 100 pieces of artillery & so materially contributed to the splendid victory of the day.

I have written thus to you for you will believe me, but I could not write an article for the paper & do this Brigade justice, without being charged with one-sidedness as I am an officer therein. I believe the 16th Vt is the only regiment from our State that has taken two stand of colors in one hour's fight.

But there is another side to the picture. In the charge we had only 425 men, yet during the day we lost in the Regiment 16 killed, over 80 wounded and about 20 missing, some of whom are undoubtedly dead, It is more difficult to determine the precise number of casualties, since the regt was not all together from Thursday PM at 5 o'clock until Saturday morning, & we were also on picket during that time.

The march we have made, and short rations, & lying in the wet grass nights has induced billiousness amounting to almost fever. I was not fit to go into the battle, but I would not have missed it for any consideration.

I am to-day stopping behind at a private house and taking thoroughwort tea, & getting cleaned up. Last night is the first that I have had my clothes off for a week, & I have slept three nights in the rain without tent or blankets. My great coat, uniform coat, all my blankets and one saddle are lost through the cowardice & carelessness of the man who was to take care of them during the battle, and Peacock, my last horse, whom I dismounted & left in the rear was killed by a shell. My carpet bag is with the teams, & I shall get it by & by, All the clothes

I have except those on me are my shirts towels & stockings. My coat that I wear is that flannel blouse made for me when I was a Lieutenant.

I shall feel better to-morrow & move on & join my regiment which I left last night with the 1st Corps, on the field of battle. As that Corps has done so much fighting here & was in the advance, it takes the rear for a while. Most of our troops have moved westerly & we suspect towards Cumberland Gap where it is rumored we are to fight again.

The rebs completely cleaned out all the stores & all the Union people here. We occupy the best Copperhead mansions for our hospitals.

Save me the papers that make mention of this great, & important battle.

Love to all & especially the little darlings.

> Your loving husband
> Charles.

"I never before was so proud of being a Vermonter"

Private Royal D. King of Benson, Company D, Fourteenth Vermont Infantry, to his sister, July 9, 1863.[1]

1. Royal D. King Papers, The Bennington Museum, Bennington, Vermont.

Near Gettysburg Pennsylvania
July 9th 1863. Thursday

Dear Sister—

I don't hear anything from you or any one else but I am a going to keep writing just the same— I have not rec'd a letter from any source since about the middle of June. I tho't it strange that I did not hear anything from home, for some time before we left the shoals.[2] I have written twice since we left there   Perhaps you have rec'd the letters. I don't expect to receive any more mail matter till we rejoin our Regiment. Our Company is left here as guard for the Division Hospital. We left the Reg't the 5th & have heard nothing from it. I suppose it is at Frederick M.D. Frederick is about 30 miles from here. Our mail I presume has been sent there, but we shall not get it till we start for home   11 days after to day will bring the 21st of July. The 13ths time is out to-morrow. There was a co of that Reg't sent here at the same time we were— They have started to rejoin their Reg't to day. I presume we shall be ordered back next week— I have not told you yet where we are. We are between 3 & 4 miles south east from the Battle Field—on the Baltimore turnpike. The whole country for 10 miles is one vast Hospital. Every Barn & almost every house has been appropriated

2. Wolf Run Shoals was the last post of the Fourteenth Vermont Infantry in the Washington defenses before the march to Gettysburg.

fo[r] hospitall purposes. The wounded suffer greatly from want of proper care. Many die, who if they had been properly cared [for] would have recovered. Ours is only a Division Hospital & there are 500 in it. Dr Woodward is the principal surgeon.[3] He does all he can & as well as he can, but that is but little compared with the care that most would get at home. They are sending the wounded off to Baltimore, Philadelphia, & Washington as fast a[s] possible   We have to stand guard six hours of the 24. That is light duty compared with anything we have had before since we left the shoals. It is hard work tho for us to do that. No one except ourselves can form any idea of how tired we were when we got here. The truth is we were completely fagged out. After marching seven days, from 20 to 25 miles each day, & lying one whole day exposed to the heat of a broiling sun, & the most terriffic canonading ever known, it [is] wonderful that so many are alive & as well as we are. The Rebs supposed they had annihilated the 2nd Vt Brigade—for they didn't suppose men could possibly live exposed to the fire that we were. They call us "fighting devils." Some of the old Reg'ts say they never saw men stand fire as we did, & old Reg'ts never could have been made to do it. We did something towards gaining the victory at Gettysburg. I [am] glad that I was there, & would willingly go thro all I have again if it would be the means of ending this inhuman war. I am proud of the "Flying Brigade," & I never before was so proud of being a Vermonter. We have not disgraced the Green Mountain State, & tho others may have done as well, I know of none who have done better. It is true we are weary & exhausted, but what of that, if we have been the means of crushing rebellion & treason. Those of us who get home will come with different looks feelings from those we left. Our experiences will have taught us many things that we never would have learned without. No money could buy mine—I would not part with them on any account.

Saturday July 11th 1863— You see it takes some time to write a letter here. I commenced this two or three days ago & have not had a chance to finish it yet. We are still at the Division Hospital but shall probably be sent away somewhere by the middle of next week. We have heard nothing from our Reg't since we left it & don't know where it is or what it has been doing. We have rec'd no mail since leaving the shoals, & probably shall not now 'till we [get] back to the Reg't. I expect that when we leave here we shall go to Baltimore & from there home. We can't get so much as a newspaper here, & know no more about what the Army has done since it left here, than the man in the moon. They are sending off the wounded as fast as possible. The greater part of them are gone & as soon as the rest are sent, we shall leave here. They send them to Baltimore first & from [there] scatter them about among the different Hospitals. Sam left yesterday with the other cripples. He is doing well & will be able to go home when the rest of us go. He lost

3. Dr. Adrian T. Woodward of Brandon, surgeon of the Fourteenth Vermont Infantry.

FIGURE 44. The charge of the Vermont cavalry at Gettysburg. Bas-relief by J. Otto Schweitzer on the monuments to William Wells at Gettysburg National Park and Battery Park, Burlington. Special Collections, University of Vermont.

his knapsack & blankets—so I went on the battlefield yesterday & got a wollen & Rubber & knapsack for him & a woollen & a knapsack for myself. I threw away my knapsack the day before the big fight. My wool Blanket I left at union mills. I am fitted up again for another march. The battlefield still shows the traces of the fierce strife waged upon it. The dead were not all buried, yesterday, they said, & hundreds of dead horses lie scattered about producing an intolerable stench. I went into the town or city of Gettysburg. It is quite a pleasant place, larger than Castleton & not so large as Rutland. About every hous I saw had bullet marks on it. We heard here last night that Lee had surrendered with his whole army—I don't credit the story. You at home know more about it than we do. If you have got a paper that has an account of the Battle of Gettysburg in it, I wish you wo'd keep it till I get home as I have not seen anything of the kind. Mr Smart has gone with the Reg't. He was well when he left here   Proctor & Steve are with the Reg't. neither of them went into the fight— I was weighed yesterday & bro't down 128 lbs. I am well as usual. I [can't] write any more now. It will not be of any use to write to me as I probably shall not get it if you do   Yours

R D King

"We marched in Thurs. and took possession"

1. Allen Family of Winhall Papers (MSA 153), folder 3, VHS.

Jonathan V. Allen of Winhall, Company H, Eighth Vermont Infantry, to his father, July 12, 1863.[1]

Dear Father;

Before recieving this you will probably hear the glorious news from the old Miss. of the capture of both Vicksburg and Port Hudson; this, I think, will be glorious news indeed to the country for things were beginning to look rather dark again. Mon. night a boat arrived at Port Hudson from Vicksburg and early Tues. morning the capture of that place was announced to us; the news was recieved with loud cheers. The news was quickly communicated to the rebs by the boys. that night a flag of truce was sent out by Gen. Gardner who wished to see the official dispatch of Gen Grant. The rumor he had heard being confirmed he demanded an interview with Gen. Banks to arrange terms of a surrender; nine oclock Wednesday was appointed and the place was surrendered. We marched in Thurs. and took possession. the rebels were good looking soldiers and as well dressed as our men but they could not possibly [have] held out much longer; they were living on mule meat and their corn was nearly gone. they had plenty of sugar and molasses. A good many of them would not believe Vicksburg was taken. We were in hopes that when Port Hudson was taken our campaign would be ended, but it seems it is not: 10000 rebs with 25 pieces of artillery were reported to be blockading the river not far from Donaldsonville so that nothing but iron clads could pass, and to capture these we were immediately started off. We landed here, where there is a fort held by our men, Friday morning and have not moved since; some of the other troops have been scouting around and had some skirmishing with the rebs who are not more than two miles from us: we are waiting for other troops to get in their rear to cut off their retreat   when things are all right we will wade in and capture what there is and then we hope to go into camp for a short time. A boat came up from N.O. this morning the first time for some while, it brought a mail. I got a letter from Henry dated 21st ult. I am sorry grandfather cannot get justice done him.

My health is very good. I have got over a diarea I had most of the time in the woods. when we came out here I pitched into the green corn hugely and I believe it cured me. we got nothing fresh in the woods and I know it is not healthy to live so. You must write me as often as possible and I shall soon be where I can write oftener. With much love to the family

Your Son
Jonathan

1. Dan Mason Papers (MSA
89), folder 4, VHS.

"I was in hopes we should damage the rebs more than we have but we have punished him severely"

**Sergeant Dan Mason of Glover, Company D, Sixth Vermont
Infantry, to Harriet, July 17, 1863.**[1]

Mason was promoted to sergeant after the battle of Chancellorsville.

Camp in the field near Berlin Md
July 17th 1863

Dear Harriet

I take this favorable opportunity to answer your last which came to
hand in due season was perused with much pleasure etc etc . . Quite
probable you have heard about the fight our Brigade had with the rebs
on the 10th   I will endeaver to give you a few particulars concerning
it . . That morning we marched from Boonsboro . . we had not gone far
when the Cavelry which our Brig was supporting run on to rebs &
skirmishing commenced   the rebs continued to fall back until within
about 1 mile of the village of Funkstown . . when the rebs made a stand
supported by Infantry which had come up . . The Cavelry dismounted
leaving their horses behind . . they held their position until near noon
when their ammunition being nearly exhausted . . Our Regt was ordered to the front to relieve them . . We had not been there long before
they opened a Battery on our line (rebs) a shower of shell & grape &
cannister was hurled among our line . . We had a good position on a
rising [piece] of ground in a piece of Oak woods near the edge fronting
an open field   After shelling us smartly a column of Gray backs were
seen moving down the road   we directed our fire in that direction
soon after they advanced across the field in line of Battle colors flying
. . as we were nothing but a skirmish line with no support near it
looked possible for us to be overpowered . . but all the time we kept
loading & firing as fast as we could . . when they got within 30 rods of
us they broke & run . . We hooted at them & they ralied & advanced
to within 20 rods of us   we poured deadly fire into them & they broke
& run . . Our ammunition was nearly exhausted & when the 4th Regt
came up & relieved us . . The rebs loss was very severe   many lay
among the Corn dead & wounded . . Our Co suffered quite severely
Sergt Moses Abbott of Troy was shot through the head killing him instantly . . Geo. Partridge was also shot dead the ball passing through
his head   Henry McGuire of Albany was wounded in the arm &
Alonzo Priest of Coventry was knocked down with a piece of spent
shell . . Our Regt lost 3 killed & 27 wounded (some have since died)
The rebs crossed Monday night . . the next morning our Cavelry pur-

sued to the river taking 1500 prisoners . . 2 . . cannon some Caisons . . I was in hopes we should damage the rebs more than we have but we have punished him severely   I dont think he will invade our soil again We have cheering news from the Mississippi such as the fall of Vicksburg Port Hudson Morris Island near Charleston etc . . it begins to look like putting down rebellion . . But I am sorry to hear of riots in New York occasioned by the draft   I should like to fight them chaps & clean them out   I have not so good opinion of them as of rebs in the South   I would shoot one quicker   I must close   give my regards to your Mother & all the friends   Dan

"I would rather die here than to be a miserable contemptible, sneaking traitor at home living in peace and casting ridicule upon our armies"

Assistant Surgeon Cornelius Chapin of Williston, Sixth Vermont Infantry, to his brother Willie, July 21, 1863.[1]

Dr. Chapin joined the Sixth after the battle of Gettysburg.

In Camp July 21st—

Dear Brother Willie—

In my letter to Alice I think the last thing I mentioned was the discovery of the escape of Lee and a brief notice of the enemy's entrenchments— They were very strong at least in some parts and as a whole were well located extending for miles along a ridge which compared with the surrounding country was like the ridge back of Lorenzo's or south of Aunt Mary's while our works were planted on a ridge something like that where Mrs Byington's house is, perhaps a little higher— thus offering a strong—but less strong position than the enemy held— To make an attack upon them would have involved a great loss, but I think the result would have offered great compensation, for our troops would have fought as they never fought before and Lee again defeated would not have had an army worth the name; indeed as it is it is but little more than a rabble for reports say oure cavalry is continually picking up stragglers and deserters— I saw about 800 of the miserable scamps as our boys were escorting them to prison   A great many swore they never would bear arms against the Flag we love so much again   There seemed to be but few who held out and they were as bitter as the most ardent admirers of southern chivalry could desire   I

FIGURE 45. Cornelius A. Chapin. Vermont Historical Society.

1. Cornelius Chapin Letters, Civil War Miscellaneous Collection, MHI.

2. Cornelius Chapin's brother Charles served in the First Vermont Cavalry. See his letter to his brother Wilbur, October 26, 1863, p. 191.

3. This story, like many told around the campfire, was completely untrue.

4. The former mayor of New York City, Fernando Wood was a leading "Peace" Democrat. The Democratic governor of New York, Horatio Seymour, opposed the conscription act.

think I mentioned my visit to the 10th Vt— I found the boys well and after staying a while with them Lieut. Holton and myself started to return to camp and after wandering about through mud kneedeep and through corn and wheat fields we succeeded in finding it & turned in wet muddy and tired— The next morning we resumed our march and after considerable fatigue we encamped at Boonsboro— Dr. Chandler & myself went to the Ambulance train to see the boys who were sick or fell out on the march— When we returned we found Charley looking for me—[2] He had just learned of my arrival and came to see me— He had not got my letters and the first thing he knew of my whereabouts he learned from a lieut of the Vt Cavalry whom I chanced to meet on the way from Washington— He was very well and glad to see me, and by invitation of Dr we went to his tent & treated him and his friend to Hospital Whiskey— After talking a while I took a lantern and we sat upon the ground for hours talking of the dangers and pleasures of a Soldiers life— His account of the cavalry charge at Gettysburgh where his horse was shot was grand and although I [he?] did not seem very anxious to make another I felt that there he did his duty   He said that Lee endeavoring to rally the North Carolina troops for a third time— being unable to do so poured the grape & cannister into them & mowed them down by thousands   That was more than they bargained for & many threw down their arms & turned in and helped our men get their guns in position when they worked with a will against the very man & cause they had suffered so much to sustain[3]—such things show the awful tyrrany the southern chivalry would bring upon our country had they the opportunity—but thanks to the brave men whom the Copperheads of the north oppose they can never succeed— New York may rave Fernando Wood, Seymour & other lesser lights may shed their tears of pitty for the land of the Southron, but mobs & things like them will be of no avail[4]   The union will be preserved and the most indellible brand of infamy in coming years will be the fact they were enemies to their country in her darkest hours—

But once let an abominable copperhead utter treason to the veterans of the Great Rebellion when they shall have returned to their homes— "with our country undivided and the many states in one" and henceforth he is marked   no generosity, no ability will free him— And you Willie must be true to our country   you are young but you cannot begin too young to love her— Do everything you can for her both you & Eddie— You must help Father & Mother all you can for they need it while Charley & myself are upon the field of danger and glory— We may neither of us return but we fall gloriously   I would rather die here than be a miserable contemptible, sneaking traitor at home living in peace and casting ridicule upon our armies— Perhaps Mother will say I talk boldly—perhaps rashly   I always did—but I always say what I think and once said I dont care who knows it and the only thing which makes me mad is that language fails me when I attempt to express my supreme contempt for Northern men who sympathize with southern principles— But to go on   nothing of interest transpired for two or three days while lying idle in camp until Sunday when we proceeded to Berlin where we crossed the Potomac upon Pontoons—

A brief description of the manner in which they are constructed may not be uninteresting to you way up in the Quiet of Vt— Well imagine a number of boats, how many I cannot give an idea—arranged side by side from one bank to the other anchored from the stern— then sleepers placed across them and planks— this Done you see we have a perfect bridge— well we had to wait an hour or two [f]or other troops to cross when we began   I mean the 2nd brigade 2 Division of the 6th Army Corps— The bridge swayed back and forth for quite a distance but we crossed with no difficulty and soon found ourselves on the Sacred Soil of Va—or rather in the mud— My next will begin with an account of my adventures this side of the Potomac— Letters directed to C. A. Chapin Asst Surgeon 6th Regt Vt. Vols. 2d Brigade 2d Division 6th army corps will find me

P.S. I wish you would send me some stamps thin paper & thin envelopes

Cornelius

"if he has got one leg and one arm he has got to come"

Private Henry J. Vaughn of Middlesex, to his brother Volney, July 24, 1863.[1]

Vaughn was a conscript assigned to Company E, Sixth Vermont Infantry.

1. Middlesex Papers (MSC 34), VHS.

Rutland Vt. July 24th/63

Well Bub I am here to day, tough & hearty but I shall probaly go to Brattleboro tomorrow, there is no use in a poor devil thinking to get off here, unless he sticks a hundred dollar greenback in the Dr.s pocket, for unless he does, if he has got one leg and one arm he has got to come. I would like to have you look after my folks and see that old put does the clean thing by them   I expect that I shall be examined again at B. but dont know.

Tell Samantha to bee a good gall and keep her nose clean, and she will see Hen when he gets home. They put the uniform right on to them here, I have just got into mine and have already had the praise of being a good looking soldier.

I expect that you will go out home Sunday for they will be anxious to hear from Hen. I shall send my things back by Omri Bruce, he will leave them at Holden's store   if they dont come right write to me, and look up Bruce, he lives on H. Hill's farm. I shall write again Sunday to the old gall herself. give my love to all, Samantha and babies in perticular and tell the ones that offered to go in my room that I feel verry thankful to them and shall always esteem them highly for it. take good care of the babies till I come.[2]

Yours in haste   Hen

2. It is unclear who he means by "my folks." Samantha was Henry's wife.

"we look for him in every minute"

Sergeant Major Perry A. Baker of Whiting, Second Vermont Light Artillery, to Asahel Hubbard, August 4, 1863.[1]

1. Hubbard Family Papers, folder 8, UVM.

Port Hudson Aug. 4th 1863

Friend Ase.

And all the rest of the famely

About one year ago to day I was writeing to you under rather differant circumstansest than what I do to day. (or this morning)

I have just eat my biscuit, and drank my coffee and now take the few moments that I have to spare, to tell you the last that I knew or heard of Frank J Hubbard.

Sunday morning (Aug 2nd) Lieut C. H. Dyer and 28 men started out, (with two pieces & Cassions) with a party of Cavelry, & Infantry, on a scout   that is the last that I saw of Frank. this morning about 3, oclock eleven of the men come back, brin[g]ing with them 5 horses. they report that they met with the rebbels at Jacson, La. which were to many for them but the rebs made the attack, surrounded, and took all of our boys, & guns, etc. Frank was taken Prisoner at the first charge. the rebs took all of his arms & bugle, horse etc. and in the next fight Frank made his escape and was seen after the firing had ceased All right and said if the rebs got him again that they would do well. we look for him in every minute. Lieut Dyer was wounded in the leg, and stoped at a [house] of the rebels, a few of the men wounded, and none of our boys killed as known   17 men & the Lieut are mising yet. 8. oclock A.M.   the fight took place about sundown last night

I am in a hurry & will write again soon if Frank does not get back. and then I will tell more of the particulars.

I remain as ever your
Obedent Servent, P. A. Baker
Sergt Maj 2nd Vt. Battery

"sholder straps cant always order us round and I guess they begin to find it out"

Private Peter M. Abbott of Barnet, Company K, Third Vermont Infantry, to his family, August 31, 1863.[1]

1. Peter M. Abbott Papers (MSS 17-2), VHS.

Tompkins Square N.Y.
Aug 31st/63

Friends at Home

I now seat myself to write you a few lines to let you know that I am well   I received 3 letters from you last week, one of them was dated, Aug 8th   I was glad to here that you was all so well at home and geting along so well with the work, you spock about me cuming home, in [y]our last letter   I should lick to very well, but, I dont think that thare is much chance for me, we still lay on the ground yet in our little tents   I had rather be in virginia if they dont do difrent from what they have, they have been guming us out of our rations, thare was a while that we did not get our diner untill about 2 or 3 o clock and then it would be coald   our Coffe is not so good as what we got in dixy, we cum very near having a mob here saturday night, thare was a very h[e]avy shower here and the water cum in to our tents and wet evry thing all up   I had to tack evry thing out of my tent right into the rain so you see we all comnced howling evry one in the holl regiment   we would have tore down the officers tents if they had not cum out and said they would get us sum boards to fix up our tents   they got boards enough to mack a shed for the horses but they are more account than we be, the officers have got nice large tents with flores layed in them and carpets on them and here we be laying in the dirt   we all had to draw new cloths when we cum here and they want us to keep them clean   thare was a boy in Co. D. tied up by the thumbs jest becauss his gloves was not clean at guard mounting   I think that is a bad way to punish them here for it makes the folks round here very mad, the last one they had tied up they had to have the guards load their guns or the boys would have cut him down   the boys are bound to have their rights and we will have them   sholder straps cant always order us round and I guess they begin to find it out, I expect my box along before a great while   I expect that thare will be sumthing to pay on it well I guess I have wrote enough this time   write as soon as you get this   so no more

From Peter M. Abbott

1. Edwin Horton Papers (MSS 21-16), VHS.

"a bad beginning makes a good ending So ... I ought to have glorius good luck from this time out"

Private Edwin Horton of Chittenden, Company C, Fourth Vermont Infantry, to his wife, Ellen, September 28, 1863.[1]

Horton's previous service in a New York regiment, he learned, did not protect him from the draft in Vermont.

Camp near Culpeper Va
Sept 28 1863

Dear wife

it is with the greatest pleasure I now Seat myself to inform you that I am well and hope this may find you the Same   I wrote to you on the 25th and enclosed you five dollars and I also enclose you too dollars to day   I havent drawed any pay yet but you know I have a great faculty for making money so I dont know as it makes any differents whether I get any pay or not   I sold my watch for Eight dollars and I owed a feller too dollars out of that and the next knight I had Sixteen dollars So you See I am getting along all right now   I told you in my last letter that I would give you a description of my journey here   when I left home on the 2nd I went direct to Mendon and from there to Rutland and I was arrested in a fiew moments after I arrived there by Sheriff Simons   I was put under guard and kept untill the next morning and then I was Sent to Brattleboro and there I was locked up in the Same room where Ike Stayed so long   I see Ike when I was there   I was taken out of there on the morning of the fourth and carried to Long Island   I was placed in the guard house there and remained there too weeks   it was the most dismal place I ever was in   there was about thirty roughs from Boston and New York imprisoned there   John Hayes was with me there about a week and then he was taken out and I have not seen him Since   while John Stayed the roughs dident dare to trouble us much but when he was gone they piched into me and took every thing I had away excepting my watch and that they Smashed all to peaces So they thought it wasent worth taking   I dident dare to report them for fear of being killed myself   I was taken out of there at the expiration of too weeks and placed on board the boat   was put on the upper deck with to guards over me and in about an hour it commenced raining and I asked the guards to take me under Shelter and they wouldent do it and I stayed there until about ten o'clock that night and it was raining awful hard and the wind blew and I was completly wet through and I commenced to swear and curse when the sargent of the guard came and put the Shackles on me and chained me up to a post where I remained all night   I caught an awful cold but I was released from the irons in the morning and put down in the hole of the boat where I stayed four days with too guards over me excepting they took me out once a day to clean the decks of the boat after the other soldiers had run over them all day. when I arrived in alexandria they called me out and released me to go with the other conscrips   I stayed in Alexandria one day and then was marched to the cars and was brought out to culpeper where we got of and had to march about three miles to the fourths camp   I was put in Co C   whether there is a-going to be any thing more to it I do not know but you know the old saying is a bad beginning makes a good ending So I think to take the whole thing into consideration I ought to have glorius good luck from this time out   this is the whole journey   please write soon and direct to the f[o]urth Vermont Co C Washington D.C.

this from your true and ever loving old friend & Husband Edwin Horton

"Som of them have no teath and the old Soldiers hafter Chaw … for them and I for one dont like to do it"

Corporal Hosea B. Williams of Concord, Company C, Third Vermont Infantry, to Moses Parker, September 28, 1863.[1]

1. Parker Family Papers, folder 10, UVM.

Camp of 3d Regt Vt Vols
Slarter [Slaughter] Mountain Verginia
Sept 28th 1863

Friend Moses   I now take this time to write you a few lines to let you [k]now that I am well and so are all the Concord boys that are hear now   Daniel has not bin heard from sinc he fel out of the ranks in Mariland   I think that he is dead but if he was not he woud have wrote to me before this time for he new that I woud not tell eny one of him if he had diserted   now that is so   if you hear from him write to me and I will keep it dark for I want to hear from him if he is a live Newell Kingbury has just got to his Co to night   he is fool [full] of his jokes as ever he was   yor ma want to [k]now how we get along with the Sconscrips or Substutes as they are   we get in our Co fifteen of them and four of them are in the Hospital and two of them are fools and the rest of them are out of som por house for they say that they are two of them are drunk all the time so if we are a gonter get such men as them we will not have eny more draft for it makes us to much work [to] take care of them and it is a grate trubale for the docter to deal out his Quinine   Som of them have no teath and the old Soldiers hafter

Chaw . . . for them and I for one dont like to do it   Well Moses how does all the Galls do in town and what is the Gene[r]al order of the day ourn [is] that there is a gonter be a nother hard battle on the Rapidan and I long for it to com on and you are of corse   Curtis Stacy Edwin Southward and Dan Adams and Luchas Reed are at our head Quarters doing ord[erli]es duty on the Staff So I see them very often   we have gut an eight days rations in our haversacks and knapsacks so I guess that we will have a hard fite out of it befour it is over with   well Moses I had a good time in new york whilst I was there   had a plenty of evry thing that a man wanted even to hide   there was som thirty men in our Regt that gut Burnt in all   that is not bad for two hundred men I tried to get a furlow but could not but I do not care for I have not but eight month and three days to stay with uncle sam   as it is geting dark I will close   write soon as you can   this is from Hosea B Williams Co C   I will send you a picture of fun

Autumn 1863

Chapter 11

The first federal draft of the Civil War, in July 1863, brought thousands of conscripts into the Union army to take the places of the fallen and discharged veterans. Among the conscripts were a scattering of conscientious objectors who would not or could not pay the $300 commutation fee to avoid service. Some declined to pay the fee on the grounds that the money contributed to the war effort. Three Quakers from Addison County, Vermont, who were drafted and assigned to the Fourth Vermont Infantry in September, refused to bear arms and equipment or to perform assigned duties, even in non-combat roles. Cyrus Pringle, Peter Dakin, and Lindley Macomber all refused to work in the military hospital. In his diary, Pringle wrote from prison that "no Friend, who is really such, desiring to keep himself clear of complicity with this system of war and to bear a perfect testimony against it, can lawfully perform service in the hospitals of the Army in lieu of bearing arms."[1]

The fighting itself showed little sign of moving toward a conclusion in the fall of 1863. The war effort in Virginia amounted to "a campaign of manoeuvres," as General Meade's biographer Richard Meade Bache put it.[2] Meade had followed Lee's Army of Northern Virginia as far as the Rappahannock River after the Confederate retreat from Gettysburg, but the Union commander declined to initiate a major conflict. General Lee withdrew south of the Rapidan River in September after a Union cavalry raid convinced him his position was vulnerable, and the Army of the Potomac soon occupied the vacated space between the two rivers.

Anxious to take the offensive, Lee planned a campaign to outflank Meade on the right and trap him near the old Manassas battlefield, as he had done to John Pope in August 1862. The Confederate army began moving on October 9. Meade soon learned of the movement and began a rapid retreat across the Rappahannock, not stopping until he was well out of danger of a flank attack. His rear guard sprang a trap at Bristoe Station on October 14, inflicting heavy casualties on two brigades of pursuing rebels.[3]

Four days later, Jeb Stuart lured the Yankee cavalry into a similar trap as the Confederate cavalry fell back rapidly from Buckland Mills, on Broad Run, in front of Judson Kilpatrick's division. Kilpatrick pursued with one brigade, leaving George Custer's brigade (including the First Vermont Cavalry) to defend the crossing at Buckland Mills. Kilpatrick suddenly found himself outflanked and outnumbered several miles from any support, while another rebel force surprised Custer. In the retreat that followed—which the rebels referred to derisively as "the Buckland Races"—more than two hundred Union cavalrymen were captured. The First Vermont was among the last units to cross Broad Run to safety, but it did so with small loss.[4]

Meade undertook a more determined but no more decisive campaign late in November. The Army of the Potomac once again moved to a position on the north side of the Rapidan River. In a movement designed to take the rebels by surprise, the Third Corps crossed the river on November 26 to lead the attack against the rebel right flank. Mismanagement and unforeseen delays ruined the surprise, however, allowing the enemy to prepare for the assault. A small but fierce battle the next day at Orange Grove (or Locust Grove) delayed the Yankee advance, after which the rebels fell back to Mine Run, a stream running north to the Rapidan.[5]

Orange Grove was "a baptism of fire" for the Tenth Vermont Infantry, which had performed picket duty faithfully but uneventfully for more than a year in the Washington defenses.[6] In this battle, the day after the first national Thanksgiving day, the Vermonters charged up a hill under heavy fire to capture a fence line. Some of the regiment went well beyond, only to find the rest of the brigade had stopped at the fence. Several men were killed or wounded stumbling back. The Tenth suffered seventy-one casualties in its first battle, of whom seventeen were killed or mortally wounded.[7]

General Meade decided to press the attack and spent the next two days searching for a weakness in the Confederate position along Mine Run. Orders were issued on November 29 to prepare for action early the next day. Forbidden to light campfires in the bitterly cold night, the Union soldiers, including the men of the Tenth Vermont Infantry and the First Vermont Brigade, made ready for what many expected would be another disaster like Fredericksburg. To attack at Mine Run they would have to wade across the cold stream under fire, then charge up a steep bank against the enemy rifle pits. Much to their relief, however, the attack was called off at the last minute when Meade decided the rebels were too strongly entrenched after all. The men would suffer through another cold night without fires, but they would live to tell about it.[8]

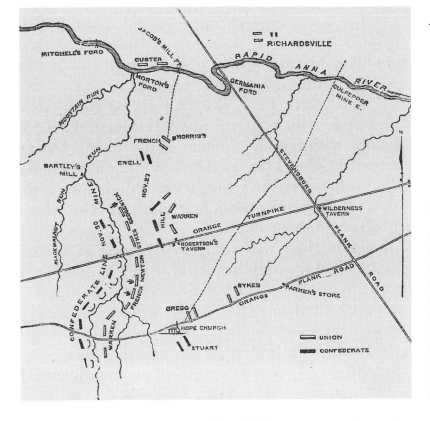

MAP 13. Union general George Meade abandoned his campaign late in November 1863, after the Confederate army withdrew to strong fortifications along Mine Run. Lossing, *Pictorial History of the Civil War in the United States of America*, vol. 3, 111. UVM.

Two days later, General Lee launched a counterstroke against Meade's left flank in the style of Stonewall Jackson's devastating attack on the Eleventh Corps at Chancellorsville. The results might have been the same had Meade not withdrawn across the Rapidan during the night. Thus ended the autumn's cat-and-mouse game, and the two armies soon settled into their winter camps.

Throughout the early fall, Vermont's Ninth regiment remained in its camp near Yorktown, growing restless on the now-quiet peninsula. Sickness increased dramatically in September until eventually the entire regiment was declared unfit for duty. Regimental officers pleaded with the War Department and political leaders for a transfer to a healthier environment. Finally, orders arrived late in October for the Ninth to move to North Carolina. The regiment was to garrison Newport Barracks, an outpost guarding the western approaches to the Union-held towns of Beaufort and Morehead City. Edward H. Ripley, now the regiment's colonel, was pleased with the move. "I propose to have a jolly winter," he wrote home. As the Vermonters regained their health in the improved conditions, they spent the remainder of the year renovating the post and participating in minor raids, including the capture of a salt works at the end of December.[9]

With the return of cold weather, Northern optimism cooled as well.

The key victories of the summer at Gettysburg and Vicksburg had not brought the war to a quick end after all. The Army of Northern Virginia continued to hold its own against the Army of the Potomac, though battle casualties and other losses were beginning to take a serious toll on Southern strength. Winter once again would provide a welcome respite for most of the combatants, but the worst of the war was yet to come.

FIGURE 46. Stephen M. Pingree. Detail from George H. Houghton photograph. Special Collections, University of Vermont.

1. Lyndon State College Collection: Pingree (Pingry)/ Hunton/Stickney Family Papers (MSA 135), folder 5, VHS.

"I see no way but to make them do duty or suffer as others do, for refusal"

Major Stephen M. Pingree of Stockbridge, Fourth Vermont Infantry, to Augustus Hunton, October 2, 1863.[1]

Near Culpepper C.H. Va. Oct. 2, 1863.

Cousin Augustus— I received yours of some days since, acknowledging the receipt of my funds. I am very much obliged to you, for the pains you have taken in this matter, as well as at all other times, to do me a kindness.

I desire you to retain enough to pay you for the use of the $75 sent to me at N.Y.—as it was a great favor to me, and, unless it was by you, must have made me some trouble & expense. I think I have not written you since we reached here, (Sep. 22) and, in fact, I have written very few letters since, as I was quite ill, with Chills & fever, for nearly two days. I was also very busy, when able, trying men who either went from N.Y. to Vt. without leave, during our stay in the city, or who were left behind on account of unwarranted absence, when we embarked to return, and reached us in from 3 to 10 or 12 days after.

I was appointed from Brigade Hd.Qrs. to try these cases, in this Regt. and have tried 22 cases, of various kinds & hues. The sentences have been generally only loss of pay, but in two or three cases, confinement in addition.

Forfeiture of one months pay, is a very common punishment for the minor offenses which omits desertion, mutiny, insubordination—disobedience of orders, cowardice, sleeping on guard & drunkenness on duty.

These are invariably tried by General C. Martial, both in cases of officers or men. I am not authorized to try officers—as by the Articles of War, they must be tried by G.C.M. Gen. Canby issued an order complimenting & thanking the troops sent to N.Y. from this army, for their attention to duty, & good behavior. They are all or nearly all back here now, but there are still many U.S. troops there, and many of the old 2 years Regts from that state, who will do good service in case of need. The 2nd Regt. has received 200 men mostly Substitutes—and 58 have deserted. The 3d has received about 200, and lost several. We have received 190 and two only have deserted.

The men we got by this process are superior to any lot of volunteer recruits ever sent to this Regt. The same is not true of the Second Regt. as I understand their men are "*scallawags,*" Nor is it hardly true of the 3d though they are [finer?] men. I hardly know how we came to get so good a lot of men. We were always unlucky in our squads of volunteer recruits, of whom we have, since we entered service, received about 200 or more. There are 3 *Quakers,* in our squad of conscripts—who will make some trouble. They are well off, but would not pay their $300 as it would help in the war,—(they admit this) and they refused to bear arms & came here with arms & equipment strapped on to them. Their uniforms had to be put on by force. They were babied, by being detailed at the Regt.l Hospital, and agreed to work there, but finally, they had a revelation, and refused this. They are now returned to their companies, and, unless they [mind], they stand a good chance, of being shot by order of a Court Martial. Reasoning does no good,—I see no way but to make them do duty or suffer as others do, for refusal. They are as much indebted to Gov't for protection as you or I—and should be ready to obey the laws. They might have paid—(as they have considerable property) but would not. I believe they are *Copperheads.* — Can you see any way out of the trouble, but do with them, as you would with others? Kind regards to Mrs. H & the children. I am very glad to receive a letter from you or them at any time.

> Very truly— S.M. Pingree

Hon. A. P. Hunton

"They refuse, <u>consciensciously, I hope,</u> to do any duty in the ranks"

Sergeant William B. Stevens of East Montpelier, Assistant Quartermaster's Office, Second Division, Sixth Corps, to his sister Ann, October 2, 1863.[1]

A year after his promotion to sergeant, Stevens received an assignment with the Assistant Quartermaster's Office.

1. Rokeby Museum, Robinson Family Papers, box 15, folder 10, Sheldon.

October 2d 1863

My dear Sister:

It is such a dismal gloomy night, that I must do something to drive awa[y] the "Blues," for, though those gentlemen have not really gaind possession of me, there is some slight possibility, of their catching one, of such a night, but what surer preventive measures can one take, than to enjoy a quiet chat with you, my dear Sister. Though this same chat may be very one-sided and consequently, very uninteresting to all, but me, I will enjoy it, as well as I may, and trust it to you, who will not judge it, harshly. Though I have received no letter from you since last I wrote you, it is *time* I had, and I will act accordingly. My health seems, once more, established, firmly, and though I am very busy this week I do suffer inconvenience. I think it is best for me to have some constant employment: am sure it is, if I will only exercise as I ought. This is my greatest failure in my search for health; I am to apt to sit, at my work, and sit—and *sit*—and <u>sit</u> till I am sick: "Forewarned, forearmed" is an old saying, and should be true, and I mean to be sure to prove it so in my own case. It has been rainy all day, and now the wind is moaning through the trees & flapping the tents, as if it were the finest sport in the world, but, for *reasons* the subscriber "does not see the sport." Yester-night an order to "move *immediately*" came, and we got all harnessed, and just ready to go the "order is countermanded" came, and we resumed our "quo status." Another Division went. We are likely to be here now a half month, or more. Yesterday I made, or rather had *forced* upon me, a discovery. Lindley Macomber & Peter Dakin are members of the Fourth Regiment, Vermont Infantry. I knew of the former as he is attached to Company "G." I had not seen him, & did not know of *Peter*. They refuse, *conscienciously*, I *hope*, to do any duty in the ranks. Lieutenant Colonel Foster thought he would rather favor them, if possible, than to prefer charges against them, as the sentence of a General Court Martial would be severe, most likely *death*, so he let them do duty in the Hospital, to which they agreed, and were to be allowed to remain there. Yesterday L. told me they had concluded not to do any more even there, as "it was very much against the judgement of the Quarterly Meeting" (his very words.) so I was lead to believe that they have sent to that body for advice *since* entering on duty in the Hospital   Foster has done his duty, so far as the matter is left to him, but if the[y] persist in their refusal they must submit to the decision of a Military Tribunal. Will not the Q.M. [Quarterly Meeting] be, in a measure responsible for it? I had a long, and though not a loud, a *plain* talk with him, but did not alter his determination, apparently. The Regiment has now gone some distance away and without particular pains I shall not see him soon. There is a more pleasant topic, for the remainder of our chat, so I will leave this one, for the present and begin the other. "What is it?" Wednesday evening I went to Culpeper, to meet Horace who was expected to arrive there that evening. He did arrive and thus for the first time in more than two years, I saw and *shook*, one who is connected with me by other, and nearer ties than *military* ones. "Was I glad to see him?" If I may judge, by this pleasure, there are some *happy* times in store for me, yet. He is as he used to be and still, not the *same*. Since first we knew him, how much he has changed, for the better, *I* think, and like the expression that you made I like him real much. He came to see me yesterday & I had a good visit with him. I hope he will like, well enough, to stay   He brought me some goodies, from home, not the least of which, was a good letter, from Mother. "*Such* a *Mother* as *ours*"   I must soon close, and will, after asking one favor   The enclosed five is one which I have carried all Summer, because "Green Backs" are *alone* "legal tender," here, so I have not been without *money*, but I do not care to be kept in funds, in this way, any longer. I have so many Photographs, they are burdensome in my pocket-case. If there is a good chance and ~~thee~~ (excuse me, since I heard from the Q. Meeting, I do not say *thee*, to many.) you are willing to get and send me such an *Album* as you would like me to have, & use the remainder, if any, for something for yourself, I shall be obligated, and promise to put your P. next to dear Fathers & Mothers and to the post of honor. Till another time,—Farewell. Thy ever loving Brother

W.B. Stevens

To Ann Stevens

"Friday in the Day time they took Capt Galt & our Dear Brother Willey & we expect they are in Richmond Ere this"

Horace A. Putnam of East Montpelier to his wife, Mary Stevens Putnam, October 19, 1863.[1]

Putnam was a civilian employee in a quartermaster's department, apparently that of the Second Division, Sixth Corps.

Centerville Oct 19/63

My Dear Wife

I am well & never felt heartier & Better apetite in my life   Day before yesterday I was helping unload Some artilery Horses & gut kicked on my left leg Just below my knee & I am quite lame now but my

FIGURE 47. Horace A. Putnam. Rokeby Museum.

1. Robinson Family Papers, box 44, folder 3, Sheldon.

2. Perley P. Pitkin of Montpelier held a series of progressively important posts as quartermaster, starting with the First Vermont Infantry in June 1861 and culminating with his election as Vermont Quartermaster General in November 1864 (Peck, *Revised Roster*, 728–29).

health is good   I guess hard tack is good for me   the armey have had & are having a hard time now fighting all the time   we have moved our head quarters & Stores 5 times Since I came out here   P[erly] P[itkin][2] Says the hardest he has Seen Since he has bin in the armey   thursday night we all Slept with nothing but the Starry canopy of heaven for atent   at 4 I woke & called all   P.P. Said I wish you had Slept one hour longer but in that one hour we had to pull up & take cars & leave   the rebs are tuff in this fight I tell you   how it will turn no one is able to tell but we hold Center ville but they pick up our men pretty fast they know the ground So well   Friday in the Day time they took Capt Galt & our Dear Brother Willey & we expect they are in Richmond Ere this   But they say they will treat them first rate for they had 3000 Dollars with them but I will risk Willey   they took 6 of Galts teams un hooked the horses or mewls from ther wagons & left the wagons & the rest of the men went & gutt them the next morning I hesitated about writing of Willeys capture but I concluded you would blame me if I did not write when you saw it in the papers & I knew you would hear of it   he was a Splendid lookin man in the Sadle & a Splendid rider but the Same good Good Willey   Just as young & Just as fair as when he left home & I think he will be treated well for they cannot treat him other wise   my Dear I know how you will feel about it & Dear mother how her Heart will blead for him but try & make her as quiet as possible   the Father of all will protect & Shield that Boy   God forbids any harm comes to him he is worshiped by all in the a.q.m [assistant quartermaster's] Department & is going to be promoted & he will come back Soon I think & all the rest think he will come soon for they had money   all that have bin taken & have had money have bin treated well & lett come back soon   be patient for such is war   I should rather be in his place than those I held the light to have their Legs & arms taken off & the bulletts cut out   lett him go whare he will or whare he is taken no one will dare to harm him for thare is a hand that Shields him from harm

I have not heard from you but once since I left home & I fear some thing has happened for I have writen four times this makes but the mail is very irregular hear   as I have said in all of my other letters I shall come home Just as soon as I make my self whole. Is it not too bad about my not seeing P & J but I have not a word to Say about it only it makes me feel happy to have you Love them   it makes my heart feel glad. I must close for the cars are coming & I must call the Boys & unload   Love to all & Kiss H & tell him father wants to see his Good little son   Write soon & send a paper for I want to see what the news is in Vermont   tell Hinkley to send me a paper

Please Except much love from husband   Horace A. Putnam

"a volley of musketry was heard and ere the smoke died away another and another and the enemy went skedaddling back pell mell"

Private Charles B. Chapin of Williston, Company L, First Vermont Cavalry, to his brother, Wilbur, Ocober 26, 1863.[1]

1. Charles B. Chapin Letters, Civil War Miscellaneous Collection, MHI.

Dismounted Camp Md. Oct 26 1863

Dear Brother Wilbur

No doubt you will be surprised to receive a letter dated in Maryland but I have been verry unlucky with horses lately. the one which I drew after my good one was shot played out beyond Culpepper. I then took sans [Sanford Marshall's] after he was wounded. *it* was taken sick the next day & was I was unable to get to the Regt. with it so I swapped for another (with one of the boys that had rather be in camp than out to the front) and started   got to the co. saturday. this horse got the sore tongue so it could not eat and played out in the fight one week ago to day. I will now commence with Sunday the 18th. we laid in camp till after dinner when we were ordered out on picket   staid about two hours and were ordered on toward gainsville   proceeded about a mile when we met the enemies pickets drove them to Ganesville fought long after dark   all we could see was the flash of their guns   we finaly halted for the night a cold stormy one without supper or fire   we waited for the morning light to resume the fight   at last gray streaks were seen in the East and we started a fire and thought to make coffee had just got the water on as we got the orders to advance   co.'s I. E. L. were deployed as skirmishers   the enemy had a heavy line so it was quite hard to start them from the town where they were sheltered by the buildings but at last we started them drove them half a mile or so and then were sent back to support a battery and give some other Regt. a chance at the advance. good success attended us till we got to Buckland Mills (about one O clock PM) where our Regt. had a chance to make coffee the first I had had since morning of the day before   we had just got bridled up when we were surprised by firing on our left. the guns were immediately turned and shell sent into the woods beyond but the firing still continued and our co. was sent to the left to keep them from flanking us. just then they made a general assault   infantry poured out of the woods like bees out of a hive and we were obliged to fall back pretty lively. our co. came pretty near being cut off the rest of the Regt.   thought we were gone sure   it was here my horse got so tired that it could only trot and I thought I should have to dismount and take to the woods. Lieut. Col. Preston told me I would be

2. The soldiers referred to
General Judson Kilpatrick as
"Kil-Cavalry" because of his
reputation for rashness.

to late if I did not look out   I told him I was looking out but that it did
not help the horse any   he laughed and said he thought I would pass.
we caught the regt. and again our co. was sent out for the same purpose   I was bound to go and so I did and again joined the Regt. by
this time Kill P2—— found out that infantry had come up so he fell
back as fast as he could to draw the enemy on   just as we got where
the woods were full of them an orderly came saying they were charging
on our rear   we did not hurry any faster but in a minute a volley of
musketry was heard and ere the smoke died away another and another
and the enemy went skedaddling back pell mell. The first brigade had
gone on while we were getting coffee and we were afraid they would
all get captured but just dark they came in all straight although they
lost some men and three waggons also two ambulances. Our Regt.
came off the field all right   our co. had one captured one of the new
recruits   Gen. Custer complimented us as coming off the field in the
best order although in the rear and consequently under the heaviest
fire. since then our Div. have done no fighting. Thursday I started for
Washington to turn over my horse but there was not cars enough for
all so our Regt. waited till the next day (34 of us) started about eight O
clock P.M.   had gone about three miles when we run off the track
eleven cars out of 13 also the engine   eight of the cars tiped over
four smashed all to peices. Lieut. of Co. I and myself were on one of
the cars which did not run off, we had a bed made on the top of the
cars and were covered up with a rubber blanket for it was raining and
dark as tar (we came verry near being thrown from them when the engine ran off)   we immediately got down to assist those unfortunate
ones which were under the broken mass   the groans and cries I shall
never forget   we worked nearly all night   there was some 20 or 25
wounded men   only one killed I believe but the poor horses fared
harder still being in the cars while the men were on top   53 of them
were killed besides as many more went hobbling about some on two
feet some on three, here we staid till noon next day before we were
ready to start again   reached Washington a little before dark   turned
over our horses and went to the soldiers rest where we stopped when
we first came down but now it is clean and neat. perhaps you remember what I wrote about it one year ago. then it was nasty, not fit for any
living thing   in the barracks that night (saturday) there was a kind of
a meeting the first I have seen since I left home. it seemed good and
made me feel lonsome to think I could not be where I could go to
church now & then. Tell Mrs. Hough I rec'd. those poscripts she sent
me and am much obliged to her   give their family my best wishes. I
have not seen Geo Miller for two weeks as he came in after a horse before I got to the co. the last time. had got one and started back before I
got here. I had a pr. of rebel spurrs which I intended to send you the
first chance I had but I lost one helping the poor fellows out from un-

der the cars. I have got to draw some boots so father need not hurry about sending any of my things. Did you get the letter with the money in   I have not had a letter from home since a week ago last thursday but think I shall get one as soon as I get back to the Regt. I shall try and get to Washington and see San before I leave but I do not know whether I can get a pass or not   I had a letter from him a few days ago he was doing well said he Lon and Phillips were going to have a furlough   I hope they will have a good time. Tell father I want him to write what he thinks about my reenlisting if the Regt. does. The first & 2nd N.Y. Vetran cavalry are here waiting to be mounted but it is getting dark and I must close. Love to all   In haste

      Charlie

Excuse mistakes
I have not time to look this over and have written verry fast

      C. B. C.

"I felt prouder of being there in my condition than I should had I been there a sound man and produced on the stage a most splendid oration"

Sergeant Henry McAllister of Stowe, Company G, Fourth Vermont Infantry, to Ann Stevens, November 1, 1863.[1]

1. Rokeby Museum, Robinson Family Papers, box 15, folder 11, Sheldon.

U.S.A. Genl. Hospital.
Burlington Vermont.
Nov. 1st 1863.

My Dear Friend:

Your kind letter announcing Willie's capture, was duly received. It gives me pain to know that he has been taken prisoner, but knowing something of the treatment of prisoners by the rebels his case does not appear at all dark to me. It is at best decidedly unpleasant to experience the tender mercies of the rebels but abating the filth and vermin of Libby prison and the poor fare our prisoners of late have been quite well treated. The greatest consolation I can offer you is that Willie is well and needs not that care and attention that a sick or wounded man would. The bare necessities of life will suffice for him and he can take care of himself and assist some poor sufferer perhaps that otherwise might be neglected. Again, he may soon be exchanged or paroled. I saw that several paroled prisoners have lately come from Richmond. he may be one of them. Let us hope for the best. I have seen very many who have seen prison life in Richmond. There are some here now. They report that a man who is well has a comparatively comfortable time. I know how anxious you must feel about him, but you must remember that he is in the Lord's hand and it will be done unto him even as He willeth. How variously we suffer. Willie is taken prisoner. I am wounded & loose a limb, another loses his life and another still escapes unharmed. I trust I love my country well enough to make such a sacrifice for her salvation. Never fear for Willie. He will come out all right.

I was much pleased with your last. It reminded me of old times when there was a freer interchange of thought, opinion and advice between us. If you will continue to write me such letters I will promise to recover speedily. I really think I am much better for that already. My abscesses are nearly healed. the bone in my leg is nearly ready to come out. I am much stronger and now able to study some & in fine I think I begin to see the sunshine breaking thro' this night of suffering. I feel that I shall yet rise up under all this and in triumph pursue my loved pursuits. I have no fears if I can gain my health and strength. I know what I can do. I intend now to devote my first strength to the completion of my Collegiate course. That accomplished I would like a Professorship in some College. That may not be so easily attained but if I am fitted for it there will some time be a demand, or if it is not attainable there are many schools in our country full as desirable as Professorships in most Colleges. There is a great demand for teachers at the West now and good situations can be readily obtained. If one succeeds in a few years he can get almost any situation he desires. I have no fears on that score. In your advice I agree with you and I know you will bid me God-speed, and success. I do not expect to be so much benefitted by my college course as I should if the War had not interrupted me, but of that interruption I will not complain

When I left College and went to the War I simply did my duty. I would do so again, and when I saw the remnant of my old class graduate last Commencement, I felt prouder of being there in my condition than I should had I been there a sound man and produced on the stage a most splendid oration. I did not envy them their honors, but I thought that this was their country as well as mine.

Permit me to say a word in regard to my College course. As you well know there were many difficulties attending it, but no one who knows what I actually accomplished will say it was a dishonor to me. At the end of the second year I came out first in Languages and second in Mathematics and counting every week I had been in College there were not more than four full terms out of six. Was that a dishonor. I can say without any vanity that my friends in College thought I did remarkably well in the circumstances. I was *perfectly* satisfied and those whose expectations in me are disappointed must go unconsoled.

But this is not a pleasant topic   I dislike to set forth my own merits or be called upon to vindicate myself. What my conscience approves that I am satisfied with if all else are displeased. I am doing nicely nòw have substituted chess for backgammon. Like it much better. Read a lot of Pope & the Bible. Am trying to be good. Please write me soon. Will write on more agreeable topics

In the hope of Willie's speedy release I am, Your Friend

      Henry

"he is known all through the Corps as the fighting chaplain"

Sergeant Walter W. Smith of Wilmington, Company H, Second U.S. Sharpshooters, to his sister, December 6, 1863.[1]

1. Walter W. Smith Papers, Duke.

Camp near Brandy Station V.A. Dec. 6 /63

Dear Sister

I received your letter last night dated the 29th Nov. We had just got back from a tramp over the Rapidan   We left here a week ago last Thursday   the troops crossed the same day & our train or our Brigade 18 ambulances from the Division crossed the next morning We crossed at Germania Ford & Friday had a fight in the woods   I dont know as there is any name for the place. The fight commenced about 3 o,clock & lasted till dark   it was pretty much all with musketry   the woods was so thick that artilery could not get into position on either side. Our Division Lieutenant is on Gen Birneys Staff & I was detailed to go with him so I was with the Gen. till the fight was nearly over   When I went back to the train I worked all night handing off the wounded   Our Brigade had to do the work for the whole Corps as the . . . trains had not got up on account of the roads being poor & Blocked up with Artilery etc. The fight was a sharp one as long as it lasted but the result was not much to the advantage of either party. We lost as near as I can judge & I was all over the field after the fight about 100 killed & 350 or 400 wounded. The Johnies I should think lost more than we did as we used some artilery while they fired but a few guns. Both parties left the ground that night. the next day we loaded up the wounded the rest of the trains having come up & went to Robinsons Tavern on the Fredericksburg & Gordonsville Pike where the whole Army was concentrated. (There was nothing but our Corps engaged Friday)   Our Regt had 5 or 6 men hurt slightly   We remained there two or three days with the enemy on one range of hills & we on another   (There was some skirmishing & some canonading but no General engagement)   when we left for this side of the River We had to stay at the Station over one day before we could get the wounded aboard of the Cars   They had been in the wagons for 7 days & carted over rough roads   a few died on the road but the most of them stood it pretty well. Our Chaplain was wounded Monday shot in the leg the bone was broken but the Doctors say it will not have to be taken off. A wounded Chaplain will be a curiosity in Washington   he is game   always goes into the fight with the Regt. he has a Rifle of his own. he says they will have to hurry up & settle the thing or he will get a chance to try his Rifle again   he thinks he is more than even with them now & I guess he is for I think the men are scarce that have killed as many Johnnies as he has. he gets his gun up to his face then says "God have mercy on your poor Soul" & lets her go & down comes Mr Johnnie   I wish the army furnished more such men. he is known all through the Corps as the fighting Chaplain[2]

We found our house just as we left it   all we had to do was to put the cover on & move in. We have been all packed up twice since we have been here   the last time was last night just before dark   We put our cover on our tent   some of the boys laid out thinking we would move early this morning but it is afternoon & we are here yet & are like to be till we are drove out. The weather is cold as greenland   it freezes water in our house half an inch thick   You wanted to know what I had for Thanksgiving   you can judge pretty near   Thanksgiving day we had Hard Tack & Coffee & the next day *Blue Pills* so you see we had a nice time of it up all night to the dance. Monday morning. I did not quite finish this last night so will do it while the boys are getting Breakfest   I suppose you will want to know what we are going to have   Well it is Fried Pork & Potatoes Coffee & some beans we had last night warmed up. When we are in camp we live as well as can be expected but on the march we have to live pretty short   My fingers are getting cold so I think I had better stop   I will write to Adin soon we expect to be paid off soon for the months Sept & Oct.   Yours Truly   From your Brother Walter W Smith

write soon

I see by the paper that Fred Streeter the man I enlisted under is under sentence to be hung the 26 of Oct for the murder of the McCoy family in Medina Ohio[3]

2. The "fighting chaplain" was the Reverend Lorenzo Barber, a Methodist minister from New York State.

3. Frederick F. Streeter of Bellows Falls enlisted as a corporal in Company F, First U.S. Sharpshooters, on September 11, 1861. According to his service records in the National Archives, he was sent home three weeks later to help recruit a company for the Second U.S. Sharpshooters. Apparently he never returned, and he was listed as a deserter on February 1, 1862. On February 26, 1864, he was hanged for the McCoy family murders.

"I never offered up a prayer with greater fervor that darkness might speedily cover the face of the earth, and put a stop to this terrible carnage"

Assistant Surgeon Joseph C. Rutherford of Newport, Tenth Vermont Infantry, to his wife, Hannah, December 13, 1863.[1]

1. Joseph C. Rutherford Papers, box 1, folder 43, UVM.

Brandy Station Va. Dec 13th 1863.

My dear wife:—

I promised myself to write to you a history of our march—and the Battle of "Lows Grove" [Orange Grove]. I shall [now] attempt to fulfill that promise. We left Brandy Station the 27th [i.e., the 26th] Nov (thanksgiving day) about 11 oclock A.M. It was a cold raw day—the wind was freezing in the extreme. We did not halt for any length of time till about 3 P.M. Here we had our *thanksgiving dinner*. Our thoughts all day had been of home and home comforts. of boards loaded with every luxury of the season till they fairly groaned with . . . their load. We thought of our friends sitting down to partake of these luxuries and wondered if while they were feasting on the delitious viands if a passing thought would flit across their memory of friends and relatives who were then going forth to do battle for their country their homes and firesides. While having these reflections we felt that many of us would never see another setting sun, or rather but one more setting sun as it was well understood that we were to meet enemy in less than 24 hours. We thought to how sad would be many a home and heart that were now happy in the plenty of Gods providence if they could see us as we were. The reflection is a sad one. While you were satisfying the cravings of the inner man with roast turkey plumb puddings mince pies—and all the luxuries that go to make up a N. E. thanksgiving dinner, we were squated on the cold ground around a smokey fire, the cold wind cutting us to the very vitals, broiling pieces of salt pork on the end of a stick, with the tears running down our cheeks from the smoke, with a "hard tack" in the other hand, and when the meat has been smoked and scorched sufficiently take it in our fingers to eat and grease our hard tack with, all of which had to be eaten hastily as we were on a forced march. How much think you would those at home enjoyed their sumptuous dinner had they known these fact[s]. This was our thanksgiving dinner. But let it be known that as meager as this fare was—a thanksgiving dinner never was eaten with more true thanksfullness to the giver of all good gifts than was ours. We were happy and content with what we had, not a murmur was heard. All were happy—and many a good joke was passed around—that seasoned our fare with the richest of spices. No grumbling tax payer at home enjoyed his feast or experienced half the thankfulness that most [   ] in our army felt. Their rotten hearts were filled with hatred and avarice. there was no room for joy nor for gratitude. They hate the war worn soldiers and they have no true love for their country. But mark it there is a terrible day of retribution coming.

Well after eating our meal we took our line of march, and came in sight of the famous Rapidan a little after sun set. By the time our Corps got across it was dark. We continued our march 2 miles back from the river—and camped for the night. We are now in a dense forest that is familliarly known as the *Wilderness*. It is well known that the woods are perfectly alive with the enemy—yet we lay down to sleep with an indifferance that is unaccountable to even the soldier himself. We were allowed to sleep till near break of day on the 27th. I would state here that we had marched 14 miles on the 26th.— We hastily eat some pork and hard tack and had a *dish* of coffee—when we took up our line of march farther into the woods. But we did not go more than 1 1/2 miles before [our] progress was checked. We found the Rebs entrenched. Here we formed a line of battle—and commenced maneuvering. But no fighting took place except by the skirmishers till a bout 3 P.M. when the great engagement took place. Our Brigade took the lead and opened the fight. Now comes my experience. There was but two surgeons for our Brig— As soon as the firing commenced we fixed a place about 6 rods in the rear of the 10th Vt as that reg. was in the center. The Brigade was on the crest of a knoll not so high as our heads as we stood in the hollow. Here we waited for work. I have told you my first feelings. We did not wait long for something to do— In about half an hour the shot came amongst us like hail storm. I did not mind it, a fact that is unaccountable to me, but I found myself experiencing feelings that I never felt before. The whole atmosphere seemed to be puffed from a heated furnace. This was not from a feeling of fear—for I had lost my whole being in my duties. The feeling is best explained by the sensation felt after the pain is gone when stung by a bee. So thick was the shot that it did not seem possible for a man to hold up his hand without its being hit. You can judge when I tell you that 30,000 muskets were being fired at us as fast as they could be loaded. I think the fighting must have lasted for nearly an hour when there seemed to be a lull. This was but momentary. But [to] my great surprise and danger the shot came from another direction and they came in a perfect shower. This is this time I have told you about when I had such a narrow escape. You will better understand how this was by a diagram [fig. 48], which I will make of our Brigade. Remember we are in a dense wood. At the time I speak of the 2 Div broke and *run* thus leaving a wide gap which the Rebs took advantage of, and undertook to turn our right flank, which was prevented by the 151st N.Y. falling back to the dotted line in their rear. I stood where the circle is beside a little stream of water, which you see would bring me directly in their line of fire and the ground is nearly level between me and the combatants, and not the length of a regiment from them. I had wounded men laying on the ground and stretchers. As strange as I may seem I thought of the safety of these poor fellow[s] more than I did of myself. I was not long in removing my quarters to a more safe and distant point. Here we were unmolested for over an hour. It was begining to be dark in the woods, and let me say here that I never offered up a prayer with greater fervor that darkness might speedily cover the face of the earth, and put a stop to this terrible carnage. The first intimation of danger here was the bursting of a shell over our heads, and followed in rapid succession by other shells. At this time we had exhausted all our dressings, and it gitting too dark to operate properly, it was thought best to leave the woods and go to the rear about half a mile where there was a clearing and a small log house which you see by looking on the map I sent you, "Gen Frenchs H. Quarters." Here we astablished our Hospital again, and I never worked harder in my life. The last wounded man was brought in after 2 A. M. next morning. One little incident occured here. There were but 2 rooms in the house   Gen French occupied one while the wounded the other. About 10 oclock P.M. he sent an orderly to me with his compliments to borrow a *candle*   I sent my compliments back to him saying that [we] had no more candles than was necessary to work with. One of the surgeons present said we had better let the Gen have one. I told him no, he nor any other Gen can have a candle when we have not enough for ourselves. The fun of the thing is that he should be there with all his train without a single candle. But to return to the battle ground— The firing ceased a little after dark and our poor exhausted men lay down among the dead and dying—to sn[ea]k a little rest and sleep, and their sleep was sounder than was ever experienced on downy pillows. Victory had perched upon their arms—the enemy was driven from the field. Before light next morning we started for "mine run."

I have given you a very imperfect history of the experience of the long to be remembered 27th Nov   I did intend to give the history of the next day but I have written till my poor old *thumb* aches like the tooth ache. I will continue this history as opportunity offers. The description of our feeling in a battle are such that language is inadequate to express them, they must be felt to know them. The 10th Vt did [fairly?] in this action   Let me say here that Capt Steele did honor to himself and his town, as well as *all* his men. Joe Daggett showed himself a brave and noble soldier. did not get a earache   Young Spafford did well—in fact not a man in his Company failed to do their duty. John Piper sent 4 horses riderless back into the enemies [   ]   He fired over 30 rounds and did not waste a shot. So Col Jewett said who stood near him all the time.

As I wrote to you yesterday I have nothing to write.

Remember me to the children.

Your Husband
J. C. Rutherford

Winter 1864

Chapter 12

The men of the First Vermont Brigade enjoyed a pleasant winter in 1864, with light work and relatively little severe weather or sickness. They participated in the usual camp diversions, but for once, religion played a significant part in camp life. Field agents of the United States Christian Commission, founded in 1861 to provide physical and spiritual comfort for soldiers, distributed tracts and held religious services in the Union camps near Brandy Station. Some revivals were reported.[1] Drinking, gambling, and other vices still had their place, however. Soldiers always seemed to find a way to supply themselves with liquor, and some of them made small fortunes doing it.

During the winter's rest from active campaigning, leaders in both the North and the South considered many options for strengthening their fighting forces. The rebel armies numbered less than half a million in total, and less than half of these were available for combat in the main theaters of war. Confederate general Patrick Cleburne went so far as to suggest freeing and arming the slaves to fight for the South. This idea was immediately rejected, but the Confederate Congress did undertake several reforms, including abolishing substitutions and expanding the draft age from eighteen to forty-five to seventeen to fifty.[2] Union forces, meanwhile, numbered almost twice as many as the rebels, but a large number of these were needed to defend the areas captured during three seasons of fighting, and to operate the machinery of supplying the far-flung armies. Furthermore, Union leaders faced the prospect of losing close to a quarter of a million experienced soldiers when their terms of enlistment expired in the coming summer.

To encourage Union veterans to reenlist, the War Department late in 1863 offered thirty-day furloughs and $402 bounties to all soldiers who had served for two years, if they signed up for another three years or the duration of the war. If three-quarters of the "old" men in a regiment reenlisted, their unit would be designated a "Veteran Regiment" and the men could wear special veteran insignias. These inducements persuaded more than half of the eligible men to reenlist, including just over a thousand men of the First Vermont Brigade.[3]

President Lincoln then called for a second draft, to be held in March, with a goal of raising five hundred thousand more soldiers. The recruitment of black troops (who were now subject to the draft) was at last moving ahead rapidly, after a cautious start in the latter half of 1862. The Colored Troops also provided opportunities for enlisted men in white regiments to win commissions, since the black regiments were to be staffed by white officers.[4] By law, African-American soldiers earned only ten dollars per month in federal pay, compared to the thirteen dollars paid to white soldiers. The issue of unequal pay caused widespread disgruntlement in the black regiments and near-mutiny in some, until Congress equalized pay with limited retroactive adjustments in June 1864.[5]

By 1864 there were 100,000 black troops in the Union army, many of whom would soon see hard service. On February 20, the 54th Massachusetts and two other black infantry regiments were among the Union troops drawn into a rebel ambush at Olustee, Florida. While some of the inexperienced troops, black and white, panicked and ran for the rear, most of the black soldiers fought back stubbornly. Of the 5,500 Union troops engaged, 1,861 were killed, wounded, or captured.[6]

One of the unintended consequences of using African-American soldiers was a hardening of policies on the exchange of prisoners. From July 1862 to May 1863, prisoners of war generally were imprisoned or released on parole only as long as it took to arrange an exchange for an equal number of prisoners from the other side (officers counting for a larger number of privates). But when the Confederacy refused to treat black prisoners the same as whites—some were murdered outright, others were sold into slavery, and none were permitted to be exchanged —Northern leaders stopped exchanges altogether. As a result, prisoners of war on both sides faced the likelihood of long stays in overcrowded prisons. Shortages of food, shelter, and medical attention in Southern prisons grew worse early in 1864, and alarming reports of sick and emaciated prisoners began to filter through to the North. Although some exchanges were arranged in 1864, rebel leaders refused to relent on the treatment of black prisoners of war until January 1865.[7]

A daring attempt was made to free some of the Union prisoners of war at the end of February, when General Judson Kilpatrick and four thousand cavalry soldiers set out on a raid to liberate Belle Isle and Libby Prisons in Richmond. The Sixth Corps marched from its camps as part of a diversion that allowed Kilpatrick to slip behind enemy lines unopposed. The cavalry force split in two when it reached Spotsylvania: a small force under Colonel Ulric Dahlgren maneuvered to approach Richmond from the west while Kilpatrick with the bulk of his men approached from the north. One hundred men of the First Vermont Cavalry accompanied Dahlgren while the rest stayed with Kilpatrick.

Kilpatrick reached the outskirts of Richmond on March 1 but received no reports from Dahlgren. After skirmishing with the defenders for several hours, still with no word from Dahlgren, Kilpatrick decided to abandon the raid. Enemy troops began to appear, pestering Kilpatrick's pickets, but the cavalrymen withdrew with few casualties.

Dahlgren's force had a much harder time. Arriving at his assigned position late on March 1, the young colonel quickly concluded that Kilpatrick had already abandoned the raid. Rebel troops rushing to the scene soon threatened the small cavalry force, which set out on an increasingly desperate retreat. Heavy rain, deep mud, and pitch darkness hampered the weary horsemen during the night of March 2. In the darkness the raiders split into two groups, and Dahlgren with 200 men ran into an ambush near King and Queen Court House. The colonel was killed in the ensuing skirmish and nearly all of his men captured. A group of 250 cavalrymen eventually found their way back to Kilpatrick and safety.

Had he followed through on his intentions, Kilpatrick might well have forced his way into the rebel capital, at least for a time, and freed some of the prisoners of war. In the end, all he managed to accomplish was some minor destruction of supplies and equipment, at the cost of 340 casualties, 300 of them prisoners. The First Vermont Cavalry lost 71 men, most of whom found themselves among the prisoners they had hoped to free.[8]

The Confederates undertook some minor raids of their own during the winter months. Late in January General George Pickett tested the Union outpost at New Bern, North Carolina, thirty miles up the Neuse River from the coastal ports of Morehead City and Beaufort. Stationed at Newport Barracks, between New Bern and Morehead City, the Ninth Vermont Infantry and a few hundred other troops defended a line in an arc from Bogue Sound to the south to the swamps bordering the Neuse to the north. Pickett sent a brigade to attack this position and capture the small fort at Newport Barracks on February 2. Lieutenant Colonel Valentine G. Barney, commanding in the absence of Colonel Edward H. Ripley, held off the enemy for several hours with fewer than a thousand men, most of them raw recruits. Finally Barney was forced to set fire to the barracks and retreat across rivers and swamps to the safety of Morehead City. The Ninth did all it could under the circumstances, narrowly avoiding the humiliation of being captured a second time.[9]

Vermont continued to raise troops with increasingly exorbitant bounties, or by conscription if necessary. Most of these new soldiers were assigned to the existing regiments. Governor Frederick Holbrook, followed by John Gregory Smith, who took office in September 1863, attempted to raise one more regiment—the Seventeenth Vermont Infantry—with the expectation that the veterans of the Second Vermont Brigade would provide ample material to fill the ranks. But the nine-month men proved largely unwilling to reenlist, and the Seventeenth's recruiting officers found it difficult to compete with those of the old regiments.[10]

Perhaps the most important development of the winter season was the appointment of a new Union army commander. In March, President Lincoln conferred on Ulysses S. Grant, the hero of Vicksburg and Chattanooga, the rank of Lieutenant General, making him the first to hold the army's highest rank since George Washington.[11] Grant was to command all of the armies of the United States and coordinate their campaigns toward the destruction of the Confederate military. George Meade would continue as commander of the Army of the Potomac, but Grant intended to travel with the army and direct its campaigns in Virginia, while he entrusted operations in the West to General William T. Sherman. Between them, the Union war effort would take on a new face of decisiveness—and bitterness.

FIGURE 49. Samuel E. Pingree. Vermont Historical Society.

1. Lyndon State College Collection, Pingree (Pingry)/Hunton/Stickney Family Papers (MSA 135), folder 6, VHS. See Stephen Pingree's letter of October 2, 1863, p. 186.

"I believe it hardly finds a rival even in the days of the bold Allens"

Lieutenant Colonel Samuel E. Pingree of Hartford, Third Vermont Infantry, to Augustus Hunton, January 14, 1864.[1]

Pingree's brother Stephen was major of the Fourth Vermont Infantry.

Camp of Third Vt. Vols.
near Brandy Station Va.
Jany. 14, 1864

Cousin Hunton

Your letter of the 10th inst. came to hand to day inclosing a dollar bill from Major Danforth, and what . . . is more pleasing still bringing news of the good health of you all and of the promptness of our noble little state in answering & more than answering all the calls of our general Govt.

I have taken great pleasure in announcing to the officers of the Regt. the fact that Vt. is still in the van in her response to the many necessary calls for troops.

We had a peculiar joy here at seeing the proud position our state has taken and will hereafter hold in history upon the question of this great rebellion.

I believe it hardly finds a rival even in the days of the bold Allens.

When I returned to my post I found the Major (Nelson) away, and Col. Seaver in command of the brigade.

Orders came immediatly for the reenlistment of troops as veterans. —no labor was spared by any of us to induce enlistments—and our success was quite equal to our expectations.

A feeling, (arising from the signs of the times) pervades most of us that the snow of this Winter will be the last that armed rebels will tread in this war,—and in our confidence in this belief the veteran business goes on with much greater facility than it otherwise would, for another three years of such hardship as has fallen to the lot of the private soldier with but 15 or even 35 days at home during the entire period does not appear to him quite so captivating as the honor of having a hand in closing the thing up and going home also, before another 12 months roll round.

148 have gone home from this Regt. and quite a number more have reenlisted and will go as soon as the rest return.

Probably 200 will enlist as veterans from us—this will be over 2/3 of those left of the "old men"

We are having recruits arrive in the brigade every few days.

Fewer come to the 3rd than to any other Regt. I am at a loss to account for this. I fear the officers & men on recruiting service from here are less efficient than others or at least less industrious. or else (what is altogether more probable) we have not done enough of "organ-grinding" in local papers to obtain a just fame.—

But it makes little odds to what Regt. men are joined if they only join some one.—

My health is quite good. If I had obtained a leave of absence for a few days, a month earlier I think I might have saved a month of sickness.— Stephen is well. Give regards to Mrs. Hunton & the children— Tell Mrs. H. if I had recd. her invitation to tea on fresh Porkchicken Pie in season I should have wished I was there, but as I have been gratified of late with several sorts of eatables, less curious, tho. probably quite as good, and all sent by her, I will express no regret at not being able to be at tea with her on the eve of the 10th— But I am going to write a line to her to send with this and will to the children also if I have time to morrow— I send you the Washington Chronicle the paper of largest circulation of any in the army here.—

"They drill excellently much better than white troops and will make splendid soldiers"

Captain Arthur P. Morey of Norwich, Company F, Twenty-Second U.S. Colored Troops, to his cousin, February 4, 1864.[1]

1. Arthur P. Morey Papers, Gertrude Mallary Collection, Bradford, Vermont.

Camp Wm Penn Philadelphia
Penn. Feb. 4th '64

My Dear Cousin

I am at last in command of a company of wooly headed gentlemen of the colored persuasion. I have got ninety eight under my special charge mostly as black as the ace of spades. My orderly sergeant is a darkey from New Jersey black as ebony. I have a little drummer fourteen years old and blacker than all the darkness of the infernal regions condensed into one little nigger   He came to me yesterday with a very consequential air and asked for a pass to go to the city saying he had some business to transact before leaving for the south   money matters and so on. I have to send one occasionally to the guard House for some misdemeaner but not near as many as would be expected from a company of whites. Here is a specimen of my style of doing things. Orderly comes in "Cap'n James K. Polk wouldnt do as I told him went to cussin me"   "Take James K Polk to the guardhouse and put a ball and chain on him for twenty four hours.["] Another man comes in "Cap'n I give head cook my money to keep when I was sick and he's been and gone to work and spent it all and wont pay me.["] Cook is sent for. Cook did you have this mans money to keep while he was sick? Yes sir. Pay him back before tomorrow morning or you go in to the guard house for a week in double irons. "But Capn" "Not a word. Leave." Thats the way we do things here. I am officer of the day to day and have to go the grand rounds at twelve. It is fun to hear some of the darkeys challenge when they first go on guard. They forget the proper methods of challengeing but it is almost impossible to get by them. They drill excellently much better than white troops and will make splendid soldiers. They all declare it . . . the height of their ambition to get a crack at Jeff. Davis who they think themselves able to bring down at an immense distance. I have been making corporals this evening or at least examining them. but very few can read or write hardly enough to get sergeants and corporals from. I beg your pardon for writing so much nonsense for I find I have filled the sheet without knowing it   give my love to all and all write soon

Your Cousin Arthur P. Morey

"I feel that I have not been disgraced even if I was obliged to destroy Every thing and retreat"

Lieutenant Colonel Valentine G. Barney of Swanton, Ninth Vermont Infantry, to his wife, Maria, February 5, 1864.[1]

Promoted to lieutenant colonel in the spring of 1863, Barney commanded the regiment in the absence of Colonel Edward H. Ripley.

1. Valentine G. Barney Papers (MS 104), folder 3, VHS.

Morehead City N.C.
Feby 5th 1864

Dear Maria

I write you a few hurried lines to go on the [vessel] Spaulding   I presume ere this you have heard of fighting in this vicinity— On the morning of Feby 2d the Enemy attacked us at Newport Ba[rrac]k's first the out posts then our main body at the Bks—their force was four times ours and we were obliged to give way and fall back across Newport River burning the Bridges in our rear but not till after a sharp fight of I think about 3 hours—   the Enemy came to our rear which gave us no chance to use our Guns in the Fort— We lost about 50 men in killed wounded and missing in our Regt   one Lt captured & one wounded Our new recruits composed nearly all our force having but about 60, or 70, of the old men present— The recruits had guns put into their hands about 3 or 4 hours before the fight—and hardly any of them knew how to right face but they fought finely considering the circumstances— Col Ripley was away at Ft Monroe so I was in command of the Post and great responsibility rested on me but I have been told by Col Jourdan Comdg this district that I done the verry best that possibly could be so I feel that I have not been disgraced even if I was obliged to destroy every thing and retreat. We came here by way of Beaufort, marching all night, leaving Newport at dusk—the men lost nearly every thing and have been on duty night and day ever since—with but little to eat and no cover whatever—   We have been expecting an attack here every hour since we arrived here so none of us have slept except by seconds since Feby 1st— I feel pretty well worn out but am in good spirits and able for any fatigue necessary— The 21st Conn. Regt have just arrived   also, Col Ripley so I will now be relieved from the command of this Post and my responsibility lessened— I can write no more at present but will give you another and more accurate account in a few days— We intend to make an advance to day but I think the Rebs are leaving   I see now large fires towards Newport which is probably the turpentine there on fire

Your Aff Husband
V. G. Barney

"There were many moistened eyes & trembling lips— That meeting rewarded me a thousand fold for all I have done or endured in coming to the army"

Reverend Charles C. Parker of Waterbury, delegate of the U.S. Christian Commission, to his wife, Elizabeth, February 24, 1864.[1]

FIGURE 50. Charles C. Parker. Special Collections, University of Vermont.

1. Parker Family Papers (Miscellaneous File 1039), Vermont Historical Society.

Brandy Camp near 2d Vermont—
Culpepper Co. Va. Feb. 24th 1864—

Dearest Lizzie

We have just dedicated our new Chapel Tent and had our first meeting at this new station & now I must tell you all about it— I think I wrote you it was determined to establish a new station for me & another Vermonter Mr. J.W.H. Baker of Greensboro— We pitched our tents Monday— The Chapel is a large tent 50 feet by 18— In the rear of it, with a narrow walk between is our tent 10 feet square— They are pitched between the 2d Vt. & the 6th Regular Cavalry— Both of these Regiments have been in the service since the war & in all the hardest battles & campaigns— The battle flag of the Cavalry fluttering before the headquarters is all in tatters— Neither of them has a Chaplain & it is on account of this our tent is pitched between them— We slept in our tent Monday night—but did not get the Chapel in order for a meeting until to-night & now we have no Seats— The tent was well filled & all seemed much interested in the services— When opportunity was given for remarks Byron Ward of Underhill—a member of Johns class—son of an old schoolmate of mine—immediately arose and made some very sensible remarks— I felt very grateful to him for this as you know how unpleasant unbroken silence is in a meeting— No other one spoke— The singing was with a will—ready—strong—earnest & all over the Chapel— Notwithstanding only one spoke & none offered prayer— we feel that we had a good meeting & that the indications are cheering— After this meeting several stopped & expressed their great joy that we had pitched our tent among them & we expect their hearty cooperation—

Saturday night—   Another weeks work is done & I will complete its record— Thursday I rode to the Station on business—visited the hospital where there are twelve sick—three very sick—visited the soldiers in their tents—or huts—& in the evening had a meeting— The Chapel was filled the men still standing on the damp earth— This evening the time was all occupied— Six made brief earnest, pointed remarks—two offered prayer— Confession of sin & the expression of a sincere desire & purpose to return to the path of truth & life characterized the remarks & prayers of every one— Men of both regiments took part & all expressed the utmost gratification at the opportunity thus to meet & worship their God once more— Friday we attended a meeting of the delegates of the commission at Brandy Station— Delegates were present from nearly all the stations & their reports were most cheering— At many of them there has been & is still a deep & extensive work of grace— Many have been hopefully converted— many wandering professors reclaimed— Both classes are numbered by hundreds—

While we were gone a squad of boys—mainly from Waterbury & Underhill volunteered & with a team furnished by Dr. Sawin, went three miles over Hazle River & cut & split for us twenty five slabs of white wood & black walnut to seat our Chapel— This was all we needed to complete our arrangements & enter fully upon our work & we felt very thankful when we saw what the noble boys had done— In the evening we had a very precious meeting— With the utmost readiness & heartiness ten soldiers spoke—mainly our noble Vermont boys— Some spoke of their wanderings & asked the forgiveness of their comrades— Others spoke of the preciousness of Jesus & the power of his religion to cheer & sustain the heart in all the perils & exposures of a soldiers life—the march—the watch—the battlefield— There were many moistened eyes & trembling lips— That meeting rewarded me a thousand fold for all that I have done or endured in coming to the army— I wish every brother & sister could have witnessed that meeting— How they would have thanked God & taken courage—

After the meeting & through the night—which was cold & windy— there was an unusual hum [and] stir in both camps & we were apprehensive what the morrow should bring— The morning came and with it the intelligence that the 2d Vt. with the whole of the 6th Corps was under marching orders & might leave at any moment— Word to be ready for an early move was passed from tent to tent immediately after the meeting & the night had been spent in getting everything in order— And now the brave fellows are gone— They took with them six days rations & have gone to reconnoitre across the Rapidan— I felt inexpressibly sad when I saw them move out of Camp to join the other Vt. Regiments & the rest of the Corps— & afterwards when from near Brandy Station I saw the long black line of them with their glittering bayonets, some two miles away—as with ceaseless tread they made their march— I am told that supply train & all the line was eight miles long—

The Maj. in command & Dr Sawin wished me to accompany them & I hastened over to Brandy Station to ask leave at headquarters so to do—as I wished much to go—but it was thought best to wait for a day

FIGURE 51. A Christian Commission chapel. Lossing, *Pictorial History of the Civil War in the United States of America*, vol. 3, 586. UVM.

2. This movement was designed to draw attention away from Kilpatrick's raid on Richmond.

or two & see how serious the movement should prove to be[2]— The boys have taken my heart with them— A guard has been left in camp & we hope to see them back in a few days & yet such are the uncertainties of war that we can predict nothing as to the future— But if these meetings are all, we shall bless God for the privilege of holding them—

This evening the meeting has been small comparatively—& not as interesting as the others & yet two young men who had not spoken before—spoke very finely & touchingly of themselves & of their interest in these meetings & of their purpose to renew their Christian life—

Sabbath evening—   Half the Sabbaths I am to spend in the field are gone—on what a swift wing time is flying! Surely what I do must be done quickly—

The Commission had partly arranged to have me preach to day at Gen Meade's head quarters & I was to go in the p.m. to preach again to the Vt Cavalry—but an Episcopal clergyman—a friend of Gen. Meade—being on a visit at head quarters—relieved the Commission— & the Vt Cavalry have taken part in this movement— The result is I have preached but once & that in our Chapel at 1 1/2 p.m. At sun down I attended the burial service of two [of] our Vt. boys—one named Holden of Reading Vt having died last night—the other— Lafayette Moore of Fayston having died today—both of Measles and Supervening Typhoid fever— To me it was a sad & novel experience, as to the mournful beat of the dead march we followed the two coffins to their graves— During the brief services at the grave the soldiers were solemn & attentive—but the moment they were away—all solemnity seemed to be gone—

Returning to my tent we heard one boom of a cannon across the Rapidan— What it imports time will develop— This evening we have had a very interesting meeting—some four or five new persons rising to speak— One of them said this was the first Sabbath he had passed in the army— It seemed like getting home once more— Hoping you have had a pleasant precious Sabbath day & all are having pleasant spacious social meetings, I bid you good night—

> Affectionately,
> C.C.P.

As the soldiers were leaving yesterday one brought me his Bible to keep for him—taking a Testament in return— Another handed me $50. to send to his motherless boy in Montreal. These little things made me very sad—

"eny thing that is licker"

Private Charles Tillison of Underhill, Company E, Second Vermont Infantry, to his son, Dudley, February 24, 1864.[1]

1. Tillison Family Papers (MSS 25-119), VHS.

Feb 24th 1864
Camp Near Brandy Stashin

Dear Son

I recived your letter last night And was glad to heare yo got the money I sent   my helth is very good   if yo send the Box bee cafule And pack it so it wont wratle for they are gitin [v]ery strick   fill the canes [cans] full And cork them tight And pack them well with saw dust   And if I can git it heare it will bring me good too hundred dolars the minet I git it   if yo cant git hy wines git what yo can   eny thing that is licker   when yo send it Direct it to Docter Sawin just as yo have the rest   now bee sure And fill the canes full   And send it Along as [soon] as yo can And write the same time yo send Box   And direct the leter to Abial Foy 2nd Vermont Regiment Hospital dep

"it was feared by the officers that they would have trouble with us, and so recourse was had to falsehood"

Private Louden S. Langley of Hinesburg, Company B, Fifty-Fourth Massachusetts Infantry, to the *Burlington Daily Free Press*, March 9, 1864.[1]

1. The letter was printed in the *Burlington Daily Free Press*, March 22, 1864, p. 2. UVM.

54th Reg't Mass. Vol.,
Jacksonville, Fla., March 9, 1864.

Editors of the Free Press:

You are aware that we (the Vermont men in this regiment) left Brattleboro' Jan 23d, for I saw it stated in the *Sentinel* that "almost a mutiny occurred among the colored soldiers when ordered to leave for their Regiment," because, while the white soldiers received $75, the black soldiers received *nothing*! This, although coming from the *Sentinel*, is nevertheless true. It is also true that "they" (the colored soldiers) "had expected to be treated in this respect the same as white soldiers, especially as *they counted on the quota of the state.*"

The boys (52 in number) at the time of their enlistment had been promised $13 per month, $302 bounty and premium, and the same allowance for clothing as white soldiers. This would have entitled each man of us to the payment of $75 before we left Brattleboro'. We would have been super-human had we sustained all of the disappointment that the *truth* conveyed without being greatly chagrined and disposed to "mutiny." Indeed, I think I may say that, if the boys had had their arms, that every man of them would have died on that spot before leaving camp without the payment of their just due. As it was they showed *un*mistakable signs that they had pluck, so much so that it was feared by the officers that they would have trouble with us, and so recourse was had to falsehood. We were told that, owing to our going into a regiment from another State, our $75 had been sent to the headquarters of our regiment, where we would be paid off as soon as we arrived there!—a falsehood that even Satan himself would blush to promulgate; but the boys, willing to believe what *should be true*, believed all would be right, and so the difficulty ended. Suffice it to say that we have sent a letter to our excellent Governor, J. Gregory Smith, complaining of our grievances, and asking for the interposition of his executive authority in our behalf.

We now number 44 effective men. We have six on the sick list at the different hospitals, both here at the Head, and have lost one by death —private John H. Freeman, whose family reside in your village, and one has been missing since the battle of Olustree (Saturday 20th ult.)— Private Charles E. Nelson of Bristol—and is supposed to have been captured by the enemy.

It is now over a month since we came on this expedition, and we have seen one battle and one defeat. From the time we landed in this city, until the day of the battle aforesaid, the rebels under Gen. Finnegan had not ceased to run; but the truth of the proverb that "it is a long road that never turns" was soon to be verified. On Wednesday the 16th ult., we left our camp with a sufficient force, as was supposed, to crush all opposition, but the rebels having been largely reinforced from

Georgia, were ready to give us a warm reception. On Saturday the 20th ult., we came up to the extreme front. It was about three P.M. when our regiment with a hearty cheer went into the fight. The enemy were strongly entrenched behind a breast-work of earth, which greatly protected them from the effect of our fire. Before we came up the rebs succeeded in capturing one of our batteries of six guns, and soon after we went into the fight they endeavored to flank us by a regiment of rebel cavalry. We wheeled and paid our respects to them, which soon set them to a "right about face." We fought bravely (i.e. the regiment— I was not in the fight, having been ordered to the rear by the Colonel, to guard the knapsacks of our men) until we were ordered to retreat. But the men had no idea of obeying the first order, and it was repeated by Col. Hallowell three times before the order was obeyed. The 54th was the last regiment that left the field, and they retreated in good order, as did the other regiments that participated in the fight. The loss of our regiment, in killed, wounded and missing, was 97 men. Among the wounded was Private Emery Anderson of Hinesburgh, who received a ball through his leg just above the ankle joint. Many of our wounded were left on the field, from which place they crawled along into the thick bushes to conceal themselves, and afterwards were discovered and captured by the enemy. However, quite a number were brought off, and those whose wounds were in the flesh only about the head and arms, retreated with the rest of our army. Many of the wounded collected at a small house about three miles from the battle field, where many of them were taken in by the ambulances and wagons that came along, and that were sent back (the number was very few) after them. The latter threw out every thing almost, that they might accommodate the wounded, to keep them from being captured by the enemy, whom it was understood were pursuing us. As our men left the field, the rebs rent the air with cheer upon cheer. It was after 8 P.M. when we left the vicinity of the battle, and before we could rest, we must march back to the place we had encamped the night before, which was a distance of 15 miles. All along the road were men who had, in the hurry and confusion, lost their regiments; some helping along the wounded, while not a few of the latter were helping along themselves, and marched the entire 15 miles without any assistance. Hard tack or army bread, was very plentifully strewn along the road for the double purpose of unburdening the teams or taking in the wounded, and of feeding the numerous stragglers that lined the road, from the rear guard (the 55th Mass., colored) to the van of the army. It was about 5 A.M. before the stragglers all came in, or when the rear guard of the army came up. The men were tired and foot-sore, having marched that day 32 miles, and had fought one battle and sustained a defeat.

At six the next morning we were on our road for the next station (Baldwin), where we arrived about 12 M., from which place we pushed on (for a short distance at double-quick) until we arrived at Camp Finnegan, which is only seven miles from this city. We arrived at this city on Monday evening, 22d ult., where we have been ever since, laboriously engaged in fortifying. The rebels have been as near to us as Camp Finnegan, and have once drove in our pickets, when we were immediately ordered to the entrenchments ready for a brush. But the rebs have thus far shown more wisdom than valor in threatening Jacksonville, and it is now very generally believed that if we see them we will have to go where they are.

The weather here for the past few days has been very cool, but today it is very warm, and owing to the sudden change the heat is somewhat oppressive. The pretty and odoriferous flowers that almost everywhere greet the eyes, remind one of June weather in Vermont. The country around this city has been stripped, and both man and beast (the swine in particular) bear evidences of great scarcity and want, and all presents a striking contrast to the thrift and abundance that everywhere greet one in Vermont.

The boys are all pleased with the draft, because they think it more than fair for all to share in the perils of the fight, as well as in the blessings of the perfect and peaceful liberty that is sure to follow.

Louden S. Langley
Co. B. 54th Mass. Vols.

"He did not advance his most ultra views, but still shewed that he was decidedly anti-slavery in his opinions"

Susan Dewey of Montpelier, to her husband, Edward, March 13, 1864.[1]

Edward Dewey was quartermaster of the Eighth Vermont Infantry and assistant quartermaster of the army post at Thibodeaux, Louisiana.

1. Edward Dewey Papers (Miscellaneous File 353), VHS.

Montpelier Mar 13th 1864.

My dear Edward,

Yours of Feb 25th was received last night, and I was very glad that you were better of your diarrhea, as I presume you are from the tone of your letter, and besides you do not mention it, and furthermore the quartermasters stores are turned over to you, which they would not probably be if you were sick.

You were fortunate in the matter of your pay, but it is only your just due, and you ought to have it.

Father thinks it strange that you should have to pay for your board when you were on duty on the Cahawba, but I suppose it was your portion of the mess—Was it not?

As to the bounty, he thinks there is not much chance for it, and Charles says they would not give it to officers who enter upon their commission at once.

Father says when your rations are given you, and you are well supplied with clothing, he does not see how your expenses can be large or take up much of your pay. He wrote you last week to be sure and not buy a horse, as you had better keep your money. Col Thomas is here, and Father has seen him, and he said he was going to call and see me, but has not yet, tho' I would like to meet him very much and hope he will come before long. Dr Greeley is here on a thirty days furlough—he came home with the N. H. regiments to vote, but was not allowed to deposit *his* vote at Nashua because Mr Bailey (who married his cousin) who was a candidate for Dem representative worked against him and said his residence was in Vermont, and so prevented him. Bailey was elected by only *five* majority, and Dr Greeley thinks they can prove fraudulent votes enough to oust him from his seat and that would be a good return upon him.

Wendell Phillips delivered a lecture last Friday evening in Depot Hall to a crowded house. We all went & enjoyed it much. I had supposed his style was more that of a harangue, but this time it was quiet, convincing and conversational. He did not advance his most ultra views, but still shewed he was decidedly anti-slavery in his opinions.

I hear that in Burlington he was more out spoken, and some left the hall and there was apprehension of a mob because he spoke of Lincoln as not enough of an anti slavery man, and not equal to the emergency. Mr Willard introduced him, and gave him a breakfast Saturday morning, to which Mr & Mrs Geo. Reed were invited, but whether anyone else I do not know. He told Mrs Keith that he remembered her father well—that he went to London with him to attend the great Anti-Slavery convention in the year thirty—only twelve went from this country—he remembered his having Byron's sword & his going to see Lady Byron.

You say that you do not wonder that the southerners thought themselves a different class from those of the north, and that you have seen a number of places that you would be willing to take if it was stocked etc—

Now it would be quite a joke if you should turn Southerner— You know Charlotte Tarbox inclined a good deal that way— However I am not much afraid of you, you have too much good northern blood in your veins.

I am glad that your masonry serves a good purpose— It serves as a sort of introduction I suppose, as much as to say "this man is to be trusted." It may help you to get friends, and once having discovered and known your true character, no one would wish to drop you. It is too bad that you can not have good water, for I know you were quite particular even here to have it pumped up very cold & fresh. I suppose *we* can not appreciate it while we have plenty of it.

You speak of a bare possibility of your coming home by July or August— Would it not be delightful! But do not let us anticipate it *too much*, for fear that leave *may* not be granted.

2. Louisiana's new pro-Union governor, Michael Hahn, took office on March 4, 1864 (Long, *The Civil War Day by Day*, 472).

The last Boston papers give a glowing account of the inauguration of Gov Hahn[2] at New Orleans & say also that a large expedition is about ready to leave Franklin probably to move up Red River. If you have gone or are going, do be careful and not get taken prisoner—do not eat too many *fruits* even if you have them or anything unwholesome, for in that warm climate you might not as soon recover from the ill effects. Take warning from raw oysters—and try to have some of my caution. Last week I put the tobacco pouch in *one* envelope, and my letter in *another* and Father was going to put on the stamps, but he found that it would save *one* stamp to put them together and did so— I should like to know whether they both reached you safely.

If all reading matter is in the same proportion as to price, as Harpers Weekly—it seems to me I would not buy much there, but I will send you whatever you think best— I could send you Harpers Magazine, but if we waited to read it first, it would be a week or two late and then the numbers would not be in a very good condition to bind afterward. Shall I do so? Mary and I are reading "Don Quixote"—I suppose you have read it—if so, you have had many a hearty laugh at its absurdities.

I do not think of any of the childrens sayings this time but presume that I shall have some by next time.

They are so pleased with any message that you send.

And now hoping soon to hear from *"Home"* (that is where the heart is) I will send you my best love (with Father's & Mother's) and a kiss from your ever affectionate wife,

Susie G. L. Dewey

"there is no better fighting material in any army, than in this"

Major William Wells of Waterbury, First Vermont Cavalry, to Anna Richardson, March 25, 1864.[1]

Wells's future wife, Anna, attended Glenwood Academy in Brattleboro.

1. William Wells Papers, carton 1, folder 2, UVM.

Camp 7th Michigan Cavalry
Stevensburg Virginia March, 25th 1864

Friend Anna

It is very wet out to night, it is raining quite hard and has been for several hours. my house which I always thought was second to none, I find leaks in several places. am oblige to spred my rubber over my bed in order to keep it dry, for your humble servant detests a wet bed although a Soldier.

It is rough for those on picket   they must stand at their posts let it rain ever so hard. am glad I am not on that duty at this time.

Lieut Genl Grant is now I am told with the "Army of the Potomac" no doubt things will undergo a change, in some departments. all have great confidence in his superior Generalship, and I hope that when the mud dries up that we may moove forward to Victory. there is no better fighting material in any army, than in this. give us good leaders, and those that work togather.

I am at present in Command of the 7th Michigan Cavalry. it is in this (2nd) Brigade. their Camp is but a short distance from 1st Vts. I am now writing in my old house with Vt Cav. but have dated my letter differently. My health for a few days past has not been the best. have a very bad cold, but shall no doubt get well of it before many days.

You have before this no doubt read all that and more than I can write you of the late Raid under Genl Kilpatrick, our Regt was with him   we lost 71 men—had 100 men with Col Dalgrun (quite a number) whom were taken prisoners killed or wounded. the ride was hard for four or five *days* and *nights* we marched without any sleep only what we got while riding horseback   I got more sleepy than I should have by sitting up the same number of nights sparking some fine young Lady, yet if one is not careful they will get sleepy sitting up to much with the females. (so I am told!)

Our expedition went within 2 1/2 miles of Richmond and if we had had double the force, we could have I think taken the City of Rebels. we only had a force of 3 508 all told, so I am informed.

Next time I go to Vermont I shall *try* and call to see you. I was very sorry I could not when last I was there, but could not. if you go to Brattleboro you must try and keep Sarah from getting so homesick. does she know you are to attend next term? if not she may not be there. it may make quite a diffirence if she knows you are to be there, for I think you two get allong first rate togather, do you not? You write me that you have not my picture in Majors uniform. you shall have one. not very well taken I think. Shall be pleased to hear from *you soon*. do not wait as long as I have. I was on Raid when your letter arrived in Camp—

Love to all—

As ever your friend
William

P.S. If I remember rightly you never have sent me your picture. all I have I have stolen from Sarah. Wid

"I would not willingly endure this again, if I knew it would place every Negro in the Confederacy in our 'Contraband Camps'"

Sergeant William B. Stevens of East Montpelier, Company G, Fourth Vermont Infantry, to Mary Stevens Putnam, March 26, 1864.[1]

Captured on October 14, 1863, Stevens was paroled on March 7, 1864.

1. Rokeby Museum, Robinson Family Papers, box 44, folder 3, Sheldon.

"Camp Parole," Annapolis.
March 26th 1864

My dear Sister:

Yours of the 22d is just before me, and I will try to reply, in "my feeble way." As you will hear by Mother's letter that my Box arrived safely, so I need only say, "Thank you all, good folks." I am not fearful of abusing my stomach, at present, as, thus far, this seems impossible. I am sorry the nine months men, were so unwise, as to kill themselves, in so foolish a way, as this is. You impose a long task on me, and one, which I must decline, in part, when you ask the particulars of my captivity. It would be a history, tedious to me and you also. I must only give some minor outlines in writing, reserving the rest, till we are "face to face." "How sick I was" is a hard query to answer, as I do not know the grades of disease in technical terms, and have no means of showing it, by comparison. I was insensible, entirely, for five days; was given up, by the Surgeons: my estate was settled & my clothing divided, by the nurses & ward-master among themselves: articles to the value of fifty dollars, to me, were distributed in this way, and they were, luckily for *them*, paroled, before I got well enough to realize their rascality. I went to sleep Nov. 5th & my first recollection was of, on the 11th passing my hand over a blister, about "seven by nine," filled to the capacity of a qt. or more, on my Bowels. I thought this rather severe at the time, but have been told, since, by the Surgeon that that, was all that saved my life, so I do not complain. This was typhoid fever: after I got so as to be dressed, after this, diarhaea captured me and held me till I was as weak as before, and oh! how poor! "Shall we believe half of the newspaper reports?" To this I reply, read all the papers say, and then, if you can *believe* it, be sure, "the half is not told." Think of me as arriving in Richmond on Oct. 21st weighing 187 pounds. Then look at me Nov. 25th so reduced, so that I could, with one hand clasp any part of my other arm, from the wrist to the shoulder, except the elbow joint. Think of one, in this condition, with nothing to eat but *four ounces* of the coursest johnny-cake: *one ounce* of meat and *one gill* of rice soup, composed of 1 part rice and nine parts "James water": no money to garnish the diet, with palatable articles, owing to the rascality of fellow prisoners, the aforesaid Nurses.

During this time I became so infested with a sort of Vermin, vulgarly called *lice* that I was ashamed to say I was a "Yank." Is such a state calculated to increase ones *patriotism*, or *abolition principles*, when one knows all the time that the only reason our Government has for leaving us in such a condition, was a miserable quibble, about the "*exchange* Negroes?" I would not willingly endure this again, if I knew it would place every Negro in the Confederacy in our "Contraband Camps," for I know that ere they had been there three weeks they would wish to be sent back to "Massa" where they "did not have to do nothin." After this what answer shall I make, to, "does thee really think it thy duty to reenlist?" If my health were again good, which it is not, and probably *never will* be, I *should* think it my *duty* to serve my Country in *some* way, but I do not think it my duty to do it now, when, by doing so, I would only serve *myself* to the amount of $24— per. mo. when I can serve my country as well, if able to be at the front again and earn *myself $75*— per. mo. Am I less patriotic than three years ago?— Now follow more queries of a furlough; to these I need not reply as I have done so fully to mother. Please do not repeat them. But I am dragging along to a weary length, so I will close soon. I need not review the list of weddings as that would be a work of time, too. "Joy to 'em all" Our snow of Wednesday is most all gone, it is a wet dirty day. I too, should somewhat enjoy a shake, with Horace, and, if he comes out shall expect him to call on me here, on his way. The Vermonters, now in "Camp Parole," are all thriving nicely. Much love to all, I am ever;

Thy loving Brother:
W.B. Stevens

Chapter 13 Spring 1864

Lieutenant General Ulysses S. Grant brought a new style of warfare to the Army of the Potomac, one that relied on the use of superior force and the relentless pursuit of the enemy. Grant intended to fight an offensive war and he meant to bring as much force to bear as he could.[1] The result was the bloodiest, costliest campaign of the war.

To increase the strength of the Army of the Potomac, Grant reassigned the heavy artillery regiments in the forts surrounding Washington to duty as infantry units. Some of these oversized regiments, including the Eleventh Vermont (or First Vermont Heavy Artillery), numbered eighteen hundred men at full strength. The "Heavies" had suffered none of the hardships of battle and relatively little of the camp sickness that had depleted the infantry ranks. They would face a great deal of taunting from their new comrades for their easy-living past, but they were welcome nonetheless.[2]

The Seventeenth Vermont Infantry, finally in the field under Lieutenant-Colonel Charles Cummings, joined the Ninth Corps on April 25, barely a week before the start of the spring campaign. The last of Vermont's infantry regiments contributed only seven companies totaling 313 men in its first fight, due to recruiting difficulties, the high rate of desertion, and sickness caused by the sudden exposure to disease, hard marching, and army food.[3] Three more companies would eventually join the regiment.

General Grant's campaign began on May 4. His plan was to cross the Rapidan River at Germanna and Ely's Fords and move southeast, starting out as Joseph Hooker had done twelve months before. Grant's route through the eight-mile stretch of tangled forest called the Wilderness would follow the Germanna Plank road, then the Brock Road to points south. Things went well for the Union commander on May 4, as three corps safely crossed the Rapidan. The next day was another story. Robert E. Lee saw the opportunity to divide and rout Grant's

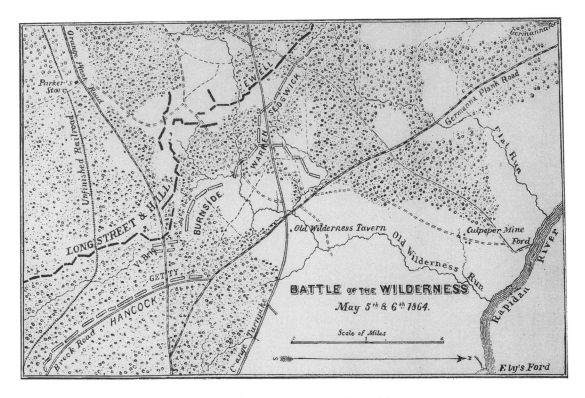

army while it was stretched out along fifteen miles of roads, and he ordered his three corps to attack along roads that intersected Grant's marching columns deep in the Wilderness.

The clash of armies in the Wilderness was cruel and desperate, and for none was it crueler than for the First Vermont Brigade. On the afternoon of May 5 the Vermonters advanced in two battle lines through the woods to the left of the Orange Plank Road to meet the approaching enemy force of A. P. Hill's corps. Fierce fighting soon erupted in the dense undergrowth. There was little advantage of numbers in the smoke-filled jungle, where an invisible enemy filled the air with lead. To remain standing for long was to risk almost certain injury or death. Companies lost contact with each other in the smoky undergrowth, and men stumbled into murderous cross fires. Officers attempting to direct and encourage their men were shot down in alarming numbers, but the Vermonters fought on. For five hours the battle flared, the Vermont Brigade advancing and falling back again, until darkness brought a merciful end to the carnage. A renewal of the fighting on May 6 took the Union force within musket range of General Lee's headquarters on the Plank Road, but Longstreet's corps arrived in time to stop the attack and fling it back to the Brock Road.[4]

The First Vermont Brigade losses were staggering. In two days of intense fighting, the Brigade lost 1,234 men, or nearly half its number. Colonels Newton Stone of the Second Vermont Infantry and Elisha

MAP 14. Detached from Sedgwick's Sixth Corps, the Vermont Brigade fought heroically to stop Hill's and Longstreet's advances along the Orange Plank Road. Benedict, *Vermont in the Civil War*, vol. 1, 416+. UVM.

Barney of the Sixth were killed, and Lieutenant Colonel John C. Tyler of the Second was mortally wounded. A majority of the brigade's company officers were killed or wounded. Not counting those who were absent due to sickness, the Fifth Vermont Infantry finished the battle with five captains and lieutenants, the Fourth with only three, out of a theoretical total of thirty each.[5]

The Army of the Potomac was badly beaten, but not routed. General Grant suffered more than seventeen thousand casualties in the Wilderness—ten thousand more than Lee. Most of the men expected this thrashing to be followed by another retreat, as had happened so many times in the past. But Grant did not intend to retreat. On the night of May 7, the Army of the Potomac resumed its march south, to the cheers of the blue-clad soldiers. In this march the heroism of the brigade did not go unnoticed. As the brigade took its position in the ranks of the Sixth Corps, George Benedict wrote, "the men nearest to it broke out into spontaneous and hearty hurrahs for the Green Mountain boys. The greeting was taken up by regiment after regiment and brigade after brigade in the line, as the Vermont Brigade moved past them, and its march to the left was made under a continuous round of cheers."[6]

The armies met next near Spotsylvania Court House. Rebel troops beat Grant's advancing columns to the strategically important village, and erected fortifications in a long, irregular semicircle. On May 12 the First Vermont Brigade took part in a concerted assault that targeted an angular salient of logs near the mid-point of the rebel works. Thousands of Yankees rushed over the salient, but could not hold the ground beyond for long. The battle degenerated into a bloody stalemate, with opposing ranks huddled on either side of the log works. For sixteen hours they fought, sometimes hand to hand, sometimes firing over or through the logs into the mass of men behind. Some jumped atop the works and fired rifles, relayed up to them in rapid form, at point-blank range, until they were themselves shot down. The carnage at the "Bloody Angle" marked a new and horrifying level of grim detachment from the work of killing.[7]

The fight on May 12 added another 254 casualties to the First Vermont Brigade's losses. The Seventeenth Infantry, engaged in a futile attack on the rebel left during the fight at the Bloody Angle, added 72 casualties to the 80 it lost in the Wilderness. The Army of the Potomac lost another 17,000 men—including Sixth Corps commander John Sedgwick, killed by a sniper on May 9. Seeing no advantage in continuing the fight at Spotsylvania, Grant once again moved the army around Lee's right, southward toward Richmond. Clashes occurred along the way on the banks of the North Anna and Totopotomoy Rivers as the armies maneuvered for position. Grant kept moving until he reached Cold Harbor, eight miles northeast of Richmond, in the midst of the battlefields of the 1862 Peninsula Campaign.

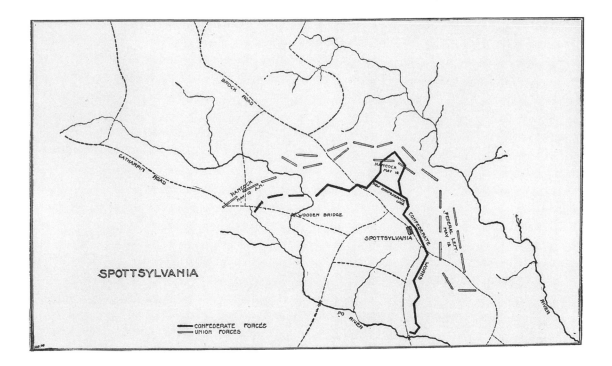

MAP 15. Fighting at the Bloody Angle lasted from before sunrise to after sunset on May 12, when the Confederates finished a new line that cut off the salient. Odell, *The Lives and Campaigns of Grant and Lee*, 443. UVM.

With each new position the rebels took up, their engineers improved the science of entrenchment. Lee had learned that strong entrenchments could more than even the odds against an enemy of superior numbers, though at the cost of limiting his own mobility.[8] The formidable rebel works west of Cold Harbor stretched seven miles south from Totopotomoy Creek to the Chickahominy River. On June 1, before this work had progressed far, the Sixth and Eighteenth Corps launched an attack on the right of the rebel line to gain better ground for the grand assault that was expected the next day. Here, the Tenth Vermont Infantry—recently transferred to the Sixth Corps—captured some rebel rifle pits, took hundreds of prisoners, and held its ground against repeated counterattacks. The Eleventh Vermont also experienced hard fighting for the first time, losing 120 men.[9]

General Grant ordered a frontal assault on the Cold Harbor entrenchments on June 3. Three infantry corps charged at dawn, but the rebels repulsed the attack in less than ten minutes. Thousands of Union soldiers lay dead or wounded on the field. Repeated orders to resume the futile charge were answered with increased firing, but no further advance, as the men hugged the ground wherever they could find shelter.[10] The First Vermont Brigade lost 104 men at Cold Harbor. The First Vermont Cavalry, meanwhile, as part of a force assigned to turn the rebel right flank to the north, fought a seesaw battle near Haw's Shop, where Colonel Addison Preston was killed.

The Cold Harbor entrenchments blocked the eastern approach to

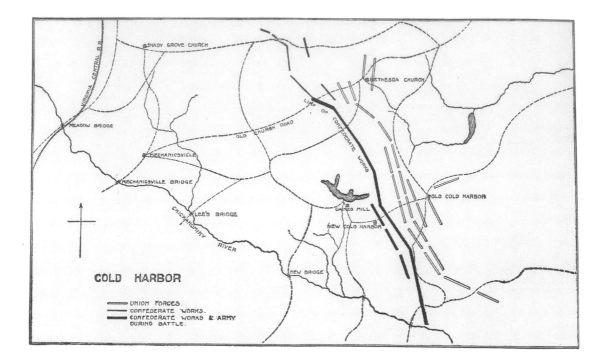

MAP 16. The futile charge at Cold Harbor, June 3, 1864, proved the value of strong entrenchments. Odell, *The Lives and Campaigns of Grant and Lee*, 474. UVM.

Richmond, but one opportunity to outflank the rebels still remained. If the city of Petersburg, twenty miles south of Richmond, could be captured, all but one of the rebel capital's railroad links would be cut off. Without a reliable supply route the Confederacy would be unable to maintain an army near Richmond for long. Accordingly, Grant ordered William F. Smith's Eighteenth Corps and Winfield S. Hancock's Second Corps to make a rapid assault on the stout but lightly-defended fortifications of Petersburg in advance of the main army. But at the critical moment Smith faltered. Having driven a handful of defenders from their first line of defensive works in the waning sunlight of June 15, Smith decided to wait for Hancock's troops, which had lost their way, before making the final assault.[11] Before long, rebel reinforcements began to arrive, and Smith's chance to "[walk] into Petersburg with bands playing" vanished.[12] The campaign against the Army of Northern Virginia now became a siege, with Union troops arrayed against a series of forts and trenches stretching between and around Richmond and Petersburg.

The Union effort for most of the next ten months would focus mainly on attempts to drive around the rebel right flank at Petersburg and cut off enemy supply routes. One of the first of these attempts resulted in another tragedy for the First Vermont Brigade. On June 23 several companies of the Fourth and Eleventh Vermont Infantry regiments were detailed to protect a party of men sent outside the Union lines to destroy a section of the Weldon Railroad running south from

Petersburg. Not long after beginning their work, the men noticed enemy troops advancing towards them. Repeated requests for support went unanswered. The enemy drew nearer, more time passed, and only one regiment arrived to challenge what appeared to be several brigades of advancing rebels. No other reinforcements arrived, nor were any orders given to retreat. Finally, after a brief fight, 401 Vermonters were surrounded and captured. Soon they were marching south, bound for the rebel prison camp at Andersonville, Georgia.[13]

"I doant think that Parker started many revivles in the armey as at least what you wrote is the first that I herd about it"

Private Tabor Parcher of Waterbury, Company B, Tenth Vermont Infantry, to his wife, Sarah, April 3, 1864.[1]

1. Tabor Parcher Papers, Manuscript Files, UVM.

3rd Div 6th Army Corps
Camp near Culpeper C H VA   April 3rd 1864

Dear Sarah

I will write you a few words to day seeing it is sunday & I have got my house remodelled over so it is pretty Cumfitable now   I received my box to day   evry thing come nice   but I would have liked more Sugar for it seames as to that you sent wont be half a taste but I will have to be contented with it   it seames as if you paid more than you nead to express on it for it did not weigh but 43 lbs & I thought they could send 50 lbs for $4.50 cts but it seams as t[h]ough they cannot how much did it cost you in the wholl for evry thing & how much money have you paid for stuff stamps & all to send to me since I came out here pleas will you tell me or near as you can   I think it must be near 25 dollars now & I doant know but what it is more but I supose you can tell very near & I wish you would as near as you can   the boys are building the officers some houses to day   they had none   it seams to bad to leave so good quarters as we did down thare & moove into such poor ones as we had to here   thare is no news to write   I did not find my files in my box for Jerome   he was some disapointed I wish I had got my box yesterday   if I had I could [have] had some waxed sugar for shore   was a plenty of snow but it is all gon now   it is quite warm to day the mud drying fast   wall now I will write a [l]ittle in answer to your last letters which I neglected to do in my last how sickly it is thare in Vt   if it was as sickly here in the armey as it is thare I doant know what we would do   I hope you & the boy (Parch)

2. John Minor Botts was a
prominent Unionist who kept a
plantation near Brandy Station.

will be well this spring   How does Rufe & Liddy get along with their
sparking   I wonder if George White got rich down to Washington   if
I was out of this I could make my fortune in 2 years   it is the greatest
place to make money thare is in the world   you wanted to know why
I doant say who goin to have baby   wall there is three girls that is a
goin to have babies that I know   *Hon* John Minor Bottss[2] Girl is a
goin to have one   she is a nice pretty girl of about 20 years of age
the safe guard knock[ed] her up   I wish it had been me   she was one
of the first girls in this vacinity before she got fucked & it doant make
much differance now   wall another is Sarah France   she lives near
the Picket line at Poney Mountain   She is about 3 1/2 months along
so she told me the last time that I see her   & the other is Alis Poland
she lives near the right of this divisions Picket line   she I am not much
aquainted with but I have seen her   I guess it is about as you say
they fuck so much that they cant have babies but thare is three girls
that I know near hear that wont fuck for money or love nor nothing
else & such a thing as the clap they are pretty much all free from it
thare is not half so meny of them got the clap hear as thare wer at Con-
rads Ferry or Rockville or eaven Brattleboro that was the rottenest
hole that ever was & so it was at Poolesville   but the clap is nothing a
man can [put?] fat on it but I supose it goze harder with women   wall
I doant know but what I have written enough of such stuff now but before I get through you will hear more of it   I wish I was at home now
I believe I would go up the brook & see what them nebraskey women
wer made of but I doant believe that I would drink much of [Menn's?]
rum for I doant like it very well   you say while the soldiers wer at
home you guess they got all they wanted   you doant think that a soldier would do such a thing as to screw do you   I doant think that
Parker started many revivles in the armey as at least what you wrote is
the first that I herd about it   I did not go to hear him while he was
here   I doant go to meating much   I have had a paper of the proced-
ings of town meeting so you will not nead to send eny   you nead not
fear of the Rebs goin into Maryland again this spring   nothing would
suit better   we had rather fight them thare than in the place they are
now   Lee is fortifing now as fast as he can but we may not go thare
you say you wanted a balmorial but I doant know what that is[3]   if
you want one I doant see why you doant get it   you think Deck looks
better than he are to [ought to?]   so do I   I am so fat a great deal fat-
ter than I ever was before   I weigh 180 pounds   I did not think I was
so fat untill I was weighed   wall I wont write eny more to night for I
have got to write to Ned so good bye

      Tabor

3. A balmoral is a Scottish cap,
petticoat, or heavy shoe.

"the Vt Brigade is all cut up"

Private Bradford P. Sparrow of Elmore, Company K, Fourth Vermont Infantry, to his family, May 13, 1864.[1]

1. Bradford P. Sparrow Papers, Manuscript Files, UVM.

Battle Field May 13th /64

Dear Parents & Brothers; I am permited by kind providence to live to see this day & write this letter, but I do not know as you will be permited [to] get it. It is awful times   I have been in a terrible battle & have been in considerable danger all the time for 8 days, but was not in the front line where I could shoot but one day, the 5th. I have not been hurt but am quite fatigued, the Vt Brigade is all cut up, I have thought of you & longed to write but no mail has gone from here untill this morning, my regiment . . . was away from the brigade & we knew nothing about it, but I write this to send the first opportunity, I suppose you [are] all suffering great anxiety by suspense & from expectation & uncertainty, My prayer is god will protect me & comfort you   I dont know how much longer this will last but I hope to see you again, Please send this picture of mine to Cousin Frances, may god watch over us all, Good Bye

> From your Son & Brother
> Bradford P. Sparrow

May 15   I am all right yet. the [   ] lays right beside us, it come this morning. I have had a good visit with the boys, the drafted men from Brattleboro came to day also, Ira was not hurt in the fight but is sick in the division hospital, Wm. Swift was killed the first day of the fight, Lenard & Luman Davis were both killed,

I dont know where I am now but between Fredirecksburg & Gordonsville I think

"It is all that I can do by hook and by crook to live ... but who cares if only we can win"

Lieutenant Colonel Charles Cummings of Brattleboro, Seventeenth Vermont Infantry, to his wife, Elizabeth, May 15, 1864.[1]

1. Charles Cummings Papers (MSA 28), folder 4, VHS.

Near Salem Church four miles from Fredericksburg May 15th 1864

My Dear Wife,

One week ago to-day I pencilled a few lines to you & forwarded them by Col Keifer to Washington, from thence to be mailed to you. I do not know whether you have received them or not. In either case I will recapitulate.

Wednesday May 4th we left Bristow & marched past Catlett's to Bealton four miles from Rappahannock Station. The next day we crossed the Rap[pahannoc]k river and marching southeasterly crossed the Rapidan at Germania Ford. marching two or three miles further we encamped for the night. At 1.30 A.M. Friday morning we renewed our march and soon after sunrise we were in line of battle. The 17th drove in a skirmish line in a short time and held the position until noon when we were withdrawn. In the forenoon we lost one killed and fifteen or twenty wounded; among the latter Capt Brown of Co. A., whose left arm was amputated in consequence thereof near the left shoulder. In the afternoon we were removed further to the left and about 2 P.M. we were hotly engaged with Longstreet's troops. It was in the woods where artillery could not be used; so the engagement was close and the musketry firing fearful. We made one charge on our own hook and carried one rifle pit but not being supported could not hold it, so were forced to withdraw ten rods. Soon after, while on one knee the better to discern the enemy and to direct the fire of my men (smoking my pipe meanwhile) a minie ball struck me on the right side of my head against my hat band. It cut a hole four inches long backwards & upwards—as my head was pitched forward at the time—and about two and a half inches long in my scalp. The blow did not make me reel but it bled with such profuseness from the breaking of a branch of the temporal artery that I concluded to go to the rear, thinking I might faint if I remained & then if repulsed I should fall into the hands of the rebels. My wound was bound up and I was sent to the Hospital in an ambulance, where my wound was dressed by Dr. Child of the 10th Vt—formerly Asst Surgeon of the 1st Vt. With other officers he dined at our house in Aug 1861.

The Regiment continued in the fight under Maj Reynolds until after dark, making considerable advance. The men fought splendidly The losses this day were 9 killed 61 wounded and 7 missing out of 313 guns and 20 officers that went into the fight. Capt Kenfield of Co. C was shot through the left arm and Lieut Martin of E through the right leg. The 1st Vt Brigade lost terribly in that fight, but they were on the right.

The 17th remained in position until Saturday morning when they were withdrawn. They marched to Chancellorville and encamped until Monday afternoon when I rejoined them. I was advised to go to Washington & remain until my wound healed but I would not consent. Monday afternoon we marched out on the Plank Road towards Fredericksburg and encamped until Tuesday noon. Then we marched southerly five miles rather towards Spottsylvania C.H., and arrived on the left of the general line of battle just as it was opening in that quarter. We lay in line of battle behind rifle pits that night, there being skirmishing all night long in front. Wednesday was much the same until four o'clock P.M. when we were moved to a new position. A long rain storm coming on and it then raining furiously[,] upon the advice of Dr. Edson I went to the teams in rear of the Hospital & have not been with the regiment since. I understand that at day-light the next morning the regiment was ordered forward with the rest of the brigade. Although it rained in torrents they drove in the enemy's skirmishers and then charged his rifle pits but unsuccessfully. Here the loss was great. I was in the Hospital assisting in dressing the wounds of my men as they came in as long as I could stand up, and the sight was fearful. The regiment continued fighting nearly all that day and part of the next, and my last report from the Adjutant was that there were less than 130 guns left. Certainly of all that went into the fight on the morning of the 6th nearly 3/5ths are killed or wounded! Some of the wounded must have fallen into the enemy's hands when we were forced to retire from that charge of Thursday morning. But the men have sustained the reputation of Vermont. They have not faltered, nor did they lose their colors as others did in the futile charge although they advanced as fast and as far.

The mortality among officers in these battle is fearful, but I do not know names well enough to particularize.

The army changed position yesterday to the left or east of Spottsylvania C.H., but the line of battle is advanced quite as much as heretofore. As a general result of last week's fighting the Union Army has taken 17,000 prisoners and nearly 50 pieces of artillery, while we have not lost but very few prisoners not re-taken say less than 1000 and but 3 guns. But here we are and there is some terrible fighting to be done unless Lee retreats which I do not apprehend.

The 11th Vt—my first regiment—reported to Gen. Meade yesterday. Mr. Crandall was well   he is 2nd Principal Musician

My wound is doing well   it will be healed in a week or ten days, but if the weather is good I shall resume command of my Rgt in a day or two.

I have not received but two letters from you—the last was handed me May 5th   It was dated May 1. To morrow a mail goes from here—the first allowed since the fighting commenced, & I have improved it to write you.

Do not give yourself uneasiness if you do not hear regularly from me for I shall be so situated that frequently I cannot write when I would nor send if I should write. It is not here as in our campaign of last summer   there are no post offices on the line of march   The country is so denuded that a lady could not exist, it is all that I can do by hook and by crook to live. Nothing can be bought   rations are cut down to a low figure, transportation reduced to three wagons to a brigade etc.—but who cares if only we can win.

My love to our dear children & to mother.

> Your loving husband
> I shall always remain
> Charles

FIGURE 52. Eri D. Wood-
bury. Special Collections,
Dartmouth College Library.

1. Eri D. Woodbury Papers,
folder 2, Dartmouth College.

"I thought this a savage initiation of a recruit"

**Private Eri D. Woodbury of St. Johnsbury, Company E,
First Vermont Cavalry, to A. J., May 17, 1864.**[1]

*Woodbury, an 1862 graduate of Dartmouth College, enlisted in the
cavalry in October 1863.*

Haxall's Landing James River Near
City Point, Va. May 17, 64.

A. J.

Have had no chance to send or receive mail matter till within day or
two since leaving Camp at Stevensburg two weeks ago. Started at midnight fortnight ago tonight. Sunrise saw us emerging from the ford of
the Rapidan & turning up the steep bank into Rebel territory in a
hurry: but little opposition met us that day. But on Thursday we
caught it in good earnest. At about 8 A.M. we were met by a strong
force of Cav. & Inf. at "Mine Run." This Co. & another were dismounted & placed behind fences, & in woods etc. as skirmishers. I had
taken position behind rail fence when one of our Co. came up on my
right & I moved about foot & half to left, he taking my place. In half
minute ball hit him in temple—& without a groan even he was "mustered out." His warm blood formed a little pool in which my knees
were steeped. Several balls cut through the rails in that very spot driving dirt into my face, but I was unharmed. After driving enemy into
woods & nearly two miles through them we fell back. I was covering
myself behind little tree, ten inches in diameter, when ball came *thud*
into opposite side of it. In the last charge made upon us by the Rebs my
horse was shot dead under me & we both went "*ker chug*" into bushes
by roadside. The Johnnys were too close at hand to allow of my stopping to take anything from saddle & so lost everything. I regret most
the loss of Port Folio & sewing materials. Meant to have written Sallie
to make & send me small needle book or bag etc. but forgot it when I
wrote & may not have chance again at present. If you write her tell her
of it.

After losing horse I did some tall travelling for about three miles before getting another; never so tired in my life & bare headed to boot, for hat was lost in a charge through woods. By the way the horse I lost was a Gov. one, as I had sold my private one. We lost from this Co. that day three killed & three wounded. I thought this a savage initiation of a recruit. Some other severe fights we had, one 3 miles from Richmond. In all this Co. has lost 3 killed, & five wounded.

Reached high bank on North side the James about four days ago. Very soon one of our Gun boats, mile off, began shelling us, but soon found out their mistake.

Wednesday morning, 18 May. Just there the bugle blew for saddling up. Left camp at 8 1/2 & arrived here about an hour ago: are stopping to feed & make coffee. Don't know where we are, but somewhere down the river for our course has been nearly parallel with it. May go to Yorktown & thence get transportation, or may not. Have been hoping that we might join Butler & Gilmore, then perhaps I could find Roger, but it does not appear likely to be the case at present.

For the last three days of our march before reaching the James we had no rations. I scarcely [ate] anything except corn sometimes raw, & again roasted; had coffee though. Got pretty hungry.

Don't know when I can mail this. Direct as heretofore.

> Yrs etc.
> Eri Davidson Woodbury

My health was never better,

"almost every one here has lost a brother or a dear friend"

Lieutenant Colonel Valentine G. Barney of Swanton, Ninth Vermont Infantry, to his wife, Maria, May 18, 1864.[1]

Barney's brother Elisha was colonel of the Sixth Vermont Infantry.

1. Valentine G. Barney Papers (MS 104), folder 3, VHS.

Newport Bks N.C.
May 18th 1864

My dear Wife

Yesterday your letter was recieved containing the sad inteligence of brother Elisha's death   I had seen in the Newyork Herald that he was wounded and had been in great anxiety for two days about him but I was not prepared to hear that it was a fatal wound and the news was almost crushing to me,   I had not seen him for nearly two years, which makes me feel worse,   this is the deepest affliction I have ever experienced   I at first almost felt disposed to murmur and to say that the lives of our noble and brave men had been sacrificed, but I soon felt that I was wrong and that perhaps it could not have been otherwise and perhaps the move in which he with so many fell was necessary to the saving of the day and the Union   I can hardly realize that my *dear brother* is gone, but know of course it must be so,   I have read your letter over & over and Oh! how my heart aches when I think I shall never see him more. The recollections of a thousand things comes up as [I] think over my past life and my associations with him. for the past day I have thought over more of my youthfull life than for years before, for that time was spent almost entirely with *him* who has given his life for his country, with him who was always *so* good, kind and noble—   It is consoling to know that he was so *perfectly prepared* to enter the next world and, that all on earth were his friends as well as all in Heaven. While I am mourning I can but think of Father, Mother and all my near and dear relatives at home. Oh I fear it will almost kill Father & Mother and as my tears flow It seems that I must fly to them that our tears might mingle together in sorrow for the Lost. I thought yesterday I would immediately request a leave of Absence and talked with Col Ripley about it but he thinks that at the present time it would be useless to attempt to get away & feared that Genl Butler might censure me for trying to get home when every thing looks so much like fighting,   We may not be called upon but no one knows when we will be called— And I hope if t'will aid in ending this wicked rebellion soon, we may start tonight,   I see by the list of casualties that nearly all my acquaintances are either killed or wounded who were in the Old Brigade—and what a feeling of sadness there must be throughout the whole state—and all over the Country in fact, but it seems that we have suffered more than any one else— I want you to write me all the particulars of Elisha's death and also of the funeral— It would be a great satisfaction for me to be there and to look upon the remains of my beloved brother but this is the fate of war— I while I am thinking and mourning of the loss of a brother I do not forget that there is one who mourns the loss of a Husband, and the best, or one of the best that the world ever knew— Oh! how she must feel, but I am glad to know she is a woman of nerve.—

A sadness pervades our whole Regiment and almost every one here has lost a brother or a dear friend. Many a prayer has assended for the fallen as well as for the success of our Army, and we shall continue till rebellion is crushed   I hope to hear from you in a day or two again, Kisses for the Children

Your Affectionate
Husband
V. G. Barney

"send me a little money so that I can acquire the bare necessities"

Private Louis Lavallée of Montreal, Canada East, Company B, Seventeenth Vermont Infantry, to Mr. Borkler, May 29, 1864.[1]

Lavallée was one of hundreds of Canadians lured into the Union army by generous bounties. He enlisted in the Seventeenth from Milton.

Lincol[n] General Hospital
Washington 29 Mai 1864

Monsieur Borkler,[2]

Je profite de ce que je suis a l'hopital pour vous annoncer que je suis blessé depuis le 6 de ce mois; et que je suis arrivé ici le 11; je suis dé-noué de tout par conséquient je vous prie de voulois bien me repondre au plus vite et de m'envoyer un peu d'argent pour me procuser les choses les plus necessaire. Veuillez faire savoir a mes parents que je suis ici et que j'esperc d'avois un farlot pour aller les voir, je compte sur votre bonté exacte pour m'envoyer ce que je vous demande, et je vous salue avec respect.   Votre devoué Louis Lavallée

Mon adresse:

>   Louis Lavallée (Pe) [Private]
>   Co. B 17th Vermont vol.
>   Lincoln Gen.l Hospital No 11
>   Washington

1. Louis Lavallée Letter (Miscellaneous File Additions), VHS.

2. "Mr Borkler,
"I'm making use of my stay at the hospital to inform you that I was injured on the 6th of this month; and that I arrived here on the 11th; as a result, I'm cut off from everything. I beg of you to please respond as quickly as possible and to send me a little money so that I can acquire the barest necessities. Please let my parents know that I'm here and that I hope to get a furlough to see them. I count on your unfailing kindness to send me what I'm requesting and I send you all due respect. Yours truly, Louis Lavallée"

"all my hopes in life are oer"

Margarett Scott of South Reading, Massachusetts, to her sister, Harriett, June 2, 1864.[1]

Margarett's husband, Erastus H. Scott, Company G, Third Vermont Infantry, was killed in action at Spotsylvania, May 12, 1864.

So. Reading June 2d

Sister Harriett

He is dead   I never shall see him again   Oh I cannot have it so all my hopes in life are oer   There is nothing but disappointment and trials in this Wourld   He was shot in the head and died instantly   oh

1. Erastus H. Scott Papers, Manuscript Files, UVM.

how like a knell it rings in my ears   I lay in a fainting condition most all night and am so weak in body and mind have pity on me   to think he lays on the Battle field far away without one moments warning and could not send no message to the wife he loved so well   My poor Mother is almost beside her self they all loved him so well

I cant write any more

Margarett

write your Father

"I am now in command of the Regt."

Major William Wells of Waterbury, First Vermont Cavalry, to his parents, June 4, 1864.[1]

1. William Wells Papers, carton 1, folder 32, UVM.

Camp near Salem Church Va
June 4th 1864

Dear Parents

Again the mail arrived and no letter from home, one from Martha & Sarah. glad to hear from them also one from Curt & Charley. the boy has enlisted for 100 days   am glad of it. he will now know wheather he likes it or not.

You no doubt get the news oftener than we do here   have not seen a paper dated later than May 30th.

You will no doubt learn before this reaches you of the death of our Noble *Col Preston*   he was killed on the skirmish line. he had just ordered me where to put my Battalion in line on our left. he says Maj don't allow your men to fire, for our men (from other Regt) are in your front   I saw nothing more of him untill I was informed that he was wounded in front of my line. several times I attempted to advance my lines to get his body but was driven back, but the third time I got his body off. he was just *alive*, not conscious, died about 15 minutes after we got posessin of him. he was shot in the left side near the heart. We also had a Captain killed Oliver F Cushman Co. E. he was instantly killed, one of the best officers in the Regt. beside one of the finest men, was very badley wounded in the face just 11 months before at Gettysburg— Two of the best officers our Regt had are *no more*. The Regt feels *sad*. their remai[n]s go to White House then home.

They were killed yestarday the 3rd at about 1 P M at Salem Church Same place that Genls Gregg & Custer had a fight several days ago.—

We Whiped the Rebs yestarday   I am now in Command of the Regt. have not mooved today. we are on the Right of the Army.

On the 1st we had a hard fight at Ashland Station   lost in killed wounded & missing 29 & two officers   Missing Lts Stone Co F & Mosher Co H.

My Battalion was s[e]nt out in advance 3 miles to wait untill the Brig came up—just as I reached Ashland I came up (at right angles) with the rear of the 1st Brigade   the Rebs were charging our men and driving pell mell. My Command was formed and I put them in   we drove the Rebs back and held them for 1/2 hour. perhaps it saved great many men from 1st Brig—   I lost one killed and six *wounded*   after this our Regt was put in dismounted and not supported. we were attacted by 3 Brigades, therefore were oblige[d] to fall back   in so doing some of our men were cut off.—

I do not know who is to take the place of Col Preston   expect that I can get the recomndatn of nearly all the officers, if I had a little help from home, or some friends in Vt   only one officer ranks me that is Maj Hall   he never has been in but one fight that was at Orange Court House in Summer 1862.

I shall not ask any one to help me. I expect Major Bennett will try for it as soon as he knows of Col Prestons death. Maj is in Vt wounded; Can you help me?

Love to all—

> Your afft Son
> William

My health is good

"it is as quiet as can be   how odd it seams   I cant write half so well as I can when the balls are whizing around my head"

Private Tabor Parcher of Waterbury, Company B, Tenth Vermont Infantry, to his wife, Sarah, June 7, 1864.[1]

1. The first part of this letter is in the Gertrude Mallary Collection, Bradford, Vermont; the second part is in the Tabor Parcher Papers, Manuscript Files, UVM.

6th Army Corps
on Skermish line in front of 1st Brig 3rd Div
June 7th 1864

Dear Wife

Seing I have got tired of shooting at the Johney Rebs & I have got a good holl dug in the ground for protection I will curl down & rest a while & I may as well be a writing as doing nothing   the little minneys go whistleing by & around me but the Rebs cant see me so if I get hit it will be by a chance shot   they take efect some whare evry little while but I guess they wont hit me   we are on the ground through hear that McCleland fought over   the trees are all full of ball holes & the tree tops are cut off by shell & sollid shott but the old ones are not so numerious as the new ones   I tell you whare the armeys go now they make a mark that will show for ages to come   never was thare such strong resistence on one side & such . . . strong determination to concor on the other side as thare is between those two great armeys they are boath determined to concor & one thing is sure if the union armey concors the rebs at this place & goes to richmond thare will not be much more fighting I believe & if the confedrate armey is successful in keeping us out of richmond & holding us at bay at this point than I doant see why all that we have done is just a Great loss but it doant seam possible that we have got to stop hear & I doant believed we have got to   I think grant will . . . put the thing further toward richmond but evry inch now has got to be contested & that strongly to but you know that Grant has got some first rate generals under him   General Mead is as good a generall as ever was in this armey   this armey never was in better spirets than they have been on this campaign   they know that Mead never was whiped & Grant never was whiped so that gives them great courage   the armey of the Potomac have not had so much as a wing turned or the center broke since the battle of Chansorville that was 13 months ago   you take an armey that has been successful in evry moove as long as the armey of the Potomac has been   why should they not have courage   wall the cannonaiding has comenced & the shells are flying so I will have to put up this for a while for they may be making a charge & I want to be prepared for them

wall the shelling has pretty much stoped but the mineys fly some but I doant care for them half so much as I do for the great shells & than have them burst & fly all around & over you & if a peace hits you you are pretty sure gon up   the Johny Rebs raised a flag of truce yesterdy & we replide to it   they wanted all fireing ceased for 2 hours & our general agreede to it so we went togather & some shook hands & swaped coffee & sugar for tabacco & exchanged papers & went togather & picked up their dead & bured them but did not bury them to gather & when the time was up they went back to their placces took down their flag & we done the same   than the fireing comenced as rappid as ever   they pitch on to us evry night some whare on the line generaly about 9 or 10 oclock   night before last they made a charge on our brest works & we let them up pretty close & then we opened a battery of grape & canestor & at the same time pourd in a volley of musketry & just piled the Johneys right up in piles   they wer glad to back off pretty quick   then last night they tride it again but a few well directed shells put them back pretty spry   it was about 12 last night when they tride it   Wall I can write a few moments in peace   all Hostilitys have ceased for 2 hours   no firing on eather side   it is as quiet as can be   how odd it seams   I cant write half so well as I can when the balls are whizing around my head   now you see I have been under fire so long that it seams real odd & quear   you wanted to know whose Picture that was wall it was Mary Stetch & now I will send you another   her name is Alzina Watts   I have several   I am a goin to send them home so if I ever get home I can look at them   they are all respectifull women enough   thare are a lots of women I am aquainted with   some have Pictires & some have not   wall I got your itty letter from you of June 1st & I got one from [Harry?] to d[a]y   I guess I wont write eny more this night   when the mail goes out I will send it

Tabor

"we have seen old Regts run but so far we have kept our place and gone where we were ordered"

First Lieutenant George G. Howe of Shoreham, Company B, Eleventh Vermont Infantry, to Lorette Wolcott, June 12, 1864.[1]

Near Cold Harbor Va.
June 12th 1864

Dear Lorette

It is Sunday and I must try and write a few lines to you   we have not had any So hard marches lately as we did when we first left Washington but we have been under a continual fire from the first dawn of day until after dark with occasionally a Shell at night   there are a great number killed and wounded by the Sharpshooters   there was one of Battery "G"[2] Shot through the body this morning   Battery "B" has been very fortunate   So far we have lost one killed Corpl. Henry H. Porter Shot in the Head and two wounded   quite a number are Sick but as a general thing we are as well as any of the Cos   this has been the most notable campaign of the war   the killed and wounded are reckoned by thousands   I was informed that there were fifteen thousand at Belle Plain at one time   I will not attempt to tell you anything about the movements as you know more about it than we do if you read the papers   the Major is all right. So is Walter. Ambroses Nephew. Sam Smith and all the Shoreham boys   it is just one month

FIGURE 53. George G. Howe. Vermont Historical Society.

1. George G. Howe Papers, Manuscript Files, UVM.

2. Some still referred to the Eleventh's companies as "batteries" though the regiment was no longer an artillery unit.

today Since we took the field and the old Soldiers Say they never had a harder time   when we first joined the Brigade a great many of the old Soldiers thought we could not Stand fire and they laughed at Heavy Artillery but they have Said nothing about our not Standing fire since the 18th of May   But they have said that when the 11th got into a place where it would run that they did not want to be there   we have seen old Regts run but so far we have kept our place and gone where we were ordered although (I *will* own to *you*) it was pretty tough Sometimes   Well what are you doing to day going to Church I Suppose wish I was there to go too   there is not much difference between Sunday and any other day here   how does Julia get along with her School and why dont She make up a dream if She is going to and write it to me   ask her if She cant dream it over again   tell her if She dont behave that She wont get any visitors to her School   has Lyd heard from Tom yet   I heard that he was wounded in the arm   there are Some Soldiers that skulk in the rear   there is no chance in front or at least not much of a chance and I have never heard that Tom Skulked   if any of the *Brave Men* of that Country think it is *funny* let them try it or else Stop their noise until they know whether there is any truth in the reports or not   I have Seen men higher in rank than any from Shoreham look for a *Safe place*   You would laugh if you could See where I am while writing this   it is in the woods behind a Breastwork   there is a place about 7 feet long and five ft wide and 18 inches deep dug in the ground a log at each end and Banked up one Side   it is covered by half a tent and a Rubber blanket to keep the Sun out   well in this *hole* are Walter & your humble Servant both writing   you and Emelie are getting to be fast friends are you not   well I am glad of it   you must have just as good times as you can   do you hear from Mrs Hall often how do they like their new home

Thank you Dear L for all your kind wishes   I hope Soon to be able to See you but we cannot tell what will happen   I pray God to give me Strength of mind and body to do my duty and having done all to be permitted to return to my friends once more

this is not a very good place to write letters and I know you will excuse anything that may seem wrong believing it to be (as it certainly would be) a mistake   there is So much talking, guns firing with the occasional Bursting of a Shell that it is rather hard to write much of a letter   Remember me to all the good folks and Believe me to be now and Forever

      Your George

one kiss

here is a Secesh Postage Stamp   dont you want to write Jeff Davis

write soon   Bye

"Try my dear child to bear this crushing affliction with the fortitude & resignation of a christian"

Rachel B. Stevens of East Montpelier to her daughter Ann, June 27, 1864.[1]

East Montpelier 27th of 6th mo. 1864
My darling Ann

I wrote to thee yesterday feeling a good deal of hope that our precious Willie would be yet spared to us—but how can I tell it to thee? to night I received a letter from the Chaplain of the 3rd div. Hosptal Alexandria stating that on the 12th instant a Steamer arrived at that place, loaded with wounded men from the front—nine of these died on the passage—among the number was one—Sargt. Wm B. Stevens—he says, "at the time I was told that the post office address of these men was not known, but last night (which was the 23rd) the surgeon of the branch hospital, where the bodies were laid till buried, brought to my room for deposit a package of valuables belonging to deceased soldiers —and among them is one marked Serg. Wm B. Stevens, & a letter is with it sealed as though ready for the office, directed to R. B. Stevens"— he then informs what course we must take to have them sent to us— Why did *he* the chaplain not send the letter at once? I think he must have written it after he was wounded—for I got the enclosed letter dated the 8th & the paper said he was wounded on the 9th— Try my dear child to bear this crushing affliction with the fortitude & resignation of a christian— I would gladly pillow thy throbbing head upon my aching bosom tonight—but the time will soon come when I hope we may meet— Mary is writing to the Chaplain for all the particulars he can give & also in relation to having the remains brought home
As ever thy very own loving mother R. B. Stevens

FIGURE 54. Rachel Stevens. Rokeby Museum.

1. Rokeby Museum, Robinson Family Papers, box 15, folder 17, Sheldon.

"my company is gone to Richmond and all of the officers with them"

Private James Frank Drenan of Woodbury, Company L, Eleventh Vermont Infantry, to his mother, June 28, 1864.[1]

Drenan's brother John was a lieutenant in Company L.

1. John S. Drenan Papers, Lewis Leigh Collection (book 8, 17), MHI.

FIGURE 55. John S. Drenan, brother of James. Vermont Historical Society.

Camp on the Weldon Railroad
June 28th 1864

Dear Mother

Think I will try and answer your letter   Mother I am lonesome to day   no one with me   my company is gone to Richmond and all of the officers with them   one of our men got a way from them   he sed it made John swear some when he had to throw Down his sword   our Cap and three Lieutenants are taken prisoners. Mother you must take this as cool as possible for if the rebs fight like this they will get the whole [Union] armey   I have got all of John's things all of his letters and everything but mother he is a prisoner   they took all of our company but 19 men but they did not get me   all I have to do is to take care of their things and [   ] my old pack Horse things   Mother John has had rather hard luck   he has been wounded twice   he had just come back to his company   he had the officers good will   he had the officers offer of going to the general Hospital but he did not want to and now he is worse than Dead I think   hope he will be exchanged before long but he may not   Mother I have sent home three or four [times] and you have not sent me any [stamps] yet   cant writ as often as I would if I had stamps.

Mother . . . we had 17 hundred men when we started from Washington and we have got eight hundred left   [   ] we are going on picket when the Rebs [   ]   Send me some [stamps?] won't you   I opened the letter that you sent John   Frank

Summer 1864

Chapter
14

The high cost of the war in lives and money caused growing dissatisfaction in the North as spring turned to summer. With no decisive results to show for the spring's terrible toll, President Lincoln's chances for reelection looked bleak. Republican Party leaders discussed finding a new candidate—even after Lincoln's renomination in June—to face the likely Democratic candidate, George McClellan. In fact, Southern hopes throughout the spring and summer rested on the possibility that Lincoln might be defeated, and a more flexible man, willing to negotiate a settlement, elected.[1]

The Vermonters captured at the Weldon Railroad on June 23 soon joined thousands of other Yankee prisoners at Andersonville Prison. The population of this twenty-six-acre stockaded campground swelled to thirty-three thousand during the summer, thanks to the stalemate over prisoner exchanges. Lack of food and medical attention resulted in great suffering and death among the prisoners, as it did in the smaller prison camps at Florence, South Carolina, and Belle Isle, near Richmond, Virginia. Photographs of paroled prisoners reduced to skin and bones by malnourishment and disease shocked the North. A century later, these images, and the tales of brutality recorded by survivors after the war, conjure up the horrors of the Holocaust. Yet it was a failure of planning, policies, and resources, not deliberate cruelty, that caused the suffering at Andersonville. Nevertheless, the suffering was real. Twenty-nine percent of the prisoners died, and of those who survived, a great many never regained their health.[2]

Grant's efforts to outflank the rebels south of Petersburg continued in the last week of June. General James H. Wilson led a five-thousand-man cavalry raid south and west of Petersburg starting on June 22, while two infantry corps prepared to extend the Union lines to the Weldon Railroad. Wilson's men inflicted heavy damage in the rebel rear, tearing up sixty miles of railroad track, burning bridges, and destroy-

FIGURE 56. Andersonville
Prison. Asa B. Isham,
*Prisoners of War and
Military Prisons*, 280+.
UVM.

ing tons of supplies. On the return trip, however, Wilson was trapped
and surrounded near Reams Station, ten miles south of Petersburg on
the Weldon Railroad. The greater part of the cavalry fought its way
out to safety, but Wilson lost fifteen hundred men and abandoned all
of his wagons, artillery, and two hundred wounded men. The First Vermont Cavalry lost ninety men in Wilson's Raid, most of whom were
taken prisoner.[3]

The Petersburg offensive came to a standstill in July as military leaders pondered how to break through or outflank the rebel defenses.
General Ambrose Burnside thought he had the answer. He forwarded
to headquarters a proposal to dig a mine under a vulnerable part of the
rebel fortifications, fill it with explosives, and blow a hole wide enough
to get a large force of troops into the rebel works. Burnside received
approval to go forward, using his own Ninth Corps troops as miners
and assault force. The digging took less than a month, and by the end
of July all was ready.

The explosion of the mine at daybreak on July 30 blew a crater two
hundred feet wide from side to side and sixty feet into the rebel fortifications. Thousands of Burnside's men were poised to rush in—including the Seventeenth Vermont Infantry, now reduced by casualties and
sickness to 120 men. But lack of preparation and coordination, and
poor field leadership doomed the assault. The attackers failed to secure
the rifle pits on either side of the crater or, beyond it, the high ground
that the panicked defenders abandoned after the explosion. Before
long, the rebels returned to these commanding positions and found the
crater packed with Union soldiers, leaderless and with no clear idea
where to go. Finding shelter as best they could, the Northern soldiers
traded fire with increasing numbers of the enemy until the futility of
the affair became apparent to the Union commanders. Ordered to
abandon the crater, the men had to run a gauntlet of fire, and some

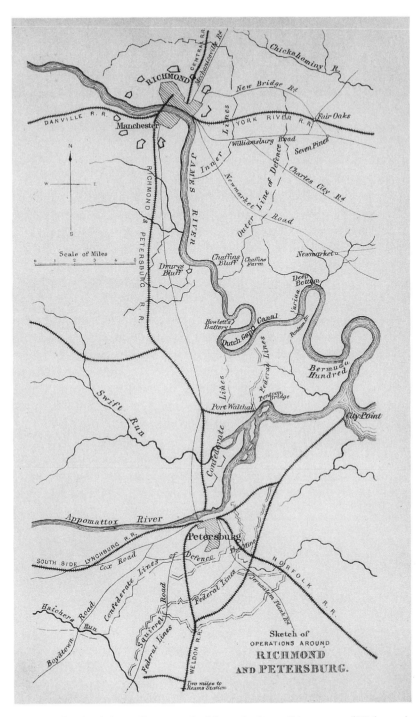

MAP 17. The Confederate lines stretched from the James River, west of Richmond, to Hatcher's Run, southwest of Petersburg, a distance of some thirty-seven miles. Fletcher, *History of the American War*, vol. 3, 259. UVM.

4,000 were shot down or captured. Of the 120 men from the Seventeenth Vermont in the battle of the Crater, 74 were killed, wounded, or captured. Out of eight officers present for duty only one, mortally wounded, returned.[4]

As the Petersburg offensive stalled, the war heated up once more in the Shenandoah Valley of western Virginia. In mid-June General Lee sent Jubal Early to the Valley with ten thousand troops to drive out an invading force of fifteen thousand Yankees under David Hunter, whom the Southerners despised for his vindictive destruction of civilian property.[5] Hunter, preparing to attack Lynchburg, thought better of it when he discovered Early's presence, and the Yankees retreated westward. This left the Shenandoah Valley open to Early, who quickly moved north toward Maryland. By the end of the first week of July, Early stood on Northern soil, with hardly a blue-clad soldier between him and Baltimore or Washington.

General Grant responded to Washington's urgent appeals for help by ordering the Sixth Corps north. The Third Division went first, arriving in Baltimore on July 7. From Baltimore the division, including the Tenth Vermont Infantry, marched west to Monocacy Junction to join a scratch force of two to three thousand men, mostly Home Guards and hundred-day militia, under General Lew Wallace. By confronting Early at this Monocacy River crossroads, some thirty-five miles west of Baltimore and an equal distance northwest of Washington, Wallace hoped to delay an attack on either city.[6]

The battle of the Monocacy began around noon on July 9. The result was never in doubt, as Early's veterans outnumbered the defenders, many of them untrained, by a wide margin.[7] Judging the Union front too strong—the men in blue held two bridges across the river, protected by a stubborn picket line of Vermonters on the west bank of the river—Early forded the river to the south, and attacked the Union left flank. Several charges on the Sixth Corps defenders were repulsed, but finally the line collapsed. All who could fled eastward toward Baltimore. The defenders lost twelve hundred men, including sixty-one members of the Tenth Vermont Infantry.[8]

Early pressed on toward Washington the next day, hoping to find the capital undefended. Battle fatigue combined with the summer heat and dust, the result of an unusually prolonged dry spell, slowed the rebels' march. Hundreds fell out, and when Early arrived at the outskirts of Washington at midday on July 11, only a fraction of his force was present and fit for battle. He knew he would have to wait for morning to attack, but before long even this hope was dashed, as a cloud of dust raised by marching columns in the city informed him that he had lost the race. The First and Second Divisions of the Sixth Corps had landed at the Potomac docks and were marching up Seventh Street toward Fort Stevens, Early's intended point of attack. After some skirmishing the next day, the rebels withdrew under cover of darkness toward the Shenandoah.[9]

The pursuit of Jubal Early's army began slowly, but in greater strength than the force Wallace had scraped together at the Monocacy. The Nineteenth Corps, recently reassigned from the Gulf Department, joined the Sixth Corps for service in western Virginia. The Eighth Vermont Infantry, after laboring in the humid heat of the Mississippi Valley for two years, now found itself marching in the dry, dusty heat of Virginia as part of the Nineteenth Corps. This force was combined with Hunter's army and put under the command of General Philip H. Sheridan, one of U. S. Grant's favorite officers. Sheridan's mission was to keep Early at bay, to destroy him if possible, and to confiscate or destroy as much of the crops and livestock of the valley as possible, in an effort to deprive the rebel armies of subsistence.[10]

Sheridan struck Early at Winchester, in the Shenandoah Valley, on the morning of September 19. Despite determined resistance, and a counterattack that threatened to drive a wedge through the center of the Yankee force, the rebels gave way in the afternoon. A cavalry charge on the rebel left flank added panic to the retreat, and the Southern soldiers fled all the way to Fisher's Hill, twenty miles to the south. Early lost four thousand men at Winchester.[11] His luck was no better at Fisher's Hill, a seemingly unassailable position near the northern extremity of Massanutten Mountain. Late in the afternoon of September 22, the Eighth Corps (formerly Hunter's men), which had worked its way undetected to the west of Fisher's Hill, fell suddenly upon the rebel left flank. Once more, the Southerners fled in panic, losing fifteen hundred men as prisoners and fourteen cannon.[12]

By the end of summer it began to appear that General Grant's strategy was finally beginning to pay off. That perception derived from a series of victories, including William T. Sherman's capture of Atlanta in early September, David Farragut's naval victory in Mobile Bay, and Sheridan's smashing triumphs in the Shenandoah Valley. President Lincoln's reelection prospects also staged a remarkable turn-around. Republican leaders who had conspired to find a stronger candidate in the summer now embraced him.[13] One more major victory before November would seal the election.

"It was such a time as we never saw before, it was a regular skedaddle"

Private Henry P. Burnham of Williamstown, Company G, Tenth Vermont Infantry, to his sister, Emma, July 8–12, 1864.[1]

1. Henry P. Burnham Papers (MSB 30), VHS.

Frederick City Md. Jul 8th 1864

Dear Sister Emma

Perhaps you will wonder how my letter came to be dated at this place, but I can tell you in a few words. it is simply because we are here and that is the most I can tell you about it. But in the first place I am well and hope [these] few lines will find you all the same. I have not had a letter from home this week, and perhaps I shall not get any before next week on account of our coming up here, but we have got to move so I must stop for now. Monday noon. I have just got round to write a little more. We are now near the Relay House nine miles from Baltimore. But to commence where I left off the last letter, I think that I finished it Saturday the 2d. Sunday morning I went on picket and stayed three days. evrything was quiet while we were out, but Wednesday morning about daylight we had orders to be ready to move immediately and Report said we were going to Harpers Ferry but we did not hardly credit the report. but between four and five we started. when we got up to camp we found that the rest of our Div had already started for City Point to take the boat so we started after them. it was 12 miles, and it was very warm and the dust was anywhere from 3 inches to half knee deep, and you may guess that it was hard marching, besides we marched pretty fast. I do not recollect what time we got there but I think not far from noon. We got aboard the boat about three oclock and started about four. We sailed all night. (there was only our Div.) We reached Baltimore thursday afternoon at four o'clock (making a ride of 24 hours, we stayed on the boat until one oclock, then we landed and took the cars. we started for Frederick City on the cars about three oclock in the morning (friday)   we reached there about 9 1/2 oclock   we marched through the city and stopped and got dinner, and there was where I began this letter   when I left off, we started and . . . marched out through the city and back again two or three times, and about eight oclock we started for Frederick Junction (where we were a few days one year ago)   we could have gone there by going three miles but instead of that they took us around as much as ten miles. we reached the Junction about 12 oclock at night (friday) (I forgot to say that the rebs were up this way and there was a small fight near Frederick thursday)   Saturday morning we moved round some and got into position and we sent out some pickets, and soon after skirmishing commenced and soon George Poor came in wounded, he was hit in the right arm just below the Elbow. it broke one bone certain dont know . . . whether it did both or not   this was sometime middle of the forenoon. the rebs soon began throwing shell and soon the fighting began in earnest. we did not get into it much before noon, but the rebs had much the larger force, the most artillery (we had only seven pieces) and the best position, and take it all in all they were too much

for us. I heard it said they had 26,000 and I dont think we had over 6,000, the rebs had three or four lines of battle and we had only one in the afternoon we had some hard fighting, neither side had any entrenchments, and we were in plain sight of each other and all we had to do was to stand up and shoot at them as fast as we could. I never want any better mark to shoot at than I had that day. I dont know as I hit any one but I done the best I could to shoot them   we fought until about four oclock when we found they had got us nearly surrounded and were going to gobble us all up if we did not leave. then we began to fall back and the rebs followed us and took a good many prisoners. we had a hard time of it for it had been a very hot day and we had been having some hard fighting and the boys were most played out. the whole Div was all scattered evry where, some went one road and some another, but we all went the same way, toward Baltimore, some went on the rail road and some by the other road. It was such a time as we never saw before, it was a regular skedaddle. I came down the rail road with five others from my Co.   we came fifteen or twenty miles on foot and then we found some hand cars and we put them on the track and came 35 or 40 miles in that way. (there was about thirty of us together in the whole. we traveled most all night. we got down to Ellicotts mills (15 miles from Baltimore) about noon Sunday. there was where our Div. came together. that night we came down here to the Relay House. today is Tuesday, and some of the boys did not get in only today and some have not got in yet, and I presume they will not for there was a good many taken prisoners, and a good good many killed and wounded. Our Division lost pretty heavy but I dont know how many, some more of the missing ones may come in yet, I dont know how many our Regt lost. our Co had two wounded and two missing. I expect there is considerable excitement in Baltimore and Washington. it is said [they] have a force of 40,000 and are within a few miles of W. they have been within four miles of Baltimore and burned the Gov. house, I suppose the rest of our Corps have come up and some others   it is thought by some that lee's whole army is coming up this way but I hardly think he would leave Richmond when Grant is so near to it, but if he does come up here I hardly think he will make much out of it in the end. it is reported tonight that they are fighting at Washington, and take it all around it is quite a time I reckon. It seems almost like getting home to get back here again, where it is civilized. the grain and hay is nearly all cut here and some of the wheat is got in. the folks are very good here when we were coming back the other day from the fight   they would give us bread and anything they had. they bring pies and such things into camp here evry day, but the trouble is we have no money. I wish they would pay us off now. I got [Lauras] last letter yesterday morning very glad to get it and to hear that you were all well.
I dont think of much more to write this time. I should like more stamps

for I have let most of mine go for change, for I did not have any money. if you have not got my last letter I wish Father would send me a couple of dollars in money. it has been so long since we have been where we could get anything that now we want to get something to eat bsides hard tack, but I dont think of much more this time. the Williamstown boys what there is here are well. there is only three Badger Wise and myself. [ ] is sick in the hospital at Baltimore. but I will close now, write often, much love to all from your brother Henry P. Burnham

Wednesday afternoon evry thing is quiet I wish if Father has got the money and he can spare that he would send me 2 or 3 dolls more when you get this letter. I presume he will send what I wrote for before, before you get this and I should like some more, and I hope we shall get paid off some time and then I will send home some money

Henry

"they got up within ten rods of us and told us to surender but I for one could not see the poin[t] and so you know I run like the old scrach"

Corporal Thomas Wiswall of Hyde Park, Company I, First Vermont Cavalry, to Vernon Fitch, July 9, 1864.[1]

1. Fitch Family Papers, carton 1, folder 16, UVM.

City Point Va. July 9th/64

Friend Vernon

I will try and answer your letter which I received just as we came of Wilsons raid and a hell of a time we had on that raid   I tell you it was the toughest soldiering I ever saw since I was a soldier   we started out the twenty second of June and got bac the second of July and we wer fiting every day all most and in the sadel almost [all] of the time [except] when we wer burning railroad and then some of us wer fiting we burnt all most sixty miles and lots of mills and mashine shops   you canot imagine how much damage we done Jef Davis and his people well Vern I am a good mind to stop just here to pay you for not writing more to me but I will tell you some more   well coming bac we got suround[ed] and had to fite all night   we lost our Capt and ten men from Co (I) and the Regt. lost some one hundred and fifty or two hundred and we left all of our artilery and Wagons and Ambulances and all of those wounded and there was nearly a hundred   if I ever was glad of any thing it was that I was not wounded to be left to the tender mercies of the rebs but they came just as near geting me in the morning they got up within ten rods of us and told us to surender but I for one could not see the poin[t] and so you know I run like the old scrach and there was four of our Co. came out   Will Hall and I wer to gather and the rebs chased us and we put to the woods and we got seperated and I came up to some of the led horses and got one but Will was not so lucky for he was in the woods thre days but came in all right   you ask if I ever hear from Cook   I never have but would like to first rate and we have some 68 from our Co Just the same as Cook no one knows any thing of them   all of us Hydepark boys are all right only Hac is wounded slightly but is with us and we are having good times now nothing to do but to take care of our horses and slep but it is the hotest weather I ever saw   O did you have a good time the fourth and where did you spend the same   well it is time to go to bed and I will close for to night

July 10th Sabath eve   perhaps you would like to know how we spend Sunday   well I have been down to the river and wash myself all over and two of us picked ten quarts of Blackbries and hade a nice super and at five our Chaplain preached to us and all of the men in the Reegt wer out to hear him and now I am writing to you   it is very hot and dusty here now   we have not had any rain for almost two months and every thing is dryd up to a terible degre   please write soon   I remain as ever your Friend

     Thomas

"I am well but A Prisnor of war"

Private Henry H. Lewis of Woodstock, Company H, Eleventh Vermont Infantry, to his parents, July 14, 1864.[1]

1. Henry H. Lewis Letter (Miscellaneous File 241), VHS.

July 14th 1864
Camp Sumpter Andersonville
Georga

Dear Parants   it is with Plaseure that I seat my self to write you A few lines to let you know that I am well but A Prisnor of war   Leander Sabin John Brow Phillip Dupheney and half of our company moses is all wright and george Shattuck   I want you to write to me as Soon as you get this   Send me my wifes picture   tell her to write Send me A box as soon as you get this and Send me Stuff that wont Spoil   Some tobaco pipe and Some tin dishes cup pail plate knife fork

and Spone   everything   my pants 2 shirts coat some Shoes Stockings Blanket 2 pound of tea and all the coffee you are A mind to   Suggar peper Salt Soda Spider pocket knife A bottol of whiskey or rum for Sickness   A large cup and Small one   A Butcher knife Spone tin dishes all of them   2 quart pail and 6 quart   Send A lot of Each kind write A good letter to me   dried apple vittiles that will keep and what Els you are A mind to   A bottol of Pepper Saus   be shure and Send them   A hat or cap to   Send my old cloths to me
fine cut tobaco to   ginger   A bottol of vinegar pickels and A good ham   A pickled one   medicine to   So good By

direct to Henry H. Lewis   11th Vt. Regt
Prisnor at Andersonville Georga

Lewis Bourdo is here

some onions

"It is hard, terrible"

1. Charles Cummings Papers (MSA 28), folder 4, VHS.

Lieutenant Colonel Charles Cummings of Brattleboro, Seventeenth Vermont Infantry, to his wife, Elizabeth, July 31, 1864.[1]

After the Sixteenth Vermont Infantry was mustered out in August 1863, Cummings was appointed to the same rank in the Seventeenth. The regiment, with only seven companies, was not allowed to muster a full colonel, so the command devolved upon Cummings.

Near Petersburg Va., July 31 '64

My Dear Wife:

Last week I received two letters from you and this morning two Harpers. Yesterday there was another severe fight with great losses in our corps & nothing accomplished. At 4:30 a.m. that mine was exploded & a terriffic bombardment commenced under cover of which we assaulted & carried a portion of the rebel line. But in our new position we were subjected to such a murderous fire from front & both flanks that in the end we were compelled to fall back with terrible loss. The 2nd Brigade is all cut up. Every officer comdg a regiment is either killed, wounded or a prisoner. The 17th went out with 8 officers including Maj. Reynolds commanding, & not one returned to the regiment. The Major & two Lieutenants were killed, one wounded & four taken prisoners. Out of about 100 men we have lost 41 to wit: 1 killed, 17 wounded & 21 missing some of whom are undoubtedly dead oth-

ers wounded and all who are alive prisoners. The adjutant just returned and two Surgeons are all the Commissioned officers present for
duty. It is hard, terrible.

My health is miserable. I have a Surgeon's certificate for a leave of
absence but I cannot use it in the present deplorable condition of things.
I *must* get the regiment in some shape before applying for leave. If I can
succeed you may expect me home for a brief period next week—say
two days hence.

I completed my ordnance returns yesterday, but I was obliged to
work on them when I ought not to for there was not a man in the regiment when the Adj't was away equal to ordering clerical duty.

Yet I am as well as I was a week since, or at least can do as much
work sitting still, but I cannot move about much. I had one day 23
bloody discharges. These I have succeeded in checking.

We have 60 men for duty in the regiment and 550 in the Brigade.
Griffin[2] feels badly & rumor fixes considerable stigma on him. The
general particulars you will get in the newspapers,

Love to all the family,

   Your loving husband
   Charles

2. Brigadier General Simon
Griffin of New Hampshire,
commanding Cummings's
brigade.

"We were fed and directed on our road by negroes always with the greatest apparant gladness"

**Captain Darius J. Safford of Morristown, Company L,
Eleventh Vermont Infantry, to his sister, August 2, 1864.[1]**

Morrisville, August 2, 1864.

Dear Sister,

I am disappointed tonight or I fear you would have to wait till tomorrow for your letter to be written. I expected Susan in to night and
she did not come. She is at Massina Springs Ny   I telegraphed to her
yesterday to come & hoped she would come tonight surely but she did
not. I got to Cambridge Sat about 12 at night came here yesterday
morning and as soon as she comes shall go to Troy if she is able & see
father and mother. I suppose of course you are anxious to hear how I
made my escape so I will give you a little information. Was taken June
23d in the evening 5 miles below Petersburg (got no food from that
time till the 26th about 11 a.m.). Were taken to Richmond by R.R. on
the 25th & incarcerated in Libby— Was robbed of field glass haver-

FIGURE 57. Darius J. Saf-
ford. Vermont Historical
Society.

1. Sherman-Safford Family
Papers (MS 23), VHS.

sack sash & $19. in greenbacks by Confederate government. Rations for a day, a piece of cornbread 4 in long & 2 in square, a piece of wormy bacon as large as two of my fingers & 1/3 pint bean soup—very small but better than none & would probably keep soul & body together & we were glad to get it. Plenty of soft water running in the prison all of the time & a trough to bathe in in each room. Left Libby June 29th for Macon Georgia taken by R.R to Lynchburg where we found Sheridan had destroyed such means of travel & we were to foot it to Danville some 75 miles. First night traveled 4 1/2 miles did not see any good chance to get away; next day marched 20 miles and crossed Staunton River and halted   between 5 & 6 P.M.   our guard was composed entirely of boys from 15 to 17 and old men from 45 to 60 years old and they got very tired indeed so they could hardly go, as the day had been oppressively warm, and they took more pains to rest themselves than to secure the prisoners so as soon as the colum halted Lt. Griswold of L Lt Fleury of K and myself took our cups and went down to the river to drink apparantly but when we had done so we kept on down the bank of the river as fast as we could in the willows which grow very thick on the bank, for some 700 yards till we came to a short bend in the river which hid us from sight of the turnpike and then we forded the river back to the side we came from, we got into some laurel bushes on that side and lay still till after dark (it was between 5 & 6 P.M. we got away) and then went up the river bluffs and over woods swamps & fields nearly a mile & lay down and kept still all that night and the next day— About night next day I went out to where a colored man was at work in the field & asked him if he would help us and he said he would and told us where to come after dark. we went there and he had all the warm corn bread we could eat and then he showed us into the turnpike and we went back over the same road we had travelled before some 11 miles & then struck off from the road to the N.W. and kept that general course all the way only when we had a guide when we went as he directed us of course. We were fed and directed on our road by negroes always with the greatest apparant gladness & none of them ever proved false to us in any way I think. We found Union people after we had been on the road about ten days and they assisted us all they could but had to be very careful in doing it for fear the rebs, would find them out in so doing and destroy their property. There are a great many Union men in the mountains of Virginia even yet and the mass of the common people would be glad to have them submit to the rule of the United States to day but the aristocracy say no and they are the ones who rule in the Confederacy. We found a great many deserters from their army in the mountains of the Blue Ridge and Alleghany Mts. and three of them came through the lines with us and were of great assistance as they knew the roads better than we did. We were pursued and fired upon by the Provost guard of Bath

County at Millboro but none of us were injured   we seperated there however and each took a seperate course to avoid capture and I have not seen Lt. Griswold since. Lt. Fleury came into our lines at Beverly W. Va. twelve hours before I got there and we only stayed about twelve hours after I got there. I confidently expect Griswold will get through but he may not.[2] I was 22 days on the road and travelled 260 miles in getting away and am very tired and pretty much used up but guess two weeks rest will bring me around all right. I wish I could see you but am afraid I shall not be able to this time   my stay is so short and Susan's being away makes it seem shorter after she gets here—   I am not as fleshy into near 50 pounds as I was when you saw me last but I did not loose it all since I was take[n] prisoner only about half of it I think. I consider myself extremely fortunate in getting away as easily as I did. I did not go over one day at any time without having something to eat, sometimes not enough and sometimes not very palatable but still so it could be eaten. The care and anxiety wore more upon me then the fatigue of the march did. I think that God has us in his especial care & keeping or we never could have made our way through the enemy's country where we did with no more trouble than we did— How is your health now? How long do you think of staying there? When you write tell me all about it and write me a good long letter as soon as you get this   if I can get it by the 15th direct to Cambridge & if not to Washington as usual.

I can write no more now.

Remember me to Alva   Your Brother

D J Safford

2. Lieutenant Edward F. Griswold of Company L was paroled in September, according to Peck (*Revised Roster*, 431), which suggests that he was recaptured.

"I guess I will have to go up and see uncle Pete if oald Abe is elected"

Corporal Peter M. Abbott of Barnet, Company K, Third Vermont Infantry, probably to his parents, August 15, 1864.[1]

1. Peter M. Abbott Papers (MSS 17-2), VHS.

Aug 15th /64,

I have been down to the Shenandoah to day and had a good swim and washed my clothes, the Boys will jump in with their clothes on and wash them out and then lay in the sun and let them dry, I have washed in the Potomac Rappahanock Shenandoah Monoccacy Rivers, and creecks to many to mention, I supose the draft will be cuming off up thare in September   that will mack sum of them lay low   this time last year we was on our way to New York and I wish we was on our way thare now   if we should go thare again I would cum home if I had to mack out my own Furlough, I expect they will be wanting me to reinlist this winter but I will never enlist to stay here 3 years longer, Higgins has not come back yet and I do not blame him, he is in Canady and I guess I will have to go up and see uncle Pete if oald Abe is elected next President   the most of the Soldiers are down on him and say that they wont vote for him and I dont think that he will be elected if thare is fare play, I cant think of any more to write at presant   we have no Chance to send mail out here but I thought I would get one ready write as soon as you get this and tell me all the news   good by   Peter M. Abbott

FIGURE 58. Silas Hall. Margaret Stone, Brookfield, Vermont.

1. Edwin C. Hall Papers (MSA 130.5), folder 18, VHS.

"The more I see of the conduct of the war the more I am convinced it is with a great many nothing but a <u>grab game</u>"

Silas Hall of Brookfield to his son, Edwin, Company G, Tenth Vermont Infantry, August 17, 1864.[1]

Brookfield August 17th 1864

Dear Son

I have waited anxiously some days to hear from you   I sent the Valise last thursday & expected you would acknowledge its receipt immediately   My conclusions are either you have not received the Valise or if you have its contents have made you sick & you are not able to write   One week ago to day sent you in [Minnies] letter five dolls & I hear nothing of the money or Valise   Nothing but absolute inability will excuse your silence   Let me know forthwith just how it is with you   If you want more money I can supply you a little while longer If not able to write yourself get some one around you to do it   We are having a fine rain this morning   It is very timely for our last spring was beginning to run low   The spring below the Schoolhouse has furnished water for three families for some time past   But it rains now & thank the Lord for it

We had a war Town Meeting monday   Voted a tax of 100 cts on the dollar to pay past bounties & left it discretionary with the Select Men to fix the price of bounties for our quota of 28 under the last call We expect the Select Men will have to pay what other town[s] are paying which is from 4 to 6 hundred dolls for one years men   And few want to go for that   There is no patriotism left   Tis all for money now & those towns that pay the most soonest fill their quotas   If we pay 500 dolls per man it will amount to the nice little sum of 14 thousand dolls & the town is now in debt for past bounties 64 hundred The whole making 20400 dolls   My proportion of the tax would be about 75 dolls   I see the necessity of economy & I hope you will   But I want all your necessary wants supplied long as the money lasts   I have got most of oats in the barn & have quite good crop of Indian wheat to cut next week   Dismissed hired boy last week   Sold the old shank of a sow for 16 dolls because had nothing to fat her on   Shall sell the oxen soon as I can get 140 dolls   Drought has made the feed short & beef has fell off in price but the rain is favorable & the prospect brightens a little   Your Mother will have your shirts ready in a few weeks   We want to know what else you will want when you come home   David Lyman was at home last week on a weeks furlough He told me that when the boys were furloughed for 30 days they were allowed to draw 7 or 8 dollars in money for their board   if this is so I hope you will not fail to secure this yourself   Advise with the Surgeon or someone who knows about it & if you are entitled to it get it if you can   The more I see of the conduct of the war the more I am convinced it is with a great many nothing but a *grab game*   And therefore I say to you look out for yourself & for your right   At the same time dont be mean about it

I shall be very anxious about you till I hear from you so dont keep me long in suspense

Praying that God would restore & preserve you I subscribe your Father

    Silas Hall

If you can remain there till pay day & then get a 30 days furlough I would advise you to do it but if by remaining you get cheated out of the furlough then come home soon as you are able

I suppose it is the Surgeon that decides the question of furloughs & if so I would inquire if it is not admissible for the Soldier to State his wishes to him & will not the Surgeon consult the wishes & conscience of the soldier in regard to all that pertains to his comfort   I would have you look after & insist upon all your rights as a Soldier & submit without a murmur to all the privations & inconveniences of your condition   Keep hope alive & believe it will all be right in the quotient

Lest you should be entirely out of money I enclose a little scrip 50 cts   tis the last of that sent by you last Ap[r]il with the exception of one 25 cnt piece   Mother wants to know if you want your shirts made as your others were with shoulder pieces

"I had the satisfaction of knowing that I was doing some good—if I did not get killed for my country"

Quartermaster Edward Dewey of Montpelier, Eighth Vermont Infantry, to his wife, Susan, September 21, 1864.[1]

FIGURE 59. Edward Dewey. Vermont Historical Society.

1. Edward Dewey Papers (Misc. File 353), VHS.

Camp near Strasburg Va. Sept. 21. 1864

My blessed wife,

As we are not on the move this morning I will write you a few words, though I cannot tell when there will be an opportunity to send it to the rear— You will have heard long before this reaches you that we have had a hard fight here & won a glorious victory . . but it may interest you to hear something about it from me— Trusting to your good nature to forgive me if it does not I will try to give my *experience*— Sunday morn I went to visit the 6th Corps, intending to write several letters when I got back, but in the meantime our train had been ordered to the rear, & of course my desk & paper was all sent with it. In the afternoon we were ordered to take down our tents—but afterwards they were put up again & we did not get on the march till 5 o'clock Monday morn— As we advanced towards Winchester the cannonading became plainer & about 11 o'clock we drew up in battle array—by noon the musketry was quite sharp & while I was away from the Regt. a few minutes they were ordered forward— By that time the "noise & confusion" was terrible— off at the left of our line, less than one half mile distant were two or three of our batteries of 12 pounders belching out the flames in a manner entirely new to me— By the way while our Regt. were drawn up in line the first time, they were in a little valley— with quite a hill on their left— Dr. Ross & I went on the top to see what could be seen—but discovered no enemy & led our horses back a little way & lay down on the grass. in a few moments hearing a devilish noise looked up & had the pleasure of seeing a cannon ball that had struck the ground on the hill & rebounded passing about 12 feet above our heads— thereupon we marched down the hill a little further— Now taking up the thread dropped above, will go on with my experience— Hearing that our Corps was engaged two Drs. & myself started for the front to find our Regt. By this time the Ambulance Corps were bringing off the men, some in the Ambulances & some on stretchers— groaning & moaning, wounded in all parts of their bodies— still we went on, till we passed a battery cutting their way through the woods, who were to play on a portion of the enemy who had got an enfilading fire on our troops— A little further on & it began to get a little worse by a good [deal more] than I had bargained for— The musket balls were whistling through among the trees & the branches were cut down above our heads by the cannon balls & shells— I then told the Drs. that I thought I could do more good in the rear than I should in front— that I was not aware that the sight would pay for the risk & turned around— at about that time some men were bringing off a Capt. who had been wounded & I took one of the handles & carried him to the hospital . . On our way one shell exploded exactly over our heads & another struck the ground about 30 feet away—near enough I thought— I then went to the hospital & offered my services— they said I was just the one they wanted— So I prepared some buildings near by—turned a family out of one, put some hay on the floors & as fast as the men had their wounds dressed had them removed to those buildings— So that I had the satisfaction of knowing that I was doing some good—if I did not get killed for my country

Our Lt Col. was wounded in the arm—A Lt. in the leg—no other officers wounded so that they left the field— about 37 men were killed & wounded— *The 8th Vt. did not take a step backwards from the time the fight commenced—always forward*   Col. Thomas sat on his horse, a little straighter than usual—"Boys give them hell"— At one time they had 4 flags in the Regt. others having left their colors, & the Genl. told them to fall in with the 8th & they would show them *how* to fight Good bye— Love to all— God bless you & the children—

> Ever yours
> Edwd. Dewey

Chapter 15 Autumn 1864

As General Grant slowly tightened his grip around the Confederate capital of Richmond and nearby Petersburg, General Sheridan embarked on a campaign of destruction in the Shenandoah Valley. Having followed Jubal Early's retreating army as far south as Staunton, Sheridan turned around and worked his way north, burning barns, storehouses, and farm equipment over an area of four hundred square miles, and confiscating livestock and crops for the army's use. Inevitably, houses were plundered and destroyed as well. Rebel guerrillas sought retaliation by ambushing Union foraging parties and supply trains, while refugees took to the road to avoid starvation in the coming winter.[1]

Sheridan thought that Jubal Early's army—now occupying Fisher's Hill again after Sheridan withdrew from the desolated southern part of the valley—posed little threat to his much larger Army of the Shenandoah. Although the Union general considered Early to be whipped, and the Union army's mission in the valley completed,[2] it was with misgivings that he left the army on October 16 to attend a War Department conference in Washington. In his absence, General Horatio G. Wright of the Sixth Corps was to command the force of more than thirty thousand men camped along Cedar Creek, north of Strasburg and south of Middletown.

The Army of the Shenandoah included an unusual proportion of Vermonters. The Sixth Corps contained the six regiments of the First Vermont Brigade, as well as the Tenth Vermont Infantry. The Nineteenth Corps included the Eighth Vermont Infantry, and the two divisions of cavalry included Vermont's only regiment of horsemen. In all, the Vermonters numbered between thirty-five hundred and four thousand, or more than one-tenth of the army.[3]

Jubal Early was determined to prove that he had not been whipped. Reinforced with artillery and a division of infantry from Richmond, he quietly marched his seventeen thousand troops north from their camps

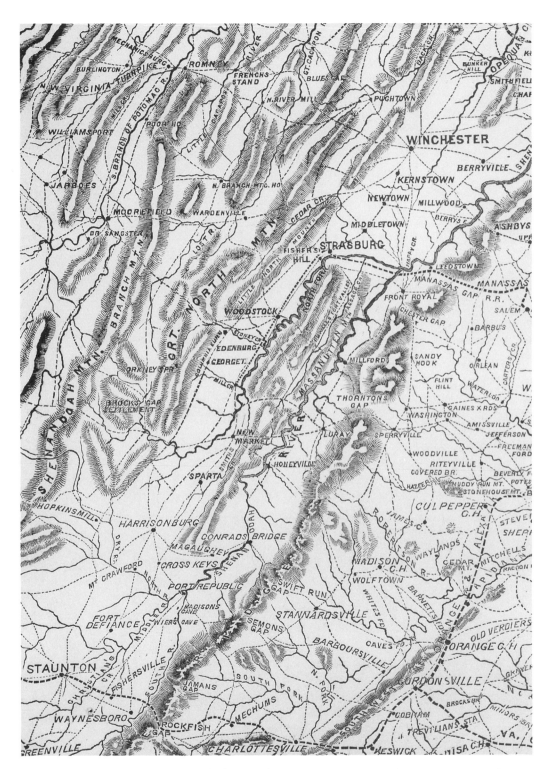

MAP 18. The Shenandoah Valley. Detail of "Map Showing Operations in Virginia, May 1864–April 1865" in Guernsey and Alden, *Harper's Pictorial History of the Civil War*, volume 2, 636. UVM.

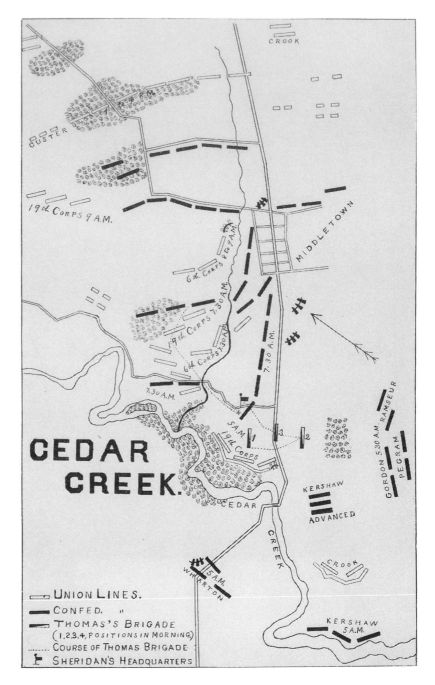

MAP 19. George Carpenter's map of Cedar Creek shows the sacrificial advance, and retreat, of Stephen Thomas's brigade, and the stubborn retreat of the Sixth Corps. Carpenter, *History of the Eighth Regiment*, 208+. UVM.

on Fisher's Hill on the night of October 18. By early morning on October 19 they were drawn up for battle opposite the left flank of the Union army. Closest to Early, in the broad angle of land north of the confluence of Cedar Creek and the Shenandoah River, the men of the Eighth Corps slumbered in their camps. Behind them, to the north, rested the Nineteenth Corps. Further on, the Sixth Corps and most of the cavalry held the right flank.

Before dawn broke Early's men rushed across Cedar Creek and the Shenandoah River into the camps of the Eighth Corps. Completely surprised, the Northerners offered little resistance, and all who could get away ran for the rear. Against a rising din of cannon and musket fire, the Nineteenth Corps scrambled into action. Quickly-organized battle lines marched to confront the attackers, but Early's men seemed to be coming from all directions in the dark morning.[4] A dangerous gap developed in the main battle line. Colonel Stephen Thomas of the Eighth Vermont Infantry, now commanding a brigade, led his four regiments into the breach on a virtual suicide mission, to buy time for the rest of the army to organize. The regimental flag of the Eighth Vermont "received a baptism of blood" at the center of the desperate hand-to-hand combat that ensued. Three color-bearers were killed in succession, but the regiment held on to its flag.[5] More than half of the men were killed, wounded, or captured. Thomas slowed the rebels, however, and when the Southerners finally overwhelmed his brigade, the Sixth Corps was forming in good order to the rear.

In the gray light and heavy fog of early morning the rebels fell upon the Sixth Corps' battle line and steadily pushed it back. Most of the fighting fell to the Second Division, consisting of the First Vermont Brigade and two others. Forming a line anchored on a graveyard northwest of Middletown, the Vermonters helped repulse several heavy assaults, but finally withdrew to the north. At midmorning the rebels halted to rest as Early considered his next move. His army had captured some twenty-four cannon and thirteen hundred prisoners, tons of food and supplies, and the personal belongings of most of the Eighth and Nineteenth Corps. Only the Sixth Corps and the two cavalry divisions remained in any shape to oppose him. Early, however, was not inclined to press the attack further, having achieved so much at relatively little expense.[6]

General Sheridan had spent the night at Winchester, twelve miles to the north, on his return from Washington. Hearing the cannon in the morning, he raced south on horseback and soon met Yankee stragglers headed north. When he arrived at the now-quiet and dispirited battle line north and west of Middletown, the soldiers erupted in cheers. Sheridan promised the men they would sleep in their old camps that night, and he set about reorganizing the ranks of the two shattered corps.[7]

The counterattack began around four o'clock. The rebels fought desperately, but their lines soon began to give way. A breakthrough on the right, in which the remaining men of the Eighth Vermont Infantry led the way, caused a general retreat. Now the Union cavalry charged on the right, with the First Vermont and Fifth New York regiments in the vanguard. The orderly retreat became a rout. Most of the rebel army retreated safely across Cedar Creek but a traffic jam on a bridge over a small brook stalled the Confederate wagons and artillery. The cavalry swept down upon them, capturing hundreds of prisoners, all of the rebel artillery—including the captured Union guns—and most of the supplies seized by the rebels from the Union camps that morning.[8]

Cedar Creek, so nearly a resounding Southern victory, instead turned out to be a mortal blow to the Confederacy. Robert E. Lee no longer had a force in Virginia, outside of Richmond and Petersburg, capable of undertaking an offensive. Although Jubal Early had lost only three thousand men at Cedar Creek, he lacked the supplies his men would need to get through the winter, and the artillery and equipment necessary to take the offensive. In December, most of his troops were transferred to Petersburg. The Union Sixth Corps soon withdrew from the valley as well, to rejoin the Army of the Potomac in the Petersburg trenches.

The same day that the Vermonters helped turn Cedar Creek into a Union triumph, another bold strike by Confederate soldiers brought the war onto Vermont soil. Some twenty rebel soldiers—prison escapees who had made their way north to Canada—invaded St. Albans and held up three banks. The raiders attempted to set fire to the city's business district before escaping with more than two hundred thousand dollars in cash and securities. One citizen was mortally wounded by gunfire as the band of raiders rode out of town on stolen horses. Outraged by the brazen attack—St. Albans was not only a bustling railroad center but the home town of Governor J. Gregory Smith—Vermonters organized Home Guard companies and armed themselves in expectation of further raids. The St. Albans raiders escaped to Canada, where they were arrested but never put on trial; most of the stolen money was never recovered.[9]

The events of October 19 reinforced the solid support for President Lincoln in Vermont, where Republicans had already made gains in September's state elections. Many of the Union soldiers voted in camp, or were given leave to vote at home. The "old" soldiers remembered George McClellan as their first great leader and some expressed their loyalty to him at the ballot box. But relatively few veterans of McClellan's campaigns remained in the ranks by the fall of 1864. On November 8 the soldiers chose Lincoln over McClellan by nearly 120,000 votes out of 154,000 cast. The Vermont Brigade voted for Lincoln 764 to 348, but the Second and Fourth regiments gave McClellan a major-

FIGURE 60. Main Street, St. Albans, shortly after the war. Stereograph by T. G. Richardson. Special Collections, University of Vermont.

ity.[10] Lincoln's wide margin of victory on November 8 signified the determination of the North to see the war through, as it signified the end of the Confederacy's last real hope for a negotiated peace.

The Union armies in Virginia had changed greatly since McClellan had been in charge. The soldiers were still patriotic, by and large, but they rarely gave rousing cheers for their generals anymore. Idealism was "played out." The thinned ranks of the veteran regiments were patched together by conscripts and high-bounty men, and too often they deserted at the first opportunity. When caught, deserters could be executed, but few were.[11] Despite desertions and diminished enthusiasm for the fight, Northern soldiers at last had good reason to be confident of victory. The balance of the war, they knew, would be measured not in years but in months.

"I think you can hardly call us very bad names in view of the attrocities committed by these infernal traitors"

Corporal George J. Howard of Mount Holly, Company G, Fifth Vermont Infantry, to his wife, Gertrude, October 9, 1864.[1]

1. George J. Howard Papers (Miscellaneous File 694), VHS.

Strausburg Va Oct 9th 1864

My Dear

Yours of Sept. 25th (No 58) was recd last eve   I had not time to reply before the departure of the mail   I was happy to get such an interesting epistle and to hear that Addie is progressing so finely with her studies   I am glad you are enjoying yourself so well

I would be happy to reply more fully to so good a letter, but we are moving back towards Harpers Ferry; halting here to draw rations & dispose of some Rebel Cavalry that has been lurking in our rear from the other end of the Valley; and I dont expect much time to write from this place; so you must excuse haste

I had not time to say to you in my last that we have a fund at Clark & Bros at Rutland Vt and you can draw on them of any fund that we may have on deposit there at any time you may need; by presenting this line for their perusal   I have good reasons to believe (I think) that Douglas Loomis is *not* married

We recd a mail last eve   I have seen the weekly Herald of date sept 29th   There is a descriptive letter published under date; copied from the new York [World?] which is the most truthfull and best illustrated schetch of any engagements that I have ever been participant of   I hope you will read it at the north; *every* person of you! The battle of: Berryville: alias: Winchester: It is now ten o'clock A.M. and heavy cannonading is now progressing in our rear

Front Royal Va Oct 11th 1864

The engagement of the 9th ended without our (the 6th corps) being called in; we lay in line of battle during the time the conflict lasted   Some of the fruits of the attact are 8 pieces of splended artillery; (one whole new battery that had not ever fired a gun)   The entire Head quarter waggon train of a Rebel genl and over three hundred prisoners   In fact it was another *rout* to the Confederate forces[2]

2. The battle of Tom's Brook on October 9 was a cavalry fight in which the rebels were driven from the field with heavy losses (Foote, *Red River to Appomattox*, 564).

At an early hour yesturday we took our line of march for this place where we are to remain until further orders

We have done a buisness for the confederacy during this campaign th[r]ough the Valley of Va that "I Recon" wont be forgotten very soon   Upon our advance, and when near Charlestown after a skirmish near that place in which corpl Jackman of Co K of this regt was killed and partially buried by the Rebls during the night time; leaving his head above ground; and inserting a *head board* into *his mouth* in which cond[it]ion his remains was found and identified by our regt soon after

While in camp near Berryville I am told by members of the 11th Regt Vt Vols that two men belonging to that regt were found murdered a short distance out of camp in the following manner   One of them was lieing upon the ground lifeless with his throat cut from ear to ear

Another was found also lifeless hanging from a tree by his feet head downwards his mouth filled with pulled wool   While we were lieing a short time in camp at Harrisonburg; Captain Meigs Chief engineer of Genl Sheridans staff was on the fourth day of this month while engaged in the duties of his position a short distance out of the infantry picket line; surprised captured and brutally murdered by a party of citizens in open day light[3]   On our cavelery advancing to & occupying Staunton we are told that a number of poor families begged our men to open the storehouses of flour in that place that they might get sufficient to keep their children from starvation as Earley had siezed all of the grain and flour in that place for the confederate use; and forbiden any one from taking a particle of it except by a written order from him Our boys overruled Earlies imperitive order; and opened the door and let the citazens take what they needed for immediate use and distroyed the bal by fire together with a large lot of other publick property claimed by the Rebel government   And now when I tell you that we have burned; by fire from staunton to Strausburg, the principal property of those persons who are engaged in this rebellion (and that includes every available male from the ages of 11 years (eleven) to near seventy years of age) and all such property as might be of immediate use to the Rebel government I think you can hardly call us very bad names in view of the attrocities committed by these infernal traitors

The property we have burned consists in the main of, Mills, shops, Factories, Tanneries, confederate Storehouses, and Barracks, Telegraphs, &, Rail way stations with some cars etc etc   Abandoned Rebel government waggons, Barnes of capazsious size filled to overflowing with Hay & grain   Multitudinous stacks of Hay grain and straw Some few dwelling houses burned by design; others caught fire by accident lit by sparks escaping from the general con, figration around, Highway bridges and some other structures of lesser note; all commingling in one grand, vast and gigantic conflagration which can be better understood when I state that its area comprised the Valley of Va from Staunton to Strausburg a distance of 75 miles with a breadth of about 5 miles on an average across   The time of the burning principally commenced on the 4th after the foul murder of Capt Meigs. The angry flames illumed high up the dark heavens of that moonless night between Staunton and Harrisonburg

But little distruction was perpetrated on the 5th preparitory to our

3. Lieutenant John Meigs and two others were surprised by a Confederate cavalry patrol on the night of October 3 and Meigs was killed. Northerners believed he was murdered by civilians. General Sheridan ordered some houses burned in retaliation (Lewis, *Guns of Cedar Creek*, 65–67).

greater work which began on the sixth ending on the 9th   The work of those three days will long be remembered by us as well   I can well rememember how awfully grand and impressive the picture of the burning of Moscow as represented in geography   The history of the distruction of Jerusalem as recorded in our early school book and the later r[e]cords of distructive confligrations occuring in London & New York and elsewhere: but as grand and awful as they were they pale into insignifficance and littleness before the burning of the fifty miles of this Valley between Harrisonburg and Strausburg as rapidly as we could pass over it with our mighty army and stupendious waggon trains of baggage and artillery

The condition of the atmosphere by nature during most of the time of those three days was a cloudless sky a wind blowing to our backs gently and a warm sun during the day time   All this blessed harmony of nature was mocked by those tall, thick volums of carbon which rapidly ascended from the burning masses to thicken and gather, and combine oer head until the rays of the sun sluggishly penetrate through the dense clouds of smoke as through a heavy eclips whilest vast sheets of flame dart and flash and tower far and high into the air seething and heating the atmosphere to threatened suffocation by day and illuminating wildly during the night time   Amidst the heavy rumbling sounds of the army waggons, the harsh rattle of the artillery wheels the loud clatter of horses hoofs upon this long macadamized "Pike" the rapidly moving and serpentine windings of our long lines of infantry and cavalry; is added the frantic shreaks of bewildered women; the frightned shrieks of children; the mingled curses and implorations of old men to save their property from distruction by the *"damnd Yankies"*

Ah! those three hundred thousand fresh soldiers *graves* in these slave states call for redress at our hands; and as true as God has a principal they shall have it, and woe to those unhappy people of this wicked rebellions conspiricy if they do not soon return to their allegiance

Amidst the many incidents of note that attracted my attention during our trip through the Valley was two features standing out prominently from one terminus of this Valley to the other   Viz—the extravigant excess of women of child bearing ages and the multitudinous numbers of children dispersed all through the laps of these same women—crops of the years of 1863–4 and yet at the same time these women as a rule claim to be widows   Surely I can't but suspect that "Hills furlough" had something to do with manifestations of this kind and their widowhood is in some instances of at least questionable character

Geo J. Howard

G B Howard

I have sent Clark & Brothers per this mail one state order $7.00 and directed them to send me pr mail one pr of Boots

I wish you would send me per mail, without delay one pr of gloves (not very expensive ones) and one pr of good suspenders

A heavy frost occured here on the morn[in]g of the tenth of this month making a Genl killing of the tender plants   Water in pails & Kettles standing in the open air th[r]ough the night previous formed ice on the surface to a thickness of one half inch

"they called themselves Confedret Oficers, Devil oficers I should think"

Ann Pierce of St. Albans to her son, Marshall, October 19, 1864.[1]

1. Ann Pierce Letter, Lynn Pierce Hughes; St. Albans Historical Society.

St Albans   Oct [19th] 1864

Marshall

My very dear son

I am feeling to night as I never felt before in my life. this day seems to bee the begining of trouble in St. Albans and the Lord knows when it will end, their was a band of men appeared in the streets   all at once comenced their awfull work   they wer Armed their was suposed to be about 30, in number   they walked in to the Banks and demanded . . . all the money and then presented revolvers & of course they got it the all three Banks were robbed of every dollar then went in to the street to kill and slay   our poor men were taken by surprise of cours and no army   what could they do but run to and fro; they then ran into Fields Barn and took all his horses also Fullers horses, mounted then they mounted them   they . . . cut the Harnesses from horses in the street & got onto them and all this time they were fireing in all directions   they shot Mr Morison just at [Marthas] door   he had hold of the lach as he fell   he is not dead the Last I heard   they also shot C. H. Huntington   they think he will die, also Mr Bingham slitly hurt and other slightly injured. they told [Ross?] Fuller to go in to the store and get them some spurs   he said he had one in his pocket that they might have so he took out A pistol which he discharged at him   he fell but they cought him up put him on his horse held him on and rode away   Steavy Conger shot at one & wounded him.   they tried to take som men prisnors but did not make much at it   after they took the money out of the one of the Banks they put Mr Beardsly into the safe and locked him in took the keys and Left   they also took 4 hundred dollars from Mr Breck just as he was about to deposit in the Bank they held a revolver at each side of his head while he got the money they said they should Fire the town before they Left   they called themselves Confedret Oficers, Devil oficers I should think, our men were runing in great confusion to colect what arms they could   the first I knew of it was Mr Eliott came runing and asked for Tell's gun   I went & got it saw he was excited   I asked if he was agoing to shoot A dog. he told me their wer raiders in town that were robbing and shooting people. just think of it all in broad day light   our men rallied all the arms and horses they could and started after them   our poor men with nothing but old guns   what will become of them this dark dark night we know not. they start[ed] off in the direction of Sheldon they threatned the town and said they had more men not far off   we have sent for Arms and men to Burlington & Vergens   you see their is great excitement   we will not go to bed to night   I now hear the train whistle   I hope it is the soldiers or the Arms or something these men have been in town for some time and several have been at Willard for a few days. [Mat] . . said she recognized the man that shot morison   had seen him at Treamont House   we fear ther is others that will rise up when our men and guns are gone but we hope for the best and trust the Lord. I just heard Kingly a going home & I asked him what news   he tells me the soldiers have come from Burlington he told us to go to bed

Tell says tell Marsh to send me a revolver.

Your Father started for Boston tusday morning   I hope he arived safe   we are well as usual here at home but wee *do not know what will be next*

we all join in sending much love to you and pa   write soon   Now Marshall you must pardon me for injureing your feelings so much when you were at home   I am very sorry I did so   I hope to do better in future

I am glad if Pa is safe   if he had been here he would had to fight   I wanted to myself   so good night my boy.

I think I will write to morrow night and let you know what became, of our men   the people are wating to heare from them   the raiders say that general Early sent them here knowing wee were with [out] Arms or Amunition so I think some of our coperhead[s] have let them know about it

from Mother Pierce   now write quick   I want to hear from Hiram

"How foolish and frantic our people have been not to heed your warning"

Ann Eliza Smith of St. Albans to her husband, Governor J. Gregory Smith, October 20, 1864.[1]

Thurs morn Oct 20   64

My Dearest—

We have had (to use *Cousin Joe's* forcible expression) a "Raid from hell!" For about half an hour yesterday afternoon I thought that we should be burnt up, and robbed— William gone to B—— and Ed—— Mr. Inglis and Joe & Eddie up to Warner's with the apples—but I hope you don't imagine I was one moment frightened, though the noise of guns, the agitated looks of the rushing men, and our powerless condition were startling enough— I ordered the house shut and locked, hunting myself for weapons, but nothing could be found but your carved pistol *empty*, however with that in my hand I stood in the door feeling *enraged* but *defiant*   I[n] a few minutes Stewart pale enough, galloped up, and asked for arms, I gave the pistol, and he told me they had turned north, but were expected back on the Sheldon road— A number of pickets ran on to Aldis hill, where they could see, and blazed away every few minutes to let the raiders know they were in readiness—

After Stewart left, we found the rifle, and I started down street to give it to somebody, but in a moment I met a man who said he was after it— We then found another pistol, and in a few moments some men rushed into the back yard for horses— I gave Mr. Beeman [of the] Car factory, Major, Ed who had just got in from the cider mill (I feared the horses and all were captured) took Kitty, and two others took the team horses— Afterward two others took Nellie and Diamond— Diamond soon came back badly scratched, by stepping through a bridge— The man took good care of him, and William came on mail train, says he is not much hurt— The other horses are still out— Worthy[2] has just been in, he will tell you all the news

I worried very much about you, thought you would suffer great anxiety on our account—but my dear, never after this, think that I shall be frightened or that I cannot do all that my best judgment dictates— that may be worthless, but it will probably be in active exercise—   I expected you and got Lawrence to meet you with a team, we had nobody here then to go—but finding by William that you did not come— I saw all secure, and went to bed and slept soundly till morning feeling that the Almighty Watcher was near me—

How foolish and frantic our people have been not to heed your

FIGURE 61. Ann Eliza Smith. St. Albans Historical Museum.

1. Smith Family Papers, St. Albans Historical Society.

2. Worthington C. Smith, Governor Smith's brother and a future Vermont Congressman.

warning— I hope this affair will settle matters at once. Good bye—
God give you grace to act wisely in these trying times

William when he heard the rumor in B groaned "Oh my God! The horses are gone!!! and ran to the Depot—

Our little Ed's spirit was superb— While Julie and some of the rest were crying terribly—he was awfully mad— "What did you let that rifle go for," says he to me "it is the only thing in the house that I can use!!"

"it is the bigest thing of the War"

1. William Wells Papers,
carton 1, folder 34, UVM.

Colonel William Wells of Waterbury, First Vermont Cavalry, to his parents, October 20, 1864.[1]

Wells had been commissioned colonel immediately after the death of Colonel Addison Preston in June 1864.

Head Quarters 3d Cav Div
Nr Middletown Va Oct. 21st [20th] 1864

Dear Parents,

Mothers letter came to hand yesterday. I was very glad to hear from you.

Thinking you have heard of our yestardays fight, and would like to know how I was, therefore I will write you a few lines. I am safe and sound, as well as ever.

Yestarday morning before day light our Cavalry picket line was at-tack[ed], they drove us back a short distance. soon after an attack was made on the extreme left against the 8th Corps. this corps was taken by surprise. they lost quite heavily in killed wounded & prisoners also some Artillery. the corps made but a short stand   they came back on the 19th Corps   this command fought them for a while but finally broke and came back in disorder through 6th Corps— this (6th) made a despirate stand but were out flanked and compeled to retire. it was done in very good order. at this time the 8 & 19th Corps were going for Winchester as fast as their legs would take them. at this time every thing looked as though we should be north of the Potomac before this. the Cav of 3d Div was massed in rear of the Infantry. (Genl Wright was in Command   Sheridan had gone to Washington)

I was sent to the right of the Infantry with one regt from 1st Div (9th N.Y.) one regt 1st Brig 3d Div (3d N.J.) the 22nd N.Y. & 1st Vt. I had comnd of the right for a distance of four miles—the enemy attact me with Cav & Artillery, but we held our ground. during this time 1st Div & remander 3d Div were on the left of the Infantry. about 2 PM Genl

Custer with 3d Div made a charge on the right (whare he had just moved) the 1st Vt was in the charge also 8th N.Y. who had rejoined the Brig. we drove the enemy, about this time Genl *Sheridan* came up and assumed Comnd, things looked better. he formed his command and moved on the enemy, drove them, soon every thing moved *forward* we pressed them back to the creek (Cedar Creek) charging several times. here the 1st Vermont charged across the stream followed by 5th N.Y. of the 1st Brig. we charged the enemy throug Strasburg distance of about four miles, capturing prisoners, Artilery Wagons etc etc I enclose list of property captured by 1st Vt Cav Comd by Lt Col Bennett of *My* Brig— it is the *bigest* thing of *the War.*

The men that Captured the battle flags have gone home on leave for *30* days. Sergt Woodbury Co "E" & Private Sweeney Co "A.".

Genl Custer started for Washington today with colors captured by the Cav Corps (8) eight in number I shall be in command of the Division untill he returns, which will be within a week. he also told me that he should reccomnd me to the Sec of War for a promotion to Brig Genl. and that he should urge the thing strongly, that I had earned the star if any one ever had.

Now is the time for my friends to work for me, if they ever intend to.

Mr Dillingham can help me very much if he will through Senators Collamer & Foot, also Woodbridge, Morrill & Baxter. letters from them to the President would help the thing— also from Gov Smith. think I can reach Col Platt.

Father is at Montpelier and can help me great *deal* through members—[2]

I can get reccomendations from Genl Custer, Genl Torbert Comdg Cav. in this Div and from Genl P. H. Sheridan the *"Hero of the Valley."*

Wish you would let me know what you can do for *me.*

I shall try and get leave for 30 days some time in November. Love to all.

> From your affectionate Son
> William Wells
> Col 1st Vermont Cav
> Comndg Div

Direct as usual

1st Vt Cav—

P.S.

The 5th N.Y. Cav capturd about the same amt of *plunder.* I never saw as Army so demoralized as was the rebs. No one knows whare they will stop. (the Army captured 62 pieces of artillery, and 2000 prisoners, & I guess 2500.—

> *Wid*

2. Wells's father, William W. Wells, represented Waterbury in the Vermont House of Representatives. State Senator Paul Dillingham, who was elected governor in 1865, was a neighbor and family friend. Lemuel B. Platt was the first colonel of the Vermont cavalry. Woodbridge, Morrill, and Baxter were Vermont's representatives in Congress.

"when the General came in sight of our lines and in the midst of hard fighting they gave rousing cheers and charged with new courage"

Musician Willard G. Smith of Williamstown, Company C, Eighth Vermont Infantry, to his family, October 23, 1864.[1]

1. Horace Smith Papers, Duke.

Cedar Creek Oct 23d 1864

Dear Friends at Home

Your letter of the 9th came to hand last eve just as I had returned from Newtown Hospital where I have been at work for the last three days— Since I last wrote you we have been through a scene of greater danger and blood-shed by far than *Winchester* or *Fishers Hill* The particulars I will give briefly as I have seen and herd from Head Qorters and perhaps more minutely than you will see in print Oct 19th at 4 o'clock I crawled out from my little tent where my comrads Wilcox & Parker lay sleeping with my canteen to go to the cook fire for our coffee though but few of the soldiers were up at that hour I had not gone more than two rods before the stillness of the morning was broken by the heaviest volly of musketry that ever greeted my ear and all as sudden as a flash. It was about 75 rods from our camp and on our right in front of the 8th Corps— The 6th C—— ocupied the left from us Our Brigade who were in front next to the Brest works started from their tents hastily taking their arms and equipments but leaving blankets haversacks tents and breakfest behind untouched and hardly having time to dress— The rebs camp had been in sight of us in the vasinity of Strasburg and Fishers Hill and our line of brest works lay across the valley north of the creek and only two miles from theirs The rebs sent out three divisions under Maj Gen Curshaw the night previus crossing the creek on our left going high up on the mountain traveling all night over its rough rocky sides and at 4 o clock had silently taken up a position on our lef[t] flank along *in and by* the village of Middletown which lays about a half mile to the left of us and 1/4 to the rear and in rear of where the 8th Corps lay When they had got fairly settled they opened in front of the 8th Corps though not till they had captured their pickets and were on their brestworks before they knew it—

At the first volley the rebs gained the brest works in front of the 8th captured all their Artillery and the 8th were retreating in the utmost confusion All that time our Brigade had started on a double quick to their assistance—. After going a few rods from camp they lay down in a hollow in the woods (where our Band had always been to practice—)

The smoke was so thick that they could not see any thing in front—
But sudenly a heavy column of Johnies who had been crawling on
hands and knees arose and discharged a heavy volley which cut up
our Reg badly— All this time the three Divisions in town had been at
work on our left flank and in the rear and our Brigade was nearly surrounded— Maj. Mead of our Reg wounded in the back the Adjutant
through the calf of the leg   Capt Ford through both legs   Capt Smith
Co. F through the hip and slight on the top of the head   Capt Howard
of my company through the arm and leg   Capt Hall mortaly through
the back and leg   Co E Lieut Seargent Co E mortaly back   Lieut Cheney back since died   Lieut Carpenter Co. F mortaly   Lieut Cooper
shot dead   Lieut Spencer Co. B leg— The Seargents Corporals and
privates I will not try to name though the loss was heavy   No Wms-
town boys were hit except Simons slightly on the wrist   Two Seargents and some privates were taken prisoners in my company other
companys I cannot tell— Capt Hall Lieut. Sargent Spencer Seargent
Lamb and some others were caried to the rear by the rebs to Fishers
Hill but were retaken by us in the evening   Lieut Carpenter is in reb
hands— Col Thomas was scratched slightly— I will now tell how we
come out and what the Band done— In less than twenty minutes from
the first shot fired the shells and minies flew in our camp like hail— as

FIGURE 62. "The Surprise
at Cedar Creek." *Battles
and Leaders of the Civil
War*, vol. 4, 515. UVM.

I stood by our cook fire to get my coffee a shell passed about two or three feet over Wilcox and my head and struck in the dirt about three rods beyond by the Col.s tent   By that time I began to think about leaving but not till I had taken down my tent and folded my blankets While Parker my chum and I were doing that a shell came and struck about a rod below us and bounded into the 12th C. I. [Connecticut Infantry] Camp but did not explode   But soon I had my traps on and shoe leather   took a quick sail for the rear though the Balls hummed about our ears at a fearful rate   The old Band boys took all their tents and rations and so did Fred Gale take tent and Bass Drum but the rest of the Barreite[s] left their tents on the field— I[n] less than fifteen minutes after we left the Johnies had posession of our camp tents and rations of all the armed men   Gen. Grover had to leave his Head Qorter tents and shoot his mules   At Brigade H——— Qorters only a few rods from us the saddler was shot dead while trying to take down the tent but saved the tent and Brig supplies except 500 pounds hard tack Such a racing of pack mules horses baggage waggons and evrything never was seen and were flying in all directions across the fields and through the woods   at times they would get stuck and snarled up and evry thing was perfect confusion   After running [through] we Band boys dared to stop and look around though the rebs were hard after us and armed men were running to the rear in swarms   The 3 Divns in town captured all of the 8th Corps Waggon train Artillery and nearly all of our ambulances   About 3 miles in the rear towards Winchester a line was formed to stop the skedadlers that had guns   The 6th Corps then helped to form a line and when the 19th had fell back to them the scales turn[ed]   At that time I was two miles beyond the line and Saw *Gen Sheridan* a coming up the road with a mounted body guard as fast as his fine black Horse could carry him under the spur and The Gen a swearing at evry bound the horse made   His Aids could hardly keep in sight   He had been to Washington the day before and when he got back to H Ferry he heard of our bad luck in holding the position he had left us [in] under the command of Gen Wright While he was coming up he [met] the scattered and scared 8th Corps and told them to turn around and go back and he would drive them over Fishers Hill before night and camp on the same ground we left in the morning   They did so and when the Gen came in sight of our lines and in the midst of hard fighting they gave rousing cheers and charged with new courage— (This was about [10 o clock])   Soon the Johnies began to falter in their lines and were driven slowly back till we gained our old camp ground evry rod of ground being dearly bought by us but with a great slaughter to the Johnies   At last our men charged on them and with the help of our noble cavelry force succeeded in driving them at a double quick across the creek a scattering and a slaughtering them in a way you can not immagine   Our Cavelry took at the creek

42 pieces of heavy Napoleon guns and retaking all the guns we lost and 2 miles of baggage train beside a large line of Ambulances   At last accounts our Cavelry had driven them through Woodstock there taking 8 more pieces and driving them on towards Harrisonburg the place we fell back from when we burned evry thing in the Valley   They have scattered to the mountains in evry direction— We took between two and three thousand prisoners that night beside quite a number since Nearly all of our wounded fell into their hands at first and were carried back to Fishers Hill but nearly all of the wounded that could not walk were retaken that evening One Captain who was shot through the leg and taken to Fishers Hill had his leg taken off by reb physicians but they did not have time to finish before our men were on them   he is now in our Hospital and doing well   Our wounded were all taken to Newtown 5 miles from this place towards Winchester   The village was entirely filled with the wounded evry shop meeting house store and inhabitants were compeled to give up their houses besid large tents being put up in the field back of the village   Our Band worked there three days to assist in amputating and taking care and moving patients— I worked at one table nearly two days to assist in giving chloroform and holding legs and arms carrying off and bringing in to the table   I attended the sponge in several cases the 2nd day   In one instance a reb was put on the . . . table who was shot through the leg above the knee   Two reb Surgeons who were prisoners came to perform the operation   I gave the chloroform   He had lost so much blood previus that he died in the operation— Many of the reb wounded were in our Hospitals and recd the same care and attention that our soldiers did except the reb women in the place brought in luxuries for them that our soldiers did not get   The 3d day all that could be moved were carried to Winchester   At the Brick Church where I worked were 3 tables that were kept full all the time for 2 days for amputation and a board of Surgeons at each table and at work all the time except when eating   This will give you somthing of an idea of the pile of legs and arms that lay beside the tables some with boots and shoes on and some with only stockings   The rebs took the boots coats & Hats off of all of our boys that fell in to their hands   The wounds looked horrid   Mangled heads faces limbs and they smelled terrible the 2d day Many of the wounds were not touched till the 3d and they were piled in to shops and houses like hogs on the hard boards when straw could not be had and no blankets for the rebs had them all and the nights were cold and windy   Many of the 6th Corps and some of the 19th Had to lay out doors with their wounds and the cold and many were left on the field all night   It is enough to make ones blood run cold and go crazy if they allow themselves to be affected by the groans and shrieks of the wounded   But we are so used to it we can now attend to them with the utmost composure   We have eat hard tack with one

hand and held at the same time legs with the other to be cut off when hungry and could not stop to eat— Most of the boys in our Corps had nothing to eat the day of the fight and no blankets at night or tents to cover them and no rations till the next day towards night and no chance to forage in this country at the present time as it is entirely striped   The boys say that in one hour after our men were driven from Camp it was literly covered with women from Strasburg and Middletown who were there for plundering   The women from Middletown fired from their windows at our men and Ambulances when passing through town   No guards are placed on houses now and soldiers are alowed to plunder all they wish   I got the stamps all safe in the last but no papers   The papers are taken from the mail by some one on [their] way which makes it rather poor encouragment for sending them   The letters all come safe when the mail is not captured by Geriles [guerrillas]   The Thread I did not get   My health never was better weighed last night 193 lbs—

We came back from Newtown last night and our tent is on the very old spot where it stood the morning of the battle   The Sanitary Commission furnished the wounded soldiers with blankets clothes and eatables necessary for their comfort   Our Regt have drawn blankets tents etc again   I have had pleanty to eat and pleanty of blankets without drawing   Were called to serenade Gen McMillan last night after we had gone to bed   Col Thomas Commanded the Brigade during the fight and McMillan the Div   If you can read this hasty scribble you can do better than I can   Please write soon all   I am glad that Em and Bell write and very well composed and written letters   It is a good chance for their improvement   I believe Silas owes me a letter & Ellen I have not had time to read all of the two last papers but will now & finish this   I hardly think it worth a while to send any thing here till we are in to winter quarters as it will be uncertain about my getting it   I shall write to Uncles folks   let them read this   Such a pile of old [   ] you never saw in shape of old harnesses Ambulance Waggons poor mules horses etc tatters straps and strings   I had a long talk with a reb Seargent yesterday who is prisoner at Sheridans head quarters— Two large squads of reb prisoners have been marched of to Winchester and more ready to go   Reb Gen Curshaw who led the flank movement was wounded taken prisoner and died at Sheridans Head Quarters yesterday[2]   Will

McClellan is getting along finely in the principal states   if soldiers are alowed to vote Abe will loose it   I think they are grabing at straws when they try to make Mc withdraw from that Chicago nomination I have learned that Gen Grover of 2nd Div did not loose his tents as supposed but is wounded in the shoulder   I have found the shell a few

2. It was General Stephen Dodson Ramseur, not General Joseph B. Kershaw, who died at Sheridan's headquarters.

minutes since that struck near my tent before I left Camp it is a round percussion shell but did not burst

I shall write again soon In haste

"The State is full of strangers prowling around with no apparent business"

Ben H. Dewey of Waterbury to Colonel William Wells of the First Vermont Cavalry, November 5, 1864.[1]

Dewey was a bank clerk and freemason in Wells's home town.

Waterbury Vermont
Nov 5th 1864.

Dear Col.

Your favor of the 26th ult came to hand last evening and I was right glad to hear from you and that you are safe and well. Your last campaigns in the Valley have told on our community as never before. We cannot hardly realize now that the little Maj. and Capt. Thompson are dead[2] Lucian was buried on Tuesday of this week. An immense concourse turned out. A detachment of 30 soldiers and 2 officers came down from Montpelier with arms and the funereal was a military one— Dea Thompson requested the members of our Lodge to turn out with gloves and aprons as mourners which of course we did. Parker as usual gave us the cold shoulder making no allusion to the fraternity, although he addressed every body else.[3] Of course every body noticed it, and our boys are mad enough— I had supposed he was man enough under the circumstances to have said something but it seems he was not— My opinion of him is growing small, and beautifully less.

It has about used Dea Thompson up in loosing Lucian— He seems all unstrung. I pity him and his family—

We have now got one of the prettiest Lodge rooms in the State, and it is furnished up to the handle— I presume you knew we were going into a new one. If you are coming home soon, we shall be pleased to shew you what we have got—

Presume you have heard of the raid on St. Albans. It was a rough affair—and undoubtedly it is not the last of the kind— The towns in the northern part of the state are armed, and in fact, generally the towns

1. William Wells Papers, carton 1, folder 34, UVM.

2. Major Edwin Dillingham of the Tenth Vermont Infantry was killed at the battle of Winchester on September 19, 1864; Captain Lucian D. Thompson of the Tenth died in battle a month later at Cedar Creek (Peck, *Revised Roster*, 382, 391). Dillingham was the son of state senator, soon-to-be governor Paul Dillingham.

3. Presumably the man who snubbed the masons was the Reverend Charles C. Parker, Waterbury's Congregational minister. See Parker's letter of February 24, 1864, p. 208.

are taking measures to protect themselves— Our town has started a company and we are daily expecting our arms— Revolvers have been in good demand, and a great many are carried here— The State is full of strangers prowling around with no apparent business. some arrests have been made—was told this morning that in St. Johnsbury a man was arrested who had letters upon his person by which they learned it was contemplated to pitch in there A lot of arms passed through here this morning for Morrisville Hyde Park and Johnson—

I want you to *seize for me*, a Spencer rifle. *Confiscate* it and bring it home to me— Do not know that any of the hounds have made me a visit yet though on the day of the St. Albans raid I had a suspicious customer—who was visiting Banks for the purpose of teaching them to detect counterfiet money   *I dident see* it, and consequently he remained on the other side of the counter. Hoping that we shall see you home soon and that, [as] a *Brig Genl!* I remain in haste,

Fraternally   Ben H. Dewey

FIGURE 63. Isaac N. Watts. Special Collections, University of Vermont.

1. Isaac N. Watts Papers, folder 2, UVM.

"McLellan men were, as a general thing, rather inclined to the rufscuff of the lot"

Corporal Isaac N. Watts of Peacham, Company M, Eleventh Vermont Infantry, to his sister, November 10, 1864.[1]

Camp near Kernstown, Va. Nov. 10th/64.

Dear Sister:

Though I haven't anything in particular to write about yet thought I would write a little today. You will see by this that we have changed our position again. Yesterday morning we were routed up early and started soon after daylight falling back and again crossing Cedar Creek, I hope for the last time, we marched about fourteen miles and camped here about five miles from Winchester   This place consists of a mill and half a dozen houses with a big name like all southern towns. We have crossed the Creek six times going both ways since Aug. 1st and I think that is about enough for one year. Yesterday we passed back over the old battle field. It didn't look much as it did three weeks before. All that showed marks of a battle was occasionally a cluster of graves, a few dead horses scattered around and houses that were in range perforated with bullets till they looked some like a pepper box. I saw where our Orderly Sergt. was buried. He was wounded and died next day. But I guess I've written enough of this. I am well and have not stood a march so well for a long time as I did yesterday though it was some muddy and my load heavier than common. The common report now is that we are going back in the vicinity of Winchester and Martinsburg and go into winter quarters. I rather think this is the case but it is hard telling what will turn up next. I hope it is so for I want to get back a little nearer to civilization. We had a very quiet election last Tues. I voted for "Abe" of course and our reg. gave him 220 majority. Some of the old regiments went for McLellan but in the Brig. Lincoln had about 450 majority. I think that is pretty well considering how many there are that are not voters. McLellan men were, as a general thing, rather inclined to the rufscuff of the lot and I guess it is so through the country. The wind is blowing pretty hard and smoke and cinders fly from the fire into my tent so I can hardly write. But as you are a pretty good hand to pick out bad writing perhaps you can this. I have never recd. the picture you said father sent though it may come next mail. Harris had two pairs of nice socks come to him the other day and I took possession. his things always come when he is away. It was so last summer and is now. Letters and papers in abundance have come since he left. I have now got clothes that look fit to be seen. I couldn't draw them and bought a part. I wont go ragged when I have money and can buy with it what I want. We have been having warm, rainy weather for a few days but to day it has cleared off and is real windy though not cold. Va. is a great place for wind and some times I think worse than Vt. If there were a few inches of light snow now there would be a gay time. Do you hear from Minnesota now. If I remember right I haven't heard anything from them for some time. I suppose everyone is excited about the raid nowadays. Has Peacham got any home guard yet. That was a pretty bold strike and a little to bold to last long. I am very sorry your letters are so *uninteresting* as you try to make them out. But I guess they will pass if the quality is poor   At any rate it wont pay to stop writing on that account. Mail day is the greatest day we have and I always like to get a letter from somewhere. But I must close. My love to all and write often to your Brother,   Isaac N Watts

"I have seen death in many forms on the battle field but never anything so horrible as to see those men swinging in the air giving their lives as a penalty for their treason"

Captain Darius J. Safford of Morristown, Company L, Eleventh Vermont Infantry, to his sister, December 17, 1864.[1]

1. Sherman-Safford Family Papers (MS 23), VHS.

Camp near Patrick Station, Va. (A.P.)
December 17, 1864.

Dear Sister,

I got your most welcome letter from the first mail we received after joining the Army of the Potomac and I need not inform you I was very glad to receive it as I am to get letters from you at any time. I hardly expected to direct my step to this place where I wrote the last time before this to you but still here I am and am better suited than I expected to be in these works. We are in the works erected by the 5th Corps south west of Petersburg and about three and 1/2 miles from the city, when we came here we came within a very few rods of the place where I was captured in June but so much had it altered that I should have hardly known it had I not been looking for it then it was covered with timber which is all gone now and a road built directly through the place where our lines were formed during the engagement. Gen. Meads Hd. Qrs. are only a few rods from the place and our lines are pushed out over five miles westwardly from where they were that day. The business of furnishing transportation for a large army never was carried on so systematically as it is now in this. here is a Railroad about twenty miles long built expressly to transport troops and articles for their use and once in two hours the trains come thundering in almost to us who lay in the front lines for miles the road is in easy shelling distance of the enemys works, and they can hear the train on the road almost as distinctly as we can ourselves— from some portions of the line occupied by our Division their works can be seen and the videtts of the two armies are near enough to be easy shooting range but still on our line there is no fireing or bad temper shown but some times the pickets blackguard one another as they can talk so as to be heard with ease. There are a great many deserters to our lines from the rebs, and I am sorry to be obliged to say quite a number of our bounty jumpers desert to them but nearly as many as come from them to us. Yesterday I saw three men pay the penalty of desertion to the enemy with their lives they were hung in presence of the 1st Division of the 2d Corps two of them were from the 5th New Hampshire and one from the 7th New York they deserted to the enemy and took up arms against us and after awhile were taken and tried for desertion to the enemy convicted and sentenced to be hung and were accordingly executed. I have seen death in many forms on the battle field but never anything so horrible as to see those men swinging in the air giving their lives as a penalty for their treason I could only say it is just, but deliver me from ever seeing anything of the kind again as long as I live. I am glad to write to you freely and to have you do the same I have always felt as though I could open my heart freely to you and am very glad indeed you feel so.
Sunday. This morning we were wakened by the booming of Artillery

and jumping up to see where the attack was made or to be made on either side I found they were the guns of the salute being fired in honor of Gen. Thomas' great victory in Tennessee over Gen. Hood,[2] so I lay down again, but I did not feel any the less rejoiced for all that— Forty-seven pieces of Artillery and eight to ten thousand prisoners the report is and if true it will prove a heavy blow to the Confederacy and I guess it is correct for Gen Grant sent an official dispatch to that effect and ordered the guns fired. We are having a fine spell of comfortable weather now which the men are improving to the utmost putting their log cabins in order— I mean to go and see Linus soon if I can get leave   I have not seen him for a long time and hardly know whether he would recognise me or not but guess he would. I am afraid Alvah behaves very foolishly in his love matters but he must judge of that himself but I do not like the way he manages at all. Henry Tuliper is a wagoner in Battery "D" of this Regiment and is now with the train of the 6th A. Corps

I do not think there would be any difficulty in obtaining the body of Mr. Palmeter, if some one went for it and made application to Gen Sheridan for an escort   the place where he fell is probably some seven or eight miles outside the present lines of the Army of the Shenandoah it would be necessary to know very near where he was buried so as to be able to describe the place   perhaps Col. Thomas of the 8th Vt would assist he being the only Vt Colonel in that army now. I have not yet seen Capt Perham but intend to do so as soon as I can get time and permission to do so which I guess will be soon— You must be very careful and not work so hard as to make yourself sick   try and make your health the main thing and others subservient to that.

I believe you have seen Susan's sister Caroline   if not you have heard me speak of her for she is a dear good sister to me. Well she was married the 12th in Cambridge to Madison Perry a good substantial farmer of Cambridge about twenty-five years old and a fine fellow I think and I hope will make a good husband for her for she deserves a good one   she is one of the best girls I ever saw in my life— I mean to go to Vermont sometime this winter if I can get leave of absence for a few days and if I do will see you if I can. I have got quite a company now here about fifty in all of whom about forty carry muskets— More or less of the sick ones and those wounded in the earlier part of the campaign are coming back nearly every day now and if we could only get our prisoners here from the South we should have a very good company once more— I can think of no more of interest to write this time So I will close. Please write as soon as you can for I am very lonesome here now. Remember me to Alva and all other friends there.   In Love,

    Darius J. Safford

2. This was the battle of Nashville, in which Union general George Thomas's Army of the Cumberland thrashed General John B. Hood's Confederate Army of Tennessee (Foote, *Red River to Appomattox*, 674–710).

Chapter 16

Winter 1865

onfederate military reverses late in 1864 greatly diminished the ability of the South to wage a sustained offensive in any part of the country. John B. Hood's shattered
Army of Tennessee, Edmund Kirby Smith's force west of the Mississippi, and an army soon to be commanded by Joseph Johnston in the
Carolinas still held out against the widening dominance of the Yankees, but could no longer alter the course of military events. For the
North, the key to victory remained the destruction of the Army of
Northern Virginia, holed up in the thirty-seven miles of trenches
fronting Richmond and Petersburg.

Conditions in the rebel works deteriorated in the early winter. Food
and supplies of all kinds grew short, in part because of the destruction
visited on the Shenandoah Valley by Philip Sheridan's men, but also because General Grant's tightening grip on Petersburg deprived the rebels
of important supply routes. Cold, hungry, and demoralized, rebel soldiers began to desert in large numbers. They came across the lines
singly and in groups, seeking an end to discomfort and despair. Others
left for home, troubled by the stories of widespread destruction caused
by William T. Sherman's troops in Georgia and South Carolina. The
appointment of a new commissary general in Richmond improved the
supply situation in February, but the lost troops could not be replaced.[1]

Little military activity took place in January, but there was a movement toward peace negotiations. Following the unofficial visit to Richmond by Maryland statesman Francis P. Blair, Confederate president
Jefferson Davis agreed to send three representatives to Fortress Monroe in late January to meet with members of the Lincoln administration.
Thousands of soldiers watched as the three Confederate representatives crossed the Petersburg lines, and hopes ran high that peace was at
last imminent. The three envoys were received cordially, and Lincoln
himself joined the talks. The president insisted that the country must
be reunified, the rebellious armies disarmed, and federal policies on

slavery maintained. In fact, there could be no compromise on the issue of slavery, even if Lincoln were so inclined. Congress, in its lame-duck session, was about to approve the Thirteenth Amendment abolishing slavery, already passed by the Senate. The new Congress, whose members were more radical than the old, would take office in March. The most Lincoln could offer was executive clemency for those accused of crimes against the country, and only within the limits imposed by an unsympathetic Congress. The talks thus came to nothing, much to the relief of hard-liners on both sides.[2]

If armed resistance were to continue, General Lee concluded, the Army of Northern Virginia would have to abandon Richmond and join forces with Johnston somewhere to the south. It became increasingly clear that the evacuation could not wait for long. Lee decided to buy time by attacking the Union works east of Petersburg late in March. Troops quietly withdrawn from the trenches were to assault Fort Stedman, capture nearby batteries, turn them on the Union lines to the north and south, and establish a new front along a line of secondary works the rebels detected through their field glasses to the rear of the fort. The new position would threaten the railroad that General Grant had built to supply his troops south of Petersburg and, Lee hoped, disrupt the Yankees long enough to allow an orderly evacuation of Richmond and Petersburg.[3]

The rebel leader massed twelve thousand troops for the 4 A.M. attack on March 25. At the given hour, the Southerners swarmed out of their lines and quickly overwhelmed Fort Stedman. The closest Union batteries to the north and south were taken, and their cannon turned around. It was a glorious but short-lived success. The secondary line of works, it turned out, did not exist, and the attackers had little protection in the growing light of day. Fort Haskell, to the south of Stedman, dominated the field to the north and proved too strong for the rebels to take. By 8 A.M. Lee ordered a retreat. Many of his men surrendered instead, inflating the Confederate casualties in the desperate attack to thirty-five hundred.[4]

Before the surprise attack at Fort Stedman, General Grant had planned to probe beyond the rebel right flank anchored on Hatcher's Run, southwest of Petersburg. Now, with evidence that Lee had stripped his lines for the failed attempt to the northeast, Grant ordered a frontal attack on Lee's right. Late in the afternoon of March 25 the Sixth Corps assaulted the outer line of rifle pits and, after some fierce fighting, drove the rebels from their first line of defensive works. Another thousand prisoners fell into Union hands—a loss that Lee could not afford. The First Vermont Brigade, the Tenth Vermont Infantry, and the Third Vermont Light Artillery all participated in the attack. The expected breakthrough did not materialize, but the ground secured soon proved to be important.[5]

Thus ended "the last desperate thrust of the Army of Northern Virginia before the agonies of its dissolution," in the words of a Yankee officer who witnessed the affair.[6] President Lincoln also witnessed the fight, or at least the retreat of the rebels from Fort Stedman. He had joined General Grant the night before, intending to review the troops on March 25. The battle delayed the review, but made Lincoln's appearance all the more welcome, and he was cheered by the troops wherever he went. Something was in the air, and every soldier could feel it.

"the Rebs. keep disirting and coming in a few most evry knight"

Sergeant Londus W. Haskell of Woodbury, Company I, Eleventh Vermont Infantry, to his mother, January 1, 1865.[1]

1. Londus W. Haskell Letter, Lewis Leigh Collection (book 5, 12), MHI.

Camp near Weldon R. R.   V.A.
Jan 1st 1865

Dear Mother

Your kind letter was recived the 30st with meny kind thanks for you for thare is me[n]y things that A mother writes that come fresh to your mind when you are seting by a small camp fire in the cool midnight hours whare sleep is forbiden wating fore the morning dawn to appear those nights have been very often this fall. But good health maks them pass off and that thing I have been bless with the past year

It is very coald day for new years   it rained yesterday   last night it snowed a bit   to day is rather rough   keep prety clost to our shanteys today a fire is pretty good friend   I have got as good one as thare is in camp it is about six feet Esq. and as good a fire plase as you have got it is made of wood and Va. mud   thare is no stone in this part of Va. thare is not eny stone hear as big as a birds egg   the wood is mostly pitch Pine some scatering Oaks and white woods   the Pines are free to split   mak good shanteys out of them   thare is only two of us Frank Marsh is with me   good felow to and duty is going to be eas[ier] then it has been   thare is good meny come back since we came down hear

Lieut. E. L. Foster came to the Regt. week go last Friday and also lieut A. J. Dudley came night before last looking as if he had just been taken out of a drawr with a smile on his brow   To day he is Oficer of the Brigade Guard   rather cool day for the first time. The line in front of us is very quiet but the left of us in the 2d. Corps. thare is some firing most evry night   the Rebs. keep trying them dashing on to thare pickets   the Rebs. keep disirting and coming in a few most evry knight night before last thay tried our first Division   charged on them   thay did get up grate ways before thay went back for some reson   thare was quite number wounded   our men said thay co[u]ld hear them groning when thay went back   Thay will find thay have got the same Six Corps. that was in the Valley to fight if thay pitch on   thay will have to bee the atacting partey   down hear we shal hold our own and catch what we can   down on our right thare was quite a sqad of them come in and gave selves up.

There is not much news hear   thare is three men hung hear evry Friday   thare is going to bee till thay hang fifty   thay are Diserters we cot most of the[m] up in the Valley thay was fighting against Uncle Sam   thay dont get much pity hear

How does Uncle Abraham get along with his Jane   Elder Rickerd his woman is to be pited if she knows enything if she does not God pitty the simple

Nothing more this time

     From L. W. Haskell

Give my love to all and Write often as you can.

"at the word ready their muskets were leveled at his breast, and quicker than it takes me to write it, the command of 'fire' was given and he fell to rise no more"

Private Moses A. Parker of Concord, Company H, Second U.S. Sharpshooters, to Eliza Hale, January 5, 1865.[1]

Discharged for disability from the Third Vermont Infantry in September 1862, Parker enlisted two years later in the Sharpshooters.

1. Parker Family Papers, folder 13, UVM.

Jan 5th 1865

Dear Eliza

With the greatest pleasure I once more resume the pen in order to communicate a few lines to you   I have but little time to write to anyone, but, believe me, you shall have your share of it   We have to drill a large share of the time, besides what it takes to "tote" up our wood and water and cook our grub   But this afternoon it is raining quite hard so there will be no drill   At 12.o.clock to day we were drawn up to witness a painful sight; even to the long tried soldier who has stood unmoved under the shower of leaden hail while the air is thick with the larger missels of death, now striking in front of him and then at his sides, ploughing deep gutters in the earth, while his comrads are fast falling on his right & left   Such scenes are bad enough but are not compared to the one we witnessed to day; the shooting of a comrade for desertion. A private in the 184th N. Y   The troops were drawn up in a hollow square two regiments deep facing each other, and, he, who once stood and fought so nobly, but in a moment of despondency, deserted his countrys flag, was marched betwen them, preceded by the band "playing the dead march" and a strong guard, seated on his coffin & drawn by two milk white horses; then he was marched into the center of the squad   took a look into his grave   Ah! did he not shudder when he thought of his home and friends, and ere many minutes must sleep in its bosom; he was left alone with the chaplain a few minutes, shook hands with him and the officer who was to give the fatal word "fire" then was seated upon his coffin & the guards were at their posts, at the word ready their muskets were leveled at his breast, and quicker than it takes me to write it, the command of 'fire' was given and he fell to rise no more; this is the 2nd one who has been shot here this winter and six have been hung in the 6th Corps that I know of for the same offence   But I fear I weary your patience   I received yours of the 25th the night I posted my last   I thank you for your Christmas wish, and wished you the same, also new years (but I guess you did not hear me)   I think you get first rate wages teaching this winter and if my letters will help you any from being homesick, you will not be troubled with the disease *much* if I send them as often as I have thus far; but I cant send many more until I get some stamps from home   We have been pretty short for rations but have a plenty to eat just now   I have never been troubled with that disease you spoke of   My health is very good now   Has your mother anyone to work for her this winter and how does your cousin Charley Stoddard and wife get along

Hoping that you are prospering well in the duties of your school I remain your loving friend

     Moses

P.S. I think you misunderstood me   What I wrote about my brother seein you with a beau he did not see you at all, but said so in order to pester me and to hear himself talk

     M. A. P.

"Slavery is dead, & past resurection, & that.s what we have been fighting about"

Private Henry E. Dunbar of Newbury, Company A, Third Massachusetts Heavy Artillery, to his wife, Mary, February 4, 1865.[1]

Discharged from the Third Vermont Infantry in 1862, Dunbar reenlisted in a Massachusetts regiment two years later.

Fort Totten D.C. Feb. 4th 1865
Saturday. 10..A.M.

My Dear Wife, Have got a few minutes leisure & will commence to write a little. Dont have so much time to write sundays as I *used to* for *Ball*[2] has quite a notion of having us out on Inspections, now days. Am happy to tell you that my cold is a good deal better & dont cough but little now have cured, or helped it, eating molasses. The *Old set* are *still* in *the Cook house* & Capt. B. says they *will remain* for the present. "Ive" had a talk with him & he said he was perfectly satisfied & if he was not he shouldnt put us out now to please 3 or 4 *grumblers* & *Irishmen* at that so you see the *little Mickey* cut his own fingers, for the Capt. has *fixed* it so its much better for us & he says if they grumble & *swear* at us now he.l *put them in the Guard House* & they begin to think they havent made much. But the *hash* is all settled now so enough "about.that." & now how is it about "Peace" "are the People all excited there about it." *We are.* The Papers say that Stephens Hunter & Campbell[3] from Richmond *are now in Washington determined to make Peace if possible.* Everybody here is *anxiously waiting* the result. "*Can* it be that *Peace* is *so near.* I dont dare to *believe* it, but cant help *hoping* that it may come & I dont see why we should not have now that the *bone* of contention is out of the way. *Slavery is dead, & past resurection,* & that.s what we have been fighting about. But I must adjourn for its time to set the tables for dinner. H.
3..P..M.. We have had a tough time getting dinner to day & it was a *tough* dinner after we did get it (*salt Horse*) our wood is *green pine* & the stove dont *draw* good to day either. "how would you like to cook with *green pine wood*, & if you would not like it, what do you think of our cooking for 100 men, & now we are trying to heat the oven to bake beans for dinner tomorrow but guess some of us will have to set up to night. My "*bunkie*" is quite sick, has got cold I guess, & is feverish. he.s a hard fellow to doctor for he dont like to take anything tho we have made out to get some Pills into him & if they operate guess he.l soon be better We have our *Old head Cook* to help in his place, guess you.l remember him at Ft. *Impudence.* he.s a fat *chuncky* fellow. I like him, but he.s not *neat enough* for me in the mess room & shall be

1. Henry E. Dunbar Papers, MHI.

2. Captain Benjamin H. Ball of Company A.

3. The three Confederate government representatives sent to meet with officials of the Lincoln administration were Vice President Alexander Stephens, Assistant Secretary of War John A. Campbell, and Senator Robert Hunter.

glad when [John?] gets well. "Did I tell you" about our Col.s having a letter from the Adj.t. Gen.l & that if he got any more *papers* from our Reg.t he would send us to the "Tortugas" Well *that* story has proved to be [ ] as we have just learned that it.s the *same old story* from *Adj.t* [Jehouler?] instead of Adj.t Breck, which is another thing entirely. *But* if we are going to have *Peace* this spring they may [as] well I wont say what, for it "*wouldnt be pretty Mr.* Chamberlin" Guess I cant write much more till eve. "Shall I get a letter tonight." *hope so.* I want to hear what you think about "*Peace*" as I suppose Boston Papers will be *full* of it, & much more so than *ours* are here. "The Chronicle" is an *Administration Paper*, & whatever is published there we can rely upon. "*Farney*" is very carefull about what he publishes. But I must again adjourn, for its most supper time *Yours in love.* H.

8 1/2 P.M. Dear "Moe" Its after "Tattoo" almost "Taps" but I must write a few lines more before I go to bed. I did.nt get a letter to night & am *sorry as a Dog*, for I had got my *mouth made up for one*, but however guess I shall stand it. The Papers dont give us but little additional "Peace" news to night tho. what little there is, *is encouraging.* It seems Seward went down to meet them first, & then sent for the President, & that.s pretty good evidence that they hoped to accomplish something, but since the Papers came, we have heard that "Old Abe" has returned, but what the result, or prospect is nobody knows yet, but guess something will *leak* out tomorrow. But if this *trial* amounts to nothing & we have to *fight* it out, *we can do it in 3 months.* so they had better dry up now before they lose Charleston & Richmond, as lose them *they must*, & *soon too.* But I must close for to night for "Taps" have *just gone*, so "good night" & "God bless you all."

Pray for "Peace" & you.l *pray for me. Your own,*

H.

"never mind the soap Yank, I am going where there is plenty of it"

Assistant Surgeon Joseph C. Rutherford of Newport, Tenth Vermont Infantry, to his wife, Hannah, February 19, 1865.[1]

1. Joseph C. Rutherford Papers, box 1, folder 70, UVM.

3d Div 6th Corps Hospital Feb 19th 1865

My dear wife:—

I am sitting here all alone with a good cheerful fire and nothing to do having just made my evening rounds of the hospital and thought that I could do no better than to write a few lines to you. But I hardly know what to write about.

This afternoon I called on Genl Grant (our Blackstone friend)[2] and had a very pleasant time talking over old times together   We handled Dr Kimball rather roughly—and some others.

It is no small matter in a military sense for one of my rank to be on equal terms with a general. It makes my social position much pleasanter than you would naturally suppose. Not but I think myself as good as any of them but such are military rules and Ettiquette that such attentions have their due weight.

The feeling is gaining ground daily here that war is nearly done with. Some think there will be some big fighting yet but more think otherwise. I am inclined to think that Lee will make one more desperate effort though he knows for a certainty that his destruction would be the result. It would be the desperation of a guilty conscience. Deserters come in daily and at all hours of the day, and they do not come singly as heretofore but in squads

There is a general good understanding between the two picket lines. They get to gether and trade knives and tobacco or any thing they have. Soap is a very scarce article among the rebs, and they will trade any thing they have for it. This morning one came over and wanted to trade a knife for some soap. After the bargain was made the Union Soldier got the soap to hand to the reb when the reb looked round behind him to see if any of his companions were looking—and said never mind the soap Yank, I am going where there is plenty of it and started and run into our lines as fast as he could leg it. The rebels pickits sung out lay down Yanks we are going to shoot. The deserter said you never mind them they wont hit any body—they fire [at,] for that, they want to come as bad as I do, they'l fire over our heads—and sure enough they did high in the air. This speaks volumes for the feelings of the rebel soldiers. And I think it a queer kind of warfare anyhow   But it is much pleasenter than constant shooting. There are some singular incidents connected with our picket duty here, some of which I have related in a letter to Helen.

I saw a letter today written by Dr Thayer[3] to the Surgeon of the 11th Vt. in which he speaks very complimentery of me, and says that I am to have the first chance. There is a prospect of a vacancy in the 5th Vt. The surgeon of that regiment went home on a leave and has now been gone 20 days over his time, and is reported absent without leave, which will knock him higher than a kite. It may not be hardly christian to wish it, yet what is one man['s] luck is another['s] misfortune—and if he is a mind to be such a fool I am perfectly willing that he suffer the consequences, and *if* I *should* get his place he has no one to blame but himself. The general belief here is that I am going into the cavalry—but I should prefer an Infantry regiment.

Feb 21st 1865

My dear—I [received] yours of the 14th last evening. Was glad to

FIGURE 64. Joseph C. Rutherford. Vermont Historical Society.

2. Presumably this was General Lewis A. Grant, commander of the First Vermont Brigade. The Rutherfords resided for a time in Blackstone, Massachusetts.

3. Dr. Samuel W. Thayer was Vermont's surgeon-general.

learn that you were all well, and as usual you have done well. I was very sick last night, but am all right to day—except a slight diarrhea. I have written all the news—except [what] we got to day and you will have there before this reaches you, of Charleston being captured. We had a salute of 100 guns at 12 oclock to day.

I will [write] a letter again in a day or so.

God bless you all

> Your Affectionate
> Husband
> J. C. Rutherford

FIGURE 65. Edwin C. Hall. Vermont Historical Society.

1. Edwin C. Hall Papers (MSA 130.5), folder 21, VHS.

"We all feel as though this is to be the climax of this war"

Private Edwin C. Hall of Brookfield, Company G, Tenth Vermont Infantry, to his father, March 26, 1865.[1]

The Tenth particpated in the assault on the rebel right on March 26.

Camp near Petersburg Va
March 26th 1865

Dear Father

As there has been another battle here you will of course want to hear from me. As yet, I am all right and have thus far been lucky enough to get out of it, being on camp guard— I was detailed for guard the 23d. the 24th the Regt had to go on picket and I was left on guard. the Regt was to be relieved yesterday but on account of the fighting they were not and probably will not be to day. Our Regt and the 6th Maryland done all the fighting in front of where they were on picket. They charged twice on the enemys works. the first time, they were repulsed but the 2d time we had two Regts massed in the centre and charged and broke their line, then our Reg't charged them on the left and were successful, captureing 700 prisoners with their guns and equipments. The Jonnies did not seem to make much resistence the 2d time, they only fired once and then threw down their guns   Our loss was small, but 2 killed in our Regt, none hurt in our Co. It seems the rebels did not make as much as they calculated to when they commenced in the morning. They made an attack on our extreme left, and in the centre before daylight yesterday morning they took our boys by surprise here in the centre. they charged on Fort Sedgwick [Fort Stedman] nearly a mile on our right with 2 Divisions, and gained the fort, driving our boys back to the railroad, but they rallied, and led by 2 officers from this Corps, they drove them back with only one Brigade.

When they were on the retreat, the forts opened on them with grape and cannister and the slaughter was nearly equal to that of Spottsylvania. I have not heard the loss on either side. 500 prisoners were taken from them, and it is reported that more than that of ours were captured. I have not heard from the left yet only that we captured over 1000 there— there was considerable manouvering among the troops all day. The President, Gens Grant, Meade, and Wright were riding around during the day "taking observations". they were here to the fort opposite our camp over half an hour, and I had a good chance to see "Uncle Abe," and I beleive he is the homliest man I have seen for three years. But I guess he is good natured, for he was a grinning all the time he was here. I guess I wont say much about him, for if he should find out that I was making fun of him, he would give me 60 days furlough. At 4 oclock the whole line charged, from the extreme left, to nearly opposite our camp. the little fort here by our camp, sent their compliments in the shape of "6 second fuse shell," and the "Jons" were so (un)civil as not to return them. In half an hour there was a roar of musketry from one end of the line to the other, mingled with the cheers of our boys as they charged the rebel works. It is reported that they carried the first line, taking a good many prisoners   Dont know whether they intend holding it or not, but I should judge they do, as the intrenching tools were sent down last night. The 5th Corps were moving last night and we expect there will be another attack to day. They will have a cold time if they do, for the wind is blowing hard from the N.W. so that a fire is very comfortable this morning. John and I are lucky boys this time. John is better, but is excused from duty and I am on guard. So we can have a good fire. Our tents are standing, the boys did not take anything but their rubbers and Haversacks   the rest of the stuff is lying loose in the tents just as though there was nothing the matter. But if there is no attack to day they will be in to night   Tell the children that the boys captured a lot of trinkets yesterday, and if I can get any of them will send them home. You will probably get the news of this fight before this letter reaches you and will get the particulars more correct than I can give them as we know nothing more than what is transpiring in this vicinity and most of *that* are rumors   We all feel as though this is to be the climax of this war. They have begun the game and Grant is going to finish it for them   He has got 4 Kings now, while they have got but two and if he does not make a mismove he will soon have them cornered

Hoping success will crown our arms, and with much love to all I remain yours as ever I was

    E C Hall

Co G 10th Vt Vols
Washington D C

Dont you put this letter in the papers now!   Ed

"the cheers from regt after regt as he passed along the line were almost deafening"

Lieutenant Colonel Valentine G. Barney of Swanton, Ninth Vermont Infantry, to his wife, Maria, March 27, 1865.[1]

1. Valentine G. Barney Letters (MS 104), folder 3, VHS.

Hd Qrs 9th Vt Vols
2d Brig 3d Div 24th A.C.
March 27th 1865

My dear Maria

I have just time to write you a few lines before drill hour. I should have written you yesterday but, we were extremely busy all day   first came inspections then an order for review and the rumor was circulated that the *President* was to be present. so all were anxious to be out and get a sight at him, we formed line at 12 o.c. M. and remained waiting for him until 4 1/2 o.c. when the long, lank, form and honest countainance made their appearance on a fine horse, and the cheers from regt after regt as he passed along the line were almost deafening and made many horses—frantic with excitement, much to the discomfort of their riders— The President rode along the line with his hat in his hand, and waving to all as he passed   he was accompanied by a host of officers, women, & orderlies. The most prominent, were Genls Grant, Ord, & Gibbon,— Mrs Lincoln and other distinguished ladies were along and rode in ambulances— Old Abe looked very much careworn and emaciated   On the whole it was quite a grand affair. We are having very busy times here just now, and I expect that there will be some fighting ere long but not on this front   All the troops except our Division left this front last night during the night and our Div holds the whole line. I cant tell where they have gone, but I think that perhaps they have joined the Army of the Potomac, and that the great battle will come off over there and probably in a very few days, we will get the news of its result, It seems that the Rebels did not make very well out of their attack on our lines of the 9th Corps on the 25th inst—as they lost 2700 prisoners and all the ground they had gained— nothing is expected to be done here on this front unless the rebs—attack us which is not probable, but we expect to go in and occupy Richmond when it is Evacuated as we are the nearest troops to the place— I got a letter from you a day or two since and am sorry to learn of mothers failing condition   Excuse this hastily written sheet and accept the warmest love it is possible for husband to have for his wife

Your Affectionate
V. G. Barney

Spring 1865

Chapter 17

The long siege of Petersburg came to a sudden end early in the spring of 1865. After General Lee's failed assault on Fort Stedman on March 25, General Grant resumed his drive around the rebel right flank south of Petersburg, forcing Lee to extend his lines further to the west. Together with the losses of March 25, this extension stretched the Confederate army to a dangerous length. Philip Sheridan's April 1 victory at Five Forks, at the western extremity of the rebel defenses, in which another five thousand Southerners were captured, set the stage for the final assault on Petersburg the following day.[1]

The main thrust of the attack fell on the center of the rebel line south of the city. The Sixth Corps took the lead and, as usual, the First Vermont Brigade was first in line. Before sunrise, the Union troops cleared paths through the abatis and chevaux de frise, and charged up the steep inclines facing the rifle pits, taking heavy casualties as they advanced. Captain Charles G. Gould of the Fifth Vermont Infantry was the first man to reach the works. He jumped into a rifle pit and fought alone against its inhabitants, receiving serious bayonet and saber wounds before he was rescued by a comrade.[2] The blue soldiers swarmed on and soon forced a gap in the rebel line. Swinging to the left, the disorganized mass of Union soldiers outflanked and captured the fortifications all the way to Hatcher's Run, some four miles to the southwest. The breach was now well beyond repair. Petersburg must be abandoned, and with it the capital.

North of Richmond a division of the Twenty-Fourth Army Corps, including the Ninth Vermont Infantry, and two divisions of the U.S. Colored Troops, waited anxiously on April 2 to learn the results of the assault on Petersburg. They were poised to attack at daybreak when word came early in the morning of April 3 that Richmond was being abandoned. With the light of day a skirmish line of the Ninth Vermont Infantry and the Twelfth New Hampshire advanced through two lines of abandoned works—for a time racing against the Colored Troops—into the outskirts of Richmond. Colonel Edward H. Ripley, formerly commander of the Ninth Vermont but now in charge of a brigade in the same division, assembled his troops near the James River docks for the formal march into the city. Ripley found Richmond in a panic. Fires set by the retreating rebels burned out of control and explosions rocked the city as the arsenal went up in flames. General Godfrey Weitzel, commanding the Twenty-Fifth Corps, put Ripley in charge of the provost guards and ordered him to extinguish the fires. Before long the streets were cleared of looters and mobs, and the fires were contained, though it would be days before they burned out.[3]

Despite the rapid turn of events, Lee pulled out of the Richmond-Petersburg defenses in good order. His plan was to retreat westward along the Appomattox River twenty miles to Amelia Court House, then follow the Danville Railroad southwest and join forces with Joseph Johnston in North Carolina. At Amelia Court House, however, a shortage of rations caused a long delay. Soon the Confederate commander learned that the railroad had been captured several miles to the south. The hungry rebels pushed on westward, vigorously pursued by Northern infantry. Many rebels fell out, weary from the march and lack of food, and were scooped up by the Northerners. At Sayler's Creek on April 6, some two thousand rebels were killed or wounded in a rear guard action, and six thousand more were cut off and captured. Two days later the remainder of Lee's army—now fewer than thirty thousand men—stopped near Appomattox Court House. The Union cavalry, followed quickly by two infantry corps, had scrambled past the rebels on the south side of the Appomattox, and now lay across their road of retreat. Lee surrendered the next day.[4]

The news reached Vermont by telegram late that night, April 9. Perhaps no other event, before or since, brought such widespread, spontaneous exultation to the streets of Burlington. "By midnight," the *Daily Times* reported, "all our bells were clanging a joyous peal, and bonfires springing up with magic rapidity in our streets." Someone commandeered a brass cannon in Battery Park, and fired it continually until

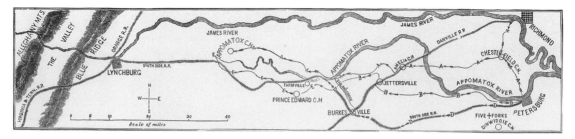

MAP 20. The retreat of Lee's army ("A") and pursuit by Union army units ("B" and "E"), April 3–8, 1865. Guernsey and Alden, *Harper's Pictorial History of the Civil War*, vol. 2, 769. UVM.

FIGURE 66. "The Village of Appomattox Court House." *Battles and Leaders of the Civil War*, vol. 4, 729. UVM.

dawn. Mobs of citizens paraded through the streets, stopping at the homes of prominent men to demand speeches.[5]

The rejoicing would last less than a week. On the night of Friday, April 14, President Lincoln was shot by John Wilkes Booth at Ford's Theater in Washington. He died the next morning, four years and a day after the surrender of Fort Sumter. Through four years of suffering and sorrow, Lincoln had been the focus of moral authority in the prosecution of the war, a symbol of perseverance in a righteous cause. He lived long enough to see the war nearly ended—to walk through the streets of Richmond, thronged by freedmen. The military question was nearly resolved, but the larger question—what was to be the role of the freed slaves in American society—remained unanswered, and now the man most responsible for raising it was gone.

The war was not yet over, of course. Joseph Johnston still commanded a sizeable army in North Carolina, and Edmund Kirby Smith still threatened the peace in the Mississippi Valley. General William T. Sherman negotiated an armistice with Johnston after Lee's surrender, but when the terms proved unacceptable to the administration, Grant acted quickly to bring more pressure to bear on Johnston. He ordered the cavalry and the Sixth Corps to join forces with Sherman and force Johnston to accept the same terms as Lee. General Horatio G. Wright of the Sixth Corps, bent on demonstrating the marching efficiency of his troops, pushed the men to the limits of their endurance. In four days the infantry marched one hundred miles, beating the cavalry to Danville. There, news of Johnston's surrender the day before reached the weary men, and the hard march came to an end.[6]

1. Valentine G. Barney Letters
(MS 104), folder 3, VHS.

"cheer after cheer are heard from every Regt"

**Lieutenant Colonel Valentine G. Barney of Swanton,
Ninth Vermont Infantry, to his wife, Maria, April 3, 1865.**[1]

Richmond Va— Hd qrs 9th Vt
Fulton Hill—
Redoubt No 2d Apr 3d 65—

My dear Maria

Here we are and I am *too much elated* to write, but will merly say
that we came into this City about nine ten.o.c. this forenoon, and are
situated as you see by my date, The enemy evacuated their line during the night and we started at daylight and came in, quick time, The
first Infantry that entered the city were 9th Vt skirmishers. We found
the City all on fire and explosions are now heard every second in all
directions
Later I have just rode through the City and visited the Capital Cus-
tom House & the Spotswood Hotel, There is intense excitement
throughout Streets thronged with houseless women & children, Col
Ripley is Provost Marshal Genl of the City & I think we are to be the
provost guard of the City— The main business part of the City is now
on fire but the fires are being allayed and I think the greater part of the
City will be preserved
We are about one mile from the Capital & my Hd qrs are at a very
fine & elegantly furnished dwelling— The people are from Massachusetts & have raised the Stars & Stripes over their house— I hear nothing from Grant yet but suppose he is in pursuit of Lee's flying mob—
all looks favorable—and we are enjoying ourselves hugely over our
success and cheer after cheer are heard from every Regt— I have no
time to write now any more but will give a detailed account of all in a
day or two Love to all

     Your Aff Husband
     V. G. Barney

"Babylon is fallen"

1. Arthur P. Morey Papers,
Gertrude Mallary Collection,
Bradford, Vermont.

**Captain Arthur P. Morey of Norwich, Company F, Twenty-
Second U.S. Colored Troops, to his cousin, April 4, 1865.**[1]

Babylon is fallen and we are going to occupy the land. We marched through Richmond yesterday in column of companies drums beating and colors flying and are now lying quietly just outside the city in an elegant bastion fort built in /61. You cannot imagine what an amount of earth works are around the city, as far as one can see and several miles farther there is a succession of forts of tremendous strength. Being in something of a hurry I cannot write much to day but will do better next time.

> Your Cousin
> Arthur P Morey

"thare are many a friend left to mourn the affects of that days battle but it was the decicive Battle"

Private Oren C. Mudge of Mount Holly, Company G, Fifth Vermont Infantry, to Mrs. Gertrude Howard, April 4, 1865.[1]

1. George J. Howard Papers (Misc. File 694), VHS.

Tuesday Apr 4th
Camp in the Field

Mrs Howard how or what shall I say   it is only a Soldiers duty but to me this is a painfull one   Sargent G. J. Howard is dead—his fighting for his country has ended— we hav lost a noble Soldier—but what is that to your loss   he went to the charg (on Sunday morn) like a bold Soldier— he was struck with a piece of Shell or Grape Shot in the left Leg near the knee and it was badly broken— he was caried back to the Division Hospital whare Dr Allen (our Regimental Surgeon) amputated it   Dr Allen told me that he died Monday morning Apr 3rd   Dr Allen has got his wallet and memoranda Book in his possesion—his knapsack was in my care at the time   I hav taken what papers he had that I deamed of any value and will send the same to you   Shad Peck was killed before George was and George had his wallet and day Book when he died   Dr Allen took them also supposeing them to be Howards   Austin Benson got a bad wound in the head the same day but is doeing well I hear—and thare are many a friend left to mourn the affects of that days battle but it was the decicive Battle   Petersburg Richmond and the most of the Confederate Army are taken   the rebellion is crushed

I write this in haste as we are on the march and dont know how soon we may start

write me if thare is any thing I can doe for you   I will doe it freely

yours with respects
O. N. Mudge

1. Edwin C. Hall Papers (MSA 130.5), folder 22, VHS.

"three cheers for Peace and three times three for U S Grant"

**Private Edwin C. Hall of Brookfield, Company G,
Tenth Vermont Infantry, to his parents, April 9, 1865.**[1]

At Parks Station on the Danville RR
Apr 9th 1865

Dear Parents

You are doubtless anxiously waiting to hear from me so I will write a few words, as I am feeling lonesome to day   Since I last wrote you we have been having rather an exciting time as you have probably been informed by the papers   Fighting and marching has been the order of exercises of the past 2 weeks, and at evry step Victory has crowned our efforts. The strongholds of the Rebellion have been broken up and Southern chivalry has nearly played out, judging from what I have seen of it   The last letter that I wrote home was dated Mar 31st. Little did I think what I was going to pass through during the next 24 hours   we were then lying in camp and hoping to get a good sleep that night as we had been kept awake 3 or 4 nights before that. But we were disappointed, for we had but just got to bed when suddenly away on the right was heard the deafening roar of artillery and soon all the cannon along the line was at work   We were ordered into the Breastworks and remained there until about 11 oclock when the Brig formed and marched out to the rear of the picket line "formed in line of battle", supported by the 2d Brigade, and laid down. Not until then did we think that we should ever attempt to carry the works in front for we supposed it impossible to do it. But we could plainly see now what was for us to do and for awhile there must have been a "powerful sight o thinking" among the boys of the 1st Brigade   But they did not have time to think long for the rebel picket thinking something was going on behind our picket line opened fire on us which was replied to by our pickets   The firing was kept up for 15 minutes when we heard their officers give the order to "Cease firing" and one of the "Jons" halloed "Haloo Yanks"   Guess its nothin but an "*April fool*" after all. Not so much of an April fool as you may think replied one of our boys. Upon this they commenced firing again which lasted for some little time this time 2 of our boys were hit Serjt Fitsgerald—in the shoulder—and Horace was hit in the leg— At 4 oclock the order to charge was given and from that time until we reached the 2d fort I hardly remember what passed (except lead) which I remember passed close enough so that I felt the heat of them)   At the 2d fort we captured 6 guns which were turned on the "retreating Jons"   At the 3d fort they rallied and made a stand   But with colors flying the 3d Div pressed on amid showers of "grape and cannister" and soon gained the ditch of the fort where we laid down   some of them got into the ditch   At the right of the fort was their barracks and a party of us were sent around to get a cross fire on them   We got there without getting hit but by this time the rebels rushed out of the fort and charged on our boys and they had to fall back to the 2d fort, thus "*flanking us*" and cutting off our retreat and in less time than I can write it your humble servant *found himself a prisoner*   Some of the boys tried to get away and one of Co K boys was shot dead. some of them got away. We were told to go to the rear   So I took my gun and started without waiting for a guard I got away a piecc watched my chance and dodged into one of the shanties, took my gun to pieces and hid it in some straw and jamed myself *under the lower bunk*   I then took my "valubles" and put them in the lining of my cap   I laid there nearly an hour during which the shot and shell flew round and through the building rather careless   I was struck on the thigh with a piece of shell, I suppose, for about that time there was one went through the building   I did not think then that it had hurt me much. But for the last 3 or 4 days I have thought different. After an hours hard fighting our boys succeeded in driving them from the fort and I crawled out of my prison put my gun together again and followed the troops   We came up with them just as they got to a swamp   Just then the old Vt Brigade appeared to them on the right flank and we soon had them in the trap   One whole Brigade with its commander was captured and marched into our lines   Gen Grant at this time came riding along the lines and such a noise as was made I have seldom heard before   The pursuit was then abandoned and the troops went up toward Petersburg and supported the 9th Corps when they charged on Petersburg   The next morning we went back to our old camp and got our knapsacks and started to head them off this way. I marched one day when my leg swelled up and was so painful that I had to ride the rest of the way   We were just in time for the Jons were here and had just commenced to intrench themselves   But the Old Sixth with "Custers Cavalry" "went in" and after a sharp fight routed them captureing Gens Ewell Fits Hugh Lee with nearly their commands together with 27 pieces of Artillery and 300 wagons   Gens Ewell F H Lee and 4 other big bugs, and 400 officers and 15000 privates left here yesterday for Washington   The troops followed up and whipped them again across the Appommattox captureing another wagon train and 6000 prisoners   It is reported that the rebel Gen Pickett was captured yesterday   The wounded are all here waiting for the cars from Petersburg. they are expected up to day   There are nearly 200 wounded rebels here and three rebel surgeons to take care of them and about 250 of our men most of them slightly wounded There is but 2 from our Reg't here. John is here   has got the mumps guess he will go to Petersburg   I shall not go any further than here if I can help it   my leg is not swelled much now but is pretty sore, but if I can get back to the Regt again I believe I shall try it   The fighting is nearly played out and now I have begun. I want to see it out   We have had 10 killed and wounded in our Co beside myself— Sam Parker from Chelsea that enlisted when I did is dead   was wounded Sunday morning and died Monday   the Brookfield boys are all well as far as I know   I have got things to send home that I captured in the fight sunday—some papers and a little money   I got a shirt and Towel but I will keep them   I might have got any amount of stuff as they left everything but I had something else to do besides foraging that day My leg begins to ache and I have got to get out and stir round some will finish this tomorrow

      E C Hall

9 oclock Monday morning

   It is raining quite hard this morning and it would be quite lonesome were it not for the glorious news that has been received here   Lee has surrendered to Grant and I should think so by the noise round here the 9th Corps is making the woods ring for miles around   It is most to good news to beleive but still it is not impossible
However I guess it is so for there was an officer just here and read the official notice to the wounded and you had ought to have been here to heard the cheers both from the rebels and our men   Hurrah! three cheers for Peace and three times three for U S Grant   I am going back to the Regt tomorrow and it is not strange if you see me in B before the 4th of July so make a lot of Maple Sugar for I am Hungry
Hurrah! Hurrah!! Hurrah!!! Hurrah!!!!

      E C Hall

"the bells are tolling which so lately rang in joy"

Ann Eliza Smith of St. Albans to her husband, Governor J. Gregory Smith, April 15, 1865.[1]

Ann Eliza was on a visit to Massachusetts.

1. Smith Family of St. Albans Papers, carton 1, folder 49, UVM.

Saturday Morn April 15 65—

Oh! my dearest, why am I not with you this morning, that we might bear this dreadful grief together! What a week of conflicting and contrasting vicissitude has this been! Victory and triumph, the wildest joy, and overflowing gratitud Thanksgiving, and fasting, the triumphant raising of the Flag at Sumter, murder by the bullet and knife of the stealthy assassin, the tolling of bells, all sights of woe, and a gloom that is almost the palsy of despair! Truly "On honors head, horrors accumulate!" There is but one comfort for the country, one hope   God still reigns and "can save by many, or by few." It is true "no one man is indespensable," but it certainly seems as if the most inextricable confusion must prevail—

Yesterday I went to Ipswich and came home about 1/2 past eight, very tired. I suppose I ought not to have gone— I went to bed early, restless and depressed—fell asleep wishing you were with me and feeling an unaccountable sadness. I woke after a few hours sleep, agitated and distressed   I could not tell why— It seemed to me something dreadful was coming, but of a personal nature   I covered my eyes as day light came & resolutely composed myself to sleep— In the morning Mrs. Millis came in before I was dressed and sank into a chair, (she had been to the door once before, but had not courage to come in) and seeing her expression, I said, "You are sick Mrs Millis?" "Oh no," she said, "but we have such sad news." Of course I thought it was from home, but in a moment she added "President Lincoln has been shot!" I was very much overcome and I dont get over it, there is a sense of personal loss, with the awfulness and horror [of] the deed— Kind, merciful man, he will I am sure find mercy with God— How kindly he treated you; my eyes will fill with tears when I think of the last evening you spent with him. If I felt well enough, I should start for home this evening—I can't bear that you should be alone tomorrow, and beside that *I* don't want [to] be without you at this moment—

I hope you will write to Mr Stanton tomorrow— Poor man, I Pray God to give him strength [to] bear the heavy burden that must inevitably come upon him— I wish you could help in some way, to steady matters . . . in this hour of awful agitation & confusion   The government has been too lenient— These arch traitors, and fiends, must be put out of the way, or there will be a scene [of] murder and midnight assasination, unparall[el]ed in the history of the world

How much I do want to see you or some body of my own kin— Mr. Millis looked sick and said he was so— The city they say is greatly agitated. I hope to go down this afternoon—and to see Lawrence if he has not left.

It is *very quiet* and pleasant here; there seems to be nothing going on— I would like to be a[t] the head of a small household for a short time and see what work I should make of it—but I would not loose one of those committed to my care—they are all too dear   I only ask for strength, if it be God's will, to take good car of them— I shall think of you all day tomorrow and hope it will be a more cheerful day to you than it will be to me—   I expect to see you next week   Mr. M thinks you will come Mon— I hope you will telegraph him so that I can get moved. I should be sorry to have you and the children come and not find me there   Give my love to them all—I want to see them very much— I hope all goes well— It [is] now 12 oclock and the bells are tolling which so lately rang in joy—

God be with you and bless all the dear ones is the prayer of yours ever

Ann Eliza

"words cannot express the loathing yes <u>hate</u> that I now feel for <u>anybody</u> that ever even <u>winked</u> at this Rebellion"

Private Henry E. Dunbar of Newbury, Company A, Third Massachusetts Heavy Artillery, to his wife, Mary, April 16, 1865.[1]

1. Henry E. Dunbar Papers, MHI.

Ft. Bunker Hill D.C.
Sunday Apr..16th 1865..10..a.m.

My Dear Wife

Our joy is turned to sorrow—mourning & indignation— Our loved President is dead, murdered & words cannot express the loathing yes *hate* that I now feel for *anybody* that ever even *winked* at this Rebellion. I can hardly contain myself now when I think of it & I can think of nothing else—& I am not alone, if we could have our own way here, we would commence *now* & *hang* without judge or jury not only every outright Rebel but every *sympathiser*, that we could get our hands upon, & I am not certain but we *shall yet*. Are anxiously awaiting "Andy.s" message to know what his Policy will be with regard to them. We are all ready here for a *complete annihilation* of the whole *cursed race*, & I am about willing to believe that God would justify such a Policy   if not, why should He permit the *fiends* to murder our good president, not to mention the attempted murder of the others. "*How can* we bear it" with any degree of patience. O it is *so* agravating & what good will it do the *incarnate Devils*, except gratifying their revenge—it will not *help* them but rather the reverse as the effect will be to exasperate the entire North, & *woe be* to the Rebs that our boys get their hands on, after this, at least if all feel as we do here. The Papers have just come & I must stop to read.   H.   Well I have read the Chronicle but cant get much consolation from it. They had.nt caught Booth at last accounts, but scouts & Detectives are scouring the country in every direction day & night & I dont believe he can escape long, but what death is there bad enough for *him*.

There is a line of Pickets stationed all round the City only 50 feet apart & not a soul allowed to leave the District for any purpose, & they are arresting everybody in citizens clothes white & black. The dinner bell is ringing & must stop again.

Well I have had some "bean *swaggle*" as the boys call it, a kind of a mongrel bean soup, & now will try & write a little more. I was some disappointed last night in not getting a letter but perhaps I shall get it to night   I went over to see Ned a few minutes ago & he had just come in from Picket. he had heard that Booth was caught & was disappointed when I told him, he was not. was in hopes Ned got a letter & dont know but he did. he had.nt had time to find out when I was there as he had to take care of his horse the *first thing* of course   am glad I dont have to take care of one. dont think I should like his place at all & finaly to tell the truth, after being where I now am dont think I could *enjoy soldiering* of any kind very well, even amid all this excitement, when everything Q. master.s men & all have to go on Guard Picket or Scouting   we have had nothing to do, & so many of the men are gone from the F.t. that we dont even have to play—& its lucky we dont for we shouldnt feel like playing anything but *dirges*   I hardly know what we could do now if we should hear that Johnson had surrendered or of any big victory. Everybody are so paralized that we couldnt *rejoice* if we wanted to, I never passed such a miserable day as yesterday in my life & very appropriately, the clouds were weeping all day, too. But I have no language to begin to Express my feelings so will not attempt it. suffice it to say that the whole Nation are mourning to gether now, even to California & the Territories & I suppose the best thing for us all to do, is to pray that God will not send any more such calamities upon us. I suppose its best to be reconciled to this, but its a *hard job* for me.

5.. o.clock P.. M. Have just been to supper & now will try & finish my letter. I rec.d yours of Friday a few minutes ago & glad to hear from you again. suppose you have heard the sad news ere this & *your* rejoicing is turned to mourning   guess there never was so sudden or sad a change before in this, or any other country, but I suppose it.s all for the best, tho, we cant see it. all I can say is that we, as a Nation must be terrible wicked to need *such* a punishment after all that we have sacrificed previously. We got the news here about 12 o.clock the same night. an orderly came out & came into our quarters & told us. We all felt like crying, & Col. Albert *did* cry like a baby but that feeling passed with me soon & then I began to grow mad & have not got over *that* yet, & if I was at the *Front* now could fight with a *good stomach.* I was glad to hear from "Lue"   guess she had.nt got my letter, as she did.nt mention it. About the Band or myself I have.nt much to tell you that.s new   Let.s see guess I have.nt told you about going to the City, again. it was Thursday. we got the Order at 4.. PM. to report at Div. Hd Qrs. (Gen.l Harding) at 7.. & we had 2—4 horse teams & all hands went in, played there some 2 hours, & then serrenaded about all over the City. The whole City was illuminated & it was a *bigger* time than when we went before, We did.nt get home till 3..o.clock. the most of us got home sober, but 2 or 3 got rather too much whiskey & I dont much wonder for we were invited in to drink 10 or 15 times. But I have sent Papers giving a full description of the whole performance. Will also send *to day.s* Chronicle, with all the Details of the Murder, & read the *Editorials* & the Poetry. I went over to see Ned again this P.M. but he was asleep & I did.nt wake him. It has been pleasant to day   no not pleasant either for the wind has blown almost a hurricane all day & blows some yet tho. not so hard & guess it will go down with the sun Guess I cant write any more this time & guess you.l be *glad of it,* with my *present feelings.* If there.s any thing new will write a little in the morning   with love to all

I am ever yours H. E. Dunbar

Monday 7. a.m.   all well & no news   H

"Many stout-hearted men were seen to weep"

1. Parker/Fleming Family Papers, carton 1, folder 12, UVM.

Catherine E. Parker of Burlington to her family, April 27, 1865.[1]

The daughter of Waterbury's Reverend Charles C. Parker, Catherine apparently was a teacher in her aunt's school in Burlington.

Burlington, Vermont, April [27] 1865

Dear Mama and all—

I have been thinking that it is high time for some of us to write you and I have not written for many weeks. I do not know whether Eddie wrote you last week or not and so I will tell about the services in our church a week ago yesterday. The church was draped in black. The Rep. flag was festooned twice—the center being fastened with black bands—to the middle of the two central pillars behind the pulpit—festooned either way—to the gallery. It was kept in place by bands of black wound around it. The galleries were trimmed with black, going straight around them. The organ was trimmed with two festoons of black. It looked finely, but very mournfully. The house was well filled —and Mr. Mix out-did himself. Many stout-hearted men were seen to weep. Auntie Brown noticed old Mr. C Blodgett crying. The ladies wished much to assist Mr. Mix in the evening—and have him repeat his sermon—which was from 11 Sam. 1.19[2]—

Some gentleman afterward came and asked him to *preach* and he consented— His text was from Matt. 6.23. last clause— I never heard him speak better. A great many are mourning, because they did not go. they thought Mr. Mix had said all that he could say. Mrs. Brinsmaid was one of the number.

On Wednesday—we had no school all day. At eleven we started for church—so as to get our places. But on the way went into the Epis. church—round Bank block—and up church street. All buildings trimmed finely. The church was filled so that they brought in setees and chairs. The choir sang an hymn—two or three verses of which Mr. Camp composed—in relation to the removal of Lincoln. They sang this both times in Sabbath also. Father Buckham, Mr. Safford offered prayer. Mr. Edmunds and Mr. Mix spoke very well indeed. In addition to the trimmings which were on the sabbath before—there was a sentence sewed onto the black shawl—(Auntie Katie's) which covered all the pulpit—"The memory of the just is blessed." The pillars all round the church were wound with black—the chairs of the pulpit covered with black—and the gas-stands wound with it also. Wednesday too there was a boquet of artificial white roses—that were beautiful—on the table in front of the pulpit and white May flowers scattered round— Our church took precedence in every thing—

Uncle went away Tuesday morning to see Mr. Boardman—taking Mr. Hickok's place. John heard Chemistry and Botany and Auntie Philosophy. He got back Saturday afternoon— I guess he did not have very good success. He said that New York was completely black from one end to the other. John thinks some of going to Troy tomorrow, to be there when the body of Lincoln passes through. He came in just this minute and said he probably would not go.

Auntie Katie has boughten Miss [Newman's?] gymnastic apparatus, and we are to practise here in school by ourselves— Mary and I called on May Smith this afternoon—she is here with her sister Mrs. Wyman, who lives in this part of N. Ballard's house— We have seen Booth's picture. He does not look as if he would do such an *awful thing*. [Janice] Bancroft of Montpelier, an old boarder called today—on her way to

FIGURE 67. Catherine E. Parker. Special Collections, University of Vermont.

2. The church was the First Congregational Church on White St. (now North Winooski Avenue), whose pastor was the Reverend Eldridge Mix.

Chicago. Mr. Lord preached Sunday— All liked him *very* much. He had to pray for the country & President—but not a word about slavery. I went to Dr. Lewis a week ago today—and got through. The front tooth that I was afraid would have the nerve exposed, did not hurt as much as some others and none of them were very bad— I gave him two $3—and the gold dollar. He said he would take it for $1.50 so I gave him $7.50. He had not the bill— Mary and I have finished our sacks— I made them from my old sack and circular. Father left three sermons here. I wonder how Uncle Reuben feels now— Auntie says she would like a tub of good maple sugar—good enough to put on the table, and for cakes— Edd has had a hard cold—so have I— We are both better.

David the [no-haired?] boy from Canada who was here last summer wrote to know if he was wanted— He is coming soon. I was glad on Auntie Brown's account.

Please send me the cloth like my circular.

I would like that straw to be sent down some time—that Mary Stone gave me once. I[t] has to be sewed in a foundation— The bonnets are so small that I hate to have mine cut up—

C. E. Parker

A week last Saturday, all that were here, went to High Bridge in 12 o'clock train. No cars till eight, so walked to Winooski   some rode from there— Very good time.

"Death to all traitors is our watch word"

1. Joseph C. Rutherford Papers, box 1, folder 75, UVM.

Surgeon Joseph C. Rutherford of Newport, Seventeenth Vermont Infantry, to his wife, Hannah, April 29, 1865.[1]

Rutherford received a long-awaited promotion to surgeon in the Seventeenth in March, 1865.

Alexandria Va   Apr 29th 1865

My dear Wife,

I have just received your letter of the 24th and hasten to reply to it.

I do not wonder at your anxiety in fact I some expected just such a letter from you for my long silence.   that is long for me. If you had been in my place for the last 10 days you would not think strange of my seeming neglect. We have marched over 300 miles besides going a long way by water and our mail facilities have been very limited and I did not feel very much like writing if I had the convenien[ce]s for doing so. Then again I had nothing particularly interesting to write. You should know by this time that if any thing was wrong with me you would be informed of it at once. Though I have not (the wind blows my paper all about) written—you may rest assured that you nor our dear children are never out of mind. I dont think I am much sorry that I did let a few days slip by without writing as you will better appreciate my poor letters. You seem to feel very anxious about my exposing myself to traitors etc   Now I can well appreciate your anxiety but as I *never* visit any of the houses of the inhabitants there can be very little danger to myself.   then what good could an injury to me do the cussed traitors?

You ask my opinion of the affairs of the nation. What can *I* say— any more than I have often said—that we are coming out all right. The thing no doubt looks dark to you who are so far from the strife and field of battle, but to us every thing is looked upon as the fulfillment of the nations destiny. God rules our nation and the events of our terrible war. let us bow in submission to his will, and act the part set for us to the best of our abilities.

If Sherman has done as it is said he did—Why I think he has *dulled* —in other words made a great blunder— But so much have I become to believe in the ultimate designs of the great Ruler of all things that I feel it was intended that greater good might accrue to the nation from it. It opens the eyes of the people to the gross folly of being too lenient to these hell born traitors not only at the South but in the midst of our N.E. homes. We are all coming home soon: and our first work will be to clean out every traitor and tory—that act as foul ulcers in the living flesh of our homes. We soldiers have *vowed* it upon the alter of our country and you may depend the poisonous blood of these treacherous villians will flow freely, for the lives of many of our noble soldiers they have been the means of sacrificing. God have mercy on them for we wont— *No! Never.*

I am more surprised that Friend Seargent did not take the life of that rotten hearted scoundrel than I should have been if he had— Robinson might as well learn now as ever that his life will not be worth the asking if he is found in the country when our troops return home.[2] You may think me excited and so I am but it is an excitement that nothing but the just punishment of traitors will allay.. The country will never be safe while they are allowed to walk its surface or breath the air of heaven— Death to all traitors is our watch word—

I am surprised that Lt Seargent should make such a mistake [having] been in the service as long as he has. Ask him if a Surgeon dont wear

the *Gold leaf*? made thus  A Surgeon ranks as Major.

A Captains badge is the two *bars*—the Strap made thus

2. The identity of "Robinson" and the exact nature of his transgression are unknown. It seems unlikely that Rutherford would make such a remark about Lucius Robinson, a prominent Newport business-man and Democrat in a heavily Republican town. (See Nelson, *Frontier Crossroads*, 169–70.) "Seargant" may have been Lieutenant Moses Sargent of Company F, Eleventh Vermont Infantry.

FIGURE 68. Oak cluster and captain's bars: details from Joseph Rutherford's letter of April 29, 1865. UVM.

A surgeon ranks as major of Cavalry which gives him more pay than major of Infantry. I am glad to learn that our friend Page is improving—dont forget to remember me to him and his excelent Wife. I have got to writing   I hardly know when to stop—but the wind flirts my paper about so much that it is next to impossible to write. I have plenty of elbow room for I am under the broad canopy of heaven where the gentle zephers have their full play.

I think you will see us all home about the 1st of June. Remember me to our dear children and accept the undying love of your

Affectionate husband
J. C. Rutherford

"I hav been in the Rebel Bull Pen in Andersonvill"

**Private Bradford Sparrow of Elmore, Company D,
Fourth Vermont Infantry, to his family, May 4, 1865.[1]**

1. Bradford P. Sparrow Papers, Manuscript Files, UVM.

Parole Hospital
Jacksonville Florida May 4th 65

Dear Father Mother & Brothers   Again I am allowed to inform you of my whereabouts. It has been a long time since we corrisponded, but that could not be avoided for it has been my fate to be deprived since the 23d of last June the privilige of writing for which I feel very sorry, but the most I think of now is whether you are all as well as when I last heard from you. I suppose you hav long wondered where I was, or if you new or imagined where I was you thought it strange that while so many were exchanged that I was not a mong them. So I suppose you hav been filled with doubt & fear all the while about my being a live, but you see now that I hav lived through it though I hav had a hard seige of it for I hav been in the Rebel Bull Pen in Andersonvill, Ga. where yankee prisoners are kept, I suppose you hav heard of this place so I will not fill my sheet with a description, but I hav got out of the Confederacy at last. My health is not verry good. I hav some cough & am weak & stiff with the scurvy. but the scurvy is easy cured. all it wants is good living or more particularly plenty of vegetables   I am thin in flesh but hav a good appetite & hav had enough to eat since I got into Gods country which was the 29th of April. I am so as to be out around but not well enough to stay at camp, all that can be done for us is being done

3000 of us come in here quite unexpected, our folks knew nothing of our coming for we were not exchanged but paroled & passed in to the lines   all the supplies here come from Hilton Head S C so they can not do as well by us here as they could a round Washington   the men hav most all got new clothes, the Sanitary Commision are doing its part   this paper & envelope was given me by one of its agents, I expect they will do better by & by, how long we shall stay here I cannot tell, not long I hope. In a few week[s] I hope I shall be at home & then I can tell you all a bout prison life. Great events have transpired of late, some for the good of the nation & some for the worse, since the surender of Lee I hav been looking for peace, minute guns were fired here every half hour one day on the death of Lincoln, I will write again as soon as I can or when I get paper   when you answer this direct to Parole Hospital, Jacksonville Florida, & in care of Dr Bundy. put in some paper & envelope. I will write more next time   Yours Truly

B. P. Sparrow.

"A joyful day it will be to us and our kindred"

Adjutant James G. Gallagher of Brookfield, Fourth Vermont Infantry, to Silas Hall, May 16, 1865.[1]

Head Qr's, 4th Vermont Vols,
Camp near Danville, Virginia
May 16 1865.

Silas Hall Esq.—

My Dear Sir—

When I promised you I would write you a letter, I never imagined that I would not have some stirring incident to relate, or at least some items of news which might be interesting to you. such however is the fact; since the occupation of this place by the Federal forces, nothing has taken place but the usual monotonous routine of drills, parade, and inspection, such as all soldiers in Camp or Garrison are subject to. In the absence then of military news I venture to give you such views as I have taken of the general features of the Country and the inhabitants, hoping they will be sufficiently interesting to bear a perusal.

The City of Danville is very pleasantly situated on the Dan River, in the midst of a fine healthy region, which by proper cultivation might produce all the necessaries of life, Fruits of all kinds too night be produced in abundance, the nature of the soil is such that it is well adapted to the production of all kinds of cereals and vegetables, the "Dan" too might be made to turn thousands of spindles, thus manufacturing at

FIGURE 69. James G. Gallagher. Vermont Historical Society.

1. Edwin C. Hall Papers (MSA 130.5), folder 23, VHS.

2. Rosinante was Don Quixote's tired old horse.

home the raw material which previous to the War went North for fabrication and was then returned south to be purchased by the producer of the raw material, thus you see paying a freight both ways which by home manufacture might be saved, with a consequent reduction in the manufactured article, but Slavery has been their bane, and the curse; the Sole cause of their present degradation, and the one thing which has kept enterprise out their country and left them to day fifty years in the van of their Northern Neighbors

It [is] somewhat amusing to a Northerner to witness their attempts at cultivation, A wooden plough with straps of Iron welded on the "sheaf," an old dilapidated negro, and a Rosinante[2] for a team composes the van guard in preparing the soil, then comes harrowing, and I assure you it is harrowing to see how it is done, but perhaps I am judging them to severely; under better circumstances they might do better and I know that their every effort for the past four years has been directed to the prosecution of the War which has just closed.

The inhabitants seem to adapt themselves to the new order of things with the utmost grace and sang froid, this may in a great measure be owing to the gentle courtesy and kindly protection extended them by Maj Gen'l Wright. They mingle freely with the Soldiers, and come and go at their option   indeed very many freely express the opinion that they did not expect such treatment from the Govt forces. By order of General Wright every man is protected in the prosecution of legitimate business. The Negroes though free to go where they please are exhorted to remain and work (for hire) for their former masters, and very many of them have done so. The climate on this region is truly delightful, and I see no reason why northern men cannot come down here and settle, I am sure that by a little application of the energy and industry which they have been accustomed to, they could in a few years become independent. I suppose that up in Vt your wheat is now coming out of the ground while down here it is headed out!! I must say a word in regard to the ladies, some of the younger portion are very fair looking, and dress them in the garb of Northern ladies of like age they would in my opinion be very fair looking. The elder portion of the female sex are as a general thing, sallow complexioned, and with tall forms without hoop's, or busses, make a rather ludicrous appearance when they go abroad. They all "dip," or to speak plainly, "chew snuff"—which lowers them much in the scale of comparison with Northern ladies. The snuff is first mixed with water or some other liquid to the consistency of mustard and is then carried to the mouth with a small stick or swab, after which it is disposed of according to the taste or inclination of the "dipper."

I have not seen any of the Brookfield boys since my arrival but Lieut Ditly and Gus Freeman   they told me however that Ed, and D. Lyman with other boys from "B" were well. I should have gone to se them but

I have been engaged every moment of the time since my arrival in arranging and trying to adjust the Regimental Records. I take pleasure in informing you that we shall start from here by Rail to Richmond to morrow or the day after. From Richmond we shall probably march to Washington and after being reviewed there be sent to Vermont to be mustered out of Service. A joyful day it will be to us and our kindred. The work for which we volunteer'd four years ago has been accomplished,—The Union is preserved—The Confederacy is a thing of the past its bogus President, is now a prisoner and if the law shall be put in force against him and he be made to suffer death for his high handed crimes I shall feel that I have not fought or my brothers blood been shed in vain   Truly Yours, J. Gallagher

"I know assuredly that no other one there ever exerted the influence for good, over my husband that Willie did"

Mattie E. Spafford of Chester to Ann Stevens, June 3, 1865.[1]

Mattie's husband, Henry W. Spafford, was commissary sergeant of the Fourth Vermont Infantry when he was taken prisoner on October 11, 1863, three days before Willie Stevens's capture. Ann Stevens was teaching at Glenwood Academy in Brattleboro.

1. Robinson Family Papers, box 40, folder 12, Sheldon.

Gassetts Station Vermont—
June 3d— 1865—

My dear *Friend*—   for thus you have granted me permission to address you—and I prize the privilige highly rest assured.—

Your kind and most welcome letter was rec'd by me yesterday afternoon, and I gladly improve this early opportunity to reply. Accept both my husband's and my own sincere thanks for the photograph of your dear Brother. We shall ever prize it highly as with a tender, sacred reverence we ever cherish the memory of the dear, departed original who crowned his pure, noble life by its last glorious sacrifice on the altar of Liberty and Righteousness. Truly his was an offering in similitude like unto Abel's and how can it prove other than acceptable to "Our Father" above? Your brother's picture is a noble one—how firmly and unmistakeably does his countenance bear the impress of the noble, manly soul within—and dear Miss Stevens, if his countenance here was so strongly stamped with purity and truth where everything is poor and imperfect at best how must it *now* shine with holiness and joy ineffable in those higher realms of bliss where his freed soul basks forevermore in the light of God's throne and the presence of *Jesus*—

"*Oh what must it be to be there?*" is often the cry of my soul as I meditate on the joys of Heaven. But your Brother *now* knows *all* the height and breadth and depth of God's love I feel assured for from what Mr. Spafford has told me of him I think he must have been an earnest, devoted christian while here—and this must be a source of unspeakable consolation to you now. I enclose another of Mr. Spafford's pictures for your Mother. the other is so poor and imperfect   Please remember me with the truest respect and regard to her. I should be pleased indeed to have your's and your Mother's photographs and hope I may soon. Willie's (I may call him so?) looks lonely in my album now— Truly *I* can say I love both yourself and your brother's memory for my husband's sake and he seemed to almost *worship* Willie. I believe he was his nearest and dearest friend in the army and he has many warm friends there. I know assuredly that no other one there ever exerted the influence for good, over my husband that Willie did, and when I heard of his death not only did I regret it much, for the sake of the near and dear friends he had left but for *my husband's* sake. I felt truly that he had lost a *true friend*, one who could he have been permitted to remain here longer would have lead him up into a purer, nobler, *higher* life than he has ever yet attained although as you so beautifully express it he is now "one of Nature's best"— oh he *is* a good and noble and *true* man, my dear friend and for much of this he has to thank your dear brother— Thank you for your kind congratulations, they are very grateful to me I assure you. Mr. Spafford was home on a short "leave" in March and we spoke of you and wished we could see you but his time was so limited we could not go to Brattleboro   He is now in Washington and expecting to be discharged the service *this month* some time. He wishes me to meet him in B. and I shall endeavor to do so. If I know in time to write you when we shall be there I will do so. We shall certainly call on you.— Truly with all the nation my heart mourns the sad death of our revered President, and with it also rejoices at the restoration of *sweet peace*— My joy is too deep for utterance and often our greatest eloquence lieth in silence— You express your gratitude for the kindness shown your brother by my husband but *we* have *greater* reason to be grateful for *his* kindness to my Husband— when released from his long confinement in Richmond's vile dungeons and but the mere shadow of his former self, weak, emaciated and with no money, *nothing* but barely clothes enough to cover his nakedness— it was *your brother* who so kindly shared with him his bed, his food, his clothing, his money until we could send him a box from home. Oh *we* have far greater cause for gratitude and truly we are grateful.— When last at home Mr. Spafford had a towel that Willie gave him—on one corner his name was marked, but he took it back with him as he wanted something that was Willie's by him— We shall always keep it if he is not so unfortunate as to lose it before he returns—

I tell you this little incident knowing how grateful it must be to you to have this proof of his love for your brother—

But forgive me if I have wearied you with this long letter and also please excuse the haste in which I have been obliged to pen it. I should be happy indeed to number you with my correspondents if it would be agreeable to you, and when we are nicely settled in life we hope to receive many and long visits from you—

Hoping that our brief acquaintance may ripen into a firm and lasting friendship I am truly—

> your friend—
> Mattie E. Spafford

Epilogue

By the end of May nothing remained for the volunteer soldiers to do but endure the irritatingly slow process of mustering out. Drilling continued for some, but there were no casualties to report and no military developments to write home about. Some wondered how they would pick up where they had left off, while others knew already that there was no going home. The main enemies now were boredom and, for many, a growing sense that the most exciting days of their lives had passed. Edward H. Ripley wrote home late in May that when a gun was fired to salute the arrival of a general in his camp, "Regt. after Regt. jumped to their feet, [and] gave cheer after cheer of grateful relief" from the boredom.[1] For better or worse, the time they had all prayed for had come at last.

Most of the Vermont regiments returned to the Green Mountain State in June or July, to be paid off and discharged. The Seventh Infantry, many of whose members had reenlisted in the summer of 1864, remained in federal service until the spring of 1866. It was assigned to the Army of Observation in Texas to keep an eye on Mexico's Emperor Maximilian, the puppet dictator supported by Napoleon III of France. The Seventh finally disbanded in Brattleboro on April 6, 1866.

For the soldiers who returned to stay, the war was soon left behind, though never forgotten. There was no wreaking of vengeance on hometown "traitors," as Doctor Rutherford of the Seventeenth Vermont had predicted, but the veterans did exercise a powerful influence in the business and political establishment for decades to come. The fifty-two hundred Vermont men who died in the service, of all causes, accounted for nearly 15 percent of those who fought. Many more returned home permanently disabled, some with limbs amputated, some suffering from recurrent malarial fevers, and some with minds and souls fractured beyond repair. Of the sacrifices on the home front—the farms abandoned, the businesses ruined, and families broken—no reckoning has ever been made. On the other hand, the war had been a boon to some—among them, industrialists, bankers and brokers, and laborers who won sizeable wage increases in a tight market.[2]

Historians such as George Benedict and the authors of numerous Vermont regimental histories can be excused if they exaggerated the accomplishments of Vermont's soldiers—unavoidably, in some cases, since to single out their parts in a panorama of events often gave undue prominence to their contributions. Surely, there were times when even some of the bravest Green Mountain boys found discretion to be the better part of valor and ran from danger. Vermont produced its share of skulkers, deserters, and bounty jumpers too. Yet the men of the Green Mountain State performed many acts of individual and collective heroism, as Howard Coffin has so effectively related in his books *Full Duty* and *Nine Months to Gettysburg*. The crossing of the Warwick River under fire at Lee's Mill by the Third, Fourth, and Sixth regiments; the smashing flank attack on Pickett's charge by the Second Brigade; the martyrdom of the First Brigade, which saved the Army of the Potomac at the Wilderness; the extremely hazardous service of the First Cavalry regiment, whose members lived and fought in the saddle almost continuously in May and June of 1864; and the stubborn resistance and eventual triumph of several Vermont units at Cedar Creek, are just a few examples. These are accomplishments of which Vermonters can be justly proud.

Whatever exaggerations nineteenth-century historians employed, they did not claim that the Vermont volunteer was motivated by inordinate bravery or the conceit of defending his state's honor. As one soldier later said, "the heroism of our boys had little of pride and pomp, of crashing music and royal banner, and 'Vive l'Empereur' boisterousness about it. It was, like themselves, homely and self-contained."[3] It was a sense that Vermont should stand up to right a terrible wrong, to restore justice and perhaps to help create a new sense of justice, that led the Vermont men to fix "their unyielding feet firmly in the earth as a badger's claws, and [make] a badger's bitter fight, simply because it was the hard but single road to their full duty."[4]

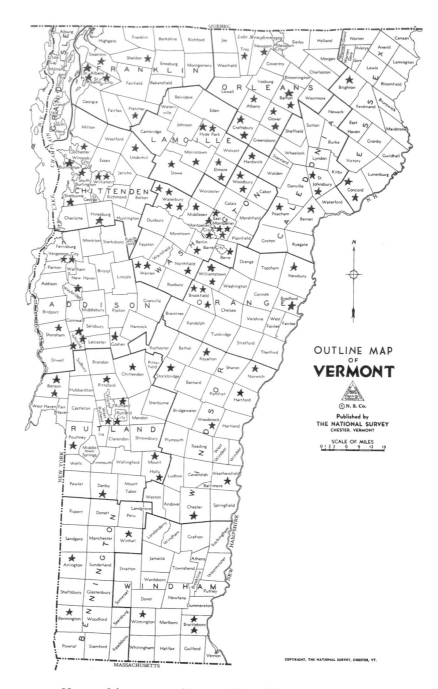

MAP 21. Homes of the correspondents are indicated by stars. Base map: Copyright, The National Survey, Inc., Chester, Vermont. Reproduced by permission of copyright owners 051898.

Appendix: Muster Roll

Of the seventy-eight soldiers represented in this collection of letters, a very high percentage—15.6—were killed in action or mortally wounded; the percentage of all Vermont soldiers killed in the Civil War was about 5.3. There was no conscious preference for selecting the letters of those who perished, but it seems likely that the soldiers at highest risk were more likely to write interesting and informative letters. The collections at the University of Vermont are similarly weighted toward the victims of war: 10 percent of the soldiers represented in the Wilbur collection were killed or mortally wounded. It may be that families were more likely to preserve the letters of loved ones they would never again see alive. Conversely, surviving soldiers may not have wished to preserve what they committed to paper during the strife.

Biographical information on prominent people of the nineteenth century is relatively easy to find, but for ordinary people who lived quiet lives, it is not. Women in particular were too often ignored in nineteenth-century histories. Official records offer fewer clues for tracing women because official business was most often conducted by, or in the names of, men. More exhaustive research, given the time to conduct it, would undoubtedly round out some of the following sketches and uncover some errors. The principal source of information is Peck's *Revised Roster* (RR), with some further reference to the Vermont adjutant general's annual reports for 1864 and 1865 (AG), pension and service records in the National Archives (NA), and U.S. Census records for Vermont (USC). Microfilms in the Vermont Vital Records Department (VR) in Middlesex provided many details. Local histories, genealogies, and obituaries in the *Burlington Free Press* (BFP) and other newspapers proved to be rich sources for biographical material. None of these sources is free from errors, but together they form a reasonably accurate base of information.

Abbott, Peter M. (1843–1922). Enlisted from Barnet on August 12, 1862, as private in Co. K, 3d Vt.; promoted to corporal, then sergeant on August 31, 1864. Wounded at Cold Harbor, June 3, 1864. Mustered out June 19, 1865. After the war he was a peddler, farmer, and horse dealer. RR; Wells, *History of Barnet*, 322. *February 28, 1863; August 31, 1863; August 15, 1864.*

Allen, Jonathan Vaile (d. 1864). Enlisted from Winhall on January 30, 1862, as private in Co. H, 8th Vt.; reenlisted on March 5, 1864, promoted to corporal, then sergeant on January 1, 1864. Killed in action at Cedar Creek, October 19, 1864. RR. *July 12, 1863.*

Ayer, Perry. Goshen. No information on Perry was found. Dana C. Perry, his brother, enlisted from Mount Holly in Co. C, 6th Vt., on October 3, 1861, giving his age as 18. He was wounded at Lee's Mill, April 16, 1862, transferred to the Veteran Reserve Corps, April 15, 1864, and discharged October 17, 1864. RR. *November 17, 1861.*

Baker, Perry Alverton (1844–). Companion of Franklin J. Hubbard. Enlisted from Whiting on October 9, 1861, as sergeant in 2d Light Artillery; promoted to sergeant-major on December 1, 1862; commissioned 2d lieutenant on July 17, 1863; and 1st lieutenant on June 20, 1864. Mustered out July 17, 1865. RR. *August 4, 1863.*

Barney, Valentine Goodrich (1834–1889). Married Marie-Louise (Maria) Hadwen ca. 1857. Enlisted from Swanton on May 2, 1861, as sergeant in Co. A, 1st Vt. Infantry, mustered out August 15, 1861. Commissioned captain of Co. A, 9th Vt., on June 14, 1862, promoted to lieutenant colonel May 24, 1863. Mustered out June 13, 1865. After the war he became a partner in his father's Swanton marble business, and had an interest in a sawmill. He later moved his family to Minneapolis, Minnesota, where he died. RR; Hemenway, *Gazetteer,* vol. 4, 1029, 1121–22. *May 19, 1861; September 22, 1862; February 10, 1863; February 5, 1864; May 18, 1864; March 27, 1865; April 3, 1865.*

Barstow, John Lester (1832–1913). Farmer and businessman. Married Laura Maeck in 1858. Commissioned from Shelburne on February 19, 1862, as adjutant of 8th Vt.; promoted to captain of Co. K on March 21, 1863, then major on December 28, 1863. Mustered out June 22, 1864. Commanded the state militia in northwestern Vermont after the St. Albans raid. Served in the Vermont Legislature from 1864 to 1867. Elected lieutenant governor 1880, governor 1882. As governor he sent the state militia to quell a labor dispute at the copper mines of Vershire. He served on a number of federal boards and commissions, and helped negotiate a treaty with the Navajos in the 1890s. RR; Ullery, *Men of Vermont,* 20–21. *May 18, 1862.*

Brainerd, Aldis Owen (1824–1906). Proprietor of a general store in St. Albans. Commissioned as quartermaster of the 5th Vt. on August 24, 1861. Resigned in March 1862 due to ill health and returned several months later to St. Albans. The brother of Ann Eliza Brainerd Smith, he was a prominent businessman for many years, with interests in railroads, a lumbering operation, and banks. RR; St. Albans *Daily Messenger,* April 25, 1906, p. 3. *June 13, 1862.*

Brockway, Stephen H. (ca. 1840–). Enlisted from St. Johnsbury on August 21, 1861, as corporal in Co. G, 4th Vt.; reduced to private on December 31, 1861. Wounded at the Wilderness, May 5, 1864. Mustered out September 30, 1864. RR; Chadwick, *Soldiers' Record . . . St. Johnsbury,* 27. *March 2, 1862.*

Bromley, James W. (ca. 1833–1865). Enlisted from Danby on May 8, 1861, as private in Co. B, 2d Vt.; reenlisted December 21, 1863. Promoted to corporal, then sergeant on February 7, 1865. Killed in action at Petersburg, April 2, 1865. RR. *July 6, 1861; December 25, 1862.*

Brown, Elijah Scott (1840–1863). From Craftsbury; enlisted from Woodbury on May 7, 1861, as private in Co. F, 2d Vt. Died of disease on February 4, 1863. RR; Sprague, *Soldiers' Record . . . Craftsbury*, 16. *July 26, 1861.*

Brown, Frances. Craftsbury. Sister of Elijah S. Brown. *February 8, 1863.*

Burnham, Henry P. (1843–1864). Enlisted from Williamstown on August 5, 1862, as private in Co. G, 10th Vt. Killed in action at Cedar Creek, October 19, 1864. RR; collection inventory, Henry P. Burnham, Papers, folder 0. *July 8–12, 1864.*

Cain, Avery B. (1840–1879). From Rutland; commissioned 2d lieutenant, 4th U.S. Infantry. Promoted to 1st lieutenant in 1863, then captain in 1864. Married Anna Cooper October 31, 1867. He remained in the service after the war, and was involved in the campaign against the Sioux and Cheyenne in the summer of 1876. Died at Fort Laramie, Wyoming Territory, on March 16, 1879. RR; BFP, March 19, 1879, p. 3. *September 4, 1862.*

Chapin, Charles B. (1842–1865). Enlisted from Williston on August 18, 1862, as private in Co. L, 1st Vt. Cavalry, promoted to corporal. Captured on May 5, 1864, and paroled on November 20, 1864. Died of disease January 17, 1865. RR; VR. *October 26, 1863.*

Chapin, Cornelius Augustus (1838–1863). An 1861 graduate of the University of Vermont, 1863 graduate of the UVM Medical College. Commissioned from Williston on July 8, 1863, as assistant surgeon of the 6th Vt. Died of disease on September 14, 1863. RR; Goodrich, *General Catalogue*, 116. *July 21, 1863.*

Cook, John F. (ca. 1836–   ). Enlisted from Hardwick on July 5, 1861, as private in Co. I, 3d Vt.; promoted to sergeant on June 1, 1862. Commissioned 2d lieutenant of Co. E, 3d Vt., October 13, 1862; 1st lieutenant, January 15, 1863; captain, November 1, 1863; and major October 18, 1864. Wounded at Spotsylvania, May 12, 1864. Discharged April 8, 1865. RR. *July 18, 1862.*

Cummings, Charles (1821–1864). An 1847 graduate of Woodstock (Vt.) Medical College. Practiced medicine, then became a journalist and editor of the *Vermont Phoenix* in Brattleboro. Commissioned lieutenant colonel of the 16th Vt. on September 27, 1862, and mustered out August 10, 1863. Commissioned lieutenant colonel of the 17th Vt. on February 9, 1864. Wounded at the Wilderness, May 6, 1864. Returned home on sick leave in August, 1864, and rejoined his regiment in September. On September 30, he was killed in action during the federal advance toward the Boydton Plank Road. Married Elizabeth B. Raynolds. RR; Waite, *Great Rebellion*, 261–63. *March 9, 1863; July 6, 1863; May 15, 1864; July 31, 1864.*

Daniels, William H. (1837–1896). Farmer in Barton. Enlisted from Sutton on September 28, 1861, as private in Co. I, 1st Vt. Cavalry; reenlisted December 28, 1863. Taken prisoner November 6, 1864, and paroled February 22, 1865. Mustered out June 21, 1865. Married Grace Forrest, May 13, 1858, was widowed; and married Martha Flint, May 13, 1867. RR; VR; AG. *February 16, 1862.*

Dewey, Ben H. (ca. 1834–   ). Waterbury. Bank clerk and freemason in Waterbury. USC. *November 5, 1864.*

Dewey, Edward (1829–1900). Merchant in Montpelier, then assistant secretary of the Vermont Mutual Fire Insurance Co. Commissioned quartermaster of the 8th Vt. on January 12, 1864. Promoted to captain and assistant quartermaster on staff of U.S. Volunteers on February 11, 1865, but declined the appointment. Resigned May 25, 1865. After the war, he became an executive of the National Life Insurance Co. of Vermont, of which his father, Dr. Julius Y. Dewey, was a co-founder. RR; *National Life*, 108–10. *September 21, 1864.*

Dewey, Susan Griggs (1834–1909). Montpelier. Married Edward Dewey on August 27, 1856, and raised six children. Montpelier *Evening Argus*, March 23, 1909, p. 2. *March 13, 1864.*

Dickinson, John Q. (1836–1871). An 1860 graduate of Middlebury College. Journalist. Commissioned from Benson on January 15, 1862, as 2d lieutenant, Co. C, 7th Vt. Promoted to 1st lieutenant, October 9, 1862; quartermaster, September 14, 1864; and captain of Co. F, August 22, 1865. Mustered out October 10, 1865. Settled in Marianne, Florida, after the war, and was a District Court Clerk. On April 3, 1871, he was assassinated by the Ku Klux Klan. RR; *Rutland Daily Herald*, April 7, 1871, p. 2. *September 1, 1862.*

Drenan, James Frank (1846–1866). Enlisted from Woodbury on May 14, 1863, as private in Co. L, 11th Vt.; promoted to corporal on June 3, 1865. Wounded at Petersburg, April 2, 1865. Discharged on August 14, 1865, for disability. Died on January 19, 1866, of consumption. Drenan's brother John (ca. 1840–1894), who was captured at the Weldon Railroad on June 23, 1864, was paroled in March 1865. John settled in Hardwick as a farmer. RR; VR; AG; BFP, June 27, 1894, p. 7. *June 28, 1864.*

Dunbar, Henry E. (1827–). Married Mary George on January 1, 1851. Enlisted from Newbury on June 1, 1861, as corporal in Co. C, 3d Vt. Wounded at Lee's Mill, April 16, 1862, and discharged for disability on May 24. Moved to Massachusetts and enlisted from Lowell as corporal in the 3d Massachusetts Heavy Artillery. RR; Wells, *History of Newbury*, 534. *July 31, 1861; April 17, 1862; February 4, 1865; April 16, 1865.*

Farnham, Roswell (1827–1903). An 1849 graduate of the University of Vermont. Married Mary Elizabeth Johnson on December 25, 1849. Taught school in Lower Canada and northern Vermont while studying law. Admitted to the Orange County Bar in 1857 and began private practice. Commissioned from Bradford on May 1, 1861, as 2d lieutenant in Co. D, 1st Vt. Infantry, and mustered out August 15, 1861. Commissioned lieutenant colonel of 12th Vt. on September 19, 1862, and mustered out July 14, 1863. He was elected to the Vermont State Senate in 1868, and elected governor in 1880. RR; Ullery, *Men of Vermont*, 134–35. *June 15, 1861; December 31, 1862.*

Gale, Justus F. (1837–1863). Enlisted from Elmore on September 23, 1861, as private in Co. A, 8th Vt. Died of disease on September 19, 1863. RR. *February 7, 1862; June 19, 1863.*

Gallagher, James G. (ca. 1830–). Enlisted from Brookfield on August 22, 1861, as corporal in Co. B, 4th Vt.; promoted to sergeant on May 1, 1862, and sergeant-major on April 1, 1863. Commissioned 2d lieutenant of Co. F on April 19, 1864, 1st lieutenant of Co. A on June 5, 1864, and adjutant on May 8, 1865. Taken prisoner at Weldon Railroad on June 23, 1864, and paroled on March 1, 1865. RR; USC. *May 16, 1865.*

Godfrey, Frederick (1841–1923). Enlisted from Bennington on August 10,

1861, as sergeant in Co. A, 4th Vt.; reduced to private September 1, 1863. Reenlisted February 9, 1864, and mustered out July 13, 1865. Employed as deputy sheriff and collector in Bennington. Married Margaret Beeman on November 10, 1894. RR; VR. *January 29, 1863.*

Green, Rollin M. (d. 1863). Enlisted from Poultney on January 9, 1862, as corporal in Co. I, 7th Vt.; promoted to sergeant on July 3, 1862. Commissioned 2d lieutenant on October 9, 1862, and 1st lieutenant on March 1, 1863. Died of disease on November 17, 1863. RR. *July 12, 1862.*

Hall, Edwin Clifton (1845–1913). Enlisted from Brookfield on September 11, 1862, as private in Co. C, 15th Vt.; mustered out August 5, 1863. Enlisted as private in Co. G, 10th Vt., on December 17, 1863. Wounded at Cold Harbor on June 1, 1864, and at Petersburg on April 2, 1865. Mustered out June 29, 1865. Married Mary A. Howe on November 21, 1872, and after her death, Mary L. Bateman on May 18, 1879. He worked as a clerk and resided in Bradford prior to his death. RR; VR; Wild, *History of Brookfield*, 235. *March 26, 1865; April 9, 1865.*

Hall, Silas (1806–1888). A farmer and carpenter in Brookfield, he was active in the Brookfield Center Church, the town library, and the Brookfield Masonic Lodge. He married three times; his first wife, Mary Bigelow, was the mother of their son Edwin C. Hall. Wild, *History of Brookfield*, 234–35. *August 17, 1864.*

Hart, James E. Enlisted from Pittsford on May 15, 1861, as musician in Co. B, 2d Vt. Deserted on October 17, 1862. RR. *June 16, 1861.*

Haskell, Londus W. (1836–1919). Farmer. Enlisted from Woodbury on July 31, 1862, as private in Co. I, 11th Vt.; promoted to corporal on March 4, 1864, and sergeant on September 27, 1864. Mustered out June 24, 1865. Married Julia A. Hall on June 22, 1879. RR; VR. *January 1, 1865.*

Heaton, Solomon G. (ca. 1840–1864). Enlisted from Brighton on April 22, 1861, as private in Co. D, 3d Vt., reenlisted on December 21, 1863. Wounded at Spotsylvania, May 12, 1864. Mortally wounded at Cold Harbor, June 3, 1864, and died June 6. RR; AG. *July 30, 1861.*

Holbrook, William Cune (1842–1904). A clerk in Boston, Holbrook returned to his home in Brattleboro at the outbreak of the war to help raise a company for the 4th Vt. Commissioned on September 7, 1861, as 1st lieutenant in Co. F, 4th Vt. Promoted to major in the 7th Vt. on January 22, 1862, and colonel on August 27, 1862. Resigned June 2, 1865. After the war he studied law at Harvard, graduating in 1869, and became a lawyer in New York City. Married Anna M. Chalmers on January 17, 1872. He won appointment as judge of the Court of Special Sessions in 1895. RR; Cabot, *Annals of Brattleboro*, vol. 2, 809–10. *August 8, 1862; April 18, 1863.*

Horton, Edwin (1841–1926). Enlisted from Chittenden as private in Co. G, 22d N.Y. Infantry for one year. Married Ellen L. Holbrook on August 4, 1862. Drafted and assigned to Co. C, 4th Vt., on July 22, 1863, and promoted to corporal on December 28, 1864. Wounded at the Wilderness, May 5, 1864. Mustered out July 13, 1865. Elected to Vermont House of Representatives and State Senate, and served as Rutland County side judge. RR; VR; Ullery, *Men of Vermont*, 208. *September 28, 1863.*

Howard, George J. (1827–1865). From Mount Holly; married Gertrude A. Thompson January 20, 1850. Enlisted from Rutland on August 11, 1862, as private in Co. G., 5th Vt., promoted to corporal, then sergeant on March 27, 1865. Wounded at the Wilderness, May 5, 1864. Mortally wounded at Petersburg, April 2, 1865, and died the next day. RR; VR; USC. *October 17, 1862; February 13, 1863; October 9, 1864.*

Howe, George Gameliel (1832–1902). Harness maker. Enlisted from Shoreham on September 1, 1862, as sergeant in Co. B, 11th Vt. Commissioned 2d lieutenant on June 7, 1863; 1st lieutenant, December 28, 1863; and captain of Co. I, May 23, 1865. Mustered out on June 24, 1865. Married Lorette Wolcott on February 20, 1866; she died two years later. Lived in Burlington for many years before moving to Weybridge, where he died of Bright's Disease. RR; VR; *Middlebury Register*, November 21, 1902, p. 2; collection description, Howe-Wolcott Correspondence, Sheldon. *June 12, 1864.*

Hubbard, Asahel Huntington, Jr. (1834?–1916). Sheep farmer in Whiting, brother of Franklin J. Hubbard. Married Jane A. Brown on February 3, 1859. VR. *November 9, 1862; May 24, 1863.*

Hubbard, Jerusha S. (1806–1877). Matriarch of the family farm in Whiting; married Asahel Hubbard, Sr., October 14, 1829. Her son Franklin, a musician in the 2nd Light Artillery, was taken prisoner August 3, 1863, and died at Andersonville on June 19, 1864, at age 26. RR; VR. *February 14, 1862.*

Hunter, Hiram Morse (1838–1896). Farmer. Enlisted from Albany on September 30, 1861, as private in Co. D, 6th Vt. Wounded at Savage's Station, June 29, 1862, and discharged March 27, 1863. Returned to Albany to farm, and married Rosaline Coburn on December 22, 1863. RR; VR. *December 22, 1861.*

Irwin, Richard James (1840–1919). The son of Irish immigrants, he began a long career with the railroads at the age of fourteen. Enlisted from Burlington on August 24, 1862, as private in Co. C, 12th Vt., mustered out July 14, 1863. After his war service he became a railway express messenger between Burlington and Boston, a job he kept for the next 45 years. Married Sarah A. Sawyer on October 10, 1871. RR; BFP, February 18, 1919, p. 8. *November 1, 1862.*

Keith, Alfred Horton (1842–1910). University of Vermont student. Commissioned from Sheldon on October 15, 1861, as 2d lieutenant in Co. K, 6th Vt.; promoted to 1st lieutenant, December 28, 1862, and captain, March 18, 1863. Wounded at Spotsylvania, May 10, 1864. After the war he was a salesman, hotel keeper, and steel manufacturer. RR; Alumni files, Archives, UVM. *July 6, 1862.*

King, Lorentio H. (ca. 1837–1865). Merchant in Northfield. Enlisted on September 17, 1861, as quartermaster sergeant in Co. C, 1st Vt. Cavalry; promoted to regimental commissary sergeant December 6, 1862. Died of consumption on March 11, 1865. RR; VR. *March 20, 1863.*

King, Royal Daniel (1824–1904). An 1846 graduate of the University of Vermont. Farmer and teacher. Enlisted from Benson on September 10, 1862, as private in Co. D, 14th Vt., and mustered out July 30, 1863. Served as town representative and state senator after the war. RR; VR; Ullery, *Men of Vermont*, 236. *June 16, 1863; July 9, 1863.*

Langley, Louden S. (1839–1881). Farmer in Hinesburg. Enlisted from Rutland on December 7, 1863, as private in Co. B, 54th Mass., transferred to 33d

U.S. Colored Troops on June 30, 1864. Promoted to sergeant-major on November 1, 1864, and mustered out January 1, 1866. After the war he stayed in Beaufort, South Carolina, where the regiment was last stationed, and was joined there by his wife Jane, whom he had married in Vermont in 1859. He found employment as a clerk and eventually became auditor of Beaufort County. Sketch provided by Jim Fuller of South Burlington, Vermont. *March 9, 1864.*

Lanpher, George M. Enlisted from Hyde Park on August 26, 1861, as private in Co. D, 5th Vt.; discharged for disability on July 11, 1862. RR. *March 16, 1862.*

Lavallée, Louis (ca. 1845–   ). From Montreal; enlisted from Milton on September 28, 1863, as private in Co. B, 17th Vt. Wounded at the Wilderness, May 6, 1864. Deserted to the enemy on March 6, 1865. RR. *May 29, 1864.*

Leach, Chester K. (1830–1909). Married Ann A. Montague October 8, 1851. Commissioned from Fletcher on May 23, 1861, as 2d lieutenant in Co. H, 2d Vt.; promoted to 1st lieutenant on September 14, 1861. Mustered out June 29, 1864. Returned to farming after the war, and served in the state senate. RR; Ullery, *Men of Vermont,* 242. *July 23, 1861.*

Lewis, Henry H. (ca. 1845–   ). Enlisted from Woodstock on December 9, 1863, as private in Co. H, 11th Vt. Taken prisoner at Weldon Railroad, June 23, 1864, and paroled on December 13, 1864. Mustered out August 25, 1865. RR; AG. *July 14, 1864.*

Mason, Dan (ca. 1839–1865). Enlisted from Glover on September 26, 1861, as corporal in Co. D, 6th Vt.; promoted to sergeant on May 1, 1862. Commissioned captain in 19th U.S. Colored Troops in March, 1865. Married Harriet B. Clark while on furlough in March, 1865. Died of disease in Brownsville, Texas, November 20, 1865. RR; AG. *May 7, 1863; July 17, 1863.*

McAllister, William Henry Harrison (1837–1915). Enlisted from Stowe on August 31, 1861, as private in Co. G, 4th Vt.; promoted to sergeant on January 20, 1862. Wounded at Fredericksburg, December 13, 1862, and discharged October 14, 1864. Married Elizabeth B. Towne on November 15, 1865. Served as deputy collector of customs in St. Albans after the war, and returned to the University of Vermont, graduating in 1880. Worked as a teacher in Virginia and Maine. He was ordained as a deacon, then elder of the Methodist Church, and served as a pastor in Portland, Maine, for a time. RR; Alumni file, Archives, UVM. *April 30, 1861; January 8, 1863; November 1, 1863.*

Morey, Arthur P. (ca. 1843–1905). Enlisted from Norwich on June 16, 1862, in the 7th Squadron, Rhode Island Cavalry, mustered out October 3, 1862. Commissioned captain of Co. F, 22d U.S. Colored Troops on January 11, 1864; discharged on October 16, 1865. After the war he moved to Sedalia, Missouri. Married Jennie Bard on May 4, 1869. Rhode Island Adjutant General, *Annual Report . . . for 1865,* 427; pension file, NA. *February 4, 1864; April 4, 1865.*

Mudge, Oren N. (ca. 1823–   ). Enlisted from Mount Holly on December 19, 1863, as private in Co. G, 5th Vt. Wounded at Cedar Creek, October 19, 1864, and Petersburg, March 27, 1865. Mustered out June 29, 1865. RR; AG. *April 4, 1865.*

Munson, William Day (1833–1903). An 1854 graduate of Norwich University. Railroad survey engineer and farmer. Commissioned from Colchester on September 6, 1862, as captain of Co. D, 13th Vt.; promoted to lieutenant colonel on May 5, 1863. Wounded at Gettysburg, July 3, 1863. Mustered out July 23, 1863. After the war he returned to Colchester and resumed farming and surveying. RR; Dodge, *Norwich University*, vol. 2, 538–40. *June 29, 1863.*

Parcher, Tabor H. (1837–1880). Laborer and farmer. Married Sarah E. Conant. Enlisted from Waterbury on July 14, 1862, as private in Co. B, 10th Vt.; promoted to corporal on July 5, 1864. Mustered out May 13, 1865. He was a farmer in Duxbury after the war. RR; VR. *April 3, 1864; June 7, 1864.*

Parker, Catherine Elizabeth (1845–1915). The daughter of the Rev. Charles Carroll Parker, she apparently boarded in Burlington with her aunt and uncle, Catherine E. and John H. Worcester, and may have taught in their school, Mrs. Worcester's Young Ladies' Academy. She moved to Gorham, Maine, with her parents in 1867 and taught in the Gorham Female Seminary. Correspondence with Mary N. DeJong of Philadelphia, Pa. *April 27, 1865.*

Parker, Charles Carroll (1814–1880). An 1841 graduate of the University of Vermont, studied at Union Theological Seminary. Congregational minister in Tinmouth and Waterbury. Appointed field delegate of the U.S. Christian Commission in the winter of 1864. In 1867 he resigned his pastorate in Waterbury to become principal of the Gorham (Maine) Female Seminary, and soon after, pastor of the Gorham Congregational Church. Alumni file, Archives, UVM. *February 24, 1864.*

Parker, Charles Edmund (1839–1924). An 1860 graduate of Dartmouth College. Commissioned from Vergennes on January 1, 1862, as adjutant of 7th Vt., promoted to captain of Co. E, December 9, 1862. Resigned October 22, 1863. After the war he was a manufacturer of doors, windows, and blinds, then president of the Vergennes Electric Co. Served as mayor of Vergennes and represented the city in the state legislature. Married Agnes W. Ripley, daughter of William Y. and Jane Warren Ripley of Rutland, in 1866. RR; Dodge, *Norwich University*, vol. 2, 631–32. *January 8, 1862; May 13, 1862.*

Parker, Henrietta Miller (1806–1887). Vergennes. Mother of Charles Edmund Parker. VR. *December 25, 1862.*

Parker, Moses A. (1839–1915). From Concord; enlisted from Waterford on June 1, 1861, as private in Co. C, 3d Vt. Wounded at Lewinsville, September 11, 1861. Wounded and taken prisoner at Savage's Station, June 29, 1862. Paroled and discharged for disability, September 24, 1862. Enlisted in Co. H, 2d U.S. Sharpshooters, August 1864. Mustered out June 19, 1865. Returned to Concord and became a farmer. Married Eliza E. Hale in 1867. RR; Jeffrey, *Successful Vermonters*, 149 (Essex County chapter). *September 19, 1861; May 26, 1862; January 5, 1865.*

Perkins, Joseph L. (1835–1906). University of Vermont student. Enlisted from Barre on May 2, 1861, as private in Co. H, 1st Vt. Infantry, mustered out August 15, 1861. Married Abbie J. Peck on November 6, 1862. Returned to the university, and graduated from the Medical College in 1867. Graduated from Pennsylvania College of Dental Surgery and became a prominent dentist with a practice in St. Johnsbury. RR; Alumni file, Archives, UVM. *April 23, 1861.*

Pierce, Ann (1819–1892). A native of Canada, she married Hiram Pierce, keeper of the American House hotel in St. Albans. VR; USC. *October 19, 1864.*

Pingree, Samuel Everett (1832–1922). An 1857 graduate of Dartmouth College. Lawyer. Commissioned from Hartford on May 24, 1861, as 1st lieutenant of Co. F, 3d Vt.; promoted to captain on August 13, 1861, major on September 27, 1862, and lieutenant colonel on January 15, 1863. Wounded at Lee's Mill, April 16, 1862. Commanded the 2d Vt. after the first day of battle at the Wilderness. Mustered out July 27, 1864. After the war he returned to his law practice, and served as Hartford town clerk for many years. Married Lydia M. Steele on September 15, 1869. Active in the Republican party, he was elected lieutenant-governor in 1882 and governor in 1884. RR; Ullery, *Men of Vermont,* 315–16. *January 14, 1864.*

Pingree, Stephen M. (1835–1892). Lawyer. Commissioned from Stockbridge on September 6, 1861, as 1st lieutenant of Co. E, 4th Vt.; promoted to captain of Co. K on April 21, 1862, major on November 11, 1862, and lieutenant colonel on April 30, 1864. Mustered out September 30, 1864. Returned to practice law in partnership with his brother Samuel in Hartford. Served in the legislature as a representative from Hartford. RR; BFP, April 20, 1892, p. 4. *October 2, 1863.*

Putnam, Horace A. (1817–1887). Farmer in East Montpelier. Married Mary Stevens on February 1, 1852. Worked for a short time in the fall of 1863 as a quartermaster's civilian assistant, apparently in the 2nd Division, Sixth Corps. VR. Brother-in-law of Willie Stevens. *October 19, 1863.*

Quimby, George Washington (1835–1862). An 1859 graduate of Dartmouth College. Teacher and law student. Commissioned from Barton on September 4, 1861, as 1st lieutenant, Co. D, 4th Vt.; promoted to captain on February 20, 1862. Killed in action at Fredericksburg, December 13, 1862. RR; Chapman, *Dartmouth College,* 444. *April 25, 1862.*

Randall, George H. (1827–1863). Enlisted from Glover on August 30, 1861, as musician in Co. D, 4th Vt. Discharged for disability February 25, 1863, and died of consumption on May 12, 1863. RR; VR. *November 8, 1861.*

Remington, Jonathan (ca. 1837–   ). Enlisted from Arlington on August 14, 1861, as musician in Co. E, 5th Vt., reenlisted December 15, 1863, mustered out June 29, 1865. RR; AG. *July 9, 1862.*

Ripley, William Young Warren (1832–1906). Commissioned from Rutland on November 28, 1859, as captain of a company that became Co. K, 1st Vt. Infantry, mustered out August 15, 1861. Commissioned lieutenant colonel of 1st U.S. Sharpshooters on January 1, 1862. Wounded at Malvern Hill, July 1, 1862, discharged August 6, 1862. Declined promotion to the colonelcy of the 10th Vt. due to continued disability. After the war, he resumed working in the marble business his father started, and was a bank executive. RR; Steele, *With Pen or Sword,* 147–67. *May 26, 1861; March 19, 1862.*

Ripley, William Young (1797–1875). Born in Middlebury, he worked as a store clerk and became the proprietor of a store in Charleston, South Carolina. Married Jane Warren on February 10, 1831. After a successful stint in a New York commission sales house, he returned to Vermont and, in the late 1830s, co-founded the first large-scale marble works in Rutland. He retired in 1865, leaving the management of the business to his sons. Hemenway, *Gazetteer*, vol. 3, 1099–1101. *July 29, 1861.*

Rutherford, Joseph Chase (1818–1902). Married Hannah W. Chase in December, 1843. An 1849 graduate of Woodstock Medical College. Practiced medicine in Blackstone, Mass., and Orleans County, Vt. He was an examining surgeon of recruits early in the war. He invented a method of invisible writing that was used by the federal government during the war. Commissioned from Newport on August 8, 1862, as assistant surgeon of 10th Vt.; promoted to surgeon of 17th Vt. on March 6, 1865. Mustered out July 14, 1865. While operating on a soldier after the battle of Orange Grove, he developed an infection in his thumb that partially disabled him for the rest of his life. Returned to his practice in Newport after the war. RR; Hemenway, *Gazetteer*, vol. 3, 300–301. *December 13, 1863; February 19, 1865; April 29, 1865.*

Safford, Darius J. (1835–1895). Commissioned from Morristown on August 12, 1862, as 1st lieutenant of Co. D, 11th Vt.; promoted to captain of Co. L on July 11, 1863, major on May 23, 1865, and lieutenant colonel on July 10, 1865. Taken prisoner at Weldon Railroad on June 23, 1864, and later escaped to return to his regiment. Wounded at Third Battle of Winchester, September 19, 1864. Mustered out August 25, 1865. RR; BFP, August 7, 1895, p. 6. *August 2, 1864; December 17, 1864.*

Scott, Margarett (ca. 1831–1910). Maiden name unknown. A native of South Reading, Mass., she married Erastus Harvey Scott of Cabot, Vermont, July 19, 1861, three days after he was mustered in to Co. G, 3rd Vt. Erastus was killed at Spotsylvania, presumably at the Bloody Angle, on May 12, 1864. Margarett never remarried. Erastus H. Scott pension file, NA. *June 2, 1864.*

Smith, Ann Eliza Brainerd (1819–1905). Presiding over the St. Albans home she shared with her husband, Governor John Gregory Smith, Ann Eliza Smith took an unusually active part in public affairs, including efforts to encourage enlistment. She was issued a lieutenant colonel's commission by Adjutant General Peter T. Washburn for "gallantry and efficient service" during the St. Albans raid of October 1864. Smith wrote numerous children's books, novels, and poetry, and gave public talks on a number of topics. She traveled throughout the United States and Europe in the postwar years. BFP, January 7, 1905, p. 1. *October 20, 1864; April 15, 1865.*

Smith, Henry A. (ca. 1843–1864). Enlisted from Royalton on September 23, 1861, as private in Co. E., 1st Vt. Cavalry. Taken prisoner July 6, 1863, and died in prison February 29, 1864. RR; AG. *June 7, 1862.*

Smith, Walter Wallace (ca. 1837–). Enlisted from Wilmington on October 17, 1861, as sergeant in Co. H, 2d U.S. Sharpshooters; reenlisted on December 21, 1863. Promoted to captain on November 11, 1864, mustered out July 13, 1865. RR. *March 9, 1862; September 15–18, 1862; December 6, 1863.*

Smith, Willard G. (1837–). Enlisted from Williamstown on December 29, 1863 as private in Co. C, 8th Vt.; mustered out June 28, 1865. RR; AG. *October 23, 1864.*

Spafford, Joseph (1837–1866). Enlisted from Weathersfield on August 16, 1861, as sergeant of Co. C, 4th Vt.; discharged for disability on May 10,

1862. Commissioned 1st lieutenant of Co. E, 16th Vt., September 1, 1862; mustered out August 10, 1863. RR; VR. *April 19, 1863.*

Spafford, Mattie E. Wife of Henry W. Spafford, quartermaster of the 4th Vt. They lived in Gassetts Station, a village in the town of Chester, where he was a railroad station agent after the war. From 1887 to 1891 the Gassetts post office was officially named Spafford in his honor. RR; Swift, *Vermont Place-Names,* 531. *June 3, 1865.*

Sparrow, Bradford Polk (1843–1920). Drafted in Elmore July 17, 1863, and assigned to Co. K, 4th Vt. Taken prisoner at Weldon Railroad, June 23, 1864. Paroled on April 28, 1865, and discharged for disability on June 17, 1865. He was a lumberman after the war. RR; VR. *May 13, 1864; May 4, 1865.*

Stevens, Ann King (1841–1920). East Montpelier. She began teaching in her home town in 1858, and at Morrisville's People's Academy in 1859. From 1861 to 1868 she taught at Glenwood Academy in Brattleboro, where she worked under the direction of the renowned educator Hiram Orcutt. In 1870 she married her distant cousin, the novelist, outdoorsman, and fellow Quaker Rowland E. Robinson, and settled with him at Rokeby, the Robinson home in Ferrisburgh, Vermont. She helped edit her husband's writings and served as Ferrisburgh town clerk for many years. Collection inventory, Robinson Family Papers, Sheldon. *April 21, 1861.*

Stevens, Rachel Byrd (1804–1868). East Montpelier. Mother of Ann and Willie Stevens. Married Stephen Foster Stevens in 1829. Collection inventory, Robinson Family Papers, Sheldon. *June 27, 1864.*

Stevens, William Byrd (1837–1864). Taught school for a time and attended the University of Vermont in the late 1850s. Enlisted from East Montpelier on August 22, 1861, as private in Co. G, 4th Vt.; promoted to sergeant on October 1, 1862. Taken prisoner on October 14, 1863, and paroled on March 7, 1864. Mortally wounded near Cold Harbor, June 4, 1864, and died June 12. RR; collection inventory, Robinson Family Papers, Sheldon. *October 9, 1861; December 22, 1862; October 2, 1863; March 26, 1864.*

Stone, Edward Payson (1830–1920). An 1853 graduate of Middlebury College. Taught school until his ordination as a Congregational minister in 1861. Commissioned from Berlin on October 10, 1861, as chaplain of 6th Vt. Resigned August 27, 1863. Served as pastor to churches in Vermont and Massachusetts, and was a missionary in Michigan. RR; Robinson, *Middlebury College,* 139. *November 15, 1862.*

Sumner, Samuel, Jr. (d. 1862). Taught school in Kentucky before the war. Commissioned from Troy on August 28, 1861, as 2d lieutenant of Co. D, 5th Vt. Killed in action at Savage's Station, June 29, 1862. RR. *April 27, 1861; November 12, 1861.*

Thayer, Esther M. (1833–1917). Warren. Maiden name unknown. Wife of Willard M. Thayer. Collection description, Esther M. Thayer Correspondence, VHS. *January 23, 1863.*

Thayer, Willard M. (1830–1864). Husband of Esther M. Thayer. Enlisted from Warren on July 19, 1862, as private in Co. B, 10th Vt.; promoted to corporal. Wounded at Orange Grove, November 27, 1863. Mortally wounded at Third Battle of Winchester, September 23, 1864. RR; collection description, Esther M. Thayer Correspondence, VHS. *October 17, 1862.*

Tillison, Charles (ca. 1817–1864). Enlisted from Underhill on August 30,

1862, as private in Co. E, 2d Vt. He became sick in May 1864 and was sent north on a hospital ship from City Point, Virginia. On the way, he apparently fell overboard and drowned. RR; AG. *February 24, 1864.*

Vaughn, Henry J. (1832–   ). Farmer in Middlesex. Drafted July 13, 1863, and assigned to Co. E, 6th Vt. Mustered out June 26, 1865. Married Samantha Vaughn (maiden name unknown). RR; VR; USC. *July 24, 1863.*

Watts, Isaac Newton (1842–1881). Drafted in Peacham on August 10, 1863, then enlisted in Co. M, 11th Vt.; promoted to corporal on March 24, 1864, sergeant on December 23, 1864, and 1st sergeant of Co. D on July 12, 1865. Mustered out August 25, 1865, and returned to the family farm. Served as town representative in the legislature for two terms. Married Lizzie S. Way in 1870, and after her death, Ellen M. Boynton, in 1877. RR; biographical material, Isaac N. Watts Papers, folder 1, UVM. *November 10, 1864.*

Wells, William (1837–1892). Commissioned from Waterbury on October 14, 1861, as 1st lieutenant of Co. C, 1st Vt. Cavalry; promoted to captain on November 16, 1861, major on October 30, 1862, colonel on June 4, 1864, and brigadier general on May 19, 1865. Taken prisoner on March 17, 1863, and paroled on May 5, 1863. Wounded at Gettysburg on July 3, 1863, and at Culpeper Court House on September 13, 1863. He commanded the Cavalry Corps in June 1865. After the war, he became a partner in the Wells-Richardson drug company and moved to Burlington. Married Arahanna (Anna) Richardson on January 18, 1866. Served in the Vermont House of Representatives and the State Senate. He was collector of customs for Vermont from 1872 to 1885, and a president or director of several Burlington-based companies. RR; Lewis, *History of Waterbury*, 133–38. *December 8, 1861; April 5, 1862; March 17, 1863; March 25, 1864; June 4, 1864; October 20, 1864.*

Wilder, Henry Harrison (ca. 1840–1862). Enlisted from Weybridge on August 23, 1861, as corporal in Co. F, 5th Vt. Killed in action at Savage's Station, June 29, 1862. RR; AG. *November 11, 1861.*

Williams, Hosea B. (ca. 1842–1864). Enlisted from Concord on June 1, 1861, as private in Co. C, 3d Vt.; reenlisted on December 21, 1863, promoted to corporal. Killed in action at Spotsylvania, May 12, 1864. RR. *May 10, 1863; September 28, 1863.*

Wiswall, Thomas (1839–1864). Enlisted from Hyde Park on October 15, 1861, as private in Co. I, 1st Vt. Cavalry; reenlisted on March 21, 1864; promoted to corporal on June 1, 1864. Taken prisoner April 1, 1863, and paroled April 7, 1863. Died of disease December 6, 1864. RR; VR. *July 9, 1864.*

Woodbury, Eri Davidson (1837–1928). Teacher. An 1863 graduate of Dartmouth College. Enlisted from St. Johnsbury on December 4, 1863, as private in Co. E, 1st Vt. Cavalry; promoted to sergeant on July 1, 1864; commissioned 2d lieutenant of Co. E, November 19, 1864; promoted to 1st lieutenant, February 9, 1865. Wounded at Appomattox Court House on April 8, 1865. Mustered out June 21, 1865. After the war he began a long career as teacher and headmaster of a private academy in Cheshire, Connecticut. Married Ann Augusta Jarvis on July 8, 1873. RR; Scales, *Biographical Sketches*, 470–73. *May 17, 1864.*

Notes

Introduction (pp. 1–15)

1. William Y. Ripley Sr. to William Ripley Jr., July 29, 1861, William Young Ripley Papers, Duke University Special Collections Library, Durham, North Carolina (hereafter Duke). Duke has about four hundred Ripley letters. Smaller Ripley collections can be found at the Bennington Museum in Bennington, Vermont, the library of the Vermont Historical Society (hereafter VHS), and the U.S. Army Military History Institute Archives at Carlisle Barracks, Pennsylvania (hereafter MHI). A selection of the letters of Edward Hastings Ripley, brother of William Jr., was published under the title *Vermont General: The Unusual War Experiences of Edward Hastings Ripley, 1862–1865* (New York: Devin-Adair Co., 1960) by Otto Eisenschiml. The location of those originals is now unknown.

2. Frederick Field to his wife, September 3, 1862, Frederick Field Papers, Manuscript Files, Special Collections, University of Vermont Library (hereafter UVM); Richard J. Irwin to his mother and sister, November 1, 1862, Richard J. Irwin Papers, Manuscript Files, UVM. Another soldier who wrote for a home-town newspaper was Wilbur Fisk of the Second Vermont Infantry, a correspondent to Montpelier's *Green Mountain Freeman*. Fisk's letters have been published by Emil and Ruth Rosenblatt in *Hard Marching Every Day: The Civil War Letters of Private Wilbur Fisk, 1861–1865* (Lawrence: University Press of Kansas, 1992).

3. Isaac N. Watts to his sister, November 10, 1864, Isaac N. Watts Papers, folder 2, UVM.

4. See Carl H. Scheele, *A Short History of the Mail Service* (Washington, D.C.: Smithsonian Institution Press, 1970), 92–95.

5. Edwin C. Hall to his father and mother, February 26, 1863, Edwin C. Hall Papers, (MSA 130.5), folder 7, VHS; on the shipping of liquor see Charles Tillison's letter of February 24, 1864, in chapter 12. Vermont's 1852 law prohibiting the manufacture and sale of alcohol lasted for fifty years, but enforcement was not always efficient.

6. Leroy S. Griswold to his wife, July 21, 1862, private collection of Donald Johnstone, Colchester, Vermont; Charles Cummings to his wife, July 3, 1864, Charles Cummings Papers (MSA 28), folder 4, VHS; Andrew H. Nor-

ton to his friend Martha, February 6, 1865, Andrew H. Norton Papers, Gertrude Mallary collection, Bradford, Vermont; John L. Barstow to his father, December 28, 1862, John L. Barstow Papers, Manuscript Files, UVM.

7. Benjamin Hatch to his wife, Lucina, October 21, 1862, Benjamin Hatch Papers, box 1, folder 3, UVM.

8. George G. Benedict, *Vermont in the Civil War: A History of the Part Taken by the Vermont Soldiers and Sailors in the War for the Union, 1861–1865*, vol. 1 (Burlington, Vt.: Free Press Association, 1886), 34–35.

9. *The Green Mountain Boys* went through at least fifty editions prior to the Civil War and sold nearly a million copies by the 1940s. Frank Luther Mott, *Golden Multitudes: The Story of Best Sellers in the United States* (New York: The Macmillan Co., 1947), 93–94.

10. *Burlington Times*, April 20, 1861, p. 2, and May 4, 1861, p. 4; J. Brown to Elijah Brown, June 7, 1861, Brown Family Papers (Miscellaneous File Additions), VHS.

11. For a thorough and thoughtful examination of the motivations of soldiers North and South see James M. McPherson, *For Cause and Comrades: Why Men Fought in the Civil War* (New York: Oxford University Press, 1997). Among the historians who assert that Vermont desired to join the Union by the 1780s is Charles Jellison; see his *Ethan Allen, Frontier Rebel* (Syracuse, N.Y.: Syracuse University Press, 1969), 288.

12. Wilbur H. Siebert, *Vermont's Anti-Slavery and Underground Railroad Record* (Columbus, Ohio: The Spahr and Glenn Co., 1937) tells many anecdotes of prowling slave-hunters outfoxed by Underground Railroad operatives, but nearly all of them were second- or third-hand accounts told many decades after the events. Siebert offers no corroborating evidence in the form of letters, diaries, newspaper accounts, or court records. Recent scholarship casts doubt on the need for secrecy among fugitives in Vermont, and suggests that the Underground Railroad was less organized and active than Siebert and others have claimed. See Raymond Paul Zirblis, *Friends of Freedom: The Vermont Underground Railroad Survey Report* (Montpelier, Vt.: Vermont Department of State Buildings and Vermont Division for Historic Preservation, 1996); Vermont, *An Act to Extend the Right of Trial by Jury*, Laws of Vermont (1840), 13–15; Vermont, *An Act, For the Protection of Personal Liberty*, Laws of Vermont (1843), 11–12.

13. See John Myers, "The Beginning of Antislavery Agencies in Vermont, 1832–1836," *Vermont History* 36, no. 3 (Summer 1968): 126–41.

14. David Ludlum, *Social Ferment in Vermont, 1791–1850* (1939; reprint, New York: AMS Press, 1966), 198; Alfred H. Keith to his father, January 16, 1864, Alfred H. Keith Papers (MSA 82), folder 11, VHS; Edward Robie to his friend Lan, August 3, 1862, Edward Robie Papers, Manuscript Files, UVM; William B. Stevens to Ann Stevens, September 7, 1862, Robinson Family Papers, box 15, folder 3, Sheldon Museum, Middlebury, Vermont (hereafter Sheldon); Roswell Farnham to his wife, July 4, 1861, Roswell Farnham Papers, box 20, volume 37, UVM.

15. Moses W. Leach letter, January 19, 1863, Lewis Leigh Collection (book 10, 77–80), MHI; Stephen W. Sears, *Landscape Turned Red: The Battle of Antietam* (Boston: Houghton Mifflin, 1983), 334; Henry E. Dunbar to his wife, February 4, 1865, Henry E. Dunbar Papers, MHI.

16. Theodore S. Peck, *Revised Roster of Vermont Volunteers and Lists of Vermonters Who Served in the Army and Navy of the United States During the War of the Rebellion, 1861–1866* (Montpelier, Vt.: Watchman Publishing Co., 1892), vi; Benedict, *Vermont in the Civil War*, vol. 1, 617.

17. See Peck, *Revised Roster*, 662–65 for rosters of black soldiers from Vermont, and 717–21 for Vermont officers of black regiments. Little information is available on Vermonters who served in other states' regiments, particularly those of the Confederacy. Ten or more of the 190 students and alumni of the University of Vermont who fought in the Civil War were rebels, according to John L. Goodrich, *General Catalogue of the University of Vermont and State Agricultural College* (Burlington, Vt.: Free Press Association, 1901). For the story of one rebel soldier from Vermont, see Harold A. Dwinell, "Vermonter in Gray: The Story of Melvin Dwinell," *Vermont History* 30, no. 3 (July 1962): 220–37.

18. Hosea B. Williams to Moses Parker, September 28, 1863, Parker Family Papers, folder 10, UVM; Valentine G. Barney to his wife, Maria, December 27, 1863, Valentine G. Barney Papers (MSA 104), folder 2, VHS; Samuel E. Pingree to Augustus Hunton, January 14, 1864, Lyndon State College Collection: Pingree (Pingry)/Hunton/Stickney Family Papers (MSA 135), folder 6, VHS.

19. For a detailed description of the recruiting process see Eugene C. Murdock, *One Million Men: The Civil War Draft in the North* (1971; reprint, Westport, Conn.: Greenwood Press, 1980).

20. Lorentio H. King to his aunt, March 20, 1863, Lorentio H. King Papers, Manuscript Files, UVM; Richard J. Irwin to his mother and sister, March 8, 1863, Richard J. Irwin Papers, Manuscript Files, UVM.

21. Murdock (*One Million Men*, 355), gives the figure of 437 Vermont men drafted and actually sent to the front, but does not cite his source. Although Peck, *Revised Roster*, does not summarize conscripts, a cursory tally of men designated as "drafted" appears to substantiate Murdock's figure. Some towns may have begun drafting on their own authority to fill quotas as early as 1862, but Peck designates no soldiers as conscripts before the federal draft of July 1863. Peter T. Washburn, in his *Report of the Adjutant & Inspector General of the State of Vermont, from Oct. 1, 1864, to Oct. 1, 1865* (Montpelier, Vt., 1865), 19, concludes that 816 men provided substitutes; Murdock puts the figure at 672. Peck, however, lists approximately 1,250 substitutes.

22. Henry J. Vaughan to his brother Volney, July 24, 1863, Middlesex Papers (MSC 34), VHS; Moses A. Parker to Eliza, September 16, 1864, Parker Family Papers, folder 11, UVM.

23. George Worthington Adams, *Doctors in Blue: The Medical History of the Union Army in the Civil War* (New York: Henry Schuman, 1952), 15.

24. George I. Hagar to Sarah Hagar, May 1, 1863, George I. Hagar Papers, Manuscript Files, UVM; Stephen H. Brockway to his friend Allard, March 2, 1862, Wendell W. Lang, Jr., Collection, MHI; Stephen Spaulding to James, July 8, 1862, Stephen Spaulding Papers (Miscellaneous File 1291), VHS.

25. Rufus Lanpher to his family, October 8, 1862, Rufus Lanpher Papers, Gertrude Mallary Collection, Bradford, Vermont; see the biographical sketch of Dr. Janes in Peck, *Revised Roster*, 726–27; Peter M. Abbott to his friends, December 9, 1862, Peter M. Abbott Papers (MSS 17-2), VHS; Willard M.

Thayer to his wife and children, October 17, 1862, in the Esther M. Thayer Papers (MSA 84), folder 1, VHS.

26. Roswell Farnham to Laura, June 19, 1863, Farnham Papers, carton 20, volume 37, UVM; William Cheney to R. A. Savage, February [18], 1863, Savage Family Papers, box 1, folder 27, UVM.

27. Chester Leach to Ann Leach, October 30, 1863, Chester Leach Papers, box 2, folder 2, UVM; William B. Stevens to Mary, December 8, 1861, in the Robinson/Stevens Family "Recent Finds" folder, Rokeby Museum, Ferrisburgh, Vermont.

28. Joseph C. Rutherford to his wife, July 19, 1863 (box 1, folder 26), and December 25, 1862 (box 1, folder 9), Joseph C. Rutherford Papers, UVM.

29. For a description of one notable snowball fight see the letter of Peter Abbott, February 28, 1863, in chapter 8; Albert F. Sawyer to his aunt, November 9, 1863, Sawyer Family Papers, UVM; Joseph C. Rutherford to his wife, January 25, 1863, Joseph C. Rutherford Papers, box 1, folder 13, UVM; Tabor Parcher to his wife, January 5, 1863, Tabor Parcher Papers, folder 2, Manuscript Files, UVM; Aldis Brainerd to his sister, Ann Eliza Smith, June 13, 1862, Smith Family of St. Albans Papers, carton 1, folder 44, UVM.

30. Edward P. Stone to his family, November 15, 1862, Edward P. Stone Papers (MSS 25-72), VHS; Charles C. Parker to Lizzie, February 24, 1864, Parker Family Papers (Miscellaneous File 1039) VHS; Tabor Parcher to his wife, April 3, 1864, Tabor Parcher Papers, folder 3, Manuscript Files, UVM.

31. Franky Brown to Elijah Brown, February 8, 1863, Brown Family Papers (Miscellaneous File Additions), VHS; Henrietta M. Parker to Charles E. Parker, December 25, 1862, Charles E. Parker Papers, carton 1, folder 14, UVM. Parker resigned in October 1863 due to ill health and returned safely to Vermont.

32. Asahel Hubbard to Frank Hubbard, May 24, 1863, Hubbard family papers, folder 8, UVM; see the discussion of the competition for recruits in T. D. S. Bassett, *Urban Penetration of Rural Vermont, 1840–1880* (Ph.D. diss., Harvard University, 1956), vol. 2, 469–73; Silas Hall to his son, August 17, 1864, Edwin C. Hall Papers, folder 18, VHS; T. M. Adams, *Prices Paid by Vermont Farmers for Goods and Services and Received by Them for Farm Products, 1790–1940; Wages of Vermont Farm Labor, 1780–1940*, Bulletin 507 of the Vermont State Agricultural Experiment Station (Burlington, Vt., 1944), 88.

33. See the communications of the First District Provost-Marshal in *The War of the Rebellion: A Compilation of the Official Records of the Union and Confederate Armies*, series 3, vol. 3 (Washington: Government Printing Office, 1899), 383–85.

34. Nellie French to her husband, January 26, 1863, George Foster French Papers, MHI; Alfred H. Keith to his sister, April 20, 1863, Alfred H. Keith Papers (MSA 82), folder 8, VHS; Franklin J. Hubbard letter, November 3, 1862, Hubbard Family Papers, folder 6, UVM; Hosea Williams to "Brother Soldier" (Moses Parker), January 8, 1863, Parker Family Papers, folder 8, UVM; George J. Howard to his family, December 18, 1862, George J. Howard Papers (Miscellaneous File 692), VHS.

35. The story of the St. Albans raid is told by Oscar A. Kinchen, *Daredevils of the Confederate Army: The Story of the St. Albans Raiders* (Boston: The

Christopher Publishing House, 1959), and Dennis K. Wilson, *Justice Under Pressure: The Saint Albans Raid and Its Aftermath* (Lanham, Md.: University Press of America, 1992).

36. Henry McAllister's letters can be found among the letters received by various member of the Robinson and Stevens families in the Robinson family papers, Sheldon; see Rutherford's letters, particularly the letter to his wife of April 29, 1865 (Joseph C. Rutherford Papers, box 1, folder 75, UVM); Stephen M. Pingree to Augustus Hunton, November 11, 1863, Lyndon State College Collection: Pingree (Pingry)/Hunton/Stickney Family Papers (MSA 135), folder 5, VHS.

37. Rachel Stevens to William B. Stevens, March 6, 1864, Robinson Family Papers, box 41, folder 13, Sheldon. More than sixty of William's letters can be found in the Robinson Papers, and another twenty in the Nancie Abbie Harriman papers at Duke.

38. Rachel Stevens to Ann Stevens, October 13, 1861, box 14, folder 16, and Ann Stevens to William B. Stevens, September 9, 1861, box 41, folder 11, Robinson Family Papers, Sheldon.

39. Sears, *Landscape Turned Red*, xi; Henry McAllister to Ann Stevens, September 16, 1862, box 15, folder 3, Robinson Family Papers, Sheldon.

1. Spring 1861 (pp. 16–33)

1. Benedict, *Vermont in the Civil War*, vol. 1, 20–25.

2. James M. McPherson, *Battle Cry of Freedom: The Civil War Era* (New York: Ballantine Books, 1989), 332.

3. On Vermont's state of preparedness see Bassett, *Urban Penetration*, vol. 2, 460–62; see sketch of Phelps in Peck, *Revised Roster*, 749, and of Washburn in the same, 744.

4. Benedict, *Vermont in the Civil War*, vol. 1, 38–39, differs slightly with Captain Ripley (see his letter of May 26, 1861) on the details of this encounter.

5. See Benedict, *Vermont in the Civil War*, vol. 1, 42–57.

6. Ibid., 61.

2. Summer 1861 (pp. 34–46)

1. See Benedict's description of the battle in *Vermont in the Civil War*, vol. 1, 69–85.

2. Allan Nevins, *The War for the Union: The Improvised War, 1861–1862*, vol. 5 of *The Ordeal of the Union* (New York: Charles Scribner's Sons, 1959), 223–24.

3. Shelby Foote, *Fort Sumter to Perryville*, vol. 1 of *The Civil War: A Narrative* (New York: Vintage Books, 1986), 85–86.

4. Benedict, *Vermont in the Civil War*, vol. 1, 127. The man killed in the fracas was Sergeant John Terrill of Canaan.

5. Ibid., 129–30.

6. See the sketches of Vermont's general officers in Peck, *Revised Roster*, 747–51.

7. Benedict, *Vermont in the Civil War*, vol. 1, 134–35.

3. Autumn 1861 (pp. 47–56)

1. Shelby Foote, *Fort Sumter to Perryville*, 69–70.

2. Benedict, *Vermont in the Civil War*, vol. 1, 236.

3. Ibid., 90–92.

4. See Kenneth Link, "Potomac Fever: The Hazards of Camp Life," *Vermont History* 51, no. 2 (Spring 1983): 69–88.

5. Benedict, *Vermont in the Civil War*, vol. 2, 533–541.

4. Winter 1862 (pp. 57–69)

1. Benedict, *Vermont in the Civil War*, vol. 1, 239–40.

2. The trials of the Seventh Vermont Infantry are related by William C. Holbrook in *A Narrative of the Services of the Officers and Enlisted Men of the 7th Regiment of Vermont Volunteers (Veterans), from 1862 to 1866* (New York, 1882).

3. Benedict, *Vermont in the Civil War*, vol. 2, 5.

4. Ibid., 6.

5. See Benedict's muted criticism of Berdan in *Vermont in the Civil War*, vol. 2, 733. Long after the war Ripley wrote *Vermont Riflemen in the War for the Union, 1861 to 1865: A History of Company F, First United States Sharp Shooters* (1883; reprint, Rochester, Mich.: Grand Army Press, 1981).

6. Benedict, *Vermont in the Civil War*, vol. 2, 735. For a description of the affair by a veteran of the Second U.S. Sharpshooters, see *The Civil War Diary of Wyman S. White*, ed. Russell C. White (Baltimore: Butternut and Blue, 1993), 36–38.

7. McPherson, *Battle Cry of Freedom*, 424.

5. Spring 1862 (pp. 70–84)

1. See Benedict, *Vermont in the Civil War*, vol. 1, 249–64.

2. Ibid., 265–66.

3. Stephen W. Sears, *To the Gates of Richmond: The Peninsula Campaign* (New York: Ticknor and Fields, 1992), 159.

4. McPherson, *Battle Cry of Freedom*, 425. See Sears, *To the Gates of Richmond*, 98–100, for a discussion of McClellan's inflated estimates of enemy strength.

5. Benedict, *Vermont in the Civil War*, vol. 2, 556–64.

6. No regimental history of the First Vermont Cavalry has been published.

A manuscript history of the regiment by one of its captains, Horace K. Ide of Barnet, is on deposit at UVM.

7. Benedict, *Vermont in the Civil War*, vol. 2, 7.

6. Summer 1862 (pp. 85–108)

1. Sears, *To the Gates of Richmond*, 281; McPherson, *Battle Cry of Freedom*, 471.

2. Benedict, *Vermont in the Civil War*, vol. 1, 295–98.

3. Sears, *To the Gates of Richmond*, 263–64.

4. Benedict, *Vermont in the Civil War*, vol. 2, 736–38.

5. Holbrook, *Narrative*, 23.

6. Ibid., 37; see also McPherson, *Battle Cry of Freedom*, 421.

7. Butler's General Orders No. 62-1/2 can be found in *The War of the Rebellion: A Compilation of the Official Records of the Union and Confederate Armies*, ser. 1, vol. 15 (Washington, D.C.: Government Printing Office, 1886), 42–46; Benedict, *Vermont in the Civil War*, vol. 2, 28.

8. For a detailed account of the battle see John J. Hennessy, *Return to Bull Run: The Campaign and Battle of Second Manassas* (New York: Simon & Schuster, 1983).

9. See Stephen W. Sears's description of the battle at Crampton's Gap in *Landscape Turned Red*, 145–49.

10. Ibid., 150–57.

11. For a full account of the battle see Sears, *Landscape Turned Red*, 181–297.

12. Benedict, *Vermont in the Civil War*, vol. 1, 329.

7. Autumn 1862 (pp. 109–27)

1. McPherson, *Battle Cry of Freedom*, 545.

2. On McClellan's removal see Sears, *Landscape Turned Red*, 336–41; on Burnside's appointment see Foote, *Fort Sumter to Perryville*, 764–65.

3. Holbrook, *Narrative*, 115–19.

4. Benedict, *Vermont in the Civil War*, vol. 2, 401.

5. Howard Coffin, *Nine Months to Gettysburg: Stannard's Vermonters and the Repulse of Pickett's Charge* (Woodstock, Vt.: Countryman Press, 1997), 35.

6. Benedict, *Vermont in the Civil War*, vol. 2, 420–24.

7. Foote, *Fredericksburg to Meridian*, vol. 2 of *The Civil War: A Narrative*, 25–26.

8. Benedict, *Vermont in the Civil War*, vol. 1, 342–46; McPherson, *Battle Cry of Freedom*, 571–72. Many historians have blamed General Burnside for the Fredericksburg fiasco. William Marvel believes General Franklin deserved a large share of the blame. See his "The Making of a Myth: Ambrose E. Burnside and the Union High Command at Fredericksburg," in *The Fredericksburg*

Campaign: Decision on the Rappahannock, ed. Gary W. Gallagher (Chapel Hill: The University of North Carolina Press, 1995).

8. Winter 1863 (pp. 128–43)

1. Stephen W. Sears, *Chancellorsville* (Boston: Houghton Mifflin, 1996), 19–20.
2. Ibid., 62–75.
3. Benedict, *Vermont in the Civil War*, vol. 1, 353–54.
4. Ibid., vol. 2, 427–30.
5. Ibid., 582–84.
6. Edward H. Ripley to his mother, February 4, 1863, as quoted in Eisenschiml, *Vermont General*, 72; Benedict, *Vermont in the Civil War*, vol. 2, 207–10.
7. McPherson, *Battle Cry of Freedom*, 558–59.
8. Sears, *Chancellorsville*, 71.

9. Spring 1863 (pp. 144–60)

1. Unless otherwise noted, the discussion of the Chancellorsville campaign follows Sears, *Chancellorsville*.
2. Sedgwick, Sears wrote, was "constitutionally . . . a McClellan disciple, careful and cautious and conservative, greatly solicitous of his men, entirely competent but happiest carrying out direct orders" (*Chancellorsville*, 249).
3. Benedict, *Vermont in the Civil War*, vol. 1, 361–66.
4. Ibid., 367–73.
5. See Foote, *Fredericksburg to Meridian*, 316–19.
6. Benedict, *Vermont in the Civil War*, vol. 1, 376.
7. George N. Carpenter, *History of the Eighth Regiment Vermont Volunteers, 1861–1865* (Boston: Press of Deland and Barta, 1886), 112–32.
8. Benedict, *Vermont in the Civil War*, vol. 2, 432.
9. Ibid., 439–40.

10. Summer 1863 (pp. 161–82)

1. Foote, *Fredericksburg to Meridian*, 450–52.
2. Edwin B. Coddington, *The Gettysburg Campaign: A Study in Command* (1968; reprint, New York: Charles Scribner's Sons, 1984), 247–50.
3. See Coffin's description of the action in *Nine Months to Gettysburg*, 200–206.
4. Benedict, *Army Life in Virginia: Letters from the Twelfth Vermont Regiment and Personal Experiences of Volunteer Service in the War for the Union, 1862–1863* (Burlington, Vt.: Free Press Association, 1895), 171–72.

5. Coffin, *Nine Months to Gettysburg*, 213–46.

6. Foote, *Fredericksburg to Meridian*, 574; Benedict, *Vermont in the Civil War*, vol. 2, 598–603.

7. Foote, *Fredericksburg to Meridian*, 578, and McPherson, *Battle Cry of Freedom*, 664.

8. Benedict, *Vermont in the Civil War*, vol. 1, 390–93.

11. Autumn 1863 (pp. 183–200)

1. Cyrus G. Pringle, *The Civil War Diary of Cyrus Pringle* (Wallingford, Pa.: Pendle Hill, 1962), 30.

2. Richard Meade Bache, *Life of General George Gordon Meade, Commander of the Army of the Potomac* (Philadelphia: Henry T. Coates & Co., 1897), 363.

3. Foote, *Fredericksburg to Meridian*, 792–94.

4. Benedict, *Vermont in the Civil War*, vol. 2, 624–25.

5. Foote, *Fredericksburg to Meridian*, 874–75.

6. So wrote the regiment's chaplain-historian, Edwin M. Haynes, in *A History of the Tenth Regiment, Vt. Vols.*, 2nd ed. (Rutland, Vt.: The Tuttle Company, 1894), 55–56.

7. Benedict, *Vermont in the Civil War*, vol. 2, 289–91.

8. Foote, *Fredericksburg to Meridian*, 875–76.

9. Eisenschiml, *Vermont General*, 164; Benedict, *Vermont in the Civil War*, vol. 2, 221–22.

12. Winter 1864 (pp. 201–19)

1. Bell Irvin Wiley, *The Life of Billy Yank: The Common Soldier of the Union* (Indianapolis: Bobbs-Merrill, 1952), 262–74.

2. Shelby Foote, *Fredericksburg to Meridian*, 953–56.

3. McPherson, *Battle Cry of Freedom*, 719–20; Benedict, *Vermont in the Civil War*, vol. 1, 410.

4. Allan Nevins, *The War for the Union: War Becomes Revolution, 1862–1863*, vol. 6 of *The Ordeal of the Union* (New York: Charles Scribner's Sons, 1960), 515–28.

5. McPherson, *Battle Cry of Freedom*, 788–89; Noah Andre Trudeau, *Like Men of War: Black Troops in the Civil War, 1862–1865* (Boston: Little, Brown, 1998), 252–55.

6. Ibid., 137–55.

7. McPherson, *Battle Cry of Freedom*, 792–800.

8. Foote, *Fredericksburg to Meridian*, 907–15; Benedict, *Vermont in the Civil War*, vol. 2, 627–31.

9. Benedict, *Vermont in the Civil War*, vol. 2, 227–32.

10. Ibid., 496–97.

11. McPherson, *Battle Cry of Freedom*, 718.

13. Spring 1864 (pp. 220–40)

1. Gordon C. Rhea, *The Battle of the Wilderness, May 5–6, 1864* (Baton Rouge: Louisiana State University Press, 1994), 46–47.

2. Foote, *Red River to Appomattox*, vol. 3 of *The Civil War: A Narrative*, 131–32.

3. Benedict, *Vermont in the Civil War*, vol. 2, 496–501.

4. See Benedict, *Vermont in the Civil War*, vol. 1, 422–32.

5. Ibid., 434–36.

6. Ibid., 439.

7. Ibid., 448–50. See Bruce Catton's description of the battle in *A Stillness at Appomattox* (Garden City, N.Y.: Doubleday, 1957), 123–28.

8. Clifford Dowdey, *Lee's Last Campaign: The Story of Lee and His Men Against Grant—1864* (Boston: Little, Brown, 1960), 300.

9. Benedict, *Vermont in the Civil War*, vol. 2, 299–301; vol. 1, 461–63.

10. Foote, *Red River to Appomattox*, 292.

11. Nevins, *The War for the Union: The Organized War to Victory, 1864–1865*, vol. 8 of *The Ordeal of the Union* (New York: Charles Scribner's Sons, 1971), 48.

12. Dowdey, *Lee's Last Campaign*, 332. Smith was soon cashiered; he devoted a great deal of time over the next three decades to clearing his name. See his *From Chattanooga to Petersburg Under Generals Grant and Butler: A Contribution to the History of the War, and a Personal Vindication* (Boston: Houghton Mifflin, 1893).

13. Benedict, *Vermont in the Civil War*, vol. 1, 473–81.

14. Summer 1864 (pp. 241–57)

1. Nevins, *The War for the Union: The Organized War to Victory*, 58–96.

2. See William Marvel, *Andersonville: The Last Depot* (Chapel Hill: University of North Carolina Press, 1994). Among the many lurid accounts of imprisonment at Andersonville is that of Simon M. Dufur, a veteran of the First Vermont Cavalry, *Over the Dead Line, or, Tracked by Blood-Hounds* (Burlington, Vt.: Free Press Association, 1902). Unpublished accounts include the diary of Bradford Sparrow and the memoirs of Luther B. Harris, both of the Fourth Vermont Infantry, at UVM.

3. Foote, *Red River to Appomattox*, 444–45; Benedict, *Vermont in the Civil War*, vol. 2, 649–55.

4. See Richard Wheeler, *On Fields of Fury: From the Wilderness to the Crater: An Eyewitness History* (New York: HarperCollins, 1991), 272–86; Benedict, *Vermont in the Civil War*, vol. 2, 511–18.

5. Charles C. Osborne, *Jubal: The Life and Times of General Jubal A. Early, CSA, Defender of the Lost Cause* (Chapel Hill, N.C.: Algonquin Books of Chapel Hill, 1992), 250–51.

6. Foote, *Red River to Appomattox*, 451.

7. Osborne, *Jubal*, 270, puts the difference at fourteen thousand to fifty-eight hundred.

8. Osborne, *Jubal*, 271–75. See Haynes, *A History of the Tenth Regiment*, 196–200, for Captain George Davis's account of the picket line's harrowing escape. Davis won a Medal of Honor for his efforts at the Monocacy.

9. Osborne, *Jubal*, 280–88.

10. Foote, *Red River to Appomattox*, 542–43.

11. Osborne, *Jubal*, 336–40.

12. Ibid., 342–44.

13. Foote, *Red River to Appomattox*, 558–59.

15. Autumn 1864 (pp. 258–81)

1. See Thomas A. Lewis, *The Guns of Cedar Creek* (New York: Harper & Row, 1988), 57–65.

2. Osborne, *Jubal*, 358.

3. The number of Vermonters is derived from Benedict, *Vermont in the Civil War*, who gives the strength of each regiment in the weeks before the battle of Cedar Creek, in the chapters devoted to each regiment.

4. See Lewis, *Guns of Cedar Creek*, 183–204.

5. See Herbert Hill's description in Carpenter, *History of the Eighth Regiment*, 214–20.

6. Lewis, *Guns of Cedar Creek*, 39.

7. Sheridan and his horse Rienzi were immortalized in Thomas Buchanan Read's poem, "Sheridan's Ride, September 19, 1864." See Lewis, *Guns of Cedar Creek*, 323–25.

8. Ibid., 265–87. For the role of the Eighth Vermont in the counterattack, see Herbert Hill in Carpenter, *History of the Eighth Vermont*, 220–29. The Vermont cavalry's role is related by Benedict, *Vermont in the Civil War,*, vol. 2, 667–69.

9. Dennis K. Wilson provides an analysis of the raid and the diplomatic crisis that followed in *Justice Under Pressure*.

10. Nevins, *The War for the Union: The Organized War to Victory, 1864–1865*, 135–43; Benedict, *Vermont in the Civil War*, vol. 1, 567.

11. Of the thousands of Union soldiers who deserted during the course of the war, only 141 were executed (Wiley, *Billy Yank*, 206). The Seventeenth Vermont Infantry was typical of the Union outfits that mustered into service late in the war in suffering high desertion rates. More than 300 of the 1,100 men on the Seventeenth's rolls deserted. Of these, 120 never even joined their companies. See Joel Lucia's assertion about deserters in Peck, *Revised Roster*, 574, and the regiment's "Final Statement" in the same, 597.

16. Winter 1865 (pp. 282–92)

1. Nevins, *The War for the Union: The Organized War to Victory, 1864–1865*, 264–67.

2. Foote, *Red River to Appomattox*, 772–78.

3. Ibid., 839–41.

4. For a detailed description of the fight at Fort Stedman, see William H. Hodgkins, *The Battle of Fort Stedman (Petersburg, Virginia), March 25, 1865* (Boston, 1889).

5. Benedict, *Vermont in the Civil War*, vol. 1, 574–78.

6. Hodgkins, *Battle of Fort Stedman*, 8.

17. Spring 1865 (pp. 293–313)

1. Foote, *Red River to Appomattox*, 864–75.

2. Benedict, *Vermont in the Civil War*, vol. 1, 586.

3. See Ripley's account in Benedict, *Vermont in the Civil War*, vol. 2, 265–71.

4. See Foote's account of the flight and surrender in *Red River to Appomattox*, 907–56.

5. The *Burlington Daily Times*, April 11, 1865, p. 3.

6. Benedict, *Vermont in the Civil War*, vol. 1, 610–11.

Epilogue (pp. 314–15)

1. Eisenschiml, *Vermont General*, 311–12.

2. For the war's effect on the Vermont home front, see Bassett, "Urban Penetration," 482–520.

3. Address of Sergeant Lucius Bigelow to the Reunion Society of Vermont Officers, October 31, 1878. *Proceedings of the Reunion Society of Vermont Officers, 1864–1884* (Burlington, Vt.: Free Press Association, 1885), 296.

4. Ibid., 289–98.

Works Cited

Secondary Sources

Adams, George Worthington. *Doctors in Blue: The Medical History of the Union Army in the Civil War.* New York: Henry Schuman, 1952.

Adams, T. M. *Prices Paid by Vermont Farmers for Goods and Services and Received by Them for Farm Products, 1790–1940; Wages of Vermont Farm Labor, 1780–1940.* Bulletin 507 of the Vermont State Agricultural Experiment Station, 1944.

Bache, Richard Meade. *Life of General George Gordon Meade, Commander of the Army of the Potomac.* Philadelphia: Henry T. Coates & Co., 1897.

Bassett, T. D. S. "Urban Penetration of Rural Vermont, 1840–1880." 2 vols. Ph.D. diss., Harvard University, 1956.

Battles and Leaders of the Civil War. 4 vols. New York: Century Co., 1887–88.

Benedict, George G. *Vermont in the Civil War: A History of the Part Taken by the Vermont Soldiers and Sailors in the War for the Union, 1861–1865.* 2 vols. Burlington, Vt.: Free Press Association, 1886, 1888.

———. *Army Life in Virginia: Letters from the Twelfth Vermont Regiment and Personal Experiences of Volunteer Service in the War for the Union, 1862–1863.* Burlington, Vt.: Free Press Association, 1895.

Cabot, Mary R. *Annals of Brattleboro, 1861–1895.* 2 vols. Brattleboro, Vt.: E. L. Hildreth & Co., 1921 and 1922.

Carpenter, George N. *History of the Eighth Regiment Vermont Volunteers, 1861–1865.* Boston: Press of Deland and Barta, 1886.

Catton, Bruce. *A Stillness at Appomattox.* Garden City, N.Y.: Doubleday, 1957.

Chadwick, Albert G. *Soldiers' Record of the Town of St. Johnsbury, Vermont, in the War of the Rebellion, 1861–5.* St. Johnsbury: C. M. Stone & Co., 1883.

Chapman, George T. *Sketches of the Alumni of Dartmouth College, from the First Graduation in 1771 to the Present Time, with a Brief History of the Institution.* Cambridge, Mass.: Riverside Press, 1867.

Coddington, Edwin B. *The Gettysburg Campaign: A Study in Command.* 1968; reprint, New York: Charles Scribner's Sons, 1984.

Coffin, Howard. *Full Duty: Vermonters in the Civil War*. Woodstock, Vt.: Countryman Press, 1993.

———. *Nine Months to Gettysburg: Stannard's Vermonters and the Repulse of Pickett's Charge*. Woodstock, Vt.: Countryman Press, 1997.

Dodge, Grenville M. *Norwich University, 1819–1911: Her History, Her Graduates, Her Roll of Honor*. 3 vols. Montpelier, Vt.: Capital City Press, 1911.

Dowdey, Clifford. *Lee's Last Campaign: The Story of Lee and His Men Against Grant—1864*. Boston: Little, Brown, 1960.

Dufur, S[imon] M. *Over the Dead Line, or, Tracked by Blood-Hounds*. Burlington, Vt.: Free Press Association, 1902.

Dwinell, Harold A. "Vermonter in Gray: The Story of Melvin Dwinell." *Vermont History* 30, no. 3 (July 1962): 220–37.

Eisenschiml, Otto. *Vermont General: The Unusual War Experiences of Edward Hastings Ripley, 1862–1865*. New York: Devin-Adair Co., 1960.

Fletcher, Henry C. *History of the American War*. 3 vols. London: Richard Bentley, 1865.

Foote, Shelby. *The Civil War: A Narrative*. 3 vols. 1958–74. Reprint, New York: Vintage Books, 1986.

Gallagher, Gary W., ed. *The Fredericksburg Campaign: Decision on the Rappahannock*. Chapel Hill: The University of North Carolina Press, 1995.

Goodrich, John L. *General Catalogue of the University of Vermont and State Agricultural College*. Burlington, Vt.: Free Press Association, 1901.

Guernsey, Alfred H., and Henry M. Alden. *Harper's Pictorial History of the Civil War*. 2 vols. Chicago: Puritan Press Co., 1894.

Haynes, Edwin M. *A History of the Tenth Regiment, Vt. Vols*. 2nd ed. Rutland, Vt.: The Tuttle Company, 1894.

Hemenway, Abby Maria. *Vermont Historical Gazetteer: A Magazine, Embracing a History of Each Town, Civil, Ecclesiastical, Biographical and Military*. 5 vols. Burlington, Vt., 1867–1891.

Hennessy, John J. *Return to Bull Run: The Campaign and Battle of Second Manassas*. New York: Simon & Schuster, 1983.

Hodgkins, William H. *The Battle of Fort Stedman (Petersburg, Virginia), March 25, 1865*. Boston, 1889.

Holbrook, William C. *A Narrative of the Services of the Officers and Enlisted Men of the 7th Regiment of Vermont Volunteers (Veterans), from 1862 to 1866*. New York, 1882.

Isham, Asa B. *Prisoners of War and Military Prisons*. Cincinnati: Lyman and Cushing, 1890.

Jeffrey, William H. *Successful Vermonters: A Modern Gazetteer of Caledonia, Essex, and Orleans Counties*. East Burke, Vt.: The Historical Publishing Co., 1904.

Jellison, Charles. *Ethan Allen, Frontier Rebel*. Syracuse, N.Y.: Syracuse University Press, 1969.

Kinchen, Oscar A. *Daredevils of the Confederate Army: The Story of the St. Albans Raiders*. Boston: The Christopher Publishing House, 1959.

Lewis, Thomas A. *The Guns of Cedar Creek*. New York: Harper & Row, 1988.

Link, Kenneth. "Potomac Fever: The Hazards of Camp Life." *Vermont History* 61, no. 2 (Spring 1983): 69–85.

Long, E. B. *The Civil War Day by Day: An Almanac, 1861–1865*. New York: Da Capo Press, 1971.

Lossing, Benson J. *Pictorial History of the Civil War in the United States of America*. 3 vols. Philadelphia: G. W. Childs, 1866.

Ludlum, David M. *Social Ferment in Vermont, 1791–1850*. 1939. Reprint, New York: AMS Press, 1966.

Marvel, William. *Andersonville: The Last Depot*. Chapel Hill: University of North Carolina Press, 1994.

———. "The Making of a Myth: Ambrose E. Burnside and the Union High Command at Fredericksburg." In *The Fredericksburg Campaign*, ed. Gary W. Gallagher.

McPherson, James M. *Battle Cry of Freedom: The Civil War Era*. New York: Ballantine Books, 1989.

———. *For Cause and Comrades: Why Men Fought in the Civil War*. New York: Oxford University Press, 1997.

Mott, Frank Luther. *Golden Multitudes: The Story of Best Sellers in the United States*. New York: The MacMillan Co., 1947.

Murdock. Eugene C. *One Million Men: The Civil War Draft in the North*. 1971. Reprint, Westport, Conn.: Greenwood Press, 1980.

Myers, John. "The Beginning of Antislavery Agencies in Vermont, 1832–1836." *Vermont History* 36, no. 3 (Summer 1968): 126–41.

National Life Insurance Company. *National Life Insurance Company: A History of its Foundation and Development, 1850–1925*. Montpelier, Vt.: National Life Insurance Co., 1925.

Nelson, Emily M., ed. *Frontier Crossroads: The People of Newport, Vermont*. Canaan, N.H.: Phoenix Publishing, 1978.

Nevins, Allan. *The Ordeal of the Union*. 8 vols. New York: Charles Scribner's Sons, 1947–71.

Odell, Samuel W. *The Lives and Campaigns of Grant and Lee: A Comparison and Contrast of the Deeds and Characters of the Two Great Leaders in the Civil War*. Chicago: Star Publishing Co., 1895.

Osborne, Charles C. *Jubal: The Life and Times of General Jubal A. Early, CSA, Defender of the Lost Cause*. Chapel Hill, N.C.: Algonquin Books of Chapel Hill, 1992.

Peck, Theodore S. *Revised Roster of Vermont Volunteers and Lists of Vermonters Who Served in the Army and Navy of the United States during the War of the Rebellion*. Montpelier, Vt.: Watchman Publishing Co., 1892.

Pringle, Cyrus G. *The Civil War Diary of Cyrus Pringle*. Wallingford, Pa.: Pendle Hill, 1962.

Proceedings of the Reunion Society of Vermont Officers, 1864–1884. Burlington, Vt.: Free Press Association, 1885.

Rhea, Gordon C. *The Battle of the Wilderness, May 5–6, 1864*. Baton Rouge: Louisiana State University Press, 1994.

———. *The Battles for Spotsylvania and the Road to Yellow Tavern, May 7–12, 1864*. Baton Rouge: Louisiana State University Press, 1997.

Rhode Island Adjutant General. *Annual Report of the Adjutant General of the State of Rhode Island, for the Year 1865*. Providence: Providence Press Co., 1868.

Ripley, William Y. *Vermont Riflemen in the War for the Union, 1861 to 1865:*

A History of Company F, First United States Sharp Shooters. 1883. Reprint, Rochester, Mich.: Grand Army Press, 1981.

Robinson, Duane L. *General Catalogue of Middlebury College.* Middlebury, Vt.: Middlebury College, 1950.

Rosenblatt, Emil and Ruth, eds. *Hard Marching Every Day: The Civil War Letters of Private Wilbur Fisk, 1861–1865.* Lawrence: University Press of Kansas, 1992.

Scheele, Carl H. *A Short History of the Mail Service.* Washington, D.C.: Smithsonian Institution Press, 1970.

Sears, Stephen W. *Landscape Turned Red: The Battle of Antietam.* Boston: Houghton Mifflin, 1983.

———. *To the Gates of Richmond: The Peninsula Campaign.* New York: Ticknor & Fields, 1992.

———. *Chancellorsville.* Boston: Houghton Mifflin, 1996.

Siebert, Wilbur H. *Vermont's Anti-Slavery and Underground Railroad Record.* 1937. Reprint, New York: Negro University Press, 1969.

Smith, William Farrar. *From Chattanooga to Petersburg Under Generals Grant and Butler: A Contribution to the History of the War, and a Personal Vindication.* Boston: Houghton Mifflin, 1893.

Sprague, George F. *Soldiers' Record, Town of Craftsbury, Vermont, 1861–1865.* n.p.: n.p., 1914.

Steele, Robert G. *With Pen or Sword: Lives and Times of the Remarkable Rutland Ripleys.* New York: Vantage Press, 1979.

Swift, Esther Munroe. *Vermont Place-Names: Footprints of History.* Brattleboro, Vt.: Stephen Greene Press, 1977.

Trudeau, Noah Andre. *Like Men of War: Black Troops in the Civil War, 1862–1865.* Boston: Little, Brown, 1998.

Ullery, Jacob G. *Men of Vermont: An Illustrated Biographical History of Vermonters and Sons of Vermont.* Brattleboro, Vt.: Transcript Publishing Co., 1894.

Waite, Otis F. R. *Vermont in the Great Rebellion, Containing Historical and Biographical Sketches, Etc.* Claremont, N.H.: Tracy, Chase and Co., 1869.

The War of the Rebellion: A Compilation of the Official Records of the Union and Confederate Armies. Washington, D.C.: Government Printing Office, 1886.

Washburn, Peter T. *Report of the Adjutant & Inspector General of the State of Vermont, from Oct. 1, 1864, to Oct. 1, 1865.* Montpelier, Vt., 1865.

Wells, Frederic Palmer. *History of Barnet, Vermont, from the Outbreak of the French and Indian War to Present Time.* Burlington, Vt.: Free Press Printing Co., 1923.

Wheeler, Richard. *On Fields of Fury: From the Wilderness to the Crater: An Eyewitness History.* New York: HarperCollins, 1991.

White, Wyman S. *The Civil War Diary of Wyman S. White.* Ed. Russell C. White. Baltimore: Butternut and Blue, 1993.

Wild, Edward P., and the Brookfield Historical Society. *The History of Brookfield.* n.p.: n.p., 1987.

Wiley, Bell Irvin. *The Life of Billy Yank: The Common Soldier of the Union.* Indianapolis: Bobbs-Merrill, 1952.

Wilson, Dennis K. *Justice Under Pressure: The Saint Albans Raid and Its Aftermath*. Lanham, Md.: University Press of America, 1992.

Zirblis, Raymond Paul. *Friends of Freedom: The Vermont Underground Railroad Survey Report*. Montpelier, Vt.: Vermont Department of State Buildings and Vermont Division for Historic Preservation, 1996.

Newspapers

Burlington Daily Free Press.
Burlington Daily Times.
Middlebury Register.
Montpelier Evening Argus.
Rutland Daily Herald.
St. Albans Daily Messenger.

Manuscript Collections

Duke University Special Collections Library, Durham, N.C.
    Ripley, William Young.
    Smith, Walter Wallace.
    Smith, Horace.

Gertrude Mallary, private collection, Bradford, Vt.
    Ayer, Perry.
    Lanpher, George.
    Lanpher, Rufus.
    Morey, Arthur P.
    Norton, Andrew H.
    Parcher, Tabor.

Military History Institute Archives, Carlisle Barracks, Pa.
    Brockway, Stephen; Wendell Lang, Jr., Collection.
    Chapin, Charles; Civil War Miscellaneous.
    Chapin, Cornelius; Civil War Miscellaneous.
    Drenan, James F.; Lewis Leigh Collection.
    Dunbar, Henry.
    French, George Foster.
    Haskell, Londus; Lewis Leigh Collection.
    Hunter, Hiram M.; Civil War Miscellaneous.
    Leach, Moses; Lewis Leigh Collection.

St. Albans Historical Society, St. Albans, Vt.
    Pierce, Ann.
    Smith Family.

Sheldon Museum, Middlebury, Vt.
    Howe-Wolcott Correspondence.
    Robinson Family.
    Stewart Family.

University of Vermont, Burlington, Vt.
    Barstow, John L.; Manuscript Files.
    Farnham, Roswell.
    Field, Frederick; Manuscript Files.
    Fitch Family.
    Hagar, George I.; Manuscript Files.
    Hatch, Benjamin.
    Heaton, Solomon; Manuscript Files.
    Holbrook, William C.
    Howe, George G.; Manuscript Files.
    Hubbard Family.
    Irwin, Richard J.; Manuscript Files.
    King, Lorentio; Manuscript Files.
    Leach, Chester K.
    Leslie, Warren; Manuscript Files.
    Parcher, Tabor; Manuscript Files.
    Parker, Charles E.
    Parker Family.
    Parker/Fleming Family.
    Perkins, Joseph L.; Manuscript Files.
    Quimby, George.
    Randall, George; Manuscript Files.
    Remington, Jonathan; Manuscript Files.
    Robie, Edward; Manuscript Files.
    Rutherford, Joseph C.
    Savage Family.
    Sawyer Family.
    Scott, Erastus H.; Manuscript Files.
    Smith Family of St. Albans.
    Sparrow, Bradford P.; Manuscript Files.
    Watts, Isaac N.
    Wells, William.
    Wilder, Henry H.; Manuscript Files.

Vermont Historical Society, Montpelier, Vt.
    Abbott, Peter M.; MSS 17-2.
    Allen Family of Winhall; MSA 153.
    Barney, Valentine G.; MS 104.
    Bromley, James W.; MSC 5-18.
    Brown Family, Miscellaneous File Additions.
    Burnham, Henry P.; MSB 30.
    Cain, Avery B.; MSC 9-2.
    Cook, John F., Letter; Miscellaneous File 235.
    Cummings, Charles; MSA 28.

Dewey, Edward; Miscellaneous File 353.

Gale and Morse Family; MSA 50.

Green, Rollin M.; MSS 27–59.

Hall, Edwin C.; MSA 130.5.

Horton, Edwin; MSS 21-16.

Howard, George J.; Miscellaneous Files 692, 693, 694.

Keith, Alfred H.; MSA 82.

Lavallée, Louis, Letter; Miscellaneous File Additions.

Lewis, Henry H., Letter; Miscellaneous File 241.

Lyndon State College Collection: Pingree (Pingry)/Hunton/Stickney; MSA 135.

Mason, Dan; MSA 89.

Middlesex; MSC 34.

Parker Family; Miscellaneous File 1039.

Sherman-Safford Family; MS 23.

Smith, Henry A.; Miscellaneous File 244, 245.

Spafford, Joseph; MSC 9-5.

Spaulding, Stephen; Miscellaneous File 1291.

Stone, Edward P.; MSS 25-72.

Thayer, Esther M.; MSA 84.

Tillison, Dudley; MSS 25-119.

Other Collections

Godfrey, Frederick; Park-McCullough House, North Bennington, Vt.

Griswold, Leroy S.; Donald Johnstone (private collection), Colchester, Vt.

King, Royal D.; Bennington Museum, Bennington, Vt.

Munson, William D.; Munson Family (private collection), Colchester, Vt.

Robinson/Stevens Family; Recent Additions, Rokeby Museum, Ferrisburgh, Vt.

Woodbury, Eri D.; Dartmouth College Archives, Hanover, N.H.

Index

Note: Numbers in italics refer to the editor's introductions and the appendix; roman entries refer to the letters.

University Press of New England publishes books under its own imprint and is the publisher for Brandeis University Press, Dartmouth College, Middlebury College Press, University of New Hampshire, Tufts University, and Wesleyan University Press.

Library of Congress Cataloging-in-Publication Data
A war of the people : Vermont Civil War letters / [edited by] Jeffrey
    D. Marshall ; foreword by Edwin C. Bearss.
        p.   cm.
    Includes bibliographical references (p.   ) and index.
    ISBN 0–87451–922–5 (cloth : alk. paper). — ISBN 0–87451–923–3
    (pbk. : alk. paper)
    1. United States—History—Civil War, 1861–1865—Personal
narratives. 2. Vermont—History—Civil War, 1861–1865—Personal
narratives. 3. Soldiers—Vermont—Correspondence. I. Marshall,
Jeffrey D.
    E464.W28   1999
    973.7′81—dc21   98–53635